The Lifework of a Labor Historian

Studies in Global Social History

Series Editor

Marcel van der Linden (*International Institute of Social History, Amsterdam, The Netherlands*)

Editorial Board

Sven Beckert (*Harvard University, Cambridge, MA, USA*)
Dirk Hoerder (*University of Arizona, Phoenix, AR, USA*)
Chitra Joshi (*Indraprastha College, Delhi University, India*)
Amarjit Kaur (*University of New England, Armidale, Australia*)
Barbara Weinstein (*New York University, New York, NY, USA*)

VOLUME 35

The titles published in this series are listed at *brill.com/sgsh*

The Lifework of a Labor Historian

Essays in Honor of Marcel van der Linden

Edited by

Ulbe Bosma
Karin Hofmeester

BRILL

LEIDEN | BOSTON

 This is an open access title distributed under the terms of the prevailing CC-BY-NC License at the time of publication, which permits any non-commercial use, distribution, and reproduction in any medium, provided the original author(s) and source are credited.

Cover illustration: Imaginary harbor in the Soviet Union (1929). Illustration for educational purposes by Georgiy Konstantinovich Savitsky (1887–1949), IISH collection.

The Library of Congress Cataloging-in-Publication Data is available online at http://catalog.loc.gov

Typeface for the Latin, Greek, and Cyrillic scripts: "Brill". See and download: brill.com/brill-typeface.

ISSN 1874-6705
ISBN 978-90-04-38658-7 (hardback)
ISBN 978-90-04-38661-7 (e-book)

Copyright 2018 by the Editors and the Authors.
This work is published by Koninklijke Brill NV incorporates the imprints Brill, Brill Hes & De Graaf, Brill Nijhoff, Brill Rodopi, Brill Sense and Hotei Publishing.
Koninklijke Brill NV reserves the right to protect the publication against unauthorized use.

This book is printed on acid-free paper and produced in a sustainable manner.

Contents

Acknowledgements   VII
List of Figures and Tables   VIII
Notes on Contributors   IX

1 Introduction   1
   Ulbe Bosma and Karin Hofmeester

2 Workers: New Developments in Labor History since the 1980s   22
   Jan Lucassen

3 "With the Name Changed, the Story Applies to You!": Connections between Slavery and "Free" Labor in the Writings of Marx   47
   Pepijn Brandon

4 Capitalism and Its Critics. A Long-Term View   71
   Jürgen Kocka

5 The ILO and the Oldest Non-profession   90
   Magaly Rodríguez García

6 The Great Fear of 1852: Riots against Enslavement in the Brazilian Empire   115
   Sidney Chalhoub

7 Driving out the Undeserving Poor   136
   Jan Breman

8 Area Studies and the Development of Global Labor History   156
   Andreas Eckert

9 Beyond Labor History's Comfort Zone? Labor Regimes in Northeast India, from the Nineteenth to the Twenty-First Century   174
   Willem van Schendel

Bibliography   209
Index   239

Acknowledgements

The publication of this book could not have been realized without the generous support of Marti Huetink, publishing director at Brill. We are grateful to Henk Wals, General Director of the IISH, and Leo Lucassen its Research Director for their unconditional support for this volume. Richard Bowles and Anne Lee perceptively edited the English-language contributions of the non-native speakers; Joppe Schaaper meticulously corrected the author's references and made the bibliography and index.

Figures and Tables

Figures

1.1   Geographical distribution of *IRSH* article topics.   6

9.1   A war captive (*sal*), 1866.   179

9.2   Mara woman and her servant pounding rice in Saikao (Serkawr), southern Mizoram.   187

9.3   Anti-slavery activist with his wife and helper, together with a Christian chief who freed his *bawi* servants in 1909.   188

9.4   "Empire on their backs": More than 30 coerced porters carrying the belongings of an official on tour, 1896.   191

9.5   Communal labor. Planing planks for a new clinic in Pukzing village, 1956.   199

9.6   Communal labor. Boys repairing a road in Sihfa village, c. 1956.   199

9.7   Communal labor. Constructing a new church in Aizawl town, 1964.   200

9.8   Communal labor. Improving the Presbyterian Hospital in Durtlang village, 1980.   200

9.9   Communal labor. Cleaning a sacred statue in Aizawl in 2012.   201

9.10   Communal labor. Smartening a college campus in Durtlang in 2016.   201

9.11   *"Tlawmngaihna is what makes being Mizo so wonderful!"* Roadside poster in Durtlang (Mizoram), 2016.   203

Tables

9.1   Mizoram. Pre-colonial labor regime.   184

9.2   Mizoram. Colonial labor regime.   196

9.3   Mizoram. Post-1955 labor regime.   202

Notes on Contributors

Ulbe Bosma

is a senior researcher at the International Institute of Social History and Professor of International Comparative Social History at the Vrije Universiteit, Amsterdam. He has published widely on colonial migrations and plantation economies. His publications in English include *"Being Dutch" in the Indies. A History of Creolisation and Empire, 1500–1920* (2008, together with Remco Raben), *The Sugar Plantation in India and Indonesia. Industrial Production 1770–2010* (2013), and *Revisiting the Periphery*, to be published by Columbia University Press.

Pepijn Brandon

is a senior researcher at the International Institute of Social History and Assistant Professor at the Vrije Universiteit, Amsterdam. In 2013, he obtained his Ph.D., which was co-supervised by Marcel van der Linden, and subsequently published as *War, Capital, and the Dutch State (1588–1795)* (2015). With Marcel, he shares an interest in the relevance of Marx' work for studying the interconnected histories of war, capitalism, and slavery. He has held fellowships at Harvard University, the University of Pittsburgh, and the Huntington Library in California, and has received two of the most prestigious early-career grants from the Dutch Research Council (NWO).

Jan Breman

has been Professor Emeritus of Comparative Sociology at the University of Amsterdam since 2001, and is continuing his academic work in South and Southeast Asian studies as Honorary Fellow at the International Institute of Social History in Amsterdam. His latest books include *At Work in the Informal Economy of India; A Perspective from the Bottom Up* (2013/2015), *Mobilizing Labour for the Global Coffee Market; Profits from an Unfree Work Regime in Colonial Java* (2015), and *On Pauperism in Present and Past* (2016).

Sidney Chalhoub

is Professor of History and of African and African American Studies at Harvard University. He has published three books on the social history of Rio de Janeiro: *Trabalho, lar e botequim* (1986), on working-class culture in the early twentieth century; *Visões da liberdade* (1990), on the last decades of slavery; and *Cidade febril* (1996), on tenements and epidemics in the second half of the nineteenth century. He also published *Machado de Assis, historiador* (2003), about the literature and political ideas of Machado de Assis. His latest book is

A força da escravidão (2012), on illegal enslavement and the precariousness of freedom in nineteenth-century Brazil.

Andreas Eckert

is Professor of African History at Humboldt University in Berlin and Director of the International Research Center "Work and Human Life Course in Global History," funded by the German Federal Ministry for Education and Research. He has published widely on nineteenth and twentieth century African history, colonialism, labor, and global history. Eckert also regularly contributes to German newspapers including the *Frankfurter Allgemeine Zeitung* and *Die Zeit*. His most recent book is *Global Histories of Work* (2016) (ed.). He is currently working on a *Short History of Colonialism*, to be published by Princeton University Press.

Karin Hofmeester

is a senior researcher at the International Institute of Social History, Amsterdam and Professor of Jewish Culture at the University of Antwerp. Her publications include *The Joy and Pain of Work. Global Attitudes and Valuations, 1500–1650* (2012, with Christine Moll-Murata, eds.), *Luxury in Global Perspective. Objects and Practices, 1600–2000* (2016, with Bernd Grewe, eds.), *Conquerors, Employers, and Arbiters: States and Shifts in Labour Relations, 1500–2000* (2016, with Gijs Kessler and Christine Moll-Murata, eds.), *Colonialism, Institutional Change and Shift in Labour Relations* (2017, with Pim de Zwart, eds), and *Handbook Global History of Work* (2017, with Marcel van der Linden, eds.).

Jürgen Kocka

taught modern history, especially social and comparative history, in Bielefeld, at the Free University of Berlin, and at UCLA. He was president of the Social Science Center Berlin (WZB), and is a Permanent Fellow of the Center "Work and Life Course in Global History," Humboldt University Berlin. His publications in English include *Industrial Culture and Bourgeois Society. Business, Labor, and Bureaucracy in Modern Germany* (1999), *Civil Society and Dictatorship in Modern German History* (2010), and *Capitalism: A Short History* (2016). Together with Marcel van der Linden, he edited *Capitalism. The Reemergence of a Historical Concept* (2016).

Jan Lucassen

is Professor Emeritus International and Comparative Social History at the Vrije Universiteit, Amsterdam. At the International Institute in Amsterdam he was Research Director (1988–2000) Senior Researcher (2000–2011), and Honorary

Fellow from 2012. He is a member of the Dutch Royal Academy of Arts and Sciences. He has published extensively on global migration and labor history, including *Migrant Labour in Europe 1600–1900* (1986), *A Miracle Mirrored. The Dutch Republic in European perspective* (1995, with Karel Davids, eds.), *Global Labour History* (2006, ed.) *Wages and Currency. Global Comparisons from Antiquity to the Twentieth Century* (2007, ed.), and *Globalising Migration History. The Eurasian Experience (16th–21st centuries)* (2014, with Leo Lucassen, eds.).

Magaly Rodríguez García
Ph.D. (2008), is Lecturer at the KU Leuven. Her main publications include "The League of Nations and the Moral Recruitment of Women," in *International Review of Social History* (2012), *On the Legal Boundaries of Coerced Labor* (2016, with Marcel van der Linden, eds.), "On the Legal Boundaries of Coerced Labor" (ibid), "Morality Politics and Prostitution Policies in Brussels: A Diachronic Comparison," in *Sexuality Research and Social Policy* (2017), and *Selling Sex in the City: A Global History of Prostitution, 1600s–2000s* (2017, with Lex Heerma van Voss and Elise van Nederveen Meerkerk, eds.).

Willem van Schendel
is Professor Emeritus Modern Asian History at the University of Amsterdam and honorary fellow at the International Institute of Social History, Amsterdam. He works in the fields of history, anthropology, and sociology of Asia. His recent publications include *Embedding Agricultural Commodities: Using Historical Evidence, 1840s–1940s* (2017, ed.), *The Camera as Witness: A Social History of Mizoram, Northeast India* (2015, with Joy L.K. Pachuau), and *The Bangladesh Reader: History, Culture, Politics* (2013, with Meghna Guhathakurta, eds.).

CHAPTER 1

Introduction

Ulbe Bosma and Karin Hofmeester

This collection of essays has been compiled on the occasion of Marcel van der Linden's sixty-sixth birthday, marking his official retirement from the International Institute of Social History (IISH) in Amsterdam, and celebrating a new phase in his academic life. The volume reflects the variety of topics that characterize his work and the golden thread that connects them. It shows how his writings on Marxist theory, capitalism, the working classes, the renewal of labor history as a discipline—including all forms of work, labor relations, and movements—and the study of labor on a global scale evolved over the years, and how they have inspired many colleagues all over the world. At the same time, the articles reveal Marcel's sources of inspiration: The colleagues and Ph.D. students he worked with, and the insights and methodological approaches that disciplines such as anthropology, ethnology, and area studies offered him.

1   The Career of a Historical Social Scientist

"We know only a single science, the science of history."[1]

Marcel van der Linden was born in Hittfeld near Hamburg in 1952 into a Dutch-German family, and grew up in Weert (Limburg province) where he attended the Gymnasium. At the age of 16, he started to develop political ideals diametrically opposed to those of his parents. In 1971 he began studying mathematics, physics, and astronomy at Utrecht University, inspired by the famous astronomer and Marxist theorist, Anton Pannekoek. He became a very

---

* The authors would like to thank Aad Blok, Mona Hilfman, Alice Mul, and Ben Stroomberg for their input regarding the biographical and *IRSH* part of this introduction.

1 "Er is maar een wetenschap en dat is de sociale wetenschap en die is historisch," Leo Noordegraaf, "In gesprek met Marcel van der Linden," in *Waarover spraken zij? Economische geschiedbeoefening in Nederland omstreeks het jaar 2000,* ed. Leo Noordegraaf (Amsterdam, 2006), 193–203, 197. For an elaboration on this idea from Marx that Marcel van der Linden used in translation, see Michael R. Krätke, "Marx and World History," *International Review of Social History* 63, no. 1 (April 2018): 91–125.

© ULBE BOSMA AND KARIN HOFMEESTER, 2018 | DOI:10.1163/9789004386617_002

This is an open access chapter distributed under the terms of the prevailing CC-BY-NC License.

active member of the student movement, and during his second year decided to switch to sociology, as this had more societal impact than the study of the stars. As one of the co-founders of the Socialist Sociologist Union (*Socialistische Sociologen Bond*), he developed close ties to the Dutch section of the Fourth International and its charismatic thinker Ernest Mandel, who became his tutor.[2] Years of intense reading and debating followed, and predominantly Marxist theory was combined with journalistic political activism. Marcel van der Linden left the Trotskyite political movement in 1980, but theoretical considerations about the foundations and conceptions of socialist thinking would remain an important part of his intellectual life. In 1978, he graduated *cum laude* in sociology, worked as an economics teacher at two high schools for three years, and then decided it was time for a change. He began thinking about Ph.D. research and met his future life partner Alice Mul during a meeting of an anti-fascist action committee in Utrecht. Western Marxism and the Soviet Union was the topic of his Ph.D. research, which he carried out "in his spare time" as he states in his own introduction. Frits de Jong Edz. was his supervisor and an impressive list of people—including Ernest Mandel—acted as commentators and sparring partners. In 1989 he received his Ph.D. *cum laude* at the University of Amsterdam.

In the meantime he had joined the IISH in 1983, and became the editorial advisor for the *International Review of Social History* (*IRSH*), the academic journal of the institute. In 1987, Arend van Woerden retired as editorial secretary of the journal and Marcel became his successor as executive editor. He would thoroughly change the publication policy of the journal, an operation that benefited both the *IRSH* and the IISH, as well as Marcel's academic development, as will be shown in the next section. At the same time, the IISH underwent a huge reorganization led by its new director Eric Fischer. The main goal of this was to rebalance the resources devoted to collections on the one hand, and research and publications on the other. These latter two functions, part of the original aims of the IISH foundation, had been neglected because of the massive growth of the collections and their use by the public.[3] The publications department, now headed by Marcel, changed its policy in accordance with this rebalancing. Traditionally, the IISH had focused on source publications based on the archival collections of the institute, now publications based on important new research questions were prepared.

---

2 Noordegraaf, "In gesprek met Marcel van der Linden," 193.
3 Eric Fischer, "The International Institute of Social History—Reorganization after fifty years," *International Review of Social History* 33, no. 3 (December 1988): 246–257.

INTRODUCTION 3

Research at the IISH received a major boost when one year later, in 1988, Jan Lucassen, a social and economic historian at Utrecht University, joined the institute. He was invited by Eric Fisher to establish a research department that would become an independent unit within the IISH.[4] At that time labor history was confined to white, male, European, or American industrial workers, often studied through the lens of their trade unions and worker's parties, and analyzed at a national level. Jan suggested using a much wider definition of work and workers—including pre-industrial, non-paid, and unfree work—to approach the subject from an international comparative perspective and to broaden the scope of labor history; both in time (going back to 1500) and in space, encompassing the whole world. Jan and Marcel became close collaborators, and research and publication strategies became so integrated that in 1993 the Research and Publications department merged, with Jan as head and Marcel as deputy. Together they wrote the *Prolegomena for a Global Labour History*, a manifesto for global labor history. How this field evolved can be traced from the overview of Marcel's work provided in this introduction, from Jan Lucassen's contribution, and from other articles in this volume. Marcel's upwardly mobile career at the IISH culminated in 2001, when he succeeded Jan as Director of the Research and Publications Department. Marcel would hold this position until 2014 when he—just like his predecessor—voluntarily stepped down and became a senior researcher.

In addition to being an editor and researcher, Marcel was also a tutor. From 1997 until 2017 he was a professor of social movement history at the University of Amsterdam. In addition, he was a visiting professor at the University of Vienna, the Université Libre in Brussels, the University of Nanjing, and the University of Oslo, which awarded him an honorary doctorate in 2008. As well as his outreach to students worldwide, he is also a networker: He is a co-founder of the Association of Indian Labour Historians, the European Labour History Network, and the Global Labour History Network. In 2014, the Ruhr University Bochum awarded him with the *Bochumer Historikerpreis* for his role as the "decisive designer of the concept of Global Labour History" and as the establisher of the "institutional foundations for a strong global network that deals with the history of labour and the labour movement, which in the 21st century has lost none of its relevance and appeal."[5]

---

4 In his contribution to this volume, Jan Lucassen elaborates on these developments, see pp. 22–23.

5 http://www.isb.ruhr-uni-bochum.de/sbr/historikerpreis/preistraeger2014.html.de.

2 The International Review of Social History

When Marcel started working for the *IRSH* as editorial advisor in 1983, his main task was to produce an extensive, annotated bibliography of the journal. This gave him the opportunity to read and digest the latest literature on social history with a focus on labor and labor movements. A firm foundation for his later well-informed work was laid in these formative years. According to his friend and colleague Karl Heinz Roth, who calls Marcel an "Encyclopaedist of critical thought," this work stimulated the development of Marcel's encyclopedic arsenal.[6] When he became executive editor of the *IRSH* in 1987, he also replaced Charles B. Timmer as Head of the Publications Department, with Mona Hilfman as editorial assistant, and from 1988 onward, Aad Blok as production and managing editor. The department was responsible for the *IRSH* and the book publication series of the IISH, including the newly established *IISG Studies and Essays* series published by the Stichting Beheer IISG publishing house, and from 1995 onward, the series *International Comparative Social History*, published by Peter Lang. Where Marcel's predecessor at the *IRSH* had been an editorial secretary, and accordingly a member of the Editorial Committee, Marcel as executive editor became a facilitator, but not a member of the committee. He could therefore operate more independently, and being in charge of the *IRSH*'s editorial office, he was now the first to decide whether an article was to be rejected immediately or sent to external referees and to the Editorial Committee for review. His position and role thereby became vital for the image and reputation of the journal. As important as this change in editorial responsibilities and procedures would turn out to be, no traces of a formal agreement or the conditions of this change can be found in the IISH and *IRSH* archives. This is illustrative of Marcel van der Linden's pragmatic strategy toward official procedures and statutes: Having fewer established rules gave him greater opportunity to operate according to his own insights.

The new Editorial Committee had already been presented in the first issue of the journal in 1987. Whereas in the past, staff members of the IISH had formed the committee, half of the appointees were now scholars from Dutch and Belgian universities, and an advisory board with an international character was announced. In the second issue that year, the new committee announced the aim to address a broader area of social history than "just" labor history of Europe from the late eighteenth century onward. From then on, the focus would also be on pre-industrial relations and non-European countries.

---

6 Karl Heinz Roth, "An Encyclopaedist of Critical Thought: Marcel van der Linden, Heterodox Marxism and Global Labour History," in *On the Road to Global Labour History. A Festschrift for Marcel van der Linden,* ed. Karl Heinz Roth (Leiden/Boston, 2017), 263–351, and here 266.

INTRODUCTION

The themes to be addressed were labor, labor markets, and labor relations. In addition, labor was to be interpreted in a broad sense, including the work of women, slaves, artisans, and peasants; personal, institutional, and cultural aspects of power relations and social functions; social and political movements; and the theoretical and methodological aspects of all these subjects.[7] An external peer review process was established and active acquisition of articles and book manuscripts was started. Review essays, book reviews, and the annotated bibliography were used to "steer the journal in its new direction" by systematically paying attention to what was then called Third World history.[8]

The internationalization of the *IRSH* continued, when in 1988 its first international advisory board was established, consisting of John Saville, Harmut Kaelbe, Charles Tilly, and David Montgomery to cover the "traditional" field of labor history: Industrial Europe and the United States. Jürgen Schlumbohm and Michel Vovelle were invited as experts for pre-industrial Europe, Ian Roxborough for South America, and Peter Gutkind for Africa. In his talk during the first meeting of this advisory board, Jan Lucassen explained how the renewal of the board should be seen as part of new publication policies, which in turn were linked to a new research policy, in fact a "revival of the International Institute of Social History."[9] The advisory board endorsed the plans for a broader interpretation of labor and labor history, the expansion in time and space and the focus on international comparisons, and promised to be "on the look-out for manuscripts."[10] In 1992, as a prelude to the merging of the research and publications departments of the IISH, the Advisory Board of the *IRSH* also became the Advisory Board of the IISH Foundation.[11]

During the annual meeting of the advisory board in 1992, Marcel gave an overview of the results of the changed policy at that point: The extension in time had not yet been very successful, and the expansion in space had been partly successful, together with the thematic expansion. Nevertheless, some interesting comparative articles had appeared. Enthusiasm characterized Marcel's remarks on the change of publisher: From 1993 on, the *IRSH* would be published by Cambridge University Press. The international marketing strategies

---

7   Editorial Committee, "Editorial," *International Review of Social History* 32, no. 2 (August 1987): 107–108.

8   Report of the Meeting of the Advisory Board of the IRSH 15-9-1992, Archief Jan Lucassen 93, Collection IISH.

9   Jan Lucassen's note for the first meeting of the International Advisory Board of the IRSH, 31-8-1988 and 1-9-1988, Archief Jan Lucassen 93, Collection IISH.

10   Remark by John Saville, Report of the Advisory Board Meeting, 31-8-1988 and 1-9-1988, Archief Jan Lucassen 93, Collection IISH.

11   The collections of the IISH, some of which concern politically sensitive materials, are the property of or have been issued on standing loan to the independent IISH Foundation.

and reputation of the new publisher were especially praised. John Saville and Peter Gutkind congratulated the editorial committee and especially Marcel van der Linden on the successful negotiations with CUP.[12] One of the reasons for this success was Marcel's professional training as a publisher: His thorough knowledge of the publishing business had made him a strong partner in the negotiations. The journal could now expand to no fewer than 174 pages, which gave it the opportunity to publish an extra issue annually. These special issues as they would be called were devoted to a particular theme, and proved to be more agenda setting than any other part of the *IRSH* content. In fact the first special issue was called an "emergency issue" by Marcel and was titled *The End of Labour History?*

Not only were the advisory board and the publisher internationalized; the editorial committee also became more global when in 2009, Ravi Ahuja joined as South Asia specialist and Michael Zeuske as Latin America specialist. Others would soon follow. Many of these editorial committee members brought in articles on the Global South as it was now called and the expansion in space began to take shape as can be seen in the geographical distribution of IRSH article topics as shown in Figure 1.1.

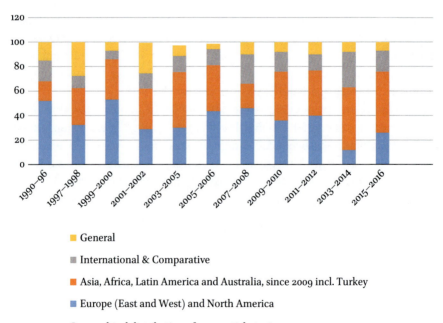

FIGURE 1.1 Geographical distribution of *IRSH* article topics.

---

12   Report of the Meeting of the Advisory Board of the IRSH 15-9-1992, Archief Jan Lucassen 93, Collection IISH.

INTRODUCTION 7

The internationalization of the *Review* ran parallel with the new global scope of the research agenda of the IISH, and last but not least, was intimately linked to Marcel's personal development as a scholar of impressive stature.

3 Marcel's Scholarly Contributions

Marcel's publishing career has resulted in more than 150 publications to date, and reflects an impressive intellectual journey. He started some key debates in the history of social resistance against capitalist exploitation and suggested productive new lines of enquiry. His publications run from evaluating the Soviet system, through Marxist perspectives, to current concerns about the massive dispossession in the global countryside and labor precarity.[13] Obviously they carry the imprint of their time. Marcel's formative years were the 1970s, when the classics were studied in working groups and fiery debates were ongoing about what qualified as Marxism and what did not. At that time, the issue was still more about what Marx *had* said than about what he *could have* said. Marcel was no outlier. In one of his articles from the 1980s, he not only denounces Lenin for being driven by a Jacobin fervor, but also attributes to the first Soviet leader a flawed understanding of basic concepts within Marx' work.[14] At that time he was working on his Ph.D. thesis, *Western Marxism and the Soviet Union*, a skillful analysis of the evolution of Marxists' critiques and apologetics of the Soviet Union. The thesis is an exercise in analyzing how political discourses are structured, in testing their consistency, and in how they should be historically contextualized. From today's perspective, one of the most noticeable features of this work, however, is that it shows Marcel's distinct interest in the anomalous unfree conditions of the workers in the Soviet Union; anomalous from a Marxist point of view, of course.

After Marcel defended his Ph.D. thesis in 1989, his work developed in thematic richness. It has radiated through a widening circle of interaction with other colleagues, particularly by posing questions and formulating topics for further research. From 1990 to date, we can trace a remarkably consistent unfolding of a research agenda. The first steps are in a methodological sense still close to Marcel's thesis, entailing projects to understand variations in

---

13   Marcel van der Linden and Karl Heinz Roth, "Introduction," in *Beyond Marx. Theorising the Global Labour Relations of the Twenty-First Century*, eds. Karl Heinz Roth and Marcel van der Linden (Leiden/Boston, 2013), 1–20, and here 4.

14   https://www.marxists.org/nederlands/van_der_linden/1983/1983kritiek_leninisme.htm.

trajectories of labor activism and how these were embedded in different economic, political, and cultural settings. An example of his investigations into nationally differentiated trajectories of labor movements is the proceedings of the 1985 conference at the IISH. Marcel edited these together with Frits van Holthoon. The conference itself was an attempt to integrate the history of labor movements in a more general historical and international setting. We see the editors using some disparaging words for the institutional history writing that was immersed in sorting out who was squabbling with whom and about what. In their highly critical introduction they take particular umbrage at the fact that among the contributions they collected, the history from below is practically absent and the history from outside Europe is entirely missing.

Their first point was certainly far from new. Social historians had earlier broken with the "old labor history" that a century before had started so gloriously with the work by Beatrice and Sidney Webb, *History of Trade Unionism*, as a homage to what had been accomplished for labor.[15] This type of history was already outdated by the 1960s, when E.P. Thompson had enforced a split between the history of the working class and the history of labor movements. Nonetheless, the conference took place in 1984, just three years before the IISH was reorganized and equipped with a research department studying social history rather than making text editions on Marxism. In the field of social history, the IISH was not exactly on the cusp of things at that time. The second point made by Van der Linden and Van Holthoon about having no input from outside Europe had far more important ramifications. After all, Thompson and his many followers at that time shared with the Webb couple an approach to labor history that stayed within the boundaries of the nation states. This point was reiterated in another volume that appeared at that time, and which Marcel had edited together with Jürgen Rojahn. Their introduction featured the objective "to break out of the still very common restriction to the national framework towards the comparative research on the one hand and the study of international connections on the other. The current project on the determinants of the working-class movements is a step in the first direction."[16] The point made here was that laborers obviously lived within different national contexts and

---

15   "Introduction," in *Class and Other Identities. Gender, Religion and Ethnicity in the Writing of European Labour History,* eds. Marcel van der Linden and Lex Heerma van Voss (New York/Oxford, 2002), 1–39, and here 4.

16   Jürgen Rojahn and Marcel van der Linden, "Introduction," in *The Formation of Labour Movements, 1870–1914. An International Perspective,* eds. Jürgen Rojahn and Marcel van der Linden. Vol. 1 (Leiden, 1990), ix–xviii, and here ix.

INTRODUCTION 9

their organizations went through a variety of trajectories, but that this did not exclude their intense connectivity.

One of the key ambitions permeating Marcel's work by around 1990 was to integrate national labor histories in a transnational framework. The already existing historiography on worker's and socialist internationalism—the Bund der Kommunisten, the First, Second and Third International—provided a suitable starting point for such an endeavor. Much of the existing work in this field was, however, unsurprisingly doctrinally informed. Pushing aside the doctrinal issues, Marcel began to advocate the comparative history of the institutional histories to find explanations for differences and commonalities in the various national trajectories of labor activism, and thus add to this field of study an urgently needed theoretical dimension. Obviously, the method had its limitations in a world which was so thoroughly interconnected, and it required a critical engagement with the methodological aspects and pitfalls of comparison.[17] It was this methodological problem that Charles Tilly, the master of the field in those days, also grappled with, but Marcel apparently did not turn to the procedures Tilly suggested or at least not explicitly. He did, however, explicitly probe other explanatory devices, as is apparent from his review essay, on Labor History and Organizational Ecology, which appeared in 1990.[18] This ecological model, designed by Michael T. Hannan and John Freeman to explain the proliferation of organizations as a sociological rather than an ideological phenomenon, seemed to promise a scientific alternative to the descriptive and un-theoretical historiography of labor organizations. However, it was an avenue not pursued further by Marcel, because this pseudo-biological format clearly had its deterministic limitations and not that much to offer in terms of explanation.

Moreover, by the late 1980s there were far more interesting questions and themes pertaining to how labor advanced its cause. Revolutionary syndicalism was a topic on which Marcel published together with Wayne Thorpe in 1990. They defined syndicalism broadly as a representation of the right of workers to "collective self-management" and as being led by the belief that ultimately, class interests were irreconcilable.[19] There is no need to read against the grain

---

17   Marcel van der Linden, "Methodologische Probleme vergleichender Sozialgeschichte: Eine Erwiderung auf Christiane Eisenbergs 'methodenkritische Bemerkungen' zu einem IISG-Projekt," *Archiv für Sozialgeschichte* 35 (1995): 231–239.

18   Marcel van der Linden, "Labour History and Organizational Ecology," *International Review of Social History* 35 (1990): 273–280.

19   See Marcel van der Linden and Wayne Thorpe, "The Rise and Fall of Revolutionary Syndicalism," in *Revolutionary Syndicalism: An International Perspective*, eds. Marcel van der Linden and Wayne Thorpe (Aldershot, 1990), 1–24.

to discover that Marcel's sympathy was with the syndicalist groups' principled struggles for workers' autonomy. The same engagement with workers' autonomy brought Marcel to the topic of mutualism as a vehicle to protect workers by limiting the effects of illness and other calamities, by strengthening self-confidence, and by educating to look ahead and to reflect on how to gain control over their lives.[20] With these lines of enquiry on syndicalism and mutualism, Marcel underscored that in addition to direct negotiations between workers and employers, there were two other collective avenues to strengthen the position of labor, namely via the political process and as consumers; both via consumer cooperatives and mutualist societies, or via boycotts.

This affinity with groups and strategies striving for autonomy is matched by inquisitiveness about the circumstances that favor or hamper their pursuits. Marcel went further down this road by starting to investigate the deeper economic and technological changes that brought about syndicalism in so many industrialized countries, which was precisely during the Second Industrial Revolution, at a time of rapidly changing living conditions for workers, sprawling urbanization, and enhanced means of communication. At the same time, there was a staggering accumulation of capital; these were the days of the trusts.[21]

The idea of mass strikes to topple the capitalist system gained credibility, as more and more workers had been turned into wage workers and had become indispensable for the proper functioning of modern society. The failure of the general strike of 1903 in the Netherlands—against the so-called strangulation laws that prohibited government employees from striking—was a time at which the moderate labor unionists and socialist politicians broke with revolutionary syndicalism in this country.[22] Further, while the immediate cause of the end of syndicalism in Europe was usually state repression, the more structural factors were the rise of the welfare state and the integration of labor in advanced capitalist economies.[23] This is what Marcel wrote about almost thirty years ago. Today this observation can raise the question of whether syndicalism could re-emerge in times of a retreating welfare state. Probably not, Marcel might say, as syndicalism attended the rise of stable wage labor relations, and today's retreat of the welfare state goes along with increasing precarity.

---

20   "Histoire comparée des Sociétés de secours mutuels," *Revue de l'économie sociale* 19 (1990): 169–179.

21   Van der Linden and Thorpe, "The Rise and Fall," 7.

22   Van der Linden, "The Many Faces of Dutch Revolutionary Trade Unionism," in *Revolutionary syndicalism*, eds. Van der Linden and Thorpe, 45–57.

23   Van der Linden, *Transnational Labour History. Explorations.* (Aldershot, 2003), 64.

INTRODUCTION

The same type of analysis of historical conjunctures was applied to the short existence of the First International (1864–1876). Moving away from the chronicles of the squabbles between the great men, and a few women, of socialism, Marcel turned his attention to the underlying causes, including economic conditions, cultural factors, and processes of nation state formation. This project resulted in a clear periodization of a pre-national phase (until the end of the 1860s), a transitional phase (from the 1860s to 1900), and ultimately a national phase. The transitional character of the First International was shaped by an ideologically internationalist outlook coupled with an organizational make-up structured into national chapters. Still, the First International was genuinely revolutionary and transnational, although within the confines of a circulation of revolutionaries on the run from Bismarck and Napoleon III. This sensitivity toward historical timing returned in Marcel's 2003 article on the Revolution of 1968, which he interprets as a transnational wave stirring many countries across the world from 1968 to 1976. He diagnosed it as a unique confluence of soaring student numbers, growing female labor participation, and the sunset of a long period of economic growth.[24]

4   The Crisis of Labor History and Decentering Wage Labor

Whereas Marcel's scholarly work of the 1980s had already transcended national boundaries and avoided the stories about doctrinal squabbles as well as the narrowly institutionalist approach, his writings were still about the world of the white male industrial worker. He considered it to be imperative for the survival of labor history that Eurocentrism should be overcome. Although the old institutionalist labor history had been rejuvenated in a social history of labor in the 1960s and blossomed in the 1970s, this renewed labor history seriously declined in the subsequent decade. It induced Marcel to question the future of labor history in the special issue of the *International Review of Social History* of 1993, now that the developments of the 1980s had "turned research on labor relations antiquarian in the eyes of many."[25] This 1993 special issue was therefore "a scholarly attempt to further the urgent integration of labor history in

---

24   Van der Linden, "The Aftermath of '1968': Interactions of Workers', Youth and Women's Movements," in *Transnational Labour History. Explorations*, ed. Van der Linden. (Aldershot, 2003), 117–141. See also *1968—A View of the Protest Movements 40 Years After, from a Global Perspective*, eds. Ven der Linden, with Angelika Ebbinghaus and Max Henninger (Leipzig, 2009).

25   Van der Linden, "Editorial," *International Review of Social History* 38, Special Issue (1993): 1–3, and here 1.

the broader discipline of social history and at the same time to highlight the field's undiminished vitality."[26] However, the problems were serious and manifold: Marcel noted a neglect of attention to gender and ethnicity, an exclusive focus on Europe and its settler colonies, an overemphasis on the white male breadwinner, and the fact that early modern history was at best treated in an anecdotal way.[27]

It was these challenges that Marcel responded to, by inviting scholars to write about new themes, mostly via special issues of the *International Review of Social History*, through a new book series he launched with Berghahn publishers, and in collaboration with his IISH colleagues Lex Heerma van Voss and Jan Lucassen. They addressed the facts that workers' identities were not just shaped by their labor relations, but also by *other* identities including gender, religion, and ethnicity, and that workers were not only workers for the market but also within households. Another major subject was the decentering of the doubly free wage laborers ("free" from the means of production and "free" to offer their labor power) as being just one among many categories of workers, and historically only recently of major importance.[28]

Marcel's participation in debates on free and unfree labor was crucial in shaping the agenda for global labor history. The theme of forced labor, which had already appeared in his Ph.D. thesis, became a recurring element in his repertoire from the mid-1990s, when the IISH organized a wide-ranging conference on "Free and Unfree Labor." This event resulted in a volume that Marcel co-edited with Tom Brass, and which marked a shift from studying labor activism to studying labor relations in world history. In his wide-ranging concluding article in that volume, titled "In Lieu of a Conclusion," Marcel asks the question of how wage labor could become the normalized labor relation. In the case study he wrote for his volume on forced labor in the Soviet Union, he points out that the existence of seven million people in the Soviet Labor Camps was part of more general labor policies under Stalin. All Soviet workers were increasingly disciplined: First by having to accept every type of work, then through a work book kept by the employer, and further through systems of penalties; all of which culminated in 1940 in "the end of free labor," meaning that workers were only allowed to quit their job or change employment with the explicit consent of the plant management.

---

26   Van der Linden, "Editorial," 2.

27   Van der Linden, "Editorial," 2.

28   See Van der Linden, "The Origins, Spread and Normalization of Free Wage Labour," in *Free and Unfree Labour. The debate Continues*, eds. Tom Brass and Van der Linden (Bern, 1997), 501–523.

INTRODUCTION

The key observation Marcel makes here is that "Against this background the GULag may be seen, not as a 'deviation' from an otherwise different type of labor system, but as the most extreme form of a far broader tendency towards bonded labor."[29] This leads him to ask whether we can describe the labor relations in the GULag as slavery. His answer tends toward the affirmative, since—despite not being the property of a person—these workers have no enforceable legal rights, and labor and other activities are totally controlled.[30] Pursuing the question further, Marcel concludes that this was a cheap way of mobilizing labor when it was in short supply.[31] Twenty years later we can see that this essay contained a crucial step toward seeking new universal explanations for labor relations that did not seem to fit within the still common evolutionist narrative of increasing freedom attending the advance of modernity.

The volume *Free and Unfree Labour* was in many ways path-breaking, not least because of an exceptionally strong line up of authors. Robert Steinfeld and Stanley Engerman, for example, contributed a joint article complicating the equivalence of wage labor and free labor, and denying the existence of neat boundaries between the two.[32] The recognition of the grey zones between "free" and "unfree" labor had become a key point in the emergence of global labor history, but at the same time a road full of pitfalls, as Marcel pointed out in one of his more recent publications. The intense renewed interest in slavery on the one hand and wage labor on the other, created a polarized body of literature in which it is precisely the grey zones that have become obfuscated.[33] These zones include an array of cases running from the masters and servants act to the massive extent of unfree labor under the Stalin and Hitler regimes. The emphasis on the binary nature of completely unfree and doubly free labor also obfuscates the fact that throughout history, unfree rather than free labor has been the rule.[34]

---

29   Van der Linden, "Forced Labour and Non-Capitalist Industrialization: The Case of Stalinism (c. 1929–c. 1956)," in *Free and Unfree Labour. The Debate Continues,* eds. Tom Brass and Van der Linden (Bern, 1997), 351–362, and here 355.

30   Van der Linden, "Forced Labour," 358.

31   Van der Linden, "Forced Labour," 362.

32   See Robert J. Steinfeld and Stanley L. Engerman, "Labor—Free or Coerced? A Historical Reassessment of Differences and Similarities," in *Free and Unfree Labour*, 107–126.

33   Van der Linden and Magaly Rodríguez García, "Introduction," in *On Coerced Labor. Work and Compulsion after Chattel Slavery*, eds. Van der Linden and Magaly Rodríguez García, (Leiden/Boston, 2016), 1–10, and here 1.

34   Jan Lucassen, "Free and Unfree Labour Before the Twentieth Century: A Brief Overview," in *Free and Unfree Labour*, 45–56.

Marcel wrote his review article (published in 1993) *Connecting Household History and Labour History*,[35] about the workers' embeddedness in the household and the need to study the household as the venue where decisions are made about what labor to take up or when to strike, and where living strategies are designed. From an interest in the household came an interest in the fact that workers often combine different labor relations; for example the smallholders who supplemented their income with sharecropping and wage work. The question of partial proletarianization, at that time a topical subject for scholars working on and in the Global South, was brought up in, again, a special issue of the *International Review of Social History* that Marcel edited together with Shahid Amin in 1997. This was part of a more general fulfilment of a promise made ten years earlier to bring the Global South into the fold of labor history, an endeavor that greatly benefited from Marcel's interactions with colleagues from South Asia as well as those in the Netherlands working on South Asia, such as Jan Breman and Willem van Schendel. The introduction to this special issue speaks of a segmentation of the labor market, showing a divide between workers who were well-off and those in the periphery whose work was insecure and floating.[36] With these discussions, Marcel guided the *International Review of Social History* toward interdisciplinary terrain, ushering in fruitful interactions with discussions featuring in publications such as the *Journal of Peasant Studies*.

Over the course of a few years, Marcel and his colleagues had demolished the boundaries set by the "old labor history" paradigm of the white male industrial wage laborer as the final agent in history. One might note that these years also marked the rise of postmodernism and the end of the grand narrative. To some extent, Marcel went along with this deconstruction of the standard Marxist narrative. His concluding essay in *Free and Unfree Labor* disavowed the Marxist orthodoxy of the capitalism-wage labor nexus by asking the question of why "free" wage labor emerged as a historical category in its own right.[37] He discarded the idea that wage labor was the "true" capitalist form of exploitation and slavery. This concluding essay developed into a *tour d'horizon*. Relying on an impressive array of sources, Marcel unsettled the generally accepted notion that specific labor relations are bound to specific stages in history, and

---

35   "Connecting Household History and Labour History," *International Review of Social History*, Supplement 1 (1993): 163–173.

36   Shahid Amin and Van der Linden, "Introduction," *"Peripheral" Labour? Studies in the History of Partial Proletarianization*, (Cambridge, 1997), 4–5.

37   Van der Linden, "The Origins, Spread and Normalization of Free Wage Labour," 501.

INTRODUCTION

suggested new connections such as the one between the rise of capitalism (print capitalism) and humanitarianism.[38] This exercise shows precisely how deconstruction served the wider purpose of developing new directions for investigation. Marcel felt little sympathy for attempts to go into postmodernist discourses on labor and micropolitics, for example. He was determined to stay attuned to the big questions of labor solidarity and why labor so often manifestly acted against its own interests.[39]

5 Global Labor History and Back to the International

The answers that followed the discussions about the 1993 special issue detailing the crisis of labor history were summarized six years later in the *Prolegomena*, the manifesto Marcel wrote together with Jan Lucassen, at that time the head of the research department of the IISH. It addressed head-on the lack of direction and program in the field of labor history, since the history of labor unionism had been replaced by the social history of workers, their families, etc. It also tabled without any ado the problem of Eurocentrism: "Our central question therefore is: how can we study the global development of labor throughout history without implicitly using (a particular interpretation of part of) European history as a model?"[40] Part of the answer lay beneath the immense variety of labor relations in the shape of a few universals, such as that people live in households, and that societies throughout history have known slavery, service for the community, and work for the market. There was, furthermore, no way to disconnect labor from social security, as this represented a crucial factor shaping labor relations; not just within the family and among peers (companionships) but also in the form of patronage.[41]

In 2003 Marcel published a selection of articles—most of which had already previously appeared—as *Transnational Labor History*. At that time, the crisis of labor history as a worn-out European brand had not yet been overcome, but there was light at the end of the tunnel in the shape of the emergence of the Association of Indian Labor Historians, a strong labor history field in South Africa, together with a boom of labor history in Latin America. This offered

---

38   Van der Linden, "The Origins," 521.

39   See Van der Linden, "Keeping Distance: Alf Lüdtke's 'Decentred' Labour History," *International Review of Social History* 40 (1995): 287–296.

40   Van der Linden and Jan Lucassen. *Prolegomena for a Global Labour History* (Amsterdam, 1999), 7.

41   Van der Linden and Lucassen, *Prolegomena*, 15.

good prospects for a transnational approach, defined in Marcel's volume as "labor history that focuses on cross-border processes and comparisons."[42] Here we see continuity with the methodological concerns expressed in his publications around 1990, but now the ambition had expanded from European to global. Marcel demonstrated a growing optimism that this would be feasible, at least this was the spirit of the special issue of the *Review* that Marcel edited with Rana Behal in 2006. The editors noted that labor history was spreading out towards India, South Africa, and Brazil and through that, the old labor history with its "vanguardism" of the industrial laborer and its uneasiness about pre-industrial and pre-colonial labor histories was gradually losing its dominant position.[43]

Old labor history indeed looked glaringly dull and parochial compared with the ambitions and cosmopolitanism of Global Labor History. A new field had been established and the time had come to relate some of the theoretical reflections of the 1990s to topical historiographical debates and the current grim sides of capitalism, which had become the only economic model after the demise of the Soviet Union and the rapid transformation of the Chinese economy. *Workers of the World. Essays Toward A Global History*, which appeared in 2008, is a concise presentation of Global Labor History in which labor relations, mutualism, workers' resistance, internationalisms, and a conversation with world systems theory are brought together in a single framework. This book is considered by most of Marcel's peers to be his most important intellectual contribution to the field. Above all, it was an overview of the field in the middle of the unfolding of Marcel's research agenda through the—by then—well-known mechanism of the editorship of special journal issues and edited volumes. One of the questions that still deserved further investigation, for example, was how capitalist expansion could be attended by a resurgence of unfree labor. On this topic, Marcel produced together with Carolyn Brown a special issue of the *International Labor and Working-Class History*, with contributions by Jan Breman on neo-bondage in India and Alessandro Stanziani on serfdom in Russia. One year later Sidney Chalhoub published an article on the grey zones of slavery in Brazil in the *Review*.[44]

---

42 Van der Linden, *Transnational Labour History. Explorations.* (Aldershot, 2003), 3–4.

43 Rana P. Behal and Van der Linden, "Preface," *International Review of Social History* 51 Supplement (2006): 1–5.

44 Carolyn Brown and Van der Linden, "Shifting Boundaries between Free and Unfree Labor: Introduction," *International Labor and Working-Class History* 78 (2010): 4–11; Sidney Chalhoub, "The Precariousness of Freedom in a Slave Society (Brazil in the Nineteenth Century)," *International Review of Social History* 56, no. 3 (2011): 405–439.

INTRODUCTION 17

6 Precarity

The decentering of stable wage labor relations was a historiographic exercise that had its parallel in the real world, where the stable wage labor contract was considered to be the norm for the industrialized world of the 1990s. For those who had not already noticed it before, the crisis of 2008 unequivocally exposed this as too complacent. The second decade of the twenty-first century witnessed a revival of Karl Marx and the rising popularity of capitalism as a field of study. Somewhat paradoxically, at the same time the open-ended character of the work of Marx was increasingly acknowledged and the relevance of the wage laborer as the vanguard of resistance against capitalist oppression called into crisis. In the North, precarity—and the related phenomenon of self-employment—has become more permanent, more akin to the informal sector in the Global South. In an essay co-authored with Jan Breman in 2014, Marcel concludes:

> The classical conceptualization of the working class, of workers' collective action and, especially, of trade unionism, was implicitly or explicitly based on the Standard Employment Relationship that, for a few decades, has been dominant in North America, Europe, Japan and Australasia. The "classical" model of collective bargaining, which has shaped the world's traditional labor movements, was based on this conceptualization. However, it is now increasingly undermined by the rapid spread of "informal" or "precarious" labor in the global North.[45]

In another publication, Marcel discussed the structural cause for this trend, namely that the labor supply shock of the 1980s and 1990s—that is, the immense influx of labor producing for the global market that was not absorbed by an equal growth in capital—had led to a general reduction of wages, including those in the most productive sectors of the global economy. On top of this Lewisian condition of an unlimited supply of labor, which informed workers' bargaining power, came another complicating factor for workers' solidarity at the global level. Since workers are positioned in different segments of the commodity chain and the division of profits over these segments is a zero-sum game, Marcel concludes that the interests of the workers down the chain in rich industrialized countries collide with those at the upper parts of the chain

---

45 Jan Breman and Marcel van der Linden, "Informalizing the Economy: The Return of the Social Question at a Global Level," *Development and Change* 45, No. 5 (2014): 920–940 and here 924.

in the Global South. This problem is further compounded in his eyes by the fact that the labor unions are shaped by their origins and are therefore burdened by institutional inflexibility, which diminishes their ability to respond adequately to rapidly changing global configurations.[46]

By linking precarity to the increasing strength of global capital vis-à-vis labor, Marcel returned—although now at a global level—to the set of questions he had addressed in the late 1980s pertaining to the trajectories of labor movements. Was it, as Mandel had once posited, that the successes of labor unionism at best benefited a mere 20 percent of the world's population, leaving by far the majority of the world under the sway of capitalism?[47] Although Marcel seemed to be susceptible to this argument, he must have noticed that it might not fit any longer, because it belonged to what was clearly divided into a first, second, and third world. At any rate, he mentions it in passing in his above-cited article co-authored with Jan Breman. More explicitly, Marcel rejects Karl Heinz Roth's argument that a bifurcation of the labor class at a global scale is transpiring, in which urban wage laborers enjoy social security and in which a much larger proletariat relies on its links with the rural countryside. He disagrees, noting that the informal sector is increasingly urban, heterogeneous, and splintered by household and ethnic and religious affinities. Even if the social-economic conditions of the precarious laborers in the Global North and the South converge, one should therefore not exaggerate their potential for labor mobilization. On the contrary, Marcel points out that "The most precarious classes in the West will be prone to falling prey to xenophobic rhetoric."[48] These points were reiterated in an article entitled *The Crisis of World labor*, in the journal *Against the Current*. Despite the massive growth of the labor force in the Global South and sometimes impressive signs of power, "The militancy of the workers has not yet been consolidated in strong organizations. In fact, 'old-style' labor is in decline, and fundamental changes will be necessary before a vibrant transnational union movement can be built."[49]

The circle has been closed. Comparative studies on labor movements and labor internationalism have gained a new currency, since it has become obsolete to talk about developing and developed countries, or rich and poor countries. The inequalities within societies and the struggles between the classes have to be placed in the foreground. At the same time, one should note that dominant

---

46 Van der Linden, "The Crisis of World Labor," *Against the Current* 176 (2015): 29–34.

47 Breman and Van der Linden, "Informalizing," 929.

48 Van der Linden, "Die neue Zusammensetzung der WeltarbeiterInnenklasse und das Problem der Solidarität," in *Die Wiederkehr der Proletarität. Dokumentation der Debatte*, ed. Karl Heinz Roth (Köln, 1994), 83–84.

49 Van der Linden, "The Crisis of World Labor."

INTRODUCTION   19

classes have been recomposed: They no longer consist of the productive industrialists and the bourgeoisie, but instead of an amalgam of bosses of public
services (education, housing, healthcare, etc.) that have been privatized, of financial and legal experts, and so on. Meanwhile, the conclusion is unavoidable
that the global working class is not a homogeneous entity but a "multiverse of
strata and social groups" embedded in a variety of kin and social networks. The
crafting of a field of global labor history has been a major accomplishment and
has enabled historians to address current social questions at the global level,
but it has also exposed the diminishing space for workers' solidarity.

7   The Contributions to this Volume

The first contribution is by *Jan Lucassen*, with whom Marcel collaborated for
many years building the research department of the IISH. They started the
intellectual journey to discover what labor history would look like once it
abandoned the confines of methodological nationalism. This reappraisal unavoidably went in many directions and brought about the inclusion of household work, slavery, and corvée as subjects for investigation. It opened the door
to an appreciation of the long and geographically diverse pedigree of wage
labor. It is the latter theme that Lucassen writes about. In his contribution he
takes stock of the literature on the nexus between wage labor and capitalism
to ground his thesis that for too long this type of labor has been held hostage
to Eurocentrism and Anglocentrism in particular. Lucassen emphasizes that
new historical evidence scattered over many nations and historical eras needs
a "framework encompassing multi-origin and therefore multilinear developments." It will render many notions and concepts obsolete, but Lucassen
would like to exclude from this clean-up one achievement of classical labor
history, namely the analytical tools to study the collective action among wage
laborers, which continue to be valuable.

No less than Marx himself was co-responsible for this unwarranted elevation of a particular configuration of wage labor and capitalism to universal
validity. *Pepijn Brandon* explains how Marcel reworked Marx' notion of commodified labor power to extend it beyond its narrow confines of proletarian
wage labor and toward a variety of coerced labor relations. This is not only of
academic relevance, but is also pivotal today, when coerced labor has proved
its resilience in the face of capitalism that has expanded to every corner of the
world. Brandon shows how Marcel's intervention has opened up the enquiry
into the full range of labor relations between slavery and "free" wage labor as
part of the history, and probably the future, of capitalism.

Jürgen Kocka starts his essay with the observation that today the "history of capitalism" stands alongside established subfields such as "women's history" and "cultural history." Capitalism has become a word that has even become *salonfähig* in evening talk shows. Kocka's contribution shows the two-sided character of the concept; being both the banner of social critique and the subject of scholarly analysis. This is not a recent phenomenon. Over the past six centuries, the perceptions and moral connotations attached to capitalism have changed considerably. From skepticism in the late Middle Ages, to merchant capitalist accumulation, to confidence in capitalism as a rational and liberating force expressed by Adam Smith and his contemporaries, and to increasing pessimism about the future of capitalism from the late nineteenth century onward. Obviously, the continuing exploitation of labor, growing inequalities, and environmental degradation have gradually overshadowed the once progressive image of capitalism.

Capitalism has commodified labor while the task of its protection is left to the state. In one sector this protection is particularly wanting, as *Magaly Rodriguez* analyzes in her contribution: Sex workers are not on an equal footing with other workers. Within the International Labor Organization opinions sharply diverge on the desirability of treating sex workers in the same way as any other workers with regard to deserving the same degree of protection. There is more than one obstacle involved in the recognition of sex workers. First, prostitution—female in particular—has been deemed problematic in most cultures. Second, the popular language of trafficking is feeding a discourse of suppression. In addition to considerations by activists that prostitution is gender-based violence, there is an unwillingness by governments that would prefer a legal ban rather than regulation of the presence of people or businesses they deem less desirable. In such an atmosphere, little can be accomplished to improve the working and living conditions of sex workers.

Labor history that is inexorably linked to the history of capitalism is not a linear history from unfree to free labor. The fact that the notion of "Second Slavery" exists is enough to make any linearity in the transition from slavery to freedom inconceivable, as *Sidney Chalhoub* points out in his contribution on Brazil. Abolition went hand in hand with new patterns of slavery and the slave trade, and the hardening of racial boundaries. First of all, because the extensive demand for slave labor in Cuba, Brazil, and the southern U.S. states prevented any smooth phasing out of slavery in the nineteenth century. Every step closer to a final ban on human trafficking across the Atlantic elicited a new frantic search by the internal slave trade in these territories. The regimes of slavery were shored up to squeeze the maximum amount of labor out of diminishing slave populations, while white anxiety increased, anticipating

INTRODUCTION 21

growing and perhaps revengeful emancipated slave populations. Against this grim backdrop, Chalhoub sheds a fascinating as well as cruel light on stories of the re-enslavement of individuals in Brazil after the ban on the Brazilian slave trade in 1850.

Jan Breman discusses the effects of capitalism on rural solidarity. Through the lens of Tocqueville's travel to Britain, Breman presents us with an early-nineteenth-century analysis of the workings of capitalism. Much of what Tocqueville found in the first industrial nation of the world in the mid-1830s prefigured what would happen in the world later on. The concept of sharing of benefits and risks, which had kept agrarian societies together for millennia, would disappear for good. Breman concludes that Tocqueville was well aware of the fact that owners of capital were not prepared to compromise their propensity to accumulate. It is an unwillingness that has been consistently exhibited by the capitalist mode of production.

In his chapter, *Andreas Eckert* argues that the interaction between labor history and the emerging field of global history has been beneficial for both sides, but that we should not overlook the indispensable role of area studies for labor history. Global histories of labor require team work, language skills, and the insertion of local specificities. Moreover, the dialogue needs to be multidirectional and non-hierarchical in the sense that models from one period, nation, or region should not be imposed on others.

Willlem van Schendel's contribution does exactly what Eckert recommends. His contribution focuses on Mizoram, a mountainous region in the extreme northeast of India, and introduces us to a world of labor that bears little resemblance to what we have previously read about India from labor historians. Local forms of servitude, forced labor, and voluntary communal labor evolved and combined here in quite distinctive ways. Last but not least, the vigor of communal labor, already sapped from the English and Irish countryside by the early nineteenth century, is still alive.

These eight contributions underscore the astonishing breadth of Marcel's work, which we have tried to reveal in the second part of this introduction. However it is not just the sprawling collections of themes that makes them valuable, but the fact that they can be seen as the result of a coherent and steadfast research agenda of liberating labor history from methodological nationalism. A field of studies has been forged that is ready to address labor history in a thoroughly connected but also immensely unequal world.

CHAPTER 2

Workers: New Developments in Labor History since the 1980s

Jan Lucassen

1 Introduction

In 1971, at the age of 19, Marcel van der Linden—who took his M.A. in sociology at Utrecht University—had already started his publishing career, initially dealing with topics concerning political economy. In 1983 he joined the International Institute of Social History (IISH) as a member of the section International Review of Social History and publications, headed by Arend van Woerden. This was just before the IISH underwent a major reorganization under Eric Fischer (in charge from 1984 to 1993), in which the regional "cabinets" were discontinued and replaced by functional departments, including a separate research department.[1] The "cabinet" staff who wished to, were given the option to become assistant researchers or researchers, which initially entailed the continuation of their source publications underway. However, Fischer wanted more: he felt the IISH research department should concentrate on analytical historical research in close connection with historical departments at universities.

Based at Utrecht University and a former colleague of Eric Fisher, in 1988 I was invited to put into practice this new research policy, which turned out not to be an easy task. However, by finding new funding and by offering part-time positions to colleagues who at the same time were able to maintain their professorial chairs at Dutch universities (for example Tony Saich for Chinese history, Eric Jan Zürcher for Turkish history, and later on Willem van Schendel for South-Asian history), a new start gradually became feasible. In this process it turned out that at the Institute, although in a different department, in Marcel I would find my natural ally. In 1987 he had succeeded Van Woerden to

---

1 Jan Lucassen, *Tracing the Past. Collections and research in social and economic history: The International Institute of Social History, the Netherlands Economic History Archive and related institutions* (Amsterdam, 1989), 47–57; Jaap Kloosterman and Jan Lucassen, *Rebels with a Cause. Five centuries of social history collected by the IISH* (Amsterdam, 2010), 24–25; for details, see the *Annual Reports* of the Institute, accessible through https://socialhistory.org/en/annualreports.

© JAN LUCASSEN, 2018 | DOI:10.1163/9789004386617_003

This is an open access chapter distributed under the terms of the prevailing CC-BY-NC License.

WORKERS: NEW DEVELOPMENTS IN LABOR HISTORY SINCE THE 1980S

become head of the Publications Section and Executive Editor of the *International Review of Social History* (*IRSH*). Over the years our cooperation became so close that the research and publications departments were merged in 1993, with me as head and Marcel as my deputy. After ten years, Marcel—though continuing his responsibilities at the *IRSH*—had fully become involved in the IISH research.

What were the main issues involved in setting up this new department? As a social historian of the early modern period with a strong inclination toward economic history, I felt an urge to expand the traditional field of interest of the Institute. By concentrating on source publications of documents acquired by the IISH since its inception in 1935, the emphasis up to that time had been placed clearly on Europe's leftist trade union and political movements in the period from 1870 to 1918, in particular the German and French-speaking countries, the Netherlands and its colonies, and also Russia. A rich field, without doubt, but at the same time only partially covering the history of work as I was used to thinking of it. The topics I had studied up to that time—the seasonal workers of Europe between 1600 and 1800 and the Moroccan and Turkish "guest workers" and immigrants more in general since 1600–only overlapped very partially with the traditional interests of the IISH.[2] Of course I could have accepted this and switched my interests, but I considered that was not the right path to follow; and the directorate (Eric Fischer, Jaap Kloosterman, and Henk Wals) fully agreed.

Instead, I developed the idea that it would be worthwhile to adopt a much wider definition of work than was usual in labor history as practiced at that time, which automatically encompassed pre-industrial and barely industrialized parts of the world.[3] This endeavor developed into the overarching project

---

2   Jan Lucassen, *Migrant Labour in Europe 1600–1900. The Drift to the North Sea* (London, 1987) (original Dutch edition 1984); Jan Lucassen and Rinus Penninx, *Newcomers. Immigrants and their Descendants in the Netherlands 1550–1995* (Amsterdam, 1997) (original Dutch edition 1985).

3   In 1989 I defined the field as follows: "The aim is to promote research on labour history in the broadest sense of the word. This comprises the history of all kinds of labour though the emphasis lies on workers, whether in paid employment, contract work or in slavery. The history of labour breaks down into three aspects: labour market; labour relations; and the organization of labour and of workers (the 'modern' socialist, anarchist, Christian, liberal and fascist labour movements, as well as workers' organizations based on ethnic, racial, gender, etc. principles). The modern and contemporaneous period will be the focus, with an emphasis on the 19th and 20th centuries. In principle, this ambitious programme will encompass the whole world." (Lucassen 1989, 51–56). For addressing the earlier centuries, see Jan Lucassen, *Jan, Jan Salie en diens kinderen. Vergelijkend onderzoek naar continuïteit en discontinuïteit in de ontwikkeling van arbeidsverhoudingen* (Amsterdam, 1991); Catharina Lis, Jan Lucassen, and

of the Research Department of the IISH on *Global Labour History* under the directorship of myself, my successor Marcel (from 2001 to 2014), and which is still currently practiced at the IISH.

What made Marcel my natural ally on this path? For me it was his methodological angle as a sociologist: always looking for conceptual precision, and also believing in the major advantages of the comparative method. This had already become clear from the conference theme of the fiftieth anniversary of the IISH in 1986: a systematic comparison of internationalism in the labor movement between 1830 and 1940, the proceedings of which were co-edited by Marcel.[4]

This essay is not intended to offer a detailed reconstruction of our long-standing cooperation (and others, in the first place Lex Heerma van Voss[5]), but instead focuses on its results. The development of three topics in particular deserves closer scrutiny: the definitions of what is work and who is a worker, the taxonomy of labor relations, and the long-term history of one specific form of labor relations more in particular, specifically wage work.

2 Definition Questions

In our search for a definition of work encompassing pre-industrial and non-industrialized societies, we were happy to discover the approach of Charles and Chris Tilly as published in 1998, and we immediately embraced it.[6] According to them:

Hugo Soly, eds., "Before the Unions. Wage earners and collective action in Europe, 1300–1850," *International Review of Social History*, Supplement 2 (1994). See also Karel Davids and Jan Lucassen, eds., *A Miracle Mirrored. The Dutch Republic in European Perspective* (Cambridge, 1995), xvii–xviii.

4 Frits van Holthoon and Marcel van der Linden, eds., *Internationalism in the Labour Movement 1830–1940* (Leiden, 1988), followed by Marcel van der Linden and Jürgen Rojahn, eds., *The Formation of Labour Movements 1870–1914. An International Perspective* (Leiden, 1990). About ten years later, he added a certain emphasis on "interconnections" or "entanglements."

5 Risking doing an injustice to many others, I would like to also mention the intellectual input from Aad Blok and Willem van Schendel, and somewhat later from Karin Hofmeester, Jan Kok, and Gijs Kessler.

6 Marcel van der Linden and Jan Lucassen, *Prolegomena for a Global Labour History* (Amsterdam, 1999), 8; Chris Tilly and Charles Tilly, *Work Under Capitalism* (Boulder, CO, 1998), 22–23. Charles Tilly played a dominant role in the International Advisory Board of the IRSH, established in 1990, and in the same year Marcel and I visited his New School for Social Research (then also joined by Eric Hobsbawm). See also Marcel van der Linden, "Charles Tilly's Historical Sociology," *International Review of Social History* 54, no. 2 (August 2009): 237–274.

> *Work* includes any human effort adding use value to goods and services. However much their performers may enjoy or loathe the effort, conversation, song, decoration, pornography, table-setting, gardening, housecleaning, and repair of broken toys, all involve work to the extent that they increase satisfactions their consumers gain from them. Prior to the twentieth century, a vast majority of the world's workers performed the bulk of their work in other settings than salaried jobs as we know them today. Even today, over the world as a whole, most work takes place outside of regular jobs. Only a prejudice bred by Western capitalism and its industrial labor markets fixes on strenuous effort expended for money payment outside the home as "real work," relegating other efforts to amusement, crime, and mere housekeeping ... Despite the rise of takeouts, fast foods, and restaurant eating, unpaid preparation of meals probably constitutes the largest single block of time among all types of work, paid or unpaid, that today's Americans do.

However, in those days mainstream labor historians—notwithstanding their general leftist political inclinations—had also come under the spell of "Western capitalism" and concentrated almost without exception on the male industrial worker, in particular in the West, and more specifically in England and its white settler colonies.

That, however, had not always been the case.[7] Many authors in the nineteenth century were interested in the history of work from the beginning of mankind as it was known by then: mainly work in Europe, North Africa, Western, and South Asia from Classical Antiquity onwards. Within these confines, most space was devoted to market economies with the unpaid work of slaves as well as paid work by free laborers. Included were all types of paid workers, such as artisans, farmers and their personnel, peasants, people engaged in cottage industries, miners, and industrial workers. The subsequent conceptual and geographical narrowing down of the history of work and its final liberation may best be followed throughout three stages in the debate on the origins of market economies: first, medieval market economies in Europe, second, exclusive English origins, and third, Eurasian origins from Antiquity onward.

---

7 Jan Lucassen, "Writing Global Labour History c. 1800–1940: A Historiography of Concepts, Periods and Geographical Scope," in *Global Labour History. A State of the Art*, ed. Jan Lucassen (Bern, 2006), 39–89.

2.1 The Origins of Market Economies in Europe: Marx and Pirenne

It is generally accepted that the traditional market economy of the Roman Empire was radically interrupted in Western Europe for half a millennium. Therefore most authors interested in its development start their narratives after 1000 CE. Marx' historical sketch of the transition from feudalism to a society characterized by markets is somewhat vague and follows the mainstream historical account of his days.[8] In this narrative, a period of feudalism was followed by one in which "capital" came to dominate first Europe and subsequently the rest of the world. It started with medieval Genoa and Venice, which were succeeded by the Dutch Republic, and finally by England. Whereas Italy and Holland were dominated by "commercial capital," it was "industrial capital" that took the lead in England.[9] Karl Marx himself did not speak of "capitalism" or of "commercial capitalism," but after him the latter term became generally accepted by Marxians and non-Marxians alike. Thanks to his Dutch family connections, Marx elaborates a little on the Dutch Republic. Parallel to what he observed in his own times, he was convinced that dominated by industrial capital, by 1648 the common people in the Dutch Republic were already more over-worked, impoverished, and brutally suppressed than anywhere else in Europe. On top of this, the Dutch exploited their subjects in Asia and their slave plantations in the West Indies. In addition to the rise of "capital" in his triplet of Northern Italy, the Dutch Republic, and England he stressed— in line with Thomas Babington Macauly's *History of England*—the demise of serfdom and the rise in fifteenth-century England of peasants, partially wage workers for the powerful farmers.

The first professional historian to study the origins of market economies at length was Henri Pirenne, in a paper read at the International Congress of Historical Studies in London in 1913.[10] In this work, he formulated a "hypothesis" (as he modestly states in his opening sentence) about the origin and nature of "the capitalist, the holder of capital" from the Middle Ages onward. He borrows

---

8   The body of literature on this topic is vast. A useful overview can be found in R.J. Holton, *The Transition from Feudalism to Capitalism* (Houndmills, Basingstoke, 1985), Ch. 3. More recently, Jürgen Kocka, "Introduction," in *Capitalism. The Reemergence of a Historical Concept*, eds. Jürgen Kocka and Marcel van der Linden (London, 2016), 1–10; Jürgen Kocka and Marcel van der Linden, eds., *Capitalism. The Reemergence of a Historical Concept* (London, 2016).

9   Piet Lourens and Jan Lucassen, "Marx als Historiker der niederländischen Republik," in *Die Rezeption der Marxschen Theorie in den Niederlanden*, ed. Marcel van der Linden (Trier, 1992), 430–454.

10   Henri Pirenne, "The Stages in the Social History of Capitalism," *American Historical Review* (1914): 494–515, reprinted in *Class, Status and Power. A Reader in Social Stratification*, eds. Reinhard Bendix and Seymour Martin Lipset (London, 1954), 501–517.

his definition from Werner Sombart's *Der moderne Kapitalismus* (1902), but at the same time fiercely rejects Sombart's idea that capitalism started only with the Renaissance. That may be the conclusion that could be reached after the study of German medieval towns, but it certainly does not apply to Northern Italy and the Low Countries. According to Pirenne "capitalism is much older than we have ordinarily thought it." But how much older? Before 1200 there were not many towns in Western Europe and those few were far more devoted to commerce than to industry, however, among the wandering merchants and their associations Pirenne already finds traces of the *spiritus capitalisticus* in the eleventh century. After 1200, migration from countryside to town and occupational specialization had an opportunity "so that all Western Europe, in the course of the thirteenth century, blossoms forth in an abundance of large and small towns." Speculative individual capitalists took their chances first, and from then on economic developments had their own logic via the Industrial Revolution until the early twentieth century. For Pirenne "the Industrial Revolution was just a more intense form of earlier development."[11]

2.2 *Exclusive English Origins?*

Contrary to this broad—if still Eurocentric—picture, from the end of the nineteenth century in England a much narrower view gained ground, which concentrated on the industrial laborer. Its most famous and eloquent spokesmen were Edward P. Thompson and Eric Hobsbawm. Brilliant intellectuals from mostly excellent universities, the English Marxist historians in the postwar years wanted to show to their fellow citizens that they were not the slavish followers of a foreign ideology that had been realized in the Soviet Union. To the contrary, the cradle of capitalism stood right in their own "good old England," and the answer to capitalist exploitation also had to be formulated in the same place. Two debates in particular were devoted to this issue: from the 1940s to the 1970s that on the transition from feudalism to capitalism, followed by the so-called Brenner debate.

If feudalism preceded capitalism—as maintained by Marx (and many contemporaries[12])—the question arises as to what "prime mover" triggered this major transition, and at what time and place it occurred. Virtually all Marxist participants in the debate agree that we have to turn to late Mediaeval England

---

11   Richard Grassby, *The Idea of Capitalism before the Industrial Revolution* (Lanham, 1999), 16–17.

12   R.J. Holton, *The Transition from Feudalism to Capitalism* (Houndmills, Basingstoke, 1985), Ch. 1.

28   JAN LUCASSEN

to find the roots of that transition, but as to how and why that happened, opinions diverge widely.[13]

The British economist Maurice Dobb (1900–1976) who started the debate, thought that somewhere between the fourteenth and seventeenth century, feudalism failed because of internal weaknesses, mainly its inability to foster capital accumulation and innovation, and its over-exploitation of peasants.[14] The American economist Paul Sweezy (1910–2004) did not agree and—relying on Henri Pirenne—instead suggested the prime mover lay in an exogenous shock caused by the blossoming of long-distance trade and the revival of towns in Western Europe, including England. The most important contributor to this debate was the medievalist Rodney Hilton (1916–2002) in his later career. With regard to the late medieval English Midlands, he concluded that "all the evidence suggests that the village economy based on the peasant household was considerably monetised."[15] The importance of the market and of wage labor for the England as a whole he then contrasted, remarkably, with continental Europe.[16]

This "Transition Debate" culminated in the so-called Brenner debate, which started with an article by Robert Paul Brenner (born in 1943), published in 1976 in the British journal *Past and Present*. A number of colleagues reacted, followed by a rebuttal, originally published in 1982.[17]

Brenner's starting point is the Late Middle Ages and in particular the thirteenth century, where he discovers "divergent paths of class formation within feudal Europe."[18] The English lords "as extractors of a surplus from their peasants" had a "superior self-organization" and were therefore more accomplished than their French counterparts "as feudal centralizers and feudal

---

13   The following after Rodney Hilton, ed., *The Transition from Feudalism to Capitalism* (London, 1976); Holton, *The Transition from Feudalism*; S.R. Epstein, "Rodney Hilton, Marxism and the Transition from Feudalism and Capitalism," *Past and Present* 195 (Supplement 2, 2007): 248–269.

14   Maurice Dobb, *Studies in the development of capitalism* (1946).

15   Rodney Hilton, *The English peasantry in the later Middle Ages: The Ford lectures for 1973, and related studies* (Oxford, 1975), 43–49 quoted by Epstein. Here, Hilton opposes Postan (a "Ricardo-Malthusian" pessimist according to Epstein) and indirectly Chayanov. See also Hilton, *The Transition from Feudalism*.

16   Hilton, *The Transition from Feudalism*, 155–158.

17   T.H. Aston and C.H.E. Philpin, eds., *The Brenner Debate. Agrarian Class Structure and Economic Development in Pre-Industrial Europe* (Cambridge, 1985).

18   Aston and Philpin, *The Brenner Debate*, quotes on 231 and 226 (where Brenner confesses himself to be "a 'political' and 'voluntarist' Marxist").

accumulators."[19] In the centuries that followed, the original differences between England and France, so Brenner stated, turned out to be persistent, as France was dominated by peasant possessors.[20]

Despite much eloquence, Robert Brenner, his supporters—among whom to a certain extent was Rodney Hilton—and his critics of all sorts (among others M.M. Postan, Guy Bois, and Emmanuel Le Roy Ladurie) were unable to convince each other. Further, after the fireworks the debate quickly petered out.[21] Brenner did not produce any new evidence, let alone firm statistical proof.[22] Instead, the debate shifted to political science. There it was most eloquently and most successfully propagated by Ellen Meiksins Wood (1942–2016).[23] It also stuck to a narrow Eurocentrism, as amply demonstrated by James Morris Blaut:

> So Brenner's theory has this simple geography: there is distance-decay of interest and relevance as we enlarge the scale, from rural England to England as a whole, to Western Europe as a whole, to Europe as a whole, to the world as a whole. The place where feudalism died and capitalism was born was a very small region indeed: rural England.[24]

This Eurocentrism was questioned at the same time from many sides, as is detailed in the next section.

---

19   Aston and Philpin, *The Brenner Debate*, 254, cf. also 238–241; 255 for earlier roots in "the 'political' organization already achieved by the Normans in Normandy" [sic].

20   Aston and Philpin, *The Brenner Debate*, 306. On the Continent he only accepts one case for the emergence of the capitalist system: late medieval Catalonia (Idem 49, 52).

21   This expression is found in Bas van Bavel, *The Invisible Hand? How Market Economies have Emerged and Declined since AD 500* (Oxford, 2016), 272.

22   Robert Brenner, *Merchants and Revolution. Commercial Change, political Conflict, and London's Overseas Traders, 1550–1653* (Princeton, 1993), 647–658, see also 33–50; Brenner in Chris Harman and Robert Brenner, "The Origins of Capitalism," *International Socialism. A quarterly review of socialist theory* 111 (2006): xxxx, http://isj.org.uk/the-origins-of-capitalism/.

23   Ellen Meiksins Wood, "Capitalism, Merchants and Bourgeois Revolution: Reflections on the Brenner Debate and its Sequel," *International Review of Social History* 41 (1996): 209–232; Ellen Meiksins Wood, *The Origin of Capitalism* (New York, 1999); Ellen Meiksins Wood, *The Origin of Capitalism. A Longer View* (London/New York, 2002). Both she and Brenner also alienated other leftist scholars such as Paul Sweezy, Andre Gunder Frank, Perry Anderson, and Immanuel Wallerstein.

24   J.M. Blaut, *Eight Eurocentric Historians* (New York/London, 2000), 56; J.M. Blaut, "Fourteen ninety-two," *Political Geography* 11, no. 4 (1992): 355–412. For Wallerstein's narrow Eurocentrism see recently Immanuel Wallerstein, "Capitalism as an Essential Concept to Understand Modernity," in *Capitalism. The Reemergence of a Historical Concept*, eds. Jürgen Kocka and Marcel van der Linden (London: Bloomsbury, 2016), 187–204, here 188.

2.3   *Eurasian Origins of Market Economies from Antiquity Onward*

Until the seventeenth and early eighteenth century, Europeans had paid serious attention to the economic achievements of countries outside Europe. Later the tide turned, and definitely so in the nineteenth century.[25] After the Second World War, Eurocentrism was questioned by historians, first and foremost Braudel, as well as by political scientists such as Samir Amin, Andre Gunder Frank, and James Morris Blaut. Very recently, this new approach received a fresh impetus from—independently of each other—Sugihara and Austen, Van Bavel, and Kocka and Van der Linden.[26]

Fernand Braudel is, without any doubt, the historian who has most successfully paved the way for the acceptance of more than one origin of economic development.[27] He is neither the first nor the only historian to challenge the unicity of Western European history, but his writings from the start have been so seductive that they were able to beat the powerful but insular Anglo-Saxon Eurocentrism. Braudel was very well aware of the growing distance between Europe, that "minuscule continent" and the rest after 1500, a phenomenon that was explained by deep history and by serious comparison. It was certainly not something that was pre-ordained. Braudel did not have a particularly special interest in the history of wage labor, but more implicitly for him is that it is part and parcel of the emergence of market economies.

Braudel attributes real dynamism and innovation to open and transparent markets that are genuinely competitive and not manipulated by only a few individuals. One can find such markets all over Eurasia; in China, Japan, and India. Importantly, according to Braudel, Japan to a certain extent did have independent cities with a powerful bourgeoisie, but China did not. Further, the Chinese state deliberately thwarted capitalism. My point is not that Braudel was right. I believe he was wrong, in particular regarding his rose-tinted idea of transparent markets with equal opportunities for all participants. Nevertheless, he opened the door to including many more places and periods in the

---

25   Frasie Hertroijs, *Hoe kennis van China naar Europa kwam. De rol van jezuïeten en VOC-dienaren, circa 1680–1795* (Ph.D. dissertation, Vrije Universiteit Amsterdam, 2014).

26   This may easily be seen from the references. In addition, Bas van Bavel wrote to me stating that he had no knowledge of the Kocka—Van der Linden volume when writing his monograph. Only Gareth Austin is involved in two out of the three books, but hardly without cross-referencing.

27   The following mainly after Peer Vries, "Europe and the rest: Braudel on capitalism," in *Aufbruch in die Weltwirtschaft: Braudel wiedergelesen*, eds. G. Garner and M. Middell (Leipzig, 2014), 81–114. For the reluctant way in which Braudel used "capitalism" see Jürgen Kocka and Marcel van der Linden, eds., *Capitalism. The Reemergence of a Historical Concept* (London, 2016).

study of economic development than most of his contemporaries were prepared to.

Partially inspired by Braudel (1902–1985), a subsequent generation of social scientists developed similar ideas criticizing Eurocentrism.[28] First of all Samir Amin (born in 1931), who himself coined the term in 1988, but also Janet Abu-Lughod (1928–2013), Andre Gunder Frank (1929–2005), James Morris Blaut (1927–2000), and others. With some success; witness in the first place the "Big Divergence Debate" about the differences between China and Europe initiated by Ken Pomeranz in 2000, and also the debate on the labor-intensive path to economic growth initiated in Japan. Illustrative of the actual situation is the content of the two-volume *Cambridge History of Capitalism* (2014), the first volume of which is devoted to the spread of capitalism before 1848. It starts with Babylonia in the first millennium BCE and includes Greece, Rome, the Silk Road, China, India, the Middle East, and even Africa.[29]

In recent years, a fresh and truly global outlook by Japanese economic historians has quickly gained ground. These historians have suggested the historical feasibility of a labor-intensive path to economic growth as an alternative to the capital-intensive path that supposedly led Britain to the First Industrial Revolution. Kaoru Sugihara, elaborating on the ideas of Akira Hayami and recently in cooperation with Gareth Austin, proposed at least an addition to the traditional theories of economic development.

Instead of explaining the success of market economies from the optimal combination of capital and labor, we have to seriously envision a second option. In Sugihara's own words:

> Classical economists ... set the framework of economics by identifying land, capital and labour as the three main factors of production. Thus, in the modern theory of economic growth, the role of labour in industrialization has been mainly discussed in the context of how and in what proportions capital and labour were combined to produce industrial goods ... The second, equally important, assumption that has been shared in the discipline is that labour was abundant, homogenous and disposable at the initial stage of economic development.[30]

---

28 For a good introduction see Blaut, "Fourteen ninety-two," and his debate with some of them (including Amin and Frank).

29 Larry Neale and Jeffrey G. Williamson, eds., *The Cambridge History of Capitalism* (2 vols, Cambridge, 2014).

30 Kaoru Sugihara, "Labour-intensive industrialization in global history. An interpretation of East Asian experiences," in *Labour-Intensive Industrialization in Global History*, eds.

Because of the highly seasonal nature of agricultural work each year, peasants had enough time to devote their efforts to other types of work. These could include improving existing agricultural practices or working inside the home or elsewhere. In many places throughout Eurasia, peasants successfully experimented in this direction, especially in the period from 1500 to 1800.[31] We can observe this process not only in Tokugawa Japan, but also in the Yangtze Delta and in Western Europe, where it is mostly discussed under the title "the industrious revolution," together with the role of women in this process.[32] For the discussion here, this broadening of cases toward a completely equal footing—implying multi-origin and multilinear histories of waged work—means nothing less than a historiographic breakthrough for labor history.

This idea also inspired Ravi Palat, who translated Sugihara's ideas from the paddy fields of Japan to those of India between 1250 and 1650.[33] At the same time, he rejected the inclination to see this monetized and labor-intensive path as a step toward "capitalism" and as an attempt at "assimilating the 'historical heritages of every people of the earth' into a master narrative based on patterns of long-term, large-scale social change in Europe and North America."[34]

In 2016, too early to take into account the Sugihara-Austin volume, another excellent example of this fresh global approach to the development of market economies is that of the Dutch mediaevalist Bas van Bavel, who compares in detail the development of factor markets (land, labor, and capital) in Early Medieval Iraq between 500 and 1100, Central and Northern Italy between 1000 and 1500, and the Low Countries between 1100 and 1800. The equal attention he pays to labor markets and other factor markets is very important, and quite rare in the field. In an epilogue he tentatively combines his insights derived from these three key examples with markets in modern states in England, the

---

Gareth Austin and Kaoru Sugihara (London/New York, 2013), 20–64, here 20–21. Note also the work of Osamu Saito.

31 Sugihara, "Labour-intensive industrialization," 59. In this context he also refers to Jan Lucassen, *Migrant Labour in Europe 1600–1900. The Drift to the North Sea* (London, 1987).

32 Jan de Vries, "The industrious revolutions in East and West," in *Labour-Intensive Industrialization in Global History*, eds. Gareth Austin and Kaoru Sugihara (London/New York, 2013), 65–84. Note that according to De Vries (p. 80) there are also important differences between Europe and its East Asian cousin; Elise van Nederveen Meerkerk, "Couples cooperating? Dutch textile workers, family labour and the 'industrious revolution,' c. 1600–1800," *Continuity and Change* 23 (2008): 237–266.

33 Ravi Palat, *The Making of an Indian Ocean World-Economy, 1250–1650. Princes, Paddy fields and Bazaars* (Houndmills, Basingstoke, 2015). This book appeared apparently too early to refer to the volume published by Sugihara and Austin in 2013.

34 Palat, *The Making of an Indian Ocean*, 223.

United States, and Western Europe from 1500 onward. His choice of cases resembles that of Fernand Braudel, with the exception of Iraq.[35]

By combining his observations with those of scholars such as, in particular, Fernand Braudel and Jack Goldstone, Van Bavel discerns several cycles of market development, all of which are basically similar, as each cycle contains the following four stages:[36] First a "market economy," in which factor markets dominate; then a stage of accumulation and growing inequality, and subsequently the stage of "capitalism" with speculation, monopolies, and a close link between capital and the state; and lastly, ending in the decline of the market economy.

Here we see capitalism not as the unavoidable outcome of a unilineal development toward or transition to the market economy, but as a stage in a cyclical process, which has occurred several times and in different places in world history. In his conclusion, Van Bavel takes this cyclical theory even further by including Babylonia and Classical Attica (though with two question marks), the Roman Empire, and Sung China.[37] Regional variations are especially apparent in the ability of small-scale peasant producers to shift their strategies between factor markets and alternative systems of exchange (in the first place the family, but also commons and guilds) or non-market economic systems.[38] In other words, labor may follow divergent paths to the subsequent stage.

In addition to Van Bavel, and Sugihara and Austin, a third recent input to the debate about the emergence of market economies is a volume with a title that is at the same time a program: *Capitalism. The Reemergence of a Historical Concept.* In his introduction, the first editor, Jürgen Kocka, proposes a compound "working definition" of the concept capitalism as a historical process.[39] Three elements together are crucial in order to define such a process:

- individual and collective actors dispose of rights which enable them to make economic decisions in a relatively autonomous and decentralized way;
- the coordination of the different economic actors takes place primarily through markets and prices ... The commodification of resources and products is central, including the commodification of labor, largely (but not exclusively) in the form of contractual ('free') labor for wages and salaries;

---

35 Van Bavel, *The Invisible Hand?* 270–276.
36 Van Bavel, *The Invisible Hand?* 273–274.
37 Van Bavel, *The Invisible Hand?* 30–35, 276–287.
38 Van Bavel, *The Invisible Hand?* 265–266, 282.
39 Jürgen Kocka, *Capitalism. A Short History* (Princeton and Oxford, 2016), 4–5; cf. Kocka, "Introduction," 21.

34   JAN LUCASSEN

– capital is central for this type of economy. This entails the investment of savings and returns in the present with the perspective of higher gains in the future.

These are not empty words, as Kocka makes clear in a smaller overview where he discusses "Merchant Capitalism," which, he emphasizes, is not simply pre-capitalist. According to him this term applies to, among others, seventh to eleventh century Arabia, tenth to fourteenth century China, and twelfth to fifteenth century Western Europe.[40]

Marcel van der Linden opens his *Final Thoughts* in the same volume with the assertion that "Capitalism is and remains a controversial idea." However, at the same time he cites Braudel's famous dictum about capitalism: "Personally, after a long struggle, I gave up trying to get rid of this troublesome intruder ... [If] capitalism is thrown out of the door, it comes in through the window."[41] Van der Linden adapts Kocka's definition by emphasizing that "capitalism cannot exist without" commodity production and commodity trade, property rights, money, and competition. Consequently, he recognizes "that capitalism knows many different forms of appearance" including merchant capitalism.

In a detailed and intelligent comment, Gareth Austin calls the three elements of Kocka's definition "dimensions [which] are related but not reducible to each other."[42] More importantly, he asserts that many of these dimensions have occurred in the past unrelated to the European genesis of industrialization and asks whether we can use the term "embryonic capitalism" in these cases.[43]

---

40   Kocka, "Introduction," 25–35, 49, 52, 127. In line with Moses Finley, he hesitates to include Classical Antiquity.

41   Marcel van der Linden, "Final Thoughts," in *Capitalism. The Reemergence of a Historical Concept*, eds. Jürgen Kocka and Marcel van der Linden (London, 2016), 251–266, here 254–255.

42   Gareth Austin, "The Return of Capitalism as a Concept," in *Capitalism. The Reemergence*, 207–234, here 215.

43   Austin, "The Return of Capitalism," 213–214. This rather hesitant formulation may have to do with his warning that for empiricist testing the concept capitalism "defies sensible measurement: we cannot meaningfully rank societies in terms of how capitalist they are, because too many elements are involved." If that is true it seems to contradict his conclusion that "the concept remains heuristically valuable, indeed unavoidable, in many historical contexts." cf. Richard Grassby, *The Idea of Capitalism before the Industrial Revolution* (Lanham, 1999), 29: "capitalism is difficult to standardize and qualify. Nor is it always clear when quantitative change should be regarded as qualitative, since only the former can be measured objectively." And (p. 64): "Capitalism cannot be defined in ways that make its empirical existence demonstrable or valid ... It cannot serve as a benchmark for operational analysis because it is not quantitative and because its functional mechanism is never described."

WORKERS: NEW DEVELOPMENTS IN LABOR HISTORY SINCE THE 1980S

If we take the broad approach by Kocka and van der Linden seriously, many more situations in which economic decisions are made autonomously by actors in markets for commodities and factors—including in particular wage labor—and with a long-term perspective, are more suitable for serious analysis than anybody could have previously envisaged. The first to have done so in a very systematic way was Bas van Bavel, and the labor-intensive path proposition shows a similar potential.

It is irrelevant whether we believe the label "capitalism" is useful, as long as we agree on the characteristics that are necessary in order to include or exclude specific cases for our comparisons.[44] I consider myself an agnostic in this regard and prefer to stick to the overarching concept of "market economies," some of which might be called "capitalist" from the point at which owners of investment capital acquire a disproportionate power. Only if academia largely agrees on where that point lies, what disproportionate means, and how it can be measured across different places, periods, and cultures, will we be able to use the concept "capitalism" for meaningful analysis. I fear that stage has not been reached yet.

For now, the far less controversial concept of "market economy" provides us with a way out, enabling us to make historical comparisons in a consistent way and encompassing all relevant cases, although I mean "comparison" conceived as "a heuristic tool that offers the historian the closest she can hope to get to controlled, testable hypotheses."[45] Formulated in the briefest possible way, and as I detail further in the last section of this paper, these cases should encompass all deeply monetized societies because this indicates that wage labor there plays a substantial enough role to be considered.

3 The Taxonomy of Labor Relations as a Tool to Study Work Worldwide

The great gains of the last decades so far discussed, regard the conceptual escape from insular Anglo-centrism and from Eurocentrism, but are still restricted to market economies. For a genuine and all-encompassing concept of work, at the IISH in approximately 2005 we realized that it was also necessary

---

44 However, considerations for including a conceptual term not only have to do with criteria, whether they are essential or not. The load of connotations that a term may have also plays a role. Personally, I think the term capitalism has become overloaded, which hinders rather than fosters a straightforward application. Attempts at redefining do not take away the noise made by all previous definitions and their applications.

45 This formulation by Epstein, "Rodney Hilton," p. 260.

to examine seriously all forms of work performed outside the market.[46] The Tillys' emphasis on the significance of unpaid household work offered a first possibility, but it was rapidly evident that more was necessary if we wanted to include all historical societies.[47]

According to classical authors, the Greeks had an inborn urge for liberty, from which followed a monetized society with free labor markets, in addition to slave labor. Their Persian enemy, by contrast, was doomed to a hierarchical society, characterized by unfree labor.[48] This contrast between "us," working from free will, and "the other," working only on command, was transmitted into the Renaissance and Enlightenment, and through the discovery voyages in the Pacific, supplemented by the concept of the "noble savage." Nineteenth century consensus only viewed Europe, subject to an internal dynamic, as evolving seemingly spontaneously from paradisiacal primitivism via feudalism to capitalism, and in the end to socialism. All the other, more primitive, societies were stuck in the phase of slavery, Asiatic despotism, or similar compulsory systems in which work was organized. A partially less negative image of the "other" societies was proposed by Max Weber, who demonstrated that in classical Egypt, the obligations of the Pharaoh's subjects were at least partially balanced by spiritual and material top-down obligations. For Mesopotamia, the great pre-Columbian societies in the Americas, and elsewhere, the same sort of interpretations have gained ground, especially in the theoretical work of Karl Polanyi. He stresses that such "centristic" societies depended not only on labor obligations by the community and taxation in kind, but equally on "redistribution."[49]

It is unfortunate that in his zeal to show how unimportant the market had been in the past, Polanyi overstretched his arguments, such as for example in his famous and detailed study on Dahomey.[50] As a consequence, his attempts

---

46　The core group consisted of Karin Hofmeester, Christine Moll-Murata, Marcel van der Linden, and myself.

47　Already in Van der Linden and Lucassen, *Prolegomena*, 9–10 "unpaid" and "autonomous" is said to "include household labor and other forms of subsistence labor" and "unpaid" and "heteronomous" work to "include feudal serfdom and chattel slavery," but both possibilities are not further elaborated.

48　Page Dubois, *Slavery. Antiquity and its Legacy* (London/New York, 2010), 54–66; cf. Catharina Lis and Hugo Soly, *Worthy Efforts: Attitudes to Work and Workers in Pre-Industrial Europe* (Leiden/Boston, 2012), Ch. 1.

49　Grassby, *The Idea of Capitalism*, 20–21; Jan Lucassen, *Outlines of a History of Labour. IISH Research Paper 51* (Amsterdam, 2013), 8–9, 20–21; Austin "The Return of Capitalism," 214–215. For Polanyi's influence on Finley see Lis and Soly, *Worthy Efforts*, 54–58.

50　Karl Polanyi in collaboration with Abraham Rotstein, *Dahomey and the slave trade; an analysis of an archaic economy* (Seattle, 1966).

to work out in a more informed and up to date way the variety of labor relations outside the market have also had less impact on the theorizing about taxonomies of work than they deserve. The same applies to a number of theoreticians of the concept of "peasantry," for example Chayanov, who tried to downplay the market involvement of the Russian peasants around 1900.[51]

All of these scholars—regardless of their shortcomings—provided us with the inspiration to come up with a proposal for a taxonomy of all types of human relations regarding work.[52] For reasons of methodical discipline, it tries to embrace all people living in a given community at a given time. Therefore the first and basic distinction is between those who work (according to the definition given above) and those who do not. A second distinction is made among those who do or do not work to produce goods or services for the market. Subsequent distinctions are made within these main categories.

This taxonomy, however, has never been an aim in itself. It is nothing more or less than a tool that enables us to compare, for any geographical area at any moment in time, the proportional distribution of labor relations in order to compare different cases, to establish commonalities and differences, and to explain continuity or change. We see this as one of the indispensable key instruments for a labor historian. In this respect we are not original, as may be exemplified by the detailed analysis of labor relations in London around 1900 by Charles Booth (1840–1916) and of the German Empire by Werner Sombart (1863–1941). Much later, Charles Tilly revived this approach covering Europe outside Russia from the sixteenth century onward.[53]

To date, the main result of this huge project is the awareness that contrary to earlier strands of labor history, major changes in labor relations as described here often take a long time, usually several generations, and they take place only gradually. Members of peasant households may perform wage work for part of a year or even for part of a day. Such combinations at the level of one person or one household may function successfully over many generations.

---

51 A.V. Chayanov, *The Theory of Peasant Economy*, eds. Daniel Thorner, Basile Kerblay, and R.E.F. Smith (Homewood, IL, 1966); Theodor Shanin, ed., *Peasants and Peasant Societies. Selected Readings* (Harmondsworth, 1971).

52 https://collab.iisg.nl/web/labourrelations. Especially see Karin Hofmeester, Jan Lucassen, Leo Lucassen, Rombert Stapel, and Richard Zijdeman, "The Global Collaboratory on the History of Labour Relations, 1500–2000: Background, Set-Up, Taxonomy, and Applications" (2015). Available at http://hdl.handle.net/10622/4OGRAD.

53 Charles Booth, *Life and labour of the people in London* (14 vols., London, 1902–1904); Werner Sombart, *Das Proletariat. Bilder und Studien* (Berlin, 1906); Charles Tilly, "Demographic Origins of the European Proletariat," in *Proletarianization and Family History*, ed. David Levine (London, 1984), 26–52.

The putting-out system in the rural textile production is one of the best-known examples. In fact, under close scrutiny, the combination of different labor relations within one household and often one person seems to have been the rule until very recently, and this certainly is still the case if we include unpaid work within the household.

By contrast, various forms of serfdom and slavery, and similar legally based systems of labor mobilization, have a much longer lifetime and may also co-exist with free labor markets for categories of workers with a different status. As long as this distinction between fundamentally and legally different categories of human beings may be upheld successfully, free and unfree labor relations can co-exist.

4   Wage Labor: Long-Term Historical Developments

With the conceptual and analytical tools forged in the past decades as described in the previous sections, it is now finally possible to come up with a new narrative of the long-term history of work worldwide. The aim here is to concentrate on wage labor in market economies—after all the classic terrain of labor history—and more specifically on the significance of coin circulation in different parts of the world for the history of work and of labor relations.

For most of human history, work was organized in small groups consisting of only a handful of households. Only many thousands of years after the first agricultural societies emerged in the Middle East did production surpluses become large enough for occupational specialization in certain households. The concomitant exchange of goods and services required more elaborate rules than those of obligation and affection that govern labor relations inside households. Such an exchange outside the reciprocal household circle can be organized locally or within larger communities. Locally, agreements can be made by obliging artisans such as blacksmiths, carpenters, potters, or priests to provide for whatever their farming co-villagers need in return for their share in the harvest of these farmers (for example in the Indian *jajmani* system). When not dozens or hundreds, but thousands or more households were involved—and not only artisans and peasants, but also specialized farmers—cities, city states, and similar polities appeared, based on obligation systems in return for maintenance. Well-known examples of these tributary labor relations include the old Mesopotamian city and later territorial states, and also classical Egypt, classical China, the Indus civilizations, and the pre-Columbian states.[54] Here

---

54   Note that there are also different usage of this term, see Amin's "tributary mode of production."

we can also find the earliest examples of waged work, paid in kind, as the soldiers of the Assyrian Empire demonstrate. However, apart from the military, there was no labor market more generally, as all the other households were aware of their obligations to as well as what they could expect from the polity.

This specialization process could reach such levels of intensity that the exchange of goods and services by fixed obligations, supervised by the polity and a shared ideology, evoked an alternative societal model. That was the market economy, which went hand in hand with the introduction of mediums of exchange. This innovation, and in particular (but not necessarily so) the introduction of coins induced the monetization process. It is not by chance that I prefer the term "introduction" rather than invention, as invention suggests a genius coming up with something new, the utility of which has to be demonstrated to his or her fellow citizens. Monetization is instead the answer to a broad societal demand for a convenient means of exchange, as its particular history suggests. Remarkably, monetization processes started at three different places around the same time, but most likely independent of each other as the regionally totally different material character and designs suggest.

4.1 Monetization and Deep Monetization

Around 500, before the Common Era, coins were introduced in the eastern Mediterranean, Northern India, and East China. From there, coinage proliferated quickly all over the subtropical and moderate parts of this huge land mass and of adjacent northern Africa, and after 1500 to the Americas and finally to tropical Africa and Oceania.[55] Although highly successful, this innovation did not simply conquer the world after its introduction. It instead shows a history of leaps and bounds of alternating periods of monetization and demonetization. Monetization in China, after its initial success between 350 BCE and 200 CE, was followed by periods of major demonetization between 600 and 1000 and again between 1200 and 1500. This periodization differs from other parts of Eurasia. Interestingly, in Northern India and Western Europe demonetization took place at a similar time, between around 400 and 1100.

---

55   Jan Lucassen, "Deep Monetization in Eurasia in the long run," in *Money, Currency and Crisis. In Search of Trust 2000 BC to AD 2000*, eds. Bert van der Speck and Bas van Leeuwen (London, 2018, forthcoming). For preconditions and actual monetization as well as wage levels in first century BCE Babylonia, see Michael Jursa, "Babylonia in the first millennium BCE—economic growth in times of empire," in *The Cambridge History of Capitalism*, eds. Larry Neale and Jeffrey G. Williamson (2 vols, Cambridge, 2014), 24–42. For England, see additionally Christine Desan, *Making Money. Coin, Currency, and the Coming of Capitalism* (Oxford, 2014). Also, several contributions to Martin Allen and D'Maris Coffman, eds., *Money, Prices and Wages. Essays in Honour of Professor Nicholas Mayhew* (Houndmills, Basingstoke, 2015).

40   JAN LUCASSEN

Crucially, after initial periods of somewhat different length, in all three original cases medium and small coins of low value—or even with a fiduciary value—were produced in large quantities. In that way, circulation patterns were adapted to the payment of wages and to their usage by wage earners to pay for goods and services in shops and market places. Consequently, the study of monetization may help us to understand the extension of waged work and labor markets in different important economic centers of Eurasia for the last 2,500 years.

Most narratives of the spread of monetization are restricted to the Mediterranean and Europe, and at the same time suppose that the concomitant "capitalist spirit" could exclusively emerge there. In the restricted framework of this essay, I provide three examples from China, Japan, and India that— to the contrary—instead suggest similarities between the different economically well-developed parts of Eurasia. The Chinese historian Sima Qian (c. 145–86 BCE) summarized the developments of the preceding centuries (exactly those in which the first monetization wave occurred) as follows:

> Society obviously must have farmers before it can eat; foresters before it can extract timber resources; artisans before it can have manufactured goods; and merchants before they can be distributed. But once these exist, what need is there for government directives, mobilizations of labor, or periodic assemblies? Each man has only to be left to utilize his own abilities and exert his strength to obtain what he wishes. Thus, when a commodity is cheap, it invites a rise in price; when it is very expensive, it invites a reduction. When each person works away at his own occupation and delights in his own business then, like water flowing downward, goods will naturally flow forth ceaselessly day and night without having been summoned, and the people will produce commodities without having been asked. Does this not tally with reason? Is this not a natural result?[56]

This early eulogy of markets by Sima Qian has a moral companion in the following observation by the Japanese Mino Masataka published in 1733; as if it was a merger of the proto-Smithian Sima Qian and the Weberian Protestant ethic:

---

56   Anthony J. Barbieri-Low, *Artisans in Early Imperial China* (Seattle/London, 2007), 43 (translation Burton Watson). Cf. Richard von Glahn, *Fountain of Fortune. Money and Monetary Policy in China, 1000–1700* (Berkeley etc., 1996), 26–43.

Though Confucianism, Buddhism and Shintoism are different respectively, in any case the fundamental value is sincerity. It is the teachings of rewarding good and punishing evil, governing the state and effecting universal peace, and setting the people at ease. Unselfishness, honesty, sympathy, ad mercy are all good attributes ... In a country there are generally three treasures, namely land, people, and politics ... persons have to be in charge of property from an ancestor and to worry about bringing up parents, wives, children and the whole family. And they must work hard at official affairs without complaining of adversity. Consequently they have no time to be glad for their lives, to fear death, or to enjoy amusements indoors.[57]

We are also given a glimpse of the filtering down of this spirit from India in some of Abdur Rahman's poems (the *Nagar Shobha*, composed while at Akbar's court at Lahore, 1580–1583) about sixty-six women, for each of whom he combines their erotic attractions and their economic activities. Economic attitudes are possibly most clearly visible in his verses devoted to the wife of the cowherd:

The Gujarin, carrying a pot of curd on her head, is exceptionally beautiful. The spilling of the curd is like the nectar of the senses, but she gives not any; She jokes with the customer and freely makes promises first stating her own price and then that of the curd.[58]

4.2 Deep Monetization and Global Labor History

The question now arises as to what the relationship is between variations in the intensity of monetization and the development of wage labor.[59] Therefore, we have to distinguish more precisely between coins of different metals and weights. There is a huge difference between on the one hand the usage of denominations that are important for long distance trade (the most valuable pieces made of gold or silver) and on the other, the small silver, copper, and other non-precious metal denominations used by the common man.

In my recent work I have proposed using the term "medium monetization" for situations in which denominations equaling *one day*'s payment are

---

57 Bettina Gramlich-Oka and Gregory Smits, eds., *Economic Thought in Early Modern Japan* (Leiden/Boston, 2010), 63–64.

58 T.C.A. Raghavan, *Attendant Lords. Bairam Khan and Abdur Rahim Courtiers and Poets in Mughal India* (Delhi, 2016), 98.

59 Holton, *The Transition from Feudalism*, 32, formulated it as follows: "Does the market economy also produce a market-oriented society?" See also 39 ff.

abundantly available. Deep monetization then applies to situations when coins equaling the value of *one hour*'s work or less are readily available. To be more precise, the value of these denominations should be more than five times the value of an hourly wage for a skilled worker in order for a society to qualify as being deeply monetized. There is no space here to explain why five times circulating per capita seems to be an acceptable threshold.[60] However, no matter what the precise threshold may be, this approach to deep monetization provides us with a practical instrument to measure and compare the intensity of monetized exchange among common people who were wage workers, or small independent producers receiving advances for their tasks at hand. These are the people who urgently needed these coins for frequent—that is, daily or weekly—payments. Much more urgently than the well-to-do who enjoyed sufficient credit to pay their bills at much larger intervals because their assets enabled them to obtain credit from shop keepers and merchants. The common man lacked property, and therefore enjoyed only very limited credit and thus used small coins most frequently.

This can be illustrated by an example from fourteenth-century India, where small denominations (half and quarter *jital* coins) equaling one hours work or less appeared. Firoz Shah, Delhi Sultan 1351–1388, introduced these as follows:

> if poor people bought something from the market and a balance in half or quarter *jitals* was left of the amount paid, the shopkeeper would not have the quarter change. If he demanded it from the shopkeeper how could he be paid when no such coin existed?[61]

Under the Suri Dynasty in Delhi (1538–1554) and under the Mughal Emperor Akbar (1556–1605), massive numbers of copper coins were produced in several small denominations. It is no wonder that the early Portuguese travelers in the subcontinent were deeply impressed by the commercial skills of the Indians, which they esteemed as being higher than those of the Italian merchants. In his description of the traders of Gujarat, Tomé Pires in his *Suma Oriental* (1512–1515) calls the Indian traders:

---

60   For the threshold see: Jan Lucassen, "Deep Monetization: The Case of the Netherlands 1200–1940," *TSEG* 11 (2014): 73–121, 75; Lucassen, "Deep Monetization in Eurasia in the long run."

61   Najaf Haider, "Fractional pieces and non-metallic monies in medieval India (1200–1750)," in *Money in Asia (1200–1900). Small Currencies in Social and Political Contexts*, eds. Kate Leonard and Ulrich Theobald (Leiden/Boston, 2015), 86–107, here 90, quoting Firoz Shah's court historian Shams Siraj Afif.

men who understand merchandise; they are so properly steeped in the sound and harmony of it that the Gujaratees say that any offence connected with merchandise is pardonable ... Those of our people who want to be clerks and factors ought to go there and learn, because the business trade is a science in itself.[62]

Consequently, the long-term history of wage labor may gain much from measuring deep monetization, especially in situations where archaeology provides good insights if written sources are meagre or lacking altogether. Archival documents on coin production figures are only available for China from the Han period onward and for Western Europe from the thirteenth century onward. Both types of information combined enable us to reconstruct developments in the remuneration of work much more accurately than before. I end by pointing to two instances when evidence about coin circulation and wage labor combined point to shifting labor relations.

To begin with in England, where as we have seen, traditional historiography greatly emphasized the phenomenon of feudalism, but where this new approach instead emphasizes monetization and the emergence of labor markets. Bolton characterizes the English society around 1250, where 40 pennies per head were in circulation, as follows:

By the mid-thirteenth century the concentrated money supply had probably reached the critical point that would allow coins to be used as the normal medium or agent of exchange. They could be used to buy and sell goods, to pay wages and other dues that peasants owed to lords. They could be collected as taxes and offered or demanded in lieu of feudal military service, and kings could now pay their much larger armies with coins.[63]

Recent archaeological evidence confirms this image.[64] According to Chris Dyer, in the fourteenth century,

The proportion of people who obtained most of their living from wage work must have exceeded one third over the whole country, rising to two-thirds in parts of the east. There were concentrations of wage-earners in

---

62   Quoted in Blaut, *Eight Eurocentric Historians*, 93.
63   J.L. Bolton, *Money in the Medieval English Economy, 973–1489* (Manchester, 2012), 27, cf. 132–135.
64   Lucassen, 2018.

large towns; in York for instance, 32 per cent of the contributors to the poll tax were called servants.[65]

The second monetization phase in China took off briskly under the Song just before the year 1000.[66] Not much later, compulsory work for the state was converted into a tax to be paid in cash, and economic progress was so impressive that some authors think that Song China was just a "hair's breadth" away from a genuine industrial revolution. In the twelfth and thirteenth century, these developments changed and only after the Ming, which increased "bond servitude," what may be called a third important wave of monetization followed in eighteenth-century China. At this time, wage labor in various industrial sectors such as mining, printing, porcelain making, and shipbuilding also increased.

Although the history of monetization has been known more or less for a very long time (India possibly excepted), it is the novel story of deep monetization that is important here.[67] Instead of attributing monetization to long-distance trade, it is instead the emergence of labor markets that brought about deep monetization. This new evidence about the circulation patterns of small coins enables us to extend substantially the history of waged work in time and space. The history of wage labor did not start in the West a few centuries ago or even in the Middle Ages. In fact, it started in the major economic centers of Eurasia 2,500 years ago.

5   In Sum

As a result of the efforts of so many, but especially of the common efforts of Marcel van der Linden and his colleagues at the research department of the IISH, and those very many engaging in and attached to its projects over the last decades, global labor history may now be seen in a different way than before.

---

65   Nicholas Mayhew, "Wages and Currency: The Case in Britain up to 1600," in *Wages and Currency. Global Comparisons from Antiquity to the Twentieth Century*, ed. Jan Lucassen (Bern, 2007), 211–220, here 213–214 (quoting Dyer). For the European continent see Bas van Bavel, "Rural wage labour in the sixteenth-century low Countries: An assessment of the importance and nature of wage labour in the countryside of Holland, Guelders and Flanders," *Continuity and Change* 21 (2006): 37–72; Bas van Bavel, "The transition in the Low Countries: Wage labour as an indicator of capitalism in the countryside, 1300–1700," *Past and Present* 195 (2007): 286–303; Van Bavel, *The Invisible Hand?*, 159–164, 174–177; cf. Tilly's estimate of one quarter for Europe as a whole around 1550, as quoted in Kocka, "Introduction," 129.

66   William Guanglin Liu, *The Chinese Market Economy, 1000–1500* (Albany, 2015).

67   See also Holton, *The Transition*, 39–46.

Tentatively the long-term history of work may provisionally be reformulated in the following way:

- Occupational specialization among agriculturalists, much more than the exigencies of long distance trade, brought about the emergence and unfolding of market economies, including labor markets and the demand for means of exchange, mostly coins.
- Such conditions emerged in several places and at several times over the last 2,500 years, often independently, sometimes mutually influenced. Leaving aside for a moment earlier periods of monetization and demonetization, monetized market economies with concomitant ideologies have been in existence uninterruptedly until now in India and in the West for the last nine centuries, and in China for the last four centuries.
- Most alternative ways of organizing work in a society with occupational specialization—such as for example state-led redistribution (pharaonic Egypt and pre-Columbian America)—have proved to be less successful in the very long term, with one exception: non-monetary reciprocity of goods and services within the household, kin groups, and similar small-scale social entities. This organizational type has always coexisted in a most intimate way with distribution via markets and it continues to do so. Marketization and monetization by no means dominate all human labor relations.
- Until one to two centuries ago, many if not most polities allowed free and unfree labor to co-exist.[68] Since then this situation has occasionally recurred, sometimes even on a massive scale, but always defined as exceptional; as punishment or as an emergency in war time (for example Russia under Stalin, Germany under Hitler, or China under Mao).
- Wage labor is certainly not a type of work of last resort where income by definition is minimal and barely enough to avoid starvation. Comparative and long-term research into wage levels shows major variations in remuneration levels resulting in many low, but also medium and high, standards of living.[69]
- Wage labor is not only flexible in its relationship with reciprocal household labor, but also shows many variations (time and piece waged work, subcontracting, share cropping, or small independent production based on advances). Furthermore, it may vary in intensity (for example the

---

68   Kocka, "Introduction," 136–137.

69   Lucassen, *Outlines*; Jursa, "Babylonia," 37; Sevket Pamuk, "Institutional change and economic development in the Middle East, 700–1800," in *The Cambridge History of Capitalism*, eds. Larry Neale and Jeffrey G. Williamson (2 vols, Cambridge, 2014), 193–224, here 195–196; Christopher Dyer, "A Golden Age Rediscovered: Labourers' Wages in the Fifteenth Century," in *Money, Prices and Wages. Essays in Honour of Professor Nicholas Mayhew*, eds. Martin Allen and D'Maris Coffman (Houndmills, Basingstoke, 2015), 180–195.

industrious revolution or the labor-intensive path to industrialization as explained below).

- Favorable wage levels were not only the result of demand for labor exceeding supply, such as for example after the Black Death in many parts of Eurasia, but also of collective action of wage workers, which to date can be testified by many examples, though not yet by systematic research.[70] Wage laborers were not by definition defenseless victims of the market.
- Lastly, wage laborers use a large repertoire of actions to foster their interests in the market. They do so in two ways: individually (by changing job or employer locally, or by migration temporarily or permanently[71]) and collectively. In the latter case they need to use the existing political structures, which has happened most successfully so far in different types of welfare states.

Early on, some historians already recognized that market economies have a long pedigree. In general not or hardly aware of the implications for labor history, they have argued at the same time that earlier and non-European market economies are very different from "modern" forms.[72] By implication, these pre-capitalist market economies supposedly also have much less, or maybe no relevance at all in terms of understanding wage labor here and now. This claim can no longer be supported, since our knowledge of the history of paid labor has grown so substantially. There is a substantial gap between this new narrative and the classic theoretical framework that is unilinear and highly Eurocentric. By comparison, the new evidence requires a framework encompassing multi-origin and therefore multilinear developments. Nevertheless, we should not throw out the baby with the bathwater. The great virtue of traditional labor history lies in its extensive analysis of collective action among wage laborers.[73] Combined with private strategies, as evident from social and geographical mobility,[74] these are aspects of labor history that now can and have to be applied to a much wider field of evidence; and the results can be ploughed back into contemporary studies. No doubt this will yield a rich harvest in the near future of this discipline.

---

70   Jan Lucassen, "Working at the Ichapur Gunpowder Factory in the 1790s," *Indian Historical Review* 39 (2012): 19–56 and 251–271.

71   For labor turnover in medieval England see Richard Britnell, "Labour Turnover and Wage rates on the Demesnes of Durham priory, 1370–1410," in *Money, Prices and Wages. Essays in Honour of Professor Nicholas Mayhew*, eds. Martin Allen and D'Maris Coffman (Houndmills, Basingstoke, 2015), 158–179.

72   Grassby *The Idea of Capitalism*.

73   For an excellent overview, see Marcel van der Linden, *Workers of the World. Essays toward a Global Labor History* (Leiden/Boston, 2008).

74   Lucassen, *Outlines*; Jan Lucassen and Leo Lucassen, eds., *Globalising Migration History. The Eurasian Experience (16th–21st centuries)* (Leiden/Boston, 2014).

CHAPTER 3

"With the Name Changed, the Story Applies to You!": Connections between Slavery and "Free" Labor in the Writings of Marx

Pepijn Brandon

1   Introduction

The field of Global Labor History that Marcel van der Linden more than any-one helped to develop, rests—among other elements—on the rejection of the idea that capitalism and "free" wage labor go hand in hand. This rejection en-tails a critique on both Marxian and Weberian approaches to labor history.[1] It forms a major challenge to the theoretical framework of classical political economy in which "free" labor holds an important place. This was true for the founders of classical liberalism as well as for Marx, although they started from different theoretical assumptions and drew completely opposite political con-clusions. Of these two, it is Marx who forms the real starting point for Van der Linden's reconceptualization. In Van der Linden's view, Marx's analysis of capi-talist development is at one and the same time "still the best we have," but also one that contains serious "limitations, errors and immanent contradictions."[2] In an act of self-conscious heterodoxy, Van der Linden expands Marx's notion of the centrality of commodified labor power to include forms of coerced la-bor that Marx explicitly excluded. This, he argues, is necessary for understand-ing capitalism's past and its future. It forms the basis for a truly global labor history that acknowledges the many intermediary forms between plantation slavery as the most extreme form of coerced labor, and an idealized version of "free" wage labor, that have operated under the control of capital. Recog-nizing such intermediary forms is of special relevance for understanding the history of capitalism in colonial and post-colonial contexts. However, it also has important consequences for understanding capitalism in the West, where

---

1   Marcel van der Linden and Jan Lucassen, *Prolegomena for a Global Labor History* (Amster-dam, 1999), 6.

2   Marcel van der Linden, *Workers of the World. Essays towards a Global Labor History* (Leiden and Boston, 2008), 18; Marcel van der Linden and Karl Heinz Roth, "Introduction," in *Beyond Marx. Theorising the global labour relations of the twenty-first century*, eds. Marcel van der Linden and Karl Heinz Roth (Leiden and Boston, 2014), 1–20, 7.

© PEPIJN BRANDON, 2018 | DOI:10.1163/9789004386617_004

This is an open access chapter distributed under the terms of the prevailing CC-BY-NC License.

unpaid, non-industrial, and precarious labor have always remained an important element of labor relations. Furthermore, it is crucial for understanding why coerced labor persists on a large scale in the present, while capitalism has expanded to every corner of the world.[3]

As could be expected, Van der Linden's critique of Marx's approach to wage labor prompted much debate among Marxist scholars.[4] Regardless of the way in which one judges the merits of the underlying theoretical argument, there is no doubt that the research program launched as a result of it has opened up important new areas for the study of labor and class struggle under capitalism.[5] In this article, I do not engage with the latter topic. Instead, I focus on a paradox in Marx's work that in my view partially helps to better position the subject of Van der Linden's critique, and partially allows for the kind of heterodox rereading that he proposes. The paradox is that in the same period in which Marx strengthened and refined his analysis of the centrality of "free" wage labor to the capitalist mode of production, he also started to put greater emphasis on the parallels and historical connections between slavery and "free" wage labor. This is shown most explicitly in a famous passage on the lengthening of the working day in *Capital*, Volume I. Marx extensively cites the American writer J.E. Cairnes's *The Slave Power* on the way in which slaveholders who have access to a steady supply of new slave laborers work their slaves to death "*durch die langsame Tortur von Ueberarbeit und Mangel an Schlaf und Erhohlung*" [through the slow torture of overwork and lack of sleep and fare].[6]

---

3 Van der Linden, *Workers of the world*, 19–20.

4 Two recent discussions of the implications of Van der Linden's re-interpretation for our understanding of *Capital* (the first highly critical, the second much more sympathetic to his approach) are Alex Callinicos, *Deciphering Capital. Marx's Capital and its destiny* (London, 2014), 197–211, and Massimiliano Tomba, *Marx's temporalities* (Leiden and Boston, 2013), 149.

5 For examples of the breadth of scholarship stimulated by the Global Labor History approach pioneered by Van der Linden at different stages of the project, see *Free and unfree labour. The debate continues*, eds. Tom Brass and Marcel van der Linden (Bern etc., 1997); *On coerced labor. Work and compulsion after chattel slavery*, eds. Marcel van der Linden and Magaly Rodríguez García (Leiden and Boston, 2016).

6 *Marx Engels Gesamt Ausgabe* (*MEGA*[2]) II.5, 209. In my research for this article, I mainly used the *Marx Engels Werke* and the *MEGA*[2], the latter being the most complete and authoritative edition of his writings. This also allowed me to check for possible changes made by Marx between the first edition of *Capital* in German, quoted here, and later editions, particularly the French edition of 1875 (reprinted in *MEGA*[2] II.7), which is the edition that contains the most substantial changes by Marx himself. For the readers' convenience, I have replaced quotations in German with the standard translations from the *Marx Engels Collected Works* (London 1974–2001) [hereafter *MECW*]. However, even in this edition there are still significant differences between the German original and the English translation. The quoted passage above is a case in point. The German edition contained Marx's own (mis-)translation

SLAVERY & "FREE" LABOR IN THE WRITINGS OF MARX

Marx then turns his attention directly to the recruitment of the "free" wage laborer for modern industry:

> *Mutato nomine de te fabula narratur!* [With the name changed, the story applies to you!] For slave trade read labour market, for Kentucky and Virginia, Ireland and the agricultural districts of England, Scotland, and Wales, for Africa, Germany. We heard how overwork thinned the ranks of the bakers in London. Nevertheless, the London labour market is always overstocked with German and other candidates for death in the bakeries.[7]

Based on a large number of passages in which Marx invokes slavery to talk about wage labor—not only in *Capital*, Volume I, but throughout his published and unpublished works, letters, notebooks, and drafts—I will show that this exclamation was not a rhetorical flourish. It expressed persistent attention to both the contrasts, and the connections and parallels between slavery and wage labor in Marx's work. This attention derived in a large part from the fact that for Marx, writing in the nineteenth century, slavery was not a historical problem, but a contemporary one. Interestingly enough, Marx's interest in this matter became more pronounced precisely at a time when real historical events—the abolition of serfdom in Russia and of slavery in North America—might easily have been taken by him as a confirmation of the necessary connection between capitalism and a linear progress toward "free" labor. Lastly, I argue that more than is often acknowledged, thinking about slavery played a role in the way Marx conceptualized wage labor itself, especially in helping him to draw a sharp line between his own, bracketed notion of "free" labor and that of liberal political economists. Such a reading is at odds with many orthodox interpretations of Marx's work, which one-sidedly stress Marx's reasons to contrast wage labor and slavery. Perhaps unexpectedly, the critique of Marx formulated by Van der Linden can thus open the way for a re-examination that reveals Marx himself as a much more nuanced thinker on the relationship between coerced labor and capitalism than is often assumed.

---

of Cairnes, which is considerably stronger in wording than Cairnes's original, to which the English edition logically reverted. Here, instead of "slow torture of overwork" it simply reads "unremitting toil," a difference that tells us something about Marx's intention in citing these lines. *MECW* 35, 272. Because of such differences, I maintain page references for the original citations taken from the *MEGA²* edition, and wherever needed, cite the German original either in the footnote or the body of the text.

7   *MECW* 35, 272 / *MEGA²* II.5, 209. The Latin phrase is taken from Horace, *Satires*, Book I, Satire 1.

2   Anti-slavery Marx

It is easy to forget that for Marx, the question of slavery and its relationship to wage labor was a matter of contemporary politics. By the time Marx entered democratic politics in the early 1840s, a strong sentiment against slavery and the slave trade had become highly influential among European liberal democrats. Slave revolts and abolitionist campaigns had firmly etched the image of cruelty inherent in slavery into public consciousness. However, at least with regard to elite perceptions, another key element of the success of anti-slavery campaigns was the conviction popularized by prominent political economists that under normal circumstances, wage labor would always prove more productive and therefore profitable than slave labor. Adam Smith had already expressed his belief, "that the work done by freemen comes cheaper in the end than that performed by slaves."[8] Referring to slavery in antiquity, James Steuart had drawn a less flattering contrast, but still one that stresses the independent agency of the wage worker: "Men were then forced to labour because they are slaves to others; men are now forced to labour because they are slaves to their own wants."[9] Three-quarters of a century later, looking back on the abolition of both the slave trade and slavery in the British colonies, John Stuart Mill was able to write with some confidence: "The history of human improvement is the record of a struggle by which inch after inch of ground has been wrung from these maleficent powers, and more and more of human life rescued from the iniquitous dominion of the law of might."[10] However, casting one's gaze a little wider, the nineteenth century did not look so bright. Slavery had rapidly expanded in the United States, Brazil, and Cuba. The possibilities of reopening the transatlantic slave trade were openly discussed in France in the late 1840s. New forms of indentured and coerced labor developed in the colonies, while penal labor became a central plank of the punishment regime of European states. Meanwhile, the realities of factory labor in the heartlands of the industrial revolution proved to be very far from the rosy perceptions of freedom of the liberal theorists.[11]

Starting their political careers on the radical fringe of liberal democracy and rapidly moving into circles of working-class socialists, Marx and Engels were acutely aware of these contradictions. In *The Poverty of Philosophy*, one

---

8   Adam Smith, *The wealth of nations. Books I–III* (London, 1999 [1776]), 184.

9   James Steuart, *An inquiry into the principles of political economy*, vol. 1 (London, 1767), 40.

10   John Stuart Mill, "The Negro question" (1850), in *The collected works of John Stuart Mill*, vol. XXI, ed. John M. Robson (London, 1984).

11   For a broad overview and recent theorization of these developments, see Dale W. Tomich, *Through the prism of slavery. Labor, capital, and the world economy* (Lanham etc., 2004).

of the first works in which Marx laid out his own economic theory in a polemic against the French anarchist Proudhon, Marx wrote that "direct slavery" in the Americas is "just as much the pivot of bourgeois industry as machinery, credits, etc. Without slavery you have no cotton; without cotton you have no modern industry."[12] Marx clearly attached some weight to this argument, since he included it verbatim in an 1846 letter to P.W. Annenkow in which he summarizes his main criticisms of Proudhon.[13] However it could be said that at this stage, Marx and Engels still approached slavery in the colonies from the same analytical distance from which they remarked on colonial developments in general.[14] In relation to slavery, this can be seen in particular from Engels' incidental adoption of an argument with strong overtones of racism then current among sections of the labor movement, presenting wage labor as a "worse kind" of slavery than plantation slavery. This literal phrase can be found in the *Condition of the Working Class in England*.[15] In an article on the struggle by the British working class for the restriction of the working day to ten hours, Engels went as far as to claim that "the fate of the slaves in the worst of the American plantations was golden in comparison with that of the English workers in that period."[16]

Furthermore, as was shown most clearly in Marx's famous article on "the future of British rule in India," in the early 1850s both Marx and Engels still held the view that capitalist development would be the main instrument of historical progress in the colonial world, although unwittingly and at great human cost. From this point of view, colonial subjects or slaves figured as the passive victims of capitalist progress. In an article written jointly by Marx and Engels in 1850, the authors repeat Marx's earlier assertion that the "crucial sector of British

---

12   *MECW* 6, 167.

13   Marx to P.W. Annenkow, 28 December 1846, *MECW* 38, 101.

14   Many writers have commented on this, especially in relation to Marx's early writings on India. For recent discussions, see Keven B. Anderson, *Marx at the margins. On nationalism, ethnicity, and non-Western societies* (Chicago and London, 2010), 11–17; Lucia Pradella, *Globalization and the critique of Political Economy. New insights from Marx's writings* (London and New York, 2014).

15   *MECW* 2, 468.

16   *MECW* 10, 291. For an extensive discussion of the notions of "white slavery" and "wage slavery" in the contemporary labor movement, including its racist connotations, see David R. Roediger, *The wages of whiteness. Race and the making of the American working class* (London, 1991), 65–92. Of course, it would be ahistorical to measure these and other statements by Marx and Engels by the standards of twenty-first-century sensitivity to language use. Nevertheless, these quotations from Engels in particular show considerable ignorance or insensitivity about the actual conditions under which slaves in the Americas lived and worked. In important respects, this attitude changed in Marx's and Engels' later writings.

industry" depended on slavery in the American South. After briefly speculating on the possibility of slave revolt, they argue that "the only feasible solution to the slave question" lay elsewhere:

> As soon as the free labour of other countries provides industry with its cotton supplies in sufficient quantity and more cheaply than the slave labour of the United States, American slavery will have been broken at the same time as the American cotton monopoly, and the slaves will be emancipated because as slaves they will have become unusable.[17]

This mechanical view, in which plantation slavery and the slaves themselves figured abstractly and passively as the backdrop to dynamics that unfolded elsewhere, would be seriously revised by Marx in the course of the 1850s and early 1860s. There were three main sources for this revision. The first was theoretical. After the defeat of the 1848–1849 revolutions, Marx decided to use the expected long lull in the class struggle to write his "critique of political economy": A task that he never managed to complete.[18] Part of this gargantuan enterprise was to revise Ricardo's theory of ground rent, which—like for example the role of money and banking in a capitalist economy—presented significant theoretical problems for the labor theory of value.[19] To strengthen the empirical basis for his arguments, Marx undertook serious studies on colonial land use, agricultural labor, and land prices, as well as on the history of colonization by European powers in general.[20] The *London Notebooks* of 1850–1853 that comprise the residue of the first of these efforts, contain many notes on slavery in European and non-European ancient empires, and in the European colonies and the U.S.[21] The notes mainly consist of long extracts from the texts of others, sometimes literally transcribed, sometimes paraphrased in Marx's unique pidgin of several living and dead languages. They hardly give a clear roadmap to his thinking during this period. However, they do indicate that his interest in

---

17   *MECW* 10, 500–501.

18   On Marx's reasons for this decision, see August H. Nimtz Jr., *Marx and Engels. Their contribution to the democratic breakthrough* (New York, 2000), 151–155.

19   Enrique Dussel, *Towards an unknown Marx. A commentary on the Manuscripts of 1861–63* (London and New York, 2001), 82–83.

20   Pradella, *Globalisation*, 104–112.

21   Examples of the former are Marx's notes on Dureau de Lamalle, *Économie politique des Romains* and W.H. Prescott, *History of the Conquest of Mexico*, MEGA² IV.9, 332, 335, 340, 406, 432. Examples of the latter are his copious notes on H.C. Carey, *The Past, the present and the future*, MEGA² IV.8, 748–749, Herman Merivale, *Lectures on colonization and colonies*, MEGA² IV.9, 436–438, 442–448, 465–472, and Th.F. Buxton, *The African slave trade*, MEGA² IV.8, 494–498.

SLAVERY & "FREE" LABOR IN THE WRITINGS OF MARX   53

slavery became more concrete and historical, and took into account the actual forms under which slavery prevailed in his own day. Among other topics, Marx paid attention to the great varieties of slavery that existed in different phases of human history, the enormous cost in terms of human life of the illegal slave trade, and the "*Cultur der jealousy zwischen* [Creoles] *und den inferior or mixed races*" in which "the place of a man in society was made to depend on his colour, even to the minutest shades."[22]

A second source for Marx's closer examination of the question of slavery was his growing engagement with colonialism. This found its clearest expression in his articles on China and India for the *New York Tribune*. Marx's large journalistic output of the 1850s and early 1860s was for a long time almost entirely ignored as a site of theoretical development. However, as Michael Krätke has argued, in these voluminous writings many topical questions relating to the operation of the capitalist system on an international scale were first developed.[23] The *Tribune* had been founded in 1841 as "a crusading organ of progressive causes," among which abolitionism took pride of place.[24] By the time he was recruited as its London correspondent in 1851, the *Tribune* had emerged as the biggest selling newspaper in the world, with more than 200,000 readers.[25] In its pages, Marx wrote with acerbic wit and great indignation about European colonialism. His greatest venom was reserved for British colonialism, which hid its brutal face behind liberal free-trade ideology. Given the importance of anti-slavery sentiments to Britain's humanitarian self-image, the way in which the global expansion of British trade continued to rely on—and even fostered—slavery while also creating misery at home, drew his special attention as proof of the hypocrisy underlying such claims.[26] Meanwhile, the Sepoy uprising in India and the Taiping rebellion in China led Marx to consider rebellion of the colonial subjects themselves as an independent force in history, leading him to break with Eurocentric notions of historical progress.[27]

---

22   *MEGA*[2] IV.8, 567; *MEGA*[2] IV.9, 495, and 438 respectively. In the cited passage, Marx paraphrases Merivale.

23   Michael Krätke, "Journalisme et science. L'importance des travaux journalistiques de Marx pour la critique de l'économie politique," *Actuel Marx*, 42, no. 2 (2007): 128–163, 129.

24   James Ledbetter, "Introduction," in Karl Marx, *Dispatches for the New York Tribune. Selected journalism of Karl Marx*, ed. James Ledbetter (London, 2007), xvii–xxvii, xvii.

25   James Ledbetter, "Introduction," in Karl Marx, *Dispatches for the New York Tribune. Selected journalism of Karl Marx*, ed. James Ledbetter (London, 2007), xviii.

26   E.g. "The Duchess of Sutherland and slavery," in Marx, *Dispatches*, 113–119; "The British government and the slave-trade," in Marx, *Dispatches*, 261–266; "The British cotton trade," in Marx, *Dispatches*, 276–280.

27   Anderson, *Margins*, 38; Lucia Pradella, "Marx and the Global South. Connecting history and value theory," *Sociology*, 51, no.1 (2017): 146–161. Marx's turn away from Eurocentric

However, by far the most important determinant of the place slavery would be given in Marx's economic studies of the 1860s was the American Civil War. Marx's writings of this period show the extent of his emotional, intellectual, and practical investment in the support for the North.[28] Long before Lincoln's Emancipation Act, at the very start of the conflict between the Confederacy and the Union, Marx insisted on the centrality of slavery as the key issue at stake. In an article written for the Vienna-based liberal newspaper *Die Presse*, he described the war as "nothing but a struggle between two social systems, the system of slavery and the system of free labour."[29] However, Marx no longer believed that the development of free trade or the proliferation of free labor would in itself solve this clash in favor of the latter. In line with his journalistic critique of British colonialism, he insisted that English trade interests led British industrialists to give full support to the South. He therefore saw it as a core task of the British and international working-class movement to oppose any move toward European intervention in support of the slaveholding states. The foundation of the International Workingmen's Association provided Marx with an opportunity to engage in practical agitation in support of the North.[30] Through his writings for the *Tribune*, and later through his connections with German revolutionary émigrés, Marx consistently stressed the need to revolutionize the war effort.[31] His confidence in the ultimate victory of the North, not always shared by his associate Engels, relied in a large part on his conviction

---

notions of progress would deepen in the 1870s and early 1880s, when he undertook major studies in Russian and Indian agricultural development to consider the various routes capitalist development could take. Tomba, *Temporalities*, 170–178.

28   This investment was shared by the entire Marx household. In December 1863, Marx's then eight-year-old daughter Eleanor wrote to her uncle Lion Philips, whom she had never met: "Do you like A.B. [Abe Lincoln]? He is a big friend of mine." *"Was ik maar weer in Bommel." Karl Marx en zijn Nederlandse verwanten*, ed. Jan Gielkens (Amsterdam, 1997), 109. Wilhelm Backhaus has argued, though in my view not entirely convincingly, that Marx's and Engels' political investment in abolitionism was so strong that it led them to considerable misreading—to the point of conscious misrepresentation—of the evidence concerning the economic viability of slavery in the Southern states. According to Backhaus, they even projected this evidence backwards onto slavery in classical antiquity. Wilhelm Backhaus, *Marx, Engels und die Sklaverei* (Düsseldorf, 1974), 248.

29   *MECW* 19, 50.

30   Robin Blackburn, *An unfinished revolution. Karl Marx and Abraham Lincoln* (London and New York, 2011), 46–49.

31   The most important of these connections was Joseph Wedemeyer, a veteran of the revolution of 1848 who became a technical aide on the staff of the Northern General John C. Frémont. August H. Nimtz, Jr., *Marx, Tocqueville, and race in America. The "Absolute Democracy" or "Defiled Republic"* (Lanham etc., 2003), 118–129.

that emancipation would boost the Northern war effort.[32] This heightened his attention to the revolutionary potential of the activity of the slaves. Marx had already written to Engels in 1860, in the wake of John Brown's famous attempt to trigger a general slave revolt by an armed raid on Harpers Ferry:

> In my view, the most momentous thing happening in the world today is the slave movement—on the one hand, in America, started by the death of Brown, and in Russia, on the other ... Thus, a "social" movement has been started both in the West and in the East ... This promises great things.[33]

The conflict in North America accompanied Marx for the entire period during which he transformed his earlier drafts into *Capital*, Volume I. It sealed the process in which, for Marx, slavery changed from one of the many distant grievances that would be violently shoved aside by the juggernaut of capitalist development, to the locus of concrete struggles intimately connected to those of the international working class. Writing to François Lafargue, the child of a Caribbean mixed relationship and father of his later son-in-law Paul Lafargue, Marx coined a phrase that would also find its way into *Capital*: "*le travail, tant qu'il est flétri dans la peau noire, ne sera jamais émancipé dans la peau blanche*" [labor in white skin will never be emancipated, where in black skin it is branded].[34]

3   Wage Labor and Capital

To understand the influence that Marx's developing insights had on the way he refers to slavery in his mature work, it is necessary to briefly discuss why, and how, Marx saw wage labor as central to capitalism. As is well known, during 1842 and 1843 the young Marx turned away from philosophy and toward the working class as the leading force for the emancipation of mankind.[35]

---

32   Nimtz, Jr., *Marx, Tocqueville, and race in America*, 104–110.

33   Marx to Engels, 11 January 1860, *MECW* 41, 4.

34   Marx to François Lafargue, 12 November 1866, *Marx Engels Correspondance*, VIII (Paris, 1981) (French original). The English translation given in *MECW* 42, 334 considerably tones down Marx's phrase, leaving out the references to both skin and branding. The French version in this letter matches the German version of the same remark in *Capital*, vol. I. *MEGA*² II.5, 239–240.

35   Shlomo Avineri, *The social and political thought of Karl Marx* (Cambridge, 1968), 41–64; Hal Draper, *Karl Marx's theory of revolution*, vol. II: The politics of social classes (New York, 1978), 33–48.

In the light of the critique of Marx's privileging of the working class formulated by Global Labor History, it deserves emphasis that through this turn, Marx primarily distanced himself from those who looked to sections of the middle class (the philosophers, philanthropists, utopian thinkers, and social improvers) as the agents of social change.[36] Marx's shift rested on a perception of the working class as a "universal class" or a "class for all classes," distinct from, but interested in and connected to the struggles of all the other subaltern groups. The proletariat was envisioned as the social sphere "which cannot emancipate itself without emancipating itself from all other spheres of society and thereby emancipating all other spheres of society, which, in a word, is the *complete loss* of man and hence can win itself only through the *complete rewinning of man*."[37] Marx's studies of political economy would soon lead him to define the relationship between the working class and the other social classes in less philosophical terms. Without losing the broad emancipatory thrust of his earlier writings, he increasingly focused on the special role of the exploitation of wage labor in capitalist production.[38]

From his preparatory work for the *Grundrisse* to the publication of *Capital*, Volume I, Marx fundamentally reworked the main concepts of classical political economy.[39] In the process, he would also fundamentally deepen his analysis of the mechanisms through which wage labor is tied to capital. Nevertheless, in a more rudimentary form, the different elements for understanding this dependency had already been outlined as early as 1847.[40] Marx did this in a short text titled *Wage Labour and Capital*, which was initially conceived as a series of lectures to the Brussels workers' association and then published in the *Neue Rheinische Zeitung* two years later. It came well before the crucial break in Marx's understanding of the categories that he inherited from classical economy: His "discovery" that the worker sells to the capitalist not labor, but labor

---

36 Michael Löwy, *The theory of revolution in the young Marx* (Leiden and Boston, 2003), 23–61.

37 *MECW* 3, 186. The German original does not speak of man, but of *der Mensch. MECW* 1, 390.

38 Enrique Dussel shows the continued presence of what he calls an "ethics of liberation" in Marx's project to revise political economy. Enrique Dussel, *La producción teórica de Marx. Un comentario a los Grundrisse* (Madrid etc., 1985), 355.

39 For the development of Marx's concepts, see V.S. Vygodski, *The story of a great discovery. How Karl Marx wrote "Capital"* (Berlin, 1973); Roman Rosdolsky, *The making of Marx's Capital* (London, 1977). For an accessible recent summary of the theoretical issues at stake, see Michael Heinrich, *An introduction to the three volumes of Karl Marx's Capital* (New York, 2004).

40 Ernest Mandel, *The formation of the economic thought of Karl Marx* (London, 1971), 54.

SLAVERY & "FREE" LABOR IN THE WRITINGS OF MARX   57

power.[41] Even so, Marx's treatment of the necessary relationship between capital and wage labor in this early text provides an excellent starting point from which to understand the later development of his thoughts. Significantly for the theme of this article, the discussion begins with an allusion to slavery. The context of this passage is an argument over whether capital is simply any collection of raw materials, work instruments, or consumption goods—as it is in a "production factors" approach—or, as Marx argued, that such commodities only become capital as a result of their function within a definite set of social relations.

> What is a Negro slave? A man of the black race. The one explanation is as good as the other. A Negro is a Negro. He only becomes a *slave* in certain relations. A cotton-spinning jenny is a machine for spinning cotton. It becomes *capital* only in certain relations.[42]

According to Marx, what changes a collection of commodities ("dead labor") into capital, is that it is posited (through market exchange) as a social power that dominates over, and reproduces itself through, the employment of commodified labor (later: Labor power). This brings into a necessary relation four different moments: (1) The moment of the sale of labor (labor power); (2) the

---

41   This is the cornerstone of Marx's explanation for the specific form taken by exploitation under capitalism. Both Adam Smith and David Ricardo grappled with a fundamental question: (1) if labor is the source of all wealth, (2) if we assume all market exchanges take place at their value, and (3) if capitalists buy labor from the workers at its value too, then where does the capitalist's profit come from? The only solution seems to be to either assume that profits are a wage for the capitalist's own labor (abandoning the fundamental distinction between profit and wage that political economy aims to explain in the first place), or to assume that profits arise from the market exchange of commodities at prices that have no inherent relation to the amount of labor they contain (abandoning the labor theory of value that formed the starting point for political economy), or to assume that under capitalism, labor is always bought at a wage that is lower than its actual value (effectively saying that no profits are possible under "average conditions"). Marx's solution is as simple as it is effective. Capitalists do not buy labor at all. They buy labor power for a certain amount of time, the "use value" of which is that it adds labor as the substance of value to the commodity during the time in which it is employed in the process of production. Paying a wage entitles the capitalist to ownership of the products produced by the use value of "labor power" during this entire period, regardless of the actual amount of "congealed labor" they contain. This makes it possible to explain the existence of a "surplus value" of unpaid labor by the worker, without abandoning either the labor theory of value or the theoretical starting-point of average exchange at prices that correspond to value. For a more complete explanation, see Rosdolsky, *Making*, 194–211, or Heinrich, *Introduction*.

42   *MECW* 9, 211.

process of production during which the laborer produces *for capital*; (3) the privatized moment of consumption through which the laborer has to expend the wage previously earned in order to "reproduce" him or herself (and his or her family); (4) forcing him or her to re-enter the labor market and allow for a new cycle of production. Marx continues to explain why this necessary relationship between the different moments constitutes the basis for the capitalist form of social domination. Capital becomes capital only in its relation to "a class which possesses nothing but its capacity to labour."[43] And it is this lack of any other options than to sell his or her labor power that turns the ostensibly "free" act of sale on the part of the laborer into an act of social subjection of the worker to capital as an alien force.[44]

One of the interesting aspects of this argument is that already at this early stage, Marx emphasized the circular nature of capitalist production. While producing commodities, it also reproduces the preconditions for its own continued existence. In this process, the subjection of the laborer is expansive and necessarily engulfs the "free" act of sale of labor power itself. In Marx's words:

> Does a worker in a cotton factory produce merely cotton textiles? No, he produces capital. He produces values which serve afresh to command his labour and by means of it to create new values. Capital can only increase by exchanging itself for labour [power], by calling wage labour to life. The wage labour [The labour power of the wage-worker] can only be exchanged for capital by increasing capital, by strengthening the power whose slave it is. *Hence, increase of capital is increase of the proletariat, that is, of the working class.*[45]

In this early text, not only does Marx already present in a very rough form the integrated levels on which he would follow the relationship between wage labor and capital in the three volumes of *Capital* (production, circulation, total

---

43 *MECW* 9, 213.

44 The notion that the worker's labor is "forced labor" because it only serves "to satisfy needs external to it" was already present in the *Manuscripts of 1844*. See Michael A. Lebowitz, *Beyond Capital. Marx's political economy of the working class* (London, 1992), 21. Also see the perceptive discussion of the relationship between (un)freedom, needs, and wants in Frédéric Lordon, *Willing slaves of capital. Spinoza and Marx on desire* (London and New York, 2014). Marcel van der Linden agrees with this categorization, and therefore includes wage labor in his taxonomy of coerced labor. Marcel van der Linden, "Dissecting coerced labor," in Van der Linden and Rodríguez García, *On coerced labor*, 293–322, 295.

45 *MECW* 9, 214. The words in brackets denote the changes made by Engels in the 1891 edition, to account for Marx's later point of view.

social reproduction), but the passage these quotations are taken from also contains a peculiar shift in the use of the concept of "slavery," which Marx would continue to employ in *Capital*. In the first quotation, slavery is invoked to underline that economic phenomena such as slavery or capital only attain their meaning under specific social relations. However, only a few pages later Marx states that the wage laborer *is*—not *is like*, or *seems to be*—the slave of capital. The easy way out of this conundrum would be to say that slavery in its first use refers to actual, historical slavery, whereas in its second use it should only be understood abstractly or rhetorically, but this is not the case. As we have seen previously, underlying *all* Marx's references to slavery in this period was a detached and to some extent a-historical notion of the actual slavery of his time. On the other hand, his growing political engagement with and historical interest in actual slavery did not persuade him to stop drawing direct parallels between the wage laborer and the slave. On the contrary, it would lead him to do so at a far greater level of concreteness.

4   Slavery and the Boundaries of the Workers' "double freedom"

In *Capital*, Volume 1, Marx argues that capital can only reproduce itself when it encounters the "free" laborer on the market. Marx famously defines this freedom in a "double sense": "that as a free man he can dispose of his labour power as his own commodity, and that on the other hand he has no other commodity for sale, is short of everything necessary for the realisation of his labour power."[46] Summarizing, the first half of this duality denotes the freedom of the laborer to sell his or her labor power, the second the "freedom from alternatives" that forces him or her to actually do so. Jairus Banaji formulated a devastating critique of attempts to ascribe to Marx the notion that this "freedom" of the wage laborer is at the same time both "formal" and "positive." Such an interpretation of the nature of "free labor" was essential to the approach of classical liberalism. In contrast to his theoretical opponents, Marx's "references to free labour have a profoundly delegitimating intent."[47] Comparing wage labor to slavery plays an important role in bringing out this purpose. It is one of the key markers by which Marx distinguishes his own approach to free labor from that

---

46   *MECW* 35, 179 / *MEGA*[2] II.5, 122.

47   Jairus Banaji, *Theory as history. Essays on modes of production and exploitation* (Leiden and Boston, 2010), 137. On the liberal interpretation of free labor, see Robert J. Steinfeld, *The invention of free labor. The employment relation in English and American law and culture, 1350–1870* (London: Chapel Hill, 1991), 147–148.

of authors such as Adam Smith, James Steuart, or John Stuart Mill, quoted in the first section of this article.

The delegitimization of the notion of the "free" wage laborer in Marx goes in three directions, each of which was already present in the earlier *Wage Labour and Capital*. First, freedom is emphatically restricted to the sphere of circulation where the capitalist buys the labor power of the wage worker. Once the act of sale is completed, and for the full duration for which the sale is concluded, the laborer is legally bound to the capitalist. Liberal writers thought that such "temporary, voluntary subjection" did not cancel out the freedom of those engaging in it.[48] However, as the designation of the laborer as the "slave" of capital in *Wage Labour and Capital* already shows, Marx thought it did. According to him, the relationship between the capitalist and the worker during the production process was not one of an equal interaction between two free agents, but one of "despotism."[49] Furthermore, as is the case in slavery, the function of this despotism is to minimize the time in which the laborer produces the necessary goods (or their equivalent in money) for his or her own upkeep and that of the family, and to maximize the time worked "for nothing" for the master/employer.[50] Clearly, it is in the derivation of surplus value from unpaid labor performed in the sphere of production that the historical connection with slavery and other forms of coerced labor runs deepest. Second, Marx only saw the sale of labor power in the process of circulation itself as a voluntary act in a very limited sense. This goes to the heart of his notion of double freedom, in which the second leg of this duality posits an ironic commentary on the first. Whereas the free disposal over one's own labor power can still be construed as a positive freedom in the liberal sense, the "freedom" from means of existence or employment outside the capital relation that complements it is purely negative. This "freedom" is not a constrained freedom. It is itself a constraint, which leaves the worker no other choice than to sell his or her labor power. Last, this force operates not just on an individual scale, in the relationship between capitalist and worker that is mediated through the market, but on a social scale. The apparent freedom granted by the market to

---

48   Steinfeld, *Invention*, 148.

49   *MECW* 35, 362.

50   Marx already emphasized the resulting change in the form of exploitation in his *Manuscripts of 1861–1863*, "The *money relation*, the sale and purchase between worker and capitalist, disguises the former's *labour for no return*, whereas with slave labour the property relation of the slave to his master disguises the former's *labour for himself.*" *MECW* 34, 98 / *MEGA*² II.3.6, 2134.

SLAVERY & "FREE" LABOR IN THE WRITINGS OF MARX

choose which capitalist in the singular will have the right to exploit the worker, results in the collective subjection of the working class to capital in general.[51]

The biting sarcasm with which Marx uses the notion of freedom finds its peak in the conclusion of the very section in which he introduces the "doubly free" wage laborer. First of all, he brutally scoffs at the liberal commentators' lofty view of the labor market. He directs his anger most of all at Jeremy Bentham, who translated political economy's celebration of the free agency and self-interest of the wage laborer into the realm of moral philosophy and contractual theory. The sphere of commodity exchange "within whose boundaries the sale and purchase of labour power goes on, is in fact a very Eden of the innate rights of man. There alone rule Freedom, Equality, Property and Bentham."[52] However, Marx leaves no room for doubt that this is only a "vulgar" perception, which starts breaking down as soon as one leaves the separate sphere of circulation and enters the sphere of capitalist production. The imagery he uses, not coincidentally, is the same he employs when describing slavery: that of the acquisition of a person's skin.

> He, who before was the money owner, now strides in front as capitalist; the possessor of labour power follows as his labourer. The one with an air of importance, smirking, intent on business; the other, timid and holding back, like one who is bringing his own hide to market and has nothing to expect but—a hiding.[53]

Here, the parallel with slavery is clearly symbolic. Nevertheless, there are other passages in which Marx goes considerably further, arguing that the sale of labor power under fully developed capitalism can under specific conditions approximate actual slavery.[54] This does not take the racist form of describing all forms of (white) wage labor as worse than (black) slavery, as in the earlier

---

51   This point is explored to great effect by Jacques Bidet, *Exploring Marx's Capital. Philosophical, economic and political dimensions* (Leiden and Boston, 2007), 27–51.

52   *MECW* 35, 186 / *MEGA*² II.5, 128.

53   *MECW* 35, 186 / *MEGA*² II.5, 128: In the German original: "*Der ehemalige Geldbesitzer schreitet voran als Kapitalist, der Arbeitskraft Besitzer folgt ihm nach als sein Arbeiter; der Eine bedeutungsvoll schmunzelnd und geschäftseifrig, der Andre scheu, widerstrebsam, wie Jemand, der seine eigne Haut zu Markt getragen und nun nichts andres zu erwarten hat als die—Gerberei.*"

54   The formulation is derived from the *Manuscripts of 1831–1863, MECW* 34, 108. In the German original, Marx uses the phrase "*sinkt hier wieder annährend zum Sklavenverhältniss hinab.*" *MEGA*² II.3.6, 2144.

remarks by Engels.[55] Instead, Marx reserves the explicit comparison only for the most exploitative types of wage labor; the extension of the working day beyond the physically sustainable limit, and the hyper-exploitation of women and children. In both cases, Marx draws his comparisons from his readings on slavery in the United States. The first case was already mentioned in the introduction, and leads on to the sentences from which the title of this article is taken. In Chapter 3, Section 4 of *Capital*, dealing with the length of the working day, Marx intends to show that if not forced to accept some limits to exploitation, capitalist production tends to extend the working day to the point of risking killing the worker. In this, he argues, the capitalists behave like slave owners, who as long as the slave trade provided the influx of new "human chattel," valued an increase in productivity above the length of the life of the slaves. Quoting J.E. Cairnes's *The Slave Power*, Marx railed against the "reckless sacrifice" of the "Negroes' life" in order to obtain "fabulous wealth, that has engulfed millions of the African race." After summing up the ways in which slave lives were expended for the sake of profit, Marx makes his injection: "*Mutato nomine de te fabula narratur!*"[56] explicitly claiming the validity of the example of slavery for the most oppressed sections of the working class.

Here, Marx is still clear that the comparison between slavery and wage labor is one between two fundamentally different phenomena (hence, "*mutato nomine*").[57] However, this changes when Marx comes to discuss the aspect of industrial exploitation that angered him most: The exploitation of child labor.[58] The argument is noteworthy, because here Marx explicitly allows for the possibility that further capitalist development would partially dispense with even the limited form of freedom entailed in the "free" sale of labor power. Focusing on the role of the male heads of the family, who according to Marx were the ones who delivered their wives and children into the hands of the factory owners, he argues that in this case, the (female or child) laborers do not in fact freely sell their labor power at all:

---

55   In the *Manuscripts of 1861–1863*, Marx still partially cited and partially paraphrased T.R. Edmonds, who argued that "the motive which impels a free man to labour is much more violent than the motive impelling a slave," MECW 34, 103n / MEGA² II.3.6, 2137–2138, but this argument did not reappear in *Capital*.

56   MECW 35, 272 / MEGA² II.5, 209.

57   In an earlier discussion of the same topic, included in the *Manuscripts of 1861–1863*, this mark of distinction was absent. Here, Marx placed examples of the detrimental results of the extension of the working day on the life expectancy of wage laborers and slaves directly next to each other. MECW 30, 183 / MEGA², II.3.1, 160.

58   On Marx's bracketing of children's labor and women's labor in the passage discussed here, and the extent to which this stems from a gendered view of labor, see Heather A. Brown, *Marx on gender and the family. A critical study* (Leiden and Boston, 2012), 78–88.

SLAVERY & "FREE" LABOR IN THE WRITINGS OF MARX

Taking the exchange of commodities as our basis, our first assumption was that capitalist and labourer met as free persons, as independent owners of commodities; the one possessing money and means of production, the other labour power. But now the capitalist buys children and young persons under age. Previously, the workman sold his own labour power, which he disposed of nominally as a free agent. Now he sells wife and child. He has become a slave-dealer.[59]

The theoretical importance can hardly be overstated. For in just a few lines, Marx emphasizes here that the representation of the meeting of capitalist and laborers as free persons was just a "first assumption," and acknowledges the possibility of "intermediary labor relations" in which labor power is sold on the market, but not sold by the laborer him- or herself. Furthermore, he does so with immediate reference to slavery. Just as in the case of the lengthening of the working day, Marx makes it clear that his comparison was not with slavery in the abstract, but with the form of slavery that had just been abolished under great acclaim in the Southern States of North America.

Die Nachfrage nach Kinderarbeit gleicht oft auch in der Form der Nachfrage nach Negersklaven, wie man sie in amerikanischen Zeitungsinseraten zu lesen gewohnt war.
[The demand for children's labor often resembles also in form the inquiries for Negro slaves, such as were formerly to be read among the advertisements in American journals.][60]

Neither was this equation of child labor with slavery accidental. Further on in *Capital*, Marx repeated it in his telegram-style summing up of the history of the cotton trade.[61] He did so again in his discussion of original accumulation, following on the heels of his extensive denunciation of slavery under the Dutch in the East Indies.[62] Bringing this history into the era of industrial capital, he emphasized "the necessity of child-stealing and child-slavery for the

---

59   *MECW* 35, 399 / *MEGA²* II.5, 324.
60   *MECW* 35, 399 / *MEGA²* II.5, 324. The English translation of *Capital* leaves out the crucial word "also" in "*auch in der Form*," which significantly changes its meaning, suggesting "in form rather than content," where Marx implies "both in form and in content."
61   *MECW* 35, 458 / *MEGA²* II.5, 371.
62   "The treasures captured outside Europe by undisguised looting, enslavement, and murder, floated back to the mother-country and were there turned into capital. Holland, which first fully developed the colonial system, in 1648 stood already in the acme of its commercial greatness." *MECW* 35, 741 / *MEGA²* II.5, 603–604.

transformation of manufacturing exploitation into factory exploitation, and the establishment of the 'true relation' between capital and labour power."[63]

Thus at the very moment that "free labor" in the classical liberal sense seemed to have gained its most significant historical breakthrough, Marx time and time again invoked the example of slavery to show this formal freedom to hide just one particular historical form of coerced labor. Further, in discussing the working day and child labor, he returned to the comparison at a greater level of concreteness in order to show that unless boundaries were enforced on it, capital's own logic impelled it to encroach on the distinction between slavery and wage labor; both in substance and in form.

5   Transitional Forms between Slavery and Capitalism

In all the examples given in the previous section, Marx placed slavery next to "free" wage labor as a tool for comparison. Even when discussed using concrete examples to highlight actual historical conditions, rather than on the plane of abstract categories, slavery still mainly served the purpose of conceptual clarification. It helped Marx to draw out what was specific to the exploitation of labor by capital, without losing sight of the elements that bound it to all other forms of coerced labor across the world and throughout history. However, Marx was also acutely aware of the actual persistence of a slave sector within the nineteenth-century world economy, and its role in the expansion of the world market and industrial capital. We have seen that in 1847, he summarized this in the pointed phrase: "without slavery no cotton, without cotton no modern industry." His sense of this mutual dependency was heightened by the sympathy for the slaveholding states expressed by important sections of the British industrial bourgeoisie during the American Civil War. This forced him to think about the historical relationship between slavery and capitalist development. Generations of Marxist historians have read Marx's reflections on this question primarily to obtain a set of solid definitions. The most important issue for them was whether in Marx's view, the commercial slavery of the American South and other regions presented a non-capitalist precursor or pedestal for "real" capitalist development outside of the capitalist system proper; a non-capitalist sector that functioned on the periphery of the capitalist world market, or was itself a form of capitalist production.[64] Quotations from Marx can

---

63   *MECW* 35, 745 / *MEGA²* II.5, 605.

64   For different perspectives, see Eugene D. Genovese, "Marxian interpretations of the slave South," in Eugene D. Genovese, *In red and black. Marxian explorations in Southern and*

be found for different, seemingly mutually exclusive positions.[65] The attempt to elevate one of them to the status of "orthodoxy" runs counter to Marx's own searching, scholarly approach, an aspect of Marx's method that Marcel van der Linden has frequently emphasized.

Equally contentious is the question of whether, for Marx, the necessity of the dominance of wage labor for the development of full capitalism meant that all other forms of exploitation would exhibit a tendency to disappear.[66] As Banaji notes, Marx's analysis explicitly excluded the possibility of "capital being founded on unfree labour (in the strict sense ...) at the level of the expansion of the total social capital."[67] However, Marx also acknowledged the possibility of the existence of slavery at "individual points" within the "bourgeois system of production," albeit as an anomaly.[68] His grappling with these questions should be understood in the context of his changing understanding of the origins, direction, and variants of capitalist development. In the introduction of *Capital*, Volume I, Marx could still insist that "the country that is more developed industrially only shows, to the less developed, the image of its own future."[69] His later studies of agricultural change in Russia and India in particular would lead him to fundamentally reconsider this statement.[70] Despite

---

Afro-American history (New York, 1968), 315–353; Robert Miles, *Capitalism and unfree labour. Anomaly or necessity?* (London and New York, 1987); Robin Blackburn, *The making of New World Slavery. From the Baroque to the modern, 1492–1800* (London and New York, 1997); Banaji, *Theory as history*; Charles Post, *The American road to capitalism. Studies in class-structure, economic development and political conflict, 1620–1877* (Leiden and Boston, 2011). The third point of view has recently made a comeback in historiographical debate, although without explicit reference to Marx, in Sven Beckert, *Empire of cotton. A global history* (New York, 2014).

65   Cf., for example, the *Grundrisse*, MECW 28, 157 / *MEGA²* II.1.1, 149, where he talks about "*Negro slavery*—a purely industrial form of slavery which in any case is incompatible with and disappears as a result of the development of bourgeois society," with the *Manuscripts of 1861–1863*, MECW 31, 516 / *MEGA²* II.3.3, 936, where he states that in plantations "commercial speculations figure from the start and production is intended for the world market, the capitalist production exists, although only in a formal sense, since the slavery of Negroes precludes free wage labour, which is the basis of capitalist production. But the business in which slaves are used is conducted by *capitalists*. The mode of production which they introduce has not arisen out of slavery but is grafted on to it."

66   As suggested by Van der Linden, *Workers*, 19n.

67   Banaji, *Theory as history*, 142.

68   Marx, *Grundrisse*, MECW 28, 392 / *MEGA²* II.1.2, 372. Cf. the *Manuscripts of 1861–1863* where the same point is approached from the diametrically opposite angle: "But so long as slavery is predominant, the capital-relation can only be sporadic and subordinate, never dominant." MECW 33, 336 / *MEGA²*, II.3.5, 1851.

69   MECW 35, 9 / *MEGA²* II.5, 12.

70   Anderson, *Marx at the margins*, 208–218; Tomba, *Marx's temporalities*, 170–186.

66 PEPIJN BRANDON

this strongly linear sentence in the introduction of *Capital*, the seeds of a much more open approach had already been sown in the early 1860s. This is shown in a particularly striking way in a passage in the *Manuscripts of 1861–1863*, where Marx introduces the notion of *"Uebergangsformen"* (transitional forms):

> I am ... speaking here of forms in which the capital-relation does not yet exist formally, i.e. under which labour is already exploited by capital before the latter has developed into the form of productive capital and labour itself has taken on the form of wage labour. Such forms are to be found in social formations which precede the bourgeois mode of production; on the other hand they constantly reproduce themselves within the latter and are in part reproduced by the latter itself.[71]

The notion of a "transitional form" does point towards a clear tendency for historical development (wage labor replacing slavery). However, the final sentence of the quotation also shows that in Marx's view, it was at least thinkable that capitalist development would never actually bring this tendency to completion. This opened up the intellectual space to discuss slavery not only as a stepping stone for capitalist development, but as a contemporaneous and connected phenomenon.

As a result of its preference for rigid definitions and clear demarcations, much of Marxist historiography has completely ignored the many areas of overlap, interaction, and combination between practices of exploitation and social struggle of "free" and unfree laborers. With regard to this neglect, Global Labor History launched an effective attack on the predominant mode of Marxist history writing. However, Marx himself was certainly not as unaware of the issue as many of his later followers were. Both his economic manuscripts and *Capital* contain extensive passages where he not only compares wage labor and slavery, but discusses the mutual historical influences and the relationships between the two. Rather than approaching slave production and capitalist production as two entities inhabiting their separate spheres, he attempted to show how their contemporaneity changed the mode of operation of both. For example, Marx discussed with considerable nuance the differences between forms of slavery in antiquity and in his own day, clearly differentiating between the nature of slave production, where this was primarily geared towards the production of use values, and slave production, where it operated for the market. Countering the Southern States' claims that slavery presented a patriarchal and therefore benevolent social system, Marx emphasized that

---

71   *MECW* 34, 117 / *MEGA*[2] II.3.6, 2152.

this might have been true in a very limited sense for an earlier period when it existed in relative isolation from capitalist markets, but not for modern slavery in its highly commercialized form:

> In proportion, as the export of cotton became of vital interest to these states, the overworking of the Negro and sometimes the using up of his life in 7 years of labour became a factor in a calculated and calculating system. It was no longer a question of obtaining from him a certain quantity of useful products. It was now a question of production of surplus labour itself.[72]

Just as the nature of slave labor changed when it came under the indirect (through the market) or direct (through the ownership of plantations) control of the capitalist, so wage labor absorbed practices that had been developed in slavery. This is clearest in Marx's treatment of the role of superintendence or "labor for the exploitation of labor" in factory production. While Marx again does not let go of the fundamental distinction between wage labor and slavery, he stresses that the role of the supervisor in the factory is closer to that of the slave supervisor than to that of the master of the small workshops that dominated urban production in Europe before the Industrial Revolution. In the latter case, discipline was enforced through the master's own participation in the work process. By contrast, a sharp division of labor between the capitalist and the overseer would come to characterize the factory hierarchy. More than that of the workshop master, the "relations of subordination" and "regimentation" of the factory were a continuation of the relations between the "working Negro slaves" and the "slave-driving Negro slaves" on the plantation.[73]

Marx paid considerable attention to the results of the interaction and intermingling of various types of labor relations. This gave historical depth to his views on wage labor, feeding back into his conceptualizations of both exploited labor in general and the sale of labor power as the dominant basis of exploitation under capitalism.[74] There was, however, an even more significant point where the sharp theoretical distinctions between historical phases broke down: The struggle for emancipation itself. This helps to explain why Marx's support for the Northern cause did not remain limited to his journalism and his political activity, but found a central place in his main theoretical work.

---

72 *MECW* 35, 244 / *MEGA²* II.5, 182.
73 In the *Manuscripts of 1861–1863*. *MECW* 33, 486 / *MEGA²* II.3.6, 2019.
74 On the function of historicity in Marx's conceptualizations, see Derek Sayer, *The violence of abstraction. The analytic foundations of historical materialism* (Oxford, 1987), 126–130.

Linking and comparing capitalism and slavery did not lead Marx to the racist perception of some sections of the workers' movement, that abolitionism was only a bourgeois distraction from the struggle of the (supposedly white) working class. Neither did it lead him back to his predictions from the 1840s, that the development of the free market and the higher productivity of "free" labor would automatically destroy the social basis for slavery. Instead, by the time he wrote *Capital*, Marx had come to see the capitalist world market as thoroughly implicated in slavery, and the fight for slave emancipation as directly connected to the emancipation of the working class internationally. In his introduction to the first edition of *Capital*, Volume I, published only four years after Lincoln's Emancipation Proclamation, Marx expressed his expectation that the fall of slavery in North America would open a new round of social struggles internationally. "As in the 18th century, the American War of Independence sounded the tocsin for the European middle class, so in the 19th century, the American Civil War sounded it for the European working class."[75] Connected to this was his belief that Emancipation would usher in a progressive era of working class gains in the US itself:

> In the United States of North America, every independent movement of the workers was paralysed so long as slavery disfigured a part of the Republic. Labour cannot emancipate itself in the white skin where in the black it is branded. But out of the death of slavery a new life at once arose. The first fruit of the Civil War was the eight hours' agitation, that ran with the seven-leagued boots of the locomotive from the Atlantic to the Pacific, from New England to California.[76]

In 1865, at the summit of Northern victory in the Civil War and in the midst of writing *Capital*, Marx's niece Nanette asked him about his personal heroes as part of a children's game. Marx' answers were Kepler and Spartacus; the astronomer who revolutionized Western science and the slave who emancipated himself to lead the largest slave revolt in antiquity.[77] Taking a detour through distant European history, the answer symbolizes the emotional chords that bound Marx's scientific endeavors to his zeal for human emancipation from slavery—of every kind.

---

75   *MECW* 35, 9 / *MEGA*² II.5, 13.
76   *MECW* 35, 305 / *MEGA*² II.5, 239–240.
77   Marx, "Confession," in Gielkens, *Bommel*, 155.

6 Conclusions

Marcel van der Linden's reinterpretation of Global Labor History draws on a lifelong interest in the work of Marx. A central idea behind the project—the rejection of the association between capitalist development and the linear extension of "free" wage labor—is formulated as a critique of both classical liberalism and orthodox Marxism. However, it is clear that of the two strands of thought, it is the one that goes back to Marx that Van der Linden most fully engages with. The self-consciously heterodox approach provided by Van der Linden opens up major theoretical questions and has undoubtedly stimulated a whole new approach to the history of labor and labor movements. It has also provided room for critically re-examining established views on the writings of Marx himself. In this article, I have attempted to do the latter, focusing on the many passages in which Marx contrasts, compares, and draws historical connections between slavery and wage labor. Whereas Marxist historiography has mainly been interested in drawing sharp distinctions between the two, I have shown that Marx himself paid considerable attention to similarities, overlaps, and intermingling. This does not mean that Marx was a "Global Labor Historian" *avant la lettre*. For important theoretical reasons that I have outlined in the article, he continued to associate capitalist development with the increasing dominance of wage labor. However, a one-sided emphasis on this aspect alone has led many later writers to ignore important nuances in his treatment of the actual relation between wage labor and slavery.

Slavery holds a paradoxical place in Marx's intellectual development. In the early 1840s, the young Marx had already turned to the working class, assigning to wage labor a central place both in capitalist development and in the struggle to overcome it. Between the first rough formulations of his economic theories in texts such as *Wage Labour and Capital* and the publication of *Capital*, Volume I, Marx would thoroughly reinterpret the main categories of classical political economy to put this connection on a firmer footing. At the same time, "free" labor seemed to make its most important global breakthrough of the nineteenth century with the abolition of serfdom in Russia and the emancipation of the slaves in North America. Marx could easily have taken this as confirmation of capitalism's inherent tendency to overcome all "antecedent" or "anomalous" forms of exploitation and subsume them under the aegis of wage labor. And yet he did not. On the contrary, nowhere in his writings was Marx so keen on comparing and connecting "free" wage labor and slavery as he was in *Capital*, Volume 1. The lengthening of the working day beyond the point where it could sustain the worker's life, could according to Marx be seen as slavery with only the name changed, and unrestricted child labor eroded even the formal freedom of the worker to such an extent that Marx was willing to describe it as slavery both in form and in content. As I have shown, these evocations of slavery were not simply rhetorical. They were instrumental in distinguishing Marx's conception of "free" wage labor from that of the classical liberal economists. In opposition to Adam Smith, John Stuart Mill, or Jeremy Bentham—but like Marcel van der Linden—Marx used the term "free" labor in a specific, highly conditional sense; as the designation of a particular type of coerced labor. In the immediate aftermath of the American Civil War, what could be a surer way of bringing home this point than showing the parallels and connections between wage labor and slavery?

Strong comparisons did not make Marx fall into the racist notion common among some sections of the workers movement that (white) wage labor in general was a form of slavery worse than actual (black) slavery. As the current article shows, the immediate background to Marx's frequent invocation of examples drawn from slavery was his growing intellectual, political, and emotional investment in the struggle against slavery in the Southern states of the U.S. The beginnings of this interest more or less coincided with his heightened attention to colonialism and the social upheavals that it produced. It led him to a much more concrete study of the actual functioning of slavery as a contemporary phenomenon, and to a more positive estimation of the potential agency of the slaves themselves. In the course of this, he largely abandoned his older mechanical conception that the development of the world market, combined with the greater efficiency of "free" labor over slavery, would be the lever for slave emancipation. Going beyond comparing slavery and wage labor as distinct historical phenomena belonging to separate phases of historical development, Marx acknowledged the contemporaneity of plantation slavery and capitalist development and reflected on the influence they had on each other. Perhaps most importantly, he increasingly drew a straight line between slave emancipation and working-class rebellion. Marx certainly continued to insist on the necessary relationship between capital and wage labor, but this did not blind him to the way capitalism drew upon and reproduced historically "transitional forms" of exploitation, or the role they could play in the struggles to come.

CHAPTER 4

Capitalism and Its Critics. A Long-Term View

Jürgen Kocka

1 The Concept

The concept "capitalism" is much younger than the historical reality it denotes. While "capital" and "capitalist" are older, the noun "capitalism" did not emerge until after the second half of the nineteenth century. The French socialist Louis Blanc used it in 1850, and defined it critically as "appropriation of capital by some, to the exclusion of others." In 1872, the German socialist Wilhelm Liebknecht railed against capitalism as a "juggernaut on the battlefields of industry." And in Britain, the Fabian John A. Hobson, a critic of imperialism, was one of the first to use the concept in the 1890s. However, it did not take long before "capitalism" moved beyond its initially critical and polemical use, becoming a central concept in the social sciences. German authors such as Albert Schäffle, Werner Sombart, Max Weber, and—in a Marxist tradition—Rudolf Hilferding, contributed much to this. Karl Marx had written a great deal about the "capitalist mode of production" and "capitalist accumulation," but he rarely used the noun "capitalism," and if so, somewhat marginally.

Presently the concept is "in," particularly among historians, and particularly in the English-speaking world. In the American Historical Association's state-of-the-field volume *American History now*, "History of capitalism" stands alongside established subfields such as "women's history" and "cultural history." A recent front-page article in the *New York Times* carried the headline, "In History Class(es), Capitalism Sees Its Stock Soar." Some authors have started to speak of a "New History of Capitalism" they see emerging. In public debates, capitalism remains controversial. As Sven Beckert recently observed:

> During the past few years, few topics have animated the chattering classes more than capitalism. In the wake of the global economic crisis of 2008,

---

* Earlier versions of this text have been presented as lectures at the Germany Institute Amsterdam, 27 October 2016 and at the Royal Flemish Academy of Belgium for Sciences and the Arts (Class of Humanities) in Brussels, 18 March 2017.

© JÜRGEN KOCKA, 2018 | DOI:10.1163/9789004386617_005

This is an open access chapter distributed under the terms of the prevailing CC-BY-NC License.

questions about the nature, past and viability of capitalism suddenly appeared on evening talk shows and in newspapers throughout the world.[1]

2 Theme and Definition

The following essay takes seriously that the concept originated in Europe before moving to other parts of the world. It takes into consideration that "capitalism" was coined as a central concept of social criticism as well as of scholarly analysis, a double function it has maintained, at least with some authors, up to the present time. It deals with the strange interplay, perhaps dialectics, between capitalism and critique of capitalism.

Although "capitalism" only became a broadly used concept after the second half of the nineteenth century, those who have been using it ever since do not doubt that it could also be applied to phenomena in periods of the past before the concept existed. I share this conviction.

In the form of *merchant capitalism*, capitalism already existed in the first millennium of our calendar, for example in Arabia, China, and Europe, though mostly just in the form of capitalist islands in a sea of predominantly non-capitalist relationships. In the form of *finance capitalism*, capitalism has existed since the high-medieval period in some parts of Europe; beginning in Northern Italy, and later moving its center to Antwerp, Amsterdam, and London. In the early modern period, West and East European *agrarian capitalism* as well as *plantation capitalism* overseas have shaped our image of capitalism as a system of repressive domination and exploitation, even violence. All of this happened before *industrial capitalism*—starting first in England in the eighteenth century, then in Europe and North America—became the decisive driving force of capitalist expansion globally. In the present era of globalization, these different types of capitalism coexist and interact.

When sketching such a scenario, I presuppose a definition of capitalism that is *narrower* than market economy in general, but *broader* than industrial capitalism based on wage work *en masse*. I want to emphasize decentralization,

---

1 Sven Beckert, "The New History of Capitalism," in Jürgen Kocka and Marcel van der Linden, eds., *Capitalism. The Reemergence of a Historical Concept* (London/New York, 2016), 235–249, here 235; Seth Rockman, What Makes the History of Capitalism Newsworthy? *Journal of the Early Republic* 34, no. 3 (2014): 439–466, esp. 439; Friedrich Lenger, "Die neue Kapitalismusgeschichte. Ein Forschungsbericht als Einleitung," *Archiv für Sozialgeschichte* 56 (2016): 3–37. Early usages of the concept are documented in: Jürgen Kocka, "Capitalism: The History of the Concept," in *International Encyclopedia of the Social & Behavioral Sciences,* 2nd ed., ed. James D. Wright, vol. 3 (Amsterdam, 2015), 105–110.

commodification, and accumulation as basic characteristics of capitalism. On the one hand, it is essential that individual and collective actors make use of (property) rights that enable them to make economic decisions in a relatively autonomous and decentralized way. On the other hand, markets serve as the main mechanisms of allocation and coordination; commodification permeates capitalism in many forms, including the commodification of labor. Further, capital is central, which means utilizing resources for investment in the present with the expectation of higher gains in the future, accepting credit besides using savings and returns, dealing with uncertainty and risk, and aiming for profit and accumulation. Change, growth, and expansion are inscribed, however, in irregular rhythms, with ups and downs, interrupted by crises.[2]

3   Christian Morale and Medieval Expansion of Capitalism

"It is easier for a camel to pass through the eye of a needle than for someone who is rich to enter the kingdom of God," quotes the Gospel of Mark (10:25). Through sermons, visual imagery, and scriptures, the moral doctrine of the Christian Church shaped the views of the educated as well as the mentalities of the broad population in medieval Europe. It is true that this doctrine could concede to the useful role of merchants and the ethical value of work and property. It could also be interpreted very flexibly. However, in this doctrine the love of money is seen as a root of evil, and the conviction was predominant that the gains of one person would always imply losses by others. Within this worldview there was much distrust of great wealth and the practices of merchants, which after all included credit taking, profit seeking, and competition. In the name of brotherly altruism and virtuous selflessness, Christian morals have distrusted the resolute orientation toward self-interest and have opposed certain capitalist practices, particularly money lending for interest. This was seen and forbidden as usury, at least if practiced vis-à-vis "thy brother," that is, members of someone's own group or religion, not necessarily vis-à-vis strangers or others (Deuteronomy 23:20).[3]

---

2 Overview and definition based on Jürgen Kocka, *Capitalism. A Short History* (Princeton, N.J., 2016), 7–24; further elaborated by Marcel van der Linden, "Final Thoughts," in *Capitalism*, eds. Kocka and van der Linden, 251–266, esp. 255–258.

3 With many differentiations: Jacques Le Goff, *La bourse et la vie: Economie et religion au Moyen Age* (Paris, 1986); Martha C. Howell, *Commerce before capitalism in Europe, 1300–1600* (London, 2010), 261–297; Giacomo Todeschini, "Credit and Debt: Patterns of Exchange in Western Christian Society," in *Europas Aufstieg. Eine Spurensuche im späten Mittelalter*, ed. Thomas Ertl (Wien, 2013), 139–160.

Certainly, this doctrine has been circumvented in many practical ways, and in many ways the Church has positively contributed to the rise of markets and capitalist practices. Nevertheless, well into the sixteenth and seventeenth centuries, a disposition that was either skeptical of or hostile toward capitalism was dominant in Europe's theologies, philosophies, and theories of society. This skepticism was amplified by the Republican humanism of the Renaissance, with its reliance on the rediscovered Aristotle, and his claim to defend public virtues and values against particularized self-interest, private wealth, and corruption.

The widespread distrust, moral rejection, and intellectual criticism, however, neither prevented nor perceptibly hindered the rise of capitalism in medieval Europe. Similar to other parts of the world such as Arabia, China, and South Asia—although a little later than there—merchant capitalism asserted itself in Europe. Long-distance trade was the leading sector, across the seas and over land in Asia. Merchants used kin-based, origin-based, ethnic and cultural ties in order to build trust, protect themselves against robbery and aggression, or to solve economic problems through non-economic means. Most of them were pious Christians. They must have shared the religiously founded reservations against profit seeking and accumulated wealth. Merchants accommodated to such prevailing attitudes, to some extent, by adopting a lifestyle and imagery compatible with religion, by donating heavily to charity, by creating foundations, and often also by making a "final penance" in old age through large transfers of wealth to monasteries and churches.

At the same time they behaved as capitalists do, though within a basically non-capitalist environment. They were ready to accept high risks, they granted and received credit, they invested and competed with one another, and they strove for profit and accumulated wealth. Particularly when combining trading with banking, they could become very rich and influential. They used different legal forms for their projects and enterprises, both in the Roman Law and in the Common Law tradition. They invented new methods of transmitting, crediting, paying, and computing such as double bookkeeping *"alla Veneziana."* Most projects and enterprises were limited in size and short lived, but some were already multi-branch and multi-local enterprises, which sometimes survived the lifespan of their founders and were transferred to heirs and others. Merchants and bankers, frequently merchant bankers, were at the core of this very dynamic system.[4]

---

4 Josef Kulischer, *Allgemeine Wirtschaftsgeschichte des Mittelalters und der Neuzeit.* vol I, 3rd ed. (Munich, 1965), 229–278; M.C. Howell, *Commerce Before Capitalism in Europe, 1300–1600* (Cambridge, 2010); K.G. Persson, "Markets and Coercion in Medieval Europe," in *The*

CAPITALISM AND ITS CRITICS

Compared with other parts of the world, especially China, merchant capitalism in medieval Europe had two characteristics that deserve to be emphasized. On the one hand, merchant capital, at some points and still to a very limited extent, transcended the sphere of distribution and penetrated the sphere of production. This happened both in mining, with its huge capital requirements and often quite extensive plant operations based on wage labor, and it happened in the cottage industries. Here and there, merchants began to exercise influence over artisans and cottage workers—that is, over the producers of goods they intended to market—by advancing raw materials to producers, placing orders, and sometimes also providing tools. We find numerous examples of this in the history of the wool trade in northern Italy, Flanders, and Brabant, starting in the thirteenth century at the latest; an early form of what was later termed proto-industrialization.

On the other hand, there were moves toward early forms of finance capitalism. From the outset, banking transactions contained elements of speculation. They were settled, to the extent that they arose, by merchants along the way. Specialization in financial business started, and banks began to emerge in North Italian cities after the twelfth century. There were already 80 banks in Florence in 1350, some of them with several branches in a number of European countries. They used the money deposited with them for financing businesses of different types. In addition, they issued bonds to city governments, landed and manorial estates, and eventually also to the highest-ranking spiritual and worldly rulers of Europe, who were in constant need of money and found it difficult to wage their wars, fulfill their ceremonial obligations, and promote their territories' expansion. State formation and the origins of financial capitalism were closely connected, and this nexus enabled prosperous urban citizens, a small elite, to establish their influence on politics while simultaneously making their entrepreneurial success dependent on powerful rulers and their shifting political fortunes. This pattern continued in the following centuries.

It seems that European capitalism was not the first, but had already become particularly vigorous before 1500. Its dynamics were linked to—and conditioned by—the peculiar dynamics of Europe's political structure, which was defined by the plurality of competing and sometimes fighting political units, in

---

Cambridge History of Capitalism, vol. 1, eds. L. Neal and J.G. Williamson (Cambridge, 2014), 225–266; Jacques Le Goff, *Marchands et Banquiers au Moyen Age* (Paris, 1956); Jacques Le Goff, *Le Moyen Age et l'Argent* (Paris, 2010); Giacomo Todeschini, "Theological Roots of the Medieval/Modern Merchants' Self-Representation," in *The Self-Perception of Early Modern Capitalists*, eds. Margaret C. Jacobs and Catherine Secretan (London, 2008), 17–46; Herman Van der Wee and G. Kurgan-van Hentenryk, eds., *A History of European Banking*, 2nd ed. (Antwerp, 2000), 71–112.

contrast for example to China and its comprehensive empire. This pluralistic political structure offered European capitalists particular incentives, opportunities, and influence.[5]

4 Business, Violence and Enlightenment: Capitalist Expansion in the Early Modern Period

The European expansion into the rest of the world since the fifteenth century had many motives and driving forces, but the resources, ambitions, greed, and enterprising spirit of West European commercial and finance capitalists were, no doubt, among them. From the sixteenth to the eighteenth century, capitalism developed a new pattern: In overseas trade, in the colonies, and connected with this, in the economic life of Europe. A new symbiosis between business and violence characterized capitalism during those centuries, particularly outside Europe—but under the influence of Europeans—as became evident in the many wars and raids, but also in the plantation system on the basis of unfree labor. Certainly, slavery was not a capitalist invention, but the capitalist plantation economy in Brazil, the Caribbean, and the southern regions of North America triggered a huge expansion of the slave trade and slavery. According to Marx, modern capitalism came into the world soaked in blood and filth, as a result of violence and suppression. This is only a half-truth historically, but none the less a correct observation when one considers the connection between the rise of capitalism and colonization. This connection is currently intensively researched.[6]

Within Europe, capitalism continued its expansion into the world of production, which was accordingly reshaped. Think of the different types of agrarian capitalism in Western and Eastern Europe, think of mining and metal-producing industries, and think of the proto-industrial reorganization of cottage industry in most industrial regions of Europe. Productivity growth was one major consequence that decisively improved the life chances—and

---

5 This essentially older argument (Max Weber, Otto Hintze, Kenneth Pomeranz, Peer Vries) is well developed in: E.H. Mielants, *The Origins of Capitalism and the "Rise of the West"* (Philadelphia, 2007); in another version in: R. Bin Wong and J.-L. Rosenthal, *Before and Beyond Divergence: The Politics of Economic Change in China and Europe* (Cambridge, MA, 2011).

6 E.g. in: E.E. Baptist, *The Half Has Never Been Told: Slavery and the Making of American Capitalism* (New York, 2014); Sven Beckert, *Empire of Cotton: A Global History* (New York, 2014); Sven Beckert and Seth Rockman, eds., *Slavery's Capitalism: A New History of American Economic Development* (Philadelphia, 2015); Karl Marx, *Das Kapital. Kritik der politischen Ökonomie,* Marx/Engels Werke, vol. 33 (Berlin, 1962), 788.

CAPITALISM AND ITS CRITICS

frequently the survival chances—of a rapidly growing population. However, new forms of inequality, dependence, and exploitation also followed, which could not be realized without some violence and many social conflicts.

The combination of merchant and finance capitalism with colonialism triggered innovations. The enterprise, a core element of capitalism in its process of consolidation, became more clearly profiled by gaining elements of a legal and institutional identity beyond the people who founded and managed it. The Dutch Vereenigde Oostindische Compagnie (the VOC, founded in 1602) was just one, but a famous example among several firms founded for the purpose of colonial trade in a number of countries, especially in the Netherlands, England, and France. An impressive capital fund (6.5 million guilders) on the basis of shares, more than 200 shareholders with limited liability, power with a board of directors, sophisticated organization with a transnational and transregional reach, a central office in Amsterdam soon with about 350 employees, a diversified portfolio of trading activities including some production units, for example a spinning mill in India: A very modern corporation, indeed. However, it rested on the foundations of political privilege and was a monopoly with extensive quasi-governmental powers. The Dutch government had conferred on the VOC the right to operate all Dutch trading business east of the Cape of Good Hope, along with the authorization to wage war, conclude treaties, take possession of land, and build fortresses. The VOC executed these rights, often in armed struggle with competitors from other countries. The distinction between conducting capitalist business and waging war was fluid. There were years in which the company apparently drew the major share of its income from the seizure of competing or enemy ships.

The VOC held together until 1799, while its shareholders continuously changed. They could easily enter and leave the corporation because they could sell and buy their shares on newly emerging stock markets; in Antwerp from 1460, in Amsterdam from 1612, and in London from 1698, with a precursor from 1571. The shares of the monopoly companies engaged in colonial business represented a considerable proportion of the commercial papers traded on the stock exchanges. Capital increasingly became a commodity, and the speculative elements associated with it grew by leaps and bounds. Not only did the prospect of spectacular profits increase as a result, but also the danger of great losses. Both the opportunities and the perils soon affected not just a small number of active, professional trade capitalists, but also an increasing number of small and large investors from wide sections of the population in western European metropolises. In the course of the seventeenth century they learned how to try their luck on the stock exchange, to bet, to invest, and to speculate, with prospects and dangers. The downfall of the English South

Sea Company in 1720 was preceded by fully-fledged speculation mania. The British government had granted the company a monopoly on trade with South America, even including all the rights to regions not yet discovered! The public expected huge gains. A run on shares set in, and the share price rose from 100 to 905 pounds within just one month. Broad segments of the population entrusted their money to the company and lost it when the bubble burst in the summer of 1720, and the share price went into free fall. Sir Isaac Newton was among the victims. He is supposed to have said: "I can calculate the motions of erratic stars, but not the madness of the multitude." The macro-economic and social consequences of such crises still remained quite limited. Yet, via stock market and speculation, larger segments of society got their first introduction to the hopes and disappointments, the gains and the losses that capitalism so abundantly held in store for them.

The rise of finance capitalism not only followed from the growing credit needs of trade and production through expansion. Rather, the services provided by banks were also requested by those in power; by city governments and ruling aristocrats, and later on above all, by the governments of the powerful territorial states just establishing themselves by competing and sometimes by fighting with one another. Step by step, the center of transnational finance capitalism moved to Western Europe, first to Antwerp and Amsterdam, then later to London.[7]

In the Netherlands and in England particularly, capitalist principles affected social life beyond the economy, sociability, consumption, leisure activities, betting and sports, the relation between the sexes, and the distribution of political power. In the seventeenth and eighteenth centuries, the Netherlands and England were the most capitalist countries in Europe and, for that matter, the world. It is worthwhile to note that they were also the most prosperous countries and certainly also the freest in Europe, on the way to constitutional government and a dynamic civil society.

I have discussed the skepticism about trade and capitalism, and the anti-capitalist sentiments dominant in medieval Europe, under the influence

---

7   Last paragraphs based on Kocka, *Capitalism*, 54–83. On European expansion to Asia: Wolfgang Reinhard, *Kleine Geschichte des Kolonialismus*, 2nd ed. (Stuttgart, 2008), 27–65, esp. 42–47 (VOC); P.A. Frentrop, *History of Corporate Governance, 1602–2002* (Amsterdam, 2002), 49–114; Newton quote: Patrick Brantlinger, *Fictions of State: Culture and Credit in Britain, 1694–1994* (Ithaca, NY, 1996), 44; C.P. Kindleberger and R. Aliber, *Manias, Panics and Crashes: A History of Financial Crises*, 5th ed. (Hoboken, NJ, 2005), 42, 58; Van der Wee and Kurgan-Van Hentenryk, eds., *History*, 117–264, esp. 260; T. Sokoll, *Europäischer Bergbau im Übergang zur Neuzeit* (Idstein, 1994); P. Kriedte et al., *Industrialization before Industrialization: Rural Industry in the Genesis of Capitalism* (Cambridge, 1981); Robert Brenner, "The Agrarian Roots of European Capitalism," *Past & Present* 97 (1982): 16–113.

CAPITALISM AND ITS CRITICS

of Christian moral doctrine and other factors. Certainly, Reformation and Counter-Reformation brought about a "modern religiosity" that stressed the "worldliness of faith"[8] and contributed to an upgraded appreciation of work and profession. Max Weber has emphasized this, not without some justification.

Nevertheless, it was not so much the Reformation, but instead the Enlightenment that brought about a re-assessment in contemporary thinking about capitalism and its reputation, at least among intellectuals and probably beyond. Under the impact of their era's destructive wars, authors such as Grotius, Hobbes, Locke, and Spinoza worked at redefining the virtues of civil society with a secularizing thrust and informed by a concern about human rights, freedom, peace, and prosperity. In 1748, in a clear withdrawal from the old European mainstream, Montesquieu praised trade as a civilizing force that contributed to overcoming barbarism, calming aggression, and refining manners. Other authors chimed in to the same tune, among them Bernard de Mandeville and David Hume, Condorcet, and of course Adam Smith; all of them West European thinkers. The common good, went the thrust of these arguments, is actually promoted by the reasonable pursuit of self-interest; the advantage of the one need not be to the disadvantage of the other. Commerce and morality were not locked into inevitable opposition. The market helped replace the war of passions with the advocacy of interests. Commerce was said to promote such virtues as diligence and persistence, uprightness, and discipline.

Overall, a fundamental affirmation of society's new capitalist tendencies was starting to emerge. It was expected not only that these tendencies would increase prosperity, but also that they would contribute to creating a new social order that was better for human cooperation, one without arbitrary state intervention, with respect for liberty and individual responsibility, and with the capacity for resolving conflicts through compromise instead of war. Certainly, these authors did not use the concept "capitalism." Adam Smith wrote about "commercial society." However, basically this was a legitimizing vision of capitalism as a civilizing promise in the spirit of Enlightenment.

With regard to appreciation by intellectuals and to public opinion, capitalism had its best time in the second half of the eighteenth century. However, again there was a wide gap between reality and discourse; now between the deep contradictions of capitalist reality and its utopian idealization in terms of "*doux commerce*" and "commercial society."[9]

---

8   Heinz Schilling, *Martin Luther. Rebell in einer Zeit des Umbruchs* (Munich, 2012), 634.

9   Most important: Albert O. Hirschman, *Rival Views of Market Society and Other Recent Essays* (Cambridge, Mass., 1992), 105–141, esp. 106; very good: Jerry Z. Muller, *The Mind and the Market: Capitalism in Western Thought* (New York, 2002; paperback 2003), 3–19 (on the older more skeptical perspectives) and 51–83 (on Smith); on changing views in the eighteenth century: J. Appleby, *The Relentless Revolution: A History of Capitalism* (New York, 2010), 87–120; on

5 Industrial Capitalism and Classical Critique in the Long Nineteenth Century

I am jumping forward by one century. In Werner Sombart's and Max Weber's analysis of capitalism, for example, there was much confidence in the *economic* superiority and the *economic* rationality of capitalism. However, these authors did not see capitalism anymore as a carrier of human progress, moral improvement, and civilizational uplift. On the contrary, liberals like Weber feared the increasing rigidity of the system that he anticipated would threaten human freedom by coercing economic actors to function according to its increasingly compulsive rules of relentless competition and growth, or to drop out of the market altogether. Among conservatives as well as on the left, capitalism was seen as an irresistible force of erosion: Custom was seen to be replaced by contract, *Gemeinschaft* by *Gesellschaft*, the traditional by the modern, and social bonds by the market. On the right, anti-capitalism frequently went hand in hand with anti-liberalism and anti-Semitism, particularly after the Great Depression of the 1870s. The socialist critique of capitalism was different, and the most powerful one. On the one hand, it attacked the exploitation of labor by capital, the increase of social inequality, the lack of a fair deal, and alienation and suppression in the workplace. On the other hand, it predicted the decline of capitalism due to its internal contradictions and its replacement by something new; namely socialism. Many of those who did not enjoy this perspective did not contest it either, but were fearful of its arrival.

The discourse of ascent and flourishing had largely been replaced by a discourse of fall and decline. I mentioned at the beginning that this was the intellectual, mental situation in which the concept of capitalism emerged, first as a critical and polemical concept; soon to be turned into a powerful analytical tool. The concept emerged, one might say, as a *concept of difference*. It was used to identify and critically underline certain features of the present, in contrast to what it was thought to have been in previous times, and to what it might become under socialism in the future. The contrast with a selectively commemorated past and with an imagined future was constitutive for the emergence of the concept "capitalism," and in a way this mechanism still works today when it comes to more basic discussions of capitalism.[10]

---

changing cultural practices in England: Christiane Eisenberg, *The Rise of Market Society in England, 1066–1800* (New York, 2014), 73–100.

10   Documentation in Kocka, "Capitalism: The History of the Concept." On the temporal structure of capitalist practices and debates about capitalism: Jens Beckert, *Imagined Futures. Fictional Expectations and Capitalist Dynamics* (Cambridge, MA, 2016). On Max Weber's notions of capitalism: Max Weber, *Economy and Society: An Outline of*

CAPITALISM AND ITS CRITICS 81

How can we explain this change in the evaluation of capitalism between the late eighteenth, late nineteenth, and early twentieth century; this change of mood from appreciation to criticism? Let me pick out three relevant issues.

1. While Adam Smith had known capitalism before industrialization, nineteenth-century capitalism mainly spread in the form of industrial capitalism, based on the factory system and wage labor *en masse*. Now the capitalist principle of commodification was fully extended into the sphere of work and labor, to the activities of human beings on a grand scale. Work relations were becoming capitalist, which meant that they became dependent on changing market mechanisms, subject to ever stricter calculation, and subordinated to supervision by employers or managers. At the same time, industrial wealth was accumulated to an unprecedented degree, due to an increasing need for large-scale fixed capital in mines, factories, railways, and other institutions of industrial capitalism. As a consequence, wealth differences became more visible, and stricter controls of profitability over time were felt to be needed and were practiced by employers and managers. The class difference had been built into capitalism as a potentiality from the start; now it became more manifest. It could be directly experienced, widely observed, and critically discussed. This was the constellation—industrial capitalism with the factory system, large-scale capital accumulation, and wage labor as a mass phenomenon—which served as the empirical base for the classic narratives of Marx and Engels, and for the rise of labor movements critical of or hostile to (basic elements of) capitalism.[11]

2. Technological and organizational innovation became much more important, frequent, and regular under industrial capitalism than ever before. In other words, what Joseph A. Schumpeter would later call "creative destruction" became the rule and a widespread experience. Factories pushed aside cottage work in the spinning of yarn and the weaving of clothes. Steamships replaced traditional forms of transportation on rivers, canals, and oceans. Producers of electrical installations gained superiority over the providers of gas-powered

---

Interpretive Sociology, eds. Guenther Roth and Claus Wittich (Berkeley, CA, 1978, reprinted 2013), 63–166, 351–54, 1094–110; Max Weber, *General Economic History*, trans. Frank H. Knight (Glencoe, IL, 1927, reprinted 1950), 275–369; Max Weber, *The Protestant Ethic and the Spirit of Capitalism*, (1920), revised, trans. and intro. Stephen Kalberg (New York, 2010); Werner Sombart, *Der moderne Kapitalismus, 3 vols.* 2nd ed. (Munich/Leipzig, 1924–1927).

11 With reference to the German case: Jürgen Kocka, *Arbeitsverhältnisse und Arbeiterexistenzen: Grundlagen der Klassenbildung im 19. Jahrhundert* (Bonn, 1990); Jürgen Kocka, *Arbeiterleben und Arbeiterkultur. Die Entstehung einer sozialen Klasse* (Bonn, 2015); Marcel van der Linden and J. Rojahn, eds., *The Formation of Labour Movements 1870–1914*, 2 vols. (Leiden, 1990).

lighting. This was a process opening up new opportunities to many and new roads towards success, but there were also numerous losers at the same time. Ascent and decline are mechanisms anchored right at the core of capitalism. Permanent competition, sustained insecurity, and threatening dangers were institutionalized; and resented. There were many losers. All of this came in cycles, with ups and downs, booms and busts. Nineteenth-century crises impacted on *large* segments of the populations. The crises helped to delegitimize capitalism and increase anti-capitalist resentment.[12]

3. There was a rise of expectations. Partly as a precondition and partly as a consequence of capitalist industrialization, previous patterns of social control were loosened, the standard of living was raised, fast historical change was experienced, and human affairs appeared—in fact proved—to be changeable. The level of education was raised, and public spaces emerged in which intellectuals and the media played a dynamic, frequently a critical, role. As a consequence, people became less patient, more demanding, and more critical. In a way, capitalism's critique followed from capitalism's success; something analyzed by Joseph Schumpeter and Albert Hirschman as capitalism's propensity to undermine itself.

All of this had surfaced by the end of the nineteenth and the start of the twentieth century, very much in contrast to the period of Adam Smith. While capitalism developed its strengths and powerfully expanded—both internally (into different spheres of life) and externally (towards different parts of the world)—its image darkened, its evaluation became increasingly pessimistic, and its past and its present were heavily criticized.

6   The Present Situation

Since then another century has passed, which has brought deep changes different from what Max Weber and his contemporaries had expected. There have been far-reaching technical and organizational innovations, the digital revolution of recent decades among them. There has been an unprecedented expansion and differentiation of consumption, including mass consumption, but also pronounced socioeconomic inequality which, within our societies, has started to grow again since the 1970s. In this "century of extremes" (Eric J. Hobsbawm), people in Europe and elsewhere have experienced unprecedented social, political, and cultural upheaval, somehow related to capitalism,

---

12   Joseph A. Schumpeter, *Capitalism, Socialism, and Democracy*, 2nd ed. (New York, 1947), 81–86 ("creative destruction").

CAPITALISM AND ITS CRITICS   83

largely initiated by Europeans, but impacting on most other parts of the world
as well, among them the deep crisis of capitalism in the interwar period facilitating the rise of fascism and World War II.

We have experienced the rise of a powerful, anti-capitalist alternative: The
Soviet type of state socialism, which radicalized the rejection of capitalism in
a very practical and effective way for decades, before it lost out in a worldwide
conflict and imploded.

Particularly in Europe, coordinated, organized, regulated forms of capitalism were invented and made concrete with the help of organized interest
groups, including organized labor, and with the welfare state as its centerpiece.
The beginnings of "organized capitalism"—others prefer to speak of "coordinated capitalism" or the "Keynesian welfare state"—can be traced back to the
late nineteenth century and World War I, but it really flourished in the third
quarter of the twentieth century, when it proved to be very compatible with
representative democracy. However, it has been questioned (though not at
all destroyed) under the more market-radical, "neo-liberal" auspices in more
recent decades, which have been characterized by an unproportional rise of
finance capitalism and financialization.

In the latter part of the twentieth and the early twenty-first century,
globalization—understood as increasing interdependence, not as increasing
convergence—proceeded with accelerated speed, across borders between
countries and world regions; conditioned by and affecting large parts of capitalism that have become more transnational and global than ever before. This
poses an unresolved problem for any form of regulation and coordination of
capitalism by political means, since political power is still largely vested in
competing national states (the criticism of capitalism and the criticism of
globalization are nowadays intrinsically mixed). The global dimension of
present-day capitalism dramatically increases its destructive impact on the
natural environment including climate; a problem largely absent in previous
centuries.[13]

---

13   The concept "organized capitalism" goes back to Rudolf Hilferding. See his *Das Finanz-*
      kapital (Vienna, 1910). The concept was successfully tried out for purposes of historical
      analysis: Heinrich August Winkler, ed., *Organisierter Kapitalismus: Voraussetzungen und*
      Anfänge (Göttingen, 1974). Also see Colin Crouch, *Industrial Relations and European State*
      Tradition (Oxford, 1993). Relevant debates in the U.S. are analyzed in: H. Brick, *Transcend-*
      ing Capitalism: Visions of a New Society in Modern American Thought (Ithaca, NY, 2006).
      On the movements away from "organized capitalism" in many Western countries since the
      1970s/1980s: Claus Offe, *Disorganized Capitalism: Contemporary Transformation of Work*
      and Politics (London, 1985); P. Mirowski and D. Plehwe, eds., *The Road from Mont Pèlerin:*
      The Making of the Neoliberal Thought Collective (Cambridge, MA, 2009); G.R. Krippner,

As mentioned in the beginning, more and more authors find the concept "capitalism" useful, in one way or another. Especially when it comes to discussing complex *connections* among economic, social, political, and cultural dimensions of historical reality, and to synthesizing or making broad comparisons across space and time, historians and historically oriented social scientists make use of the concept. On the other hand, the concept continues to serve as an interpretative concept that invites fundamental debate about the past, present, and future. It certainly plays a role in intellectual and political debates outside the scholarly world, too, as it already had around 1900.

There are authors who use the concept of capitalism with clearly positive overtones, for example economists in the tradition of the Chicago School. Take the late Gary Becker as an example, who wrote: "Capitalism with free markets is the most effective system yet devised for raising both economic well-being and political freedom." In popular literature too, the term "capitalism" is used in an affirmative sense.[14] There are also numerous examples of a primarily analytical, "neutral" use of the concept, such as in the long and ongoing debate by economists and political scientists about "varieties of capitalism." In this debate, we usually distinguish between types of capitalism according to different relationships between market and state, ranging from a relatively market-radical model, especially in the U.S., to state-capitalist forms, especially in East Asia, with different forms of coordinated or organized capitalism in combination with strong welfare state elements in the middle, especially on the European continent.[15]

Anyone who takes a serious look at the history of capitalism and, moreover, knows something about life in centuries past that were either not capitalist or were barely so, cannot but be impressed by the immense progress that has taken place in large parts of the world (though not everywhere). In spite of its very unequal distribution, this progress has also impacted on the broad masses of people who did not and do not belong to the elites and well-situated upper-strata; with regard to material living conditions and everyday life, gains in life

---

Capitalizing on Crisis: The Political Origins of the Rise of Finance (Cambridge, 2011); Ivan T. Berend, *An Economic History of Nineteenth-Century Europe* (Cambridge, 2013); Jürgen Osterhammel and N.P. Petersson, *Globalization: A Short History* (Princeton, NJ, 2009). My view on financialization, deregulation, and the changing relations between markets and states in recent decades is presented in Kocka, *Capitalism*, 114–124, 145–161.

14   G.S. Becker and G.N. Becker, *The Economics of Life: From Baseball to Affirmative Action to Immigration. How Real-World Issues Affect Our Everyday Life* (New York, 1997); J. Mackey, *Conscious Capitalism: Liberating the Heroic Spirit of Business* (Cambridge, MA, 2013).

15   Cf. P.A. Hall and D. Soskice, eds., *Varieties of Capitalism: The Institutional Foundations of Comparative Advantage* (Oxford, 2001); B. Amable, *The Diversity of Modern Capitalism* (Oxford, 2003); R. Dore, *Stock Market Capitalism, Welfare Capitalism: Japan and Germany versus the Anglo-Saxons* (Oxford, 2000).

CAPITALISM AND ITS CRITICS

span and health, opportunities for choice, and freedom.[16] It was progress of which one might say, in retrospect that it would presumably not have happened without capitalism's characteristic way of constantly stirring things up, pushing them forward, and reshaping them. To date, alternatives to capitalism have proven inferior, both with regard to the creation of prosperity and to the facilitation of freedom. The downfall of the centrally administered state-socialist economies in the last third of the twentieth century was, in this respect, a key process for evaluating the historical balance sheet of capitalism.

Nevertheless, particularly in Europe the concept continues most frequently to be used with skeptical or pessimistic overtones, in a spirit of criticism or at least of ambivalence, and with much sensitivity for the dark sides of capitalism's record. There are notable continuities in the criticism of capitalism. Take the catholic social teaching as an example, with its critique of the "idolatry of the market" and its rejection of "radical capitalist ideology" (*Centesimo Annus*, the papal encyclical of 1991). The current pope, undoubtedly against the background of his experiences of countries from the Global South, has again intensified the tone of the Catholic critique.[17] Other examples of discursive continuities can be found in different currents of (what I want to call) a totalizing critique that rejects "capitalism" as the epitome of (Western) modernity or as the outright embodiment of evil. This type of fundamentalism is hard to discuss.[18] Now, as in the nineteenth and twentieth centuries, criticism of capitalism can be raised from standpoints on the political left—for example by rejecting inequalities and dependencies coming with capitalist relations—or from standpoints on the political right—for example with anti-liberal, anti-cosmopolitan, nativist implications. Politically, *Kapitalismuskritik* is polyvalent and ambiguous.

Some critiques of capitalism that were once at the center of attention have, however, moved to the margins. This is true for the classical Marxist critique of capitalism as the site of the alienation of labor and of the immiseration of the working class. In most economically developed parts of the world, the "labor question" has ceased to have the explosive and mobilizing effects it used to display in the nineteenth and first part of the twentieth century.

---

16   Usefully summarized in J.L. Van Zanden et al., *How Was Life? Global Well-Being Since 1820* (Paris, 2014). Along a similar line: Angus Deaton, *The Great Escape: Health, Wealth, and the Origins of Inequality* (Princeton, 2013).

17   Amintori Fanfani, *Catholicism, Protestantism, and Capitalism* (Norfolk, VA, 2002); Andrea Tornielli and Giacomo Galeazzi, *This Economy Kills: Pope Francis on Capitalism and Social Justice* (Liturgical Press, 2015).

18   Examples can be found in C. Tripp, *Islam and the Moral Economy: The Challenge of Capitalism* (Cambridge, 2006), though such totalizing condemnations of capitalism are also not unknown in the West.

Nevertheless, at the global level it deserves to be rediscovered, given the massive spread of so-called "informal labor" under conditions of capitalist exploitation in the Global South.[19]

Other topics have moved to the foreground. Concrete abuses are denounced, such as "structured irresponsibility" in the financial sector. That lack of accountability has led to a widening gap—incidentally, in violation of one of capitalism's central premises—between deciding, on the one hand, and answering to the consequences of decisions, on the other. As a result, exorbitant profits for money managers are facilitated by public budgets that take on gigantic losses ("too big to fail").[20] Moreover, the contemporary critique of growing inequality as a consequence of capitalism is becoming ever more urgent. Here, public discussion has focused on the kind of inequality of income and of wealth distribution that since the 1970s has become much more severe *inside* most individual countries; there has been less interest in the much more serious inequality that exists between countries and regions of the globe. The latter grew immensely between 1800 and 1950, but no longer did so after that. Lamenting the growth of inequality blends into protest against infringements on distributive justice, which is how the critique becomes systemically relevant.[21] One criticizes the discrepancy between, on the one hand, the claim of democratic politics to shape our common destinies according to democratic principles and procedures, and on the other hand, the dynamic of capitalism that evades democratic politics. The relationship between capitalism and democracy continues to be a much discussed theme.[22] Also lamented are the perennial insecurity, unrelenting acceleration pressures, and extreme individualization that are inherent to capitalism and that may lead, in the absence of countermeasures, to the erosion of social welfare and neglect of the public

---

19　Basic: Marcel van der Linden, *Workers of the World: Essays Toward a Global Labor History* (Leiden, 2008). Cf. J. Breman, *Outcast Labour in Asia: Circulation and Informalization of the Workers at the Bottom of the Economy* (Oxford, 2012); Andreas Eckert, "Capitalism and Labor in Sub-Saharan Africa," in *Capitalism*, eds. Kocka and Van der Linden, 165–185.

20　C. Honegger et al., eds., *Strukturierte Verantwortungslosigkeit: Berichte aus der Bankenwelt* (Frankfurt, 2010).

21　Cf. A.B. Atkinson, *Inequality. What Can be Done?* (Cambridge, MA, 2015); Thomas Piketty, *Capital in the Twenty-first Century* (Cambridge, MA, 2014); Branco Milanovic, *Global Inequality. A New Approach for the Age of Globalization* (Cambridge, MA, 2016).

22　Jürgen Kocka, *Capitalism is not Democratic and Democracy not Capitalistic. Tensions and Opportunities in Historical Perspective* (Florence, 2015); Jürgen Kocka, "Kapitalismus und Demokratie. Der historische Befund," *Archiv für Sozialgeschichte* 56 (2016): 39–50: Capitalism has existed and flourished under different political systems. There is scope for political choice and shaping. Much depends on the political orientations and energies a community can mobilize.

interest. Similar, in the way it poses fundamental questions, is the critique of capitalism's intrinsic dependence on permanent growth and constant expansion beyond the attained status quo; a dependence that threatens to destroy natural resources (the environment and climate) and cultural resources (solidarity and meaning). These are resources that capitalism needs in order to survive, but that it increasingly exhausts and destroys.[23] This, in turn, raises the urgent question of where the limits of the market and of venality lie, or where—on moral or practical grounds—they should be drawn. The historical overview offers strong arguments for the case that there is a need for such boundaries: That capitalism, in other words, cannot be allowed to permeate everything, but that it needs non-capitalist abutments in society, culture, and the state.[24]

Certainly, there are those who defend capitalism in the public debate. They have good arguments, which demonstrate its achievements, its alliance with progress, and its beneficial effects over the centuries. However, by and large the critical, skeptical, pessimistic arguments, connotations, and overtones dominate—particularly since the Great Recession of 2008—both in public debates and in relevant parts of the social sciences, at least in Europe. Writings about "postcapitalism" are selling well, nowadays with frequent references to the impact of digitalization and the inclination to predict the imminent end of capitalism as we have known it.[25] With changing arguments in detail, this type of literature has a long tradition.

7   Conclusion and Coda

At any point in time, very different and even contradictory assessments of capitalism have coexisted or competed, which is why it is hard to generalize. If we

---

23   E.g., Naomi Klein, *This Changes Everything. Capitalism vs. the Climate* (New York, 2014); Jürgen Renn and Bernd Scherer, eds., *Das Anthropozän. Zum Stand der Dinge* (Berlin, 2015); Michael Mann, "The End May Be Nigh, But for Whom?" in *Does Capitalism Have a Future?* eds. Immanuel Wallerstein et al. (Oxford, 2013), 71–97. On p. 94 Mann convincingly puts the relationship between capitalism and climate change in a much broader and more complex perspective: "The three great triumphs of the modern period—capitalism, the nation-state, and citizen rights—are responsible for the environmental crisis."

24   There is something to be learned from very different authors such as Karl Polányi, *The Great Transformation*, New York, 1944); Schumpeter, *Capitalism*; M.J. Sandel, *What Money Can't Buy: The Moral Limits of Markets* (New York, 2012).

25   Wolfgang Streeck, "How will Capitalism End?" *New Left Review* 87 (2014): 35–64; Jeremy Rifkin, *The Zero Marginal Cost Society: The Internet of Things, the Collaborative Commons, and the Eclipse of Capitalism* (New York, 2015); Paul Mason, *PostCapitalism: A Guide to the Future* (London, 2016).

do nevertheless generalize, we may conclude that over the centuries in Europe, the rise, the breakthrough, and finally the triumph of capitalism have taken place in an intellectual and mental climate of pronounced *Kapitalismuskritik*, or criticism of capitalism. If this conclusion is correct, one may wonder why these skeptical and critical sentiments and convictions have not hindered or handicapped the real rise of European or European-sponsored capitalism more than is apparently the case. An achievement with a bad conscience? A typical contradiction between basis and superstructure? A century-old hypocrisy not unknown in the history of public morale and noble principles? A European *Sonderweg*?

One can offer a more constructive hypothesis and hold that the widespread criticism of capitalism has contributed to its permanent change and reform— as well as indirectly and inadvertently to its survival and success—over the centuries. One could show in detail that ideas and discourses of *Kapitalismuskritik*, once they managed to be translated into social and political energy, have led to reforms that improved and civilized capitalism, making it more compatible with human needs. This has enhanced its social acceptance and ultimately its capability to survive. It is neither guaranteed nor excluded that this mechanism will continue to work in the future.

Sometimes the difficult and ambivalent concept "capitalism" reminds me of the similarly difficult and ambivalent concept "modernity."[26] Both concepts relate to an impressive multitude of very different empirical phenomena, with respect to which one sometimes wonders why they should be assembled under one and the same conceptual roof. Both are rather abstract constructs, which were originally created by relating them to basic value judgements. Both share particular temporal structures in that they try to make present phenomena intelligible by differentiating them from past and future phenomena; from objects of remembrance on the one hand, and from objects of imagination on the other. In one case (modernity), hope and the expectation of progress stimulated the conceptual construction, in the other case (capitalism), it was criticism. In both cases, concepts emerged from acts of evaluation, but this did not prevent them from becoming instruments of sophisticated analysis.

The comparison with the concept "modernity" highlights the fact that the concept "capitalism" not only serves the purpose of understanding and

---

26   Cf. Paul Nolte, "Modernization and Modernity in History," in *International Encyclopedia of the Social and Behavioral Sciences*, vol. 15, eds. Neil J. Smelser and Paul B. Baltes (Oxford, 2001), 9954 ff.; Peter Wagner, *Modernity as Experience and Interpretation: A New Sociology of Modernity* (London, 2008).

interpreting present realities, but also serves as a conceptual foil on which very different expectations, anxieties, and hopes can be projected in order to be articulated, asserted and, if possible, accomplished. That means that the concept may tend to change the reality that it helps to represent and understand: The concept as a sort of intervention.

CHAPTER 5

The ILO and the Oldest Non-profession

Magaly Rodríguez García

1   Introduction

In June 2010, the International Labour Organization (ILO) approved the first labor standard on HIV and AIDS in the world of work, and the ratification of Recommendation No. 200 has been hailed as a step forward by various sex workers' organizations. As activists from the Global Network of Sex Work Projects write on their webpage, sex work is not specifically mentioned in the ILO recommendation, but they refer to the discussions during the drafting process and to subsequent meetings concerning HIV to emphasize the labor approach of the Geneva organization.[1] The ILO, too, stresses that the recommendation "reaches out to all workers" and highlights its community-based initiatives to train sex workers.[2] The use of the term "sex worker" instead of "prostitute" in its policy papers and communication on its HIV programs is also a clear indication of the ILO's recent approach to prostitution. Sex work, however, remains in limbo in international labor law. In spite of its recognition in some national legal contexts (e.g. Germany, New Zeeland, and the Netherlands) and the increased worldwide activism of sex workers from the 1970s onward, the ILO has never advocated the legalization of prostitution.

This paper provides a historical overview of the ILO's stance toward prostitution. It argues that the ILO's refusal to put forward an international labor standard that would place sex workers on an equal footing with other workers is linked to the generalized condemnation of commercial sex, which has deep roots. Furthermore, it highlights the divisions within the ILO that make the recognition of prostitution as a form of work difficult. The analysis unfolds in two sections. In the first part, I take the reader on a conceptual tour from

---

*   Many thanks to Dorothea Hoehtker, Liat Kozma, Richard Howard, Françoise Thébaud, and Pieter Vanhees for the provision of useful material and their helpful comments on this article.

1   "A Labour Rights Approach to HIV and Sex Work," Global Network of Sex Work Projects, accessed December 27, 2016, http://www.nswp.org/news/labour-rights-approach-hiv-and -sex-work.

2   "HIV and work. Getting to Zero through the world of work," International Labour Organization, accessed January 10, 2017, http://www.ilo.org/wcmsp5/groups/public/@ed_protect/@ protrav/@ilo_aids/documents/genericdocument/wcms_185717.pdf.

© MAGALY RODRÍGUEZ GARCÍA, 2018 | DOI:10.1163/9789004386617_006

This is an open access chapter distributed under the terms of the prevailing CC-BY-NC License.

antiquity to the present, and provide some theoretical insights that might help to demonstrate why prostitution—particularly female—has been deemed problematic in most cultures. The second part focuses on the ILO's involvement with the issue, from its inception to the present day. It concentrates on three specific periods: First, from 1919 up to the 1950s, when the organization first developed its views on sexually transmitted diseases and prostitution; second, the period after the World Employment Conference of 1976, when the ILO committed to promote the status of women in developing countries; and third, recent decades, during which two special ILO programs—on HIV/AIDS and forced labor—have given impetus to the (gendered) debates on sex work. By "prostitution," I mean the provision of physical sex for payment (in cash or in kind) and I use it synonymously with "sex work" (even though the latter includes other paid services of a sexual nature, such as stripping, pornography, and telephone sex). I also use the terms "prostitute" and "sex worker" interchangeably in the text to emphasize, regarding the former, the stigma that has stuck to people (women in particular) involved in prostitution since ancient times; and for the latter, my labor approach to prostitution. My view of prostitution owes much to Marcel van der Linden's conception of "work," which he defines as "the production of useful objects and services."[3] This broad definition of work has facilitated the entrance of a whole range of men and women into the (analytical) realm of labor. Whether society at large is prepared to treat activities such as prostitution as a form of work remains to be seen.

2 The Meaning of Prostitution[4]

The Cambridge online dictionary defines prostitution as "the work of a prostitute," and a prostitute as "a person who has sex with someone for money."[5]

---

3   Marcel van der Linden, "Studying Attitudes to Work Worldwide, 1500–1650: Concepts, Sources, and Problems of Interpretation," *International Review of Social History* 56 (2011), 25–43, 27.

4   The main ideas of this section are further developed in Magaly Rodríguez García, "Defining Commercial Sexualities, Past and Present," in *The Routledge Research Companion to Geographies of Sex and Sexualities*, eds. Gavin Browne and Kath Brown (Oxford, 2016), 321–329; Magaly Rodríguez García, "Ideas and Practices of Prostitution around the World," in *The Oxford Handbook of the History of Crime and Criminal Justice*, eds. Paul Knepper and Anja Johansen (New York, 2016), 132–154; Magaly Rodríguez Garcia, Elise van Nederveen Meerkerk and Lex Heerma van Voss, "Selling Sex in World Cities, 1600s–2000s: An Introduction," in *Selling Sex in the City: A Global History of Prostitution, 1600s–2000s*, eds. Magaly Rodríguez García, Lex Heerma van Voss, and Elise van Nederveen Meerkerk (Leiden, 2017), 1–21.

5   http://dictionary.cambridge.org/dictionary/english/prostitution; http://dictionary.cambridge.org/dictionary/english/prostitute (27 December 2016).

However, prostitution has rarely been considered a job like any other, especially when practiced by women. Perhaps its metaphorical definition found in the Oxford online dictionary provides a clearer clue to its symbolic meaning across time and space: Prostitution is "the *unworthy* or *corrupt* use of one's talents for personal or financial gain" (emphasis added).[6] Indeed, it is the moral or status connotation attached to it, and not the service provided in the exchange of sexual favors for money or in kind, that has characterized the meaning of prostitution in many societies.

The view of prostitution as an evil—a necessary one for some and an unwarranted one for others—seems to be ubiquitous. Recently, an increasing number of historians of the ancient world have started to stress the negative perception of prostitution and to question the radical distinction between *hetaira* (a free prostitute working independently and in relatively good conditions) and *pornē* (a common prostitute of slave status and confined to a brothel). According to Allison Glazebrook, the ancients did not make a clear distinction between *hetairai* or *pornai*, or between *hetairai* or adulteresses and women in atypical relationships. *Pornē* was, in any case, the more pejorative term. The word probably derives from the verb *pernēmi*, which means "to sell." Other ancient labels also emphasize the material nature of the prostitute-client relationship and the (female) prostitute's "innate immorality." For male prostitutes, not the noun *pornoi* but the verb form for prostitution, *pornos*, was commonly used. This suggests that for males, prostitution was simply perceived as a trade, whereas for women it was considered an identity.[7] In republican and imperial Rome, the most common terms for prostitute were *meretrix* and *scortum*. *Meretrix* derives from *mereo*, meaning "to earn" or "to merit," and stresses the economic aspect of prostitution. Derivatives from the Latin *meretrix* are also preferred in some contemporary societies. In Bolivia, for example, prostitutes prefer to be called *meretrices*, as the word highlights the labor aspect of prostitution and depicts them as working women.[8]

In some other regions and time periods, too, prostitution has been perceived as a form of work—albeit morally condemned. Indeed, although some forms

---

6 https://en.oxforddictionaries.com/definition/prostitution (27 December 2016).

7 Allison Glazebrook, "The Bad Girls of Athens: The Image and Function of *Hetairai* in Judicial Oratory," in *Prostitutes & Courtesans in the Ancient World*, eds. Christopher A. Faraone and Laura K. McClure (Madison, 2006), 125–138; Allison Glazebrook, "Prostitution," in *A Cultural History of Sexuality in the Classic World*, eds. Mark Golden and Peter Toohey (Oxford/New York, 2011), 145–168.

8 Pascal Absi, "The Future of an Institution from the Past: Accommodating Regulationism in Potosí (Bolivia) from the Nineteenth to Twenty-First Centuries," in *Selling Sex in the City*, eds. Rodríguez García, Heerma van Voss, and van Nederveen Meerkerk, 466–489.

THE ILO AND THE OLDEST NON-PROFESSION   93

of high-level prostitution in earlier times commanded respect and prestige, most societies have treated prostitutes with contempt. For hundreds of years in pre-colonial India, common prostitutes formed part of the mainstream labor population but were perceived as "sinners." Furthermore, the caste-based, hierarchical society accorded them a low social status and placed them just above sweepers.[9] During most of Chinese history, prostitution was legal and monitored by the imperial or local state. Within this highly patriarchal society, providing sex commercially was recognized as an occupation, but one that was meant to distinguish "good" women from those who provided social companionship and sexual services to men.[10] In Cairo, prostitutes were taxed, had access to court, and were allowed to participate in guild processions—albeit marching at the end of the parade.[11] In medieval Europe, municipal authorities of most large cities regulated prostitution and tolerated prostitutes because they supposedly served as outlets for male sexual drives and protected "honest" women from rape.[12] Advocates of the modern system of regulation (installed in France by Napoleon) followed this Augustinian logic.[13] However, the nineteenth-century system of regulation, with its enclosed brothels, compulsory registration, harsh medical treatment, confinement to specialized hospitals for the treatment of venereal diseases, or imprisonment for clandestine prostitutes, treated women as quasi criminals or, in the best case, as filthy workers. For instance, the French hygienist Alexandre Parent-Duchâtelet described prostitutes "as inevitable as sewers."[14]

Moreover, comparative studies of prostitution demonstrate that some sex workers internalized this general scorn for prostitution. When a group of prostitutes demanded better working and living conditions in Buenos Aires during

---

9   Raelene Frances, "Prostitution: The Age of Empires," in *A Cultural History of Sexuality in the Age of Empire*, eds. Chiara Beccalossi and Ivan Crozier (Oxford, 2011), 145–170.

10   Sue Gronewold, "Prostitution in Shanghai," in *Selling Sex in the City*, eds. Rodríguez García, Heerma van Voss, and van Nederveen Meerkerk, 567–593.

11   Hahan Hammad and Francesca Biancani, "Prostitution in Cairo," in *Selling Sex in the City*, eds. Rodríguez García, Heerma van Voss, and van Nederveen Meerkerk, 234–260.

12   Ruth Mazo Karras, *Common Women: Prostitution and Sexuality in Medieval England* (New York, 1996); Mary Elizabeth Perry, *Gender and Disorder in Early Modern Seville* (New Jersey, 1990); Richard Trexler, "La prostitution florentine au XVe siècle: patronages et clientèles," *Annales. Économies, Sociétés, Civilisations* 36 (1981): 983–1015.

13   The fourth-century Christian theologian Augustine of Hippo once wrote: "Suppress prostitution, and capricious lusts will overthrow society," quoted in Nicky Roberts, *Whores in History: Prostitution in Western Society* (London, 1992), 61.

14   Alexandre Parent-Duchâtelet, *De la prostitution dans la ville de Paris, considérée sous le rapport de l'hygiène publique, de la morale et de l'administration* (London/Brussels, 1838), 336.

the 1930s, one of them told a reporter: "we have not all become what we wanted to become, but the fact is that we are workers, the worst class of workers, but we have a right to live as *gente decente.*"[15] Later on in the twentieth century, the development of the sex workers' rights movement helped to build self-esteem among the women, men, and trans people engaged in prostitution. Increasingly since the mid-1970s, confident sex workers have contributed to a multitude of (printed and online) publications and public manifestations worldwide that demand state protection and an end to discrimination. In 2015, a Dutch union for sex workers was created, calling itself "PROUD."[16] However, even in countries where prostitution is legal, such as the Netherlands, the main actors (sex workers, clients, and intermediaries) continue to be stigmatized. In a recent call to demonstrate against the compulsory interviews and illegal registration of sex workers in Groningen (a city in the north of the Netherlands), PROUD activists promised to distribute red umbrellas and masks to protect the privacy of the participants.[17] The red umbrella was first used by sex workers in Venice in 2001; in 2005, the International Committee on the Rights of Sex Workers in Europe adopted it as a symbol of "protection from the abuse and discrimination faced by sex workers everywhere."[18]

Indeed, from antiquity to the present, the mandatory use of distinguishable clothing or ornaments and the establishment of zoning laws have served the purpose of singling out sex workers and keeping them at a safe distance from "respectable" society. The poor reputation of prostitution has deep roots. Throughout time and space, the notions used to describe commercial sex have nearly always involved the condemnation of atypical sex acts. In spite of the geographical and temporal differences in the way the sex trade has been practiced and policed, available literature demonstrates that unorthodox sexual desire has been deemed disruptive in most cultures. As it became increasingly

---

15   "La vida miserable y trágica de las cabareteras revelada ante varios funcionarios oficiales," *El Gráfico,* 19 October 1937: 12, quoted in Donna J. Guy, *Sex and Danger in Buenos Aires. Prostitution, Family and Nation in Argentina* (Lincoln, 1991), 200; Lex Heerma van Voss, "'The Worst Class of Workers': Migration, Labor Relations and Living Strategies of Prostitutes Around 1900," in *Working on Labor: Essays in Honor of Jan Lucassen,* eds. Marcel van der Linden and Leo Lucassen (Leiden, 2012), 153–170.

16   PROUD Belangenvereniging voor en door sekswerkers accessed December 28, 2016, http://wijzijnproud.nl/.

17   "Sekswerkers Groningen protesteren tegen illegale registratie," PROUD, accessed December 28, 2016, http://wijzijnproud.nl/2016/09/05/sekswerkers-groningen-protesteren-tegen-illegale-registratie/.

18   "Under the red umbrella," International Committee on the Rights of Sex Workers in Europe, accessed December 28, 2016, http://www.sexworkeurope.org/campaigns/red-umbrella-campaigns.

commodified with the rise of industrial societies, the growth of national armies, and increased migration, commercial sex became a constant preoccupation of the elites and the bourgeoisie. In particular, women using sex for purposes other than procreation were (and still are in many places) openly or less openly incriminated.[19] Female promiscuity has been commonly condemned in all patriarchal societies, as it threatens the ability to ascertain paternity on the part of men and, from women's point of view, to secure faithful and healthy husbands or partners. Moreover, the nexus between female licentiousness and financial or material gain exacerbates the anxiety of men regarding their traditional role as head of the family and breadwinner. In short, the "female capacity of opportunistic promiscuity threatens the very premise of the patriarchal family, and the prostitute is a constant reminder of this ability."[20]

The idea of the prostitute as a deviant, a threat, or an outright criminal in the nineteenth and twentieth centuries was not, however, universal. The notion of the fallen woman could refer not only to sinful or unruly behavior for which she was responsible, but also to situations of vulnerability in which women fell prey to malevolent men. From the second half of the nineteenth century, women involved in prostitution became increasingly perceived as victims in Western countries where the feminist movement gained ground. In the UK, feminists and libertarians helped publicize a series of sexual scandals in the 1880s, which ended with the reporting of Jack the Ripper and the murder of five prostitutes. William Stead's newspaper publication on the abduction of English girls, who were subsequently sold to continental brothels, as well as the media attention given to the Ripper murders, rendered all men suspect and strengthened the notions of urban danger and female fragility.[21] The link between (migration for) prostitution, male violence, and trafficking was established at the time. By the end of the nineteenth century, a movement for the suppression of "white slave traffic" had emerged in Britain and had been disseminated internationally. From the early twentieth century onward,

---

19   Michel Foucault, *Histoire de la sexualité: La volonté de savoir* (Paris, 1976); Robert Barker, Kathleen Wininger, and Frederick Elliston, *The Philosophy of Sex* (New York, 1984); Nina Peršak and Gert Vermeulen, "Faces and Spaces of Prostitution," in *Reframing Prostitution. From Discourse to Description, from Moralisation to Normalisation?*, eds. Nina Peršak and Gert Vermeulen (Antwerp, 2014), 13–24.

20   Lena Edlund and Evelyn Korn, "A Theory of Prostitution," *Journal of Political Economy* 110 (2002): 181–214, here: 208.

21   Judith Walkowitz, "Jack the Ripper and the Myth of Male Violence," *Feminist Studies* 8 (1982): 542–574.

national and international initiatives to curtail trafficking for prostitution rose to a crescendo.[22]

The perception of prostitution as a harmful activity, in which women are the main victims, has become increasingly influential since the last decades of the twentieth century. In the U.S., certain feminists view prostitution as the sexual oppression of women and demand the decriminalization[23] of prostitutes as a short-term solution, and the radical transformation of the socioeconomic structure of society to eliminate prostitution in the long run. Some radical feminist writers and activists linked to networks such as the European Women's Lobby refuse to define prostitution in terms of labor. They understand prostitution as "sexual slavery," and prefer to speak of "prostituted women" instead of "prostitutes," as the former term "brings the perpetrator into the picture"[24] and emphasizes, in their view, the male sexual violence involved in it.[25]

In Sweden, a similar logic has been applied, but with a new strategy. Focusing on the demand side of prostitution, some Swedish feminists called for the criminalization of clients. After a long debate, the purchase of sex was made illegal in Sweden in 1999.[26] In that context, prostitution is viewed as a crime, but one committed by men on women. Hence the idea of women as victims and men as predators is strengthened. With some variations, the so-called Swedish model has spread to several European countries. As was the case at the turn of the nineteenth century, contemporary supporters of this interpretation of prostitution are of the opinion that commercial sex fuels human trafficking. In February 2014, the European Parliament approved a non-binding resolution, which recommends that EU countries re-evaluate their prostitution policies to reduce the demand for commercial sex and trafficking, by punishing clients. Since prostitution is seen as inherently exploitative and as a violation of human rights, supporters of the Swedish model make no distinction between voluntary and forced prostitution. In their view, women are forced into prostitution by third parties, poverty, or both, so that prostitution cannot possibly be understood as a form of work.

---

22 In 1921, the League of Nations replaced the racialized term "white slavery" by "traffic in women and children." Stephanie Limoncelli, *The Politics of Trafficking: The First International Movement to Combat the Sexual Exploitation of Women* (Stanford, 2010).

23 Advocates of decriminalization are not in favor of legalizing prostitution.

24 Sheila Jeffreys, *The Idea of Prostitution* (North Melbourne, 1997), 5.

25 Kathleen Barry, *Female Sexual Slavery* (Englewood Cliffs, 1979).

26 Yvonne Svanström, "Criminalising the John: A Swedish Gender Model," in *The Politics of Prostitution: Women's Movements, Democratic States and the Globalisation of Sex Commerce*, ed. Joyce Outshoorn (Cambridge, 2004), 225–244.

The idea of "unusual" or "immoral" sexuality inherent in prostitution and the representation of prostitutes as threats or victims have not only reinforced its bad reputation, but they have also made it more difficult to study. Until recently, very few people directly involved in the sex trade left first-hand accounts of their activities and motivations. Scientific analyses containing information about the social backgrounds and the working and living conditions of prostitutes in the past are usually based on sources that originated within normative contexts such as policy making or policing of the trade. However, although difficult to find, primary sources about the people involved in prostitution do exist. Moreover, recent decades have witnessed a significant increase in the amount of personal testimonies of sex workers worldwide. Various historians, sociologists, and other social scientists are currently making great efforts to present alternative narratives of prostitution.[27] Bottom-up analyses of prostitution and first-hand accounts have not, however, led to the inclusion of the views of the people concerned in policy making at the national and international levels.[28]

Accordingly, the problem in studying sex work is not necessarily related to a lack of sources, but to the perception of prostitution. In contrast to the analysis of other human activities, it appears that the study of prostitution is heavily influenced by emotions and personal views about sexuality and intimacy.[29] This tendency has often reduced prostitution debates and policy formation to "normative claims that are presented as self-evidenced truths that need no

---

27 See among others: Julia Laite, *Common Prostitutes and Ordinary Citizens: Commercial Sex in London, 1885–1960* (London, 2011); Julia Laite, "Traffickers and Pimps in the Era of White Slavery," *Past & Present* 237 (2017): 237–269; P.G. Macioti and Giulia Garofalo Geymonat, "Sex workers speak. Who listens?" *openDemocracy*, last modified 2016, accessed December 28, 2016, http://www.nswp.org/sites/nswp.org/files/Sex%20Workers%20Speak.%20 Who%20Listens%3F%2C%20Macioti%20and%20Geymonat%20-%202016.pdf.

28 The recent #AreWeNotWomen campaign of the Global Network of Sex Work Projects "seeks to highlight how sex workers are being excluded and silenced by some of the women's movements in the development of the new UN Women sex work policy," 9 December 2016, accessed December 29, 2016, http://www.nswp.org/news/arewenotwomen-campaign.

29 I am thankful to Jan Lucassen for bringing this point to my attention during the European Social Science History Conference, Vienna, April 2014. Hendrik Wagenaar and Sietske Altink, "Prostitution as Morality Politics or Why it is Exceedingly Difficult To Design and Sustain Effective Prostitution Policy," *Sexuality Research and Social Policy* 9, no. 3 (2012): 279–292. The authors argue that prostitution policy can be understood as an instance of morality politics. As such, much of prostitution policy is influenced by ideology, is emotionally charged, and is resistant to empirical evidence.

justification or evidential explanation."[30] As the following paragraphs demonstrate, personal views on prostitution also influenced the discourse and initiatives of international actors.

3 Prostitution in Geneva

3.1 *The Interwar Years*

The interpretations of prostitution described above are clearly discernable in ILO material. Soon after their foundation in 1919, the League of Nations and the ILO touched upon the issue but in an indirect way. Since prostitution was perceived as a matter of national authority, both organizations dealt with it through their campaigns on borderless issues: Phenomena that (allegedly) involve international criminal networks and the spread of bacteria and viruses.[31] While article 23c of the League of Nations' Covenant entrusted the organization with monitoring the international agreements on trafficking in women and children, the preamble of the ILO's Constitution placed it in charge of the protection of workers against disease. The League also agreed on the creation of a technical committee to specifically deal with health concerns and founded in 1921 the League of Nations' Health Organization (LNHO). Venereal disease and its link with prostitution received a great deal of attention in all of these Geneva based organizations.

Concerns regarding "loose morals," the spread of sexually transmitted diseases (STDs), and physical degeneration have intensified since the modern period. A healthy labor force and army were crucial to protect the nascent nation-states and to guarantee the realization of imperialist projects. This preoccupation was reflected in the installation of systems for the regulation of prostitution in various cities in Europe and the Americas. By the end of the nineteenth century, medical authorities, the police, voluntary organizations, and others agreed that the spread of STDs called for international analysis and response. Various initiatives took place during the first years of the new

---

30   Isabel Crowhurst, "Troubling Unknowns and Certainties in Prostitution Policy Claims-Making," in *Prostitution Research in Context: Methodology, Representation and Power*, eds. May-Len Skilbrei and Marlene Spanger (Oxford, 2017), 47–63.

31   Magaly Rodríguez, Davide Rodogno, and Liat Kozma, "Introduction," in *The League of Nations' Work on Social Issues: Visions, Endeavours and Experiments*, eds. Magaly Rodríguez, Davide Rodogno, and Liat Kozma (Geneva, 2016), 13–28, accessed December 29, 2016, http://www.un-ilibrary.org/united-nations/the-league-of-nations-work-on-social-issues_43045dc7-en.

THE ILO AND THE OLDEST NON-PROFESSION 99

century.[32] The experience of the First World War gave further impetus to local, national, and international action against STDs.

Under the leadership of its energetic first secretary-general, the French socialist Albert Thomas, the ILO created its own medical division. It focused initially on sailors, whose "nomadic" and "promiscuous" life made them particularly vulnerable to infection.[33] After the Genoa maritime conference of 1920, the ILO attempted to promote itself as one of the key players in an international network for the treatment and prevention of STDs among seamen.[34] It conducted a first survey of treatment centers in ports and harbors and sponsored the International Agreement respecting Facilities to be given to Merchant Seamen for the Treatment of Venereal Diseases, signed in Brussels in 1924. The agreement was meant to guarantee free treatment to all merchant seamen or watermen without distinction. It also provided for issuing an individual but anonymous health card, which enabled the patient to continue treatment in the next port of call. Masters of ships, ship owners, and sanitary inspection officers were required to inform the crews about the treatment facilities, and times and places for consultations.[35]

Although the ILO had initially focused on medical treatment and the prevention of STDs, its discourse became more moralistic after the late 1920s. Increased cooperation with the *Union Internationale contre le Péril Vénérien* (UIPV) and the League's anti-traffic committee may explain this change. The UIPV was established in Paris in 1923, and was composed of state representatives, various specialist societies, and technical representatives from the LNHO, the International Council of Women, and the ILO. From 1927, it was headed by Dr. J.A. Cavaillon—a French public health official—and was strongly

---

32 Josep L. Barona, "The emergence of venereal diseases in the international agenda (ca. 1900)," paper presented at the European Social Science History Conference, Valencia, 30 March 2016.

33 Bureau international du travail, *La protection de la santé des marins contre les maladies vénériennes*. Etudes et documents, Series P. (Marins), no. 2 (Geneva, 1926), 1–2. I am extremely thankful to Liat Kozma for providing these sources and for sharing with me her views on the international policing of "men on the move."

34 Paul Weindling, "The Politics of International Co-ordination to Combat Sexually Transmitted Diseases, 1900–1980s," in *AIDS and Contemporary History*, eds. Virginia Berridge and Philip Strong (New York, 1993), 93–107.

35 International Agreement respecting Facilities to be given to Merchant Seamen for the Treatment of Venereal Diseases, Brussels, 1 December 1924 accessed December 29, 2016, http://treaties.fco.gov.uk/docs/fullnames/pdf/1926/TS0020%20(1926)%20CMND-27 27%201924%201%20DEC,%20BRUSSELS%3B%20AGREEMENT%20RESPECTING%20 FACILITIES%20TO%20BE%20GIVEN%20TO%20MERCHANT%20SEAMEN%20 FOR%20TREATMENT%20OF%20VENEREAL%20DISEASE.pdf.

supported by Sybil Neville-Rolfe—"the formidable Secretary-General of the [British] National Council for Combating Venereal Disease and eugenicist."[36] By the early 1930s, the UIPV had tried to find a balance between the medical approach and social hygiene. Its suggestions served as an inspiration for the drafting of the 1931 report on the *"Amélioration des conditions de séjour des marins dans les ports,"* in which the ILO recommended, among other things, the closing down of establishments that served alcohol around ports by 10 p.m., the reduction of the number of taverns, a ban on the employment of female waitresses in establishments that served alcohol, and severe medical control of women who had illegitimate relationships with men.[37]

Around the same time, the League's experts finalized their enquiries into international trafficking in women and children.[38] They reached the conclusion that among the main causes of the global trafficking and prostitution in general were the intermediaries of prostitution and the regulation system.[39] This allowed them to go beyond their competence and to call for the abolition of the system which, they argued, maintained women in "a position of terrible slavery."[40] During the anti-traffic committee's meetings of the 1930s, its members no longer discussed trafficking, but turned their attention to the relationship between women's low wages, unemployment, and prostitution, the best means to rehabilitate women who were no longer allowed to work in licensed brothels, and the "prevention of immorality."[41] Among the new invitees to those debates was Marguerite Thibert, the French socialist and feminist

---

36   Weindling, "The Politics of International Co-ordination," 96. See also: Angelique Richardson, *Love and Eugenics in the Late Nineteenth Century. Rational Reproduction and the New Woman* (New York, 2003).

37   Annex: Report presented by the Sub-commission sur les conditions de séjour des marins dans les port, by J. Havelock Wilson and T. Salveson. *Venereal Diseases: Correspondence respecting Treatment of sailors in port*, League of Nations Archives (hereafter LNA), 8A/8227/1525; "Amélioration des conditions de séjour des marins dans les ports," Genève, 1931, accessed December 29, 2016, http://staging.ilo.org/public/libdoc/ilo/1931/31B09_14 _fren.pdf.

38   Report of the Special Body of Experts on Traffic in Women and Children (two parts), Geneva, League of Nations Advisory Committee on Traffic in Women and Children, 1927; League of Nations Commission of Enquiry into Traffic of Women and Children in the East—Report to the Council, Geneva, 1932.

39   Magaly Rodríguez García, "La Société des Nations face à la traite des femmes et au travail sexuel à l'échelle mondiale," *Le Mouvement Social* 241 (2012): 105–125.

40   League of Nations Advisory Committee on Traffic in Women and Children (hereafter "Committee"), Minutes of the Ninth Session, Eighth Meeting, Geneva, 5 April 1930, 49, LNA C.246M.121.1930.IV.

41   Miss Whitton, Canadian representative, Committee, Minutes of the Fifteenth Session, Fifth Meeting, Geneva, 22 April 1936, 10, LNA, CTFE/15th Session/PV.5.

who, after 1931, led the ILO's Section on Conditions of Employment of Women and Children.[42]

The Great Depression and its impact on women's work did not pass unnoticed by the ILO. In particular, domestic work received much attention, as it constituted the largest occupation for women at the time.[43] The League's anti-traffic committee also paid attention to that branch of labor, because its members had found sufficient evidence that domestic servants furnished a large proportion of prostitutes. The Belgian representative Isidore Maus had already in 1927 asked his colleagues to pay more attention to the "considerable influence of low wages on the development of prostitution," but not everyone seemed to agree.[44] This was an issue that resurfaced in each annual meeting, yet no consensus was reached. According to the British delegate S.W. Harris, too much emphasis was laid on the connection between wages and prostitution[45] and in 1929, the French abolitionist Avril de Sainte-Croix informed the members of the committee that the letters she had received from British colleagues suggested that "poverty was not the only cause of prostitution, but that idleness, coquetry, greed and bad company also play a part."[46] They all agreed, however, that the issue of wages paid to young women was part of a larger economic question, and that it needed to be studied in coordination with the ILO. Louis Varlez, ILO's representative in the League's anti-traffic committee during the 1920s, supported Maus' proposal to study the question of wages, but warned that it "covered an enormous field, of which the investigation would require hundreds of volumes."[47] Nevertheless, he promised to give all his support to any investigation on the theme as long as it was clearly defined. To my knowledge, no joint study emerged from those discussions.

---

42   On Thibert, see: Françoise Thébaud, "Construire un espace européen ou construire un espace international. L'exemple de Marguerite Thibert (1886–1982)," in *Les rôles transfrontaliers joués par les femmes en Europe*, ed. Guyonne Leduc (Paris, 2012), 267–282; Françoise Thébaud, "Les femmes au BIT: l'exemple de Marguerite Thibert," in *Femmes et relations internationales*, eds. Jean-Marc Delaunay and Yves Denéchère (Paris, 2006), 177–187. I am thankful to Françoise Thébaud for providing me with these publications.

43   Eileen Boris and Jennifer N. Fish, "Decent Work for Domestics: Feminist Organizing, Worker Empowerment, and the ILO," in *Towards a Global History of Domestic and Caregiving Workers*, eds. Dirk Hoerder, Elise van Nederveen Meerkerk, and Silke Neunsinger (Leiden, 2015), 530–552.

44   Committee, Minutes of the Sixth Session, Third Meeting, 26 April 1927, 16, LNA C.338.M.113.1927.IV. Similar discussions took place within the feminist movement. See: Christine Machiels, *Les féminismes et la prostitution (1860–1960)* (Rennes, 2016), particularly the chapter on the feminist lobby within the League of Nations, 143–176.

45   Committee, Minutes of the Sixth Session, Third Meeting, 26 April 1927, 17.

46   Committee, Minutes of the Eight Session, Geneva, 19–27 April 1929, 116, LNA C.294. M.97.1929.IV.

47   Committee, Minutes of the Sixth Session, Third Meeting, 26 April 1927, 16.

102   MAGALY RODRÍGUEZ GARCÍA

Thibert seemed more determined to tackle the problems faced by working women, but her conclusions on prostitution did not differ from the ideas of her abolitionist colleagues inside and outside the League. During a meeting of the League's anti-traffic committee in 1934, a discussion arose about the effects of unemployment and the economic crisis on women. The representative of the International Union of Catholic Women's Leagues, Ms. Lavielle, reported on an investigation conducted in various countries by Catholic women's associations and stated that "it was evident that unemployment, and even the inadequacy of women's earnings, constituted one of the factors of prostitution."[48] Nevertheless, she emphasized that the union "was convinced that the demoralization of young people was due to deeper causes than those of an economic character." She added that only a few women had mentioned unemployment as the cause of prostitution, and believed that "the replies of prostitutes were often merely pretexts." In her view, many of them simply refused to work. Although the Polish delegate, Mrs. Grabinska, disagreed by arguing that unemployment "constituted a serious danger" for young women, the ILO representative chose the middle way. Thibert said that she had tried to study the subject, but that an analysis based on statistics had led to no satisfactory results. In her view, the initiatives undertaken by voluntary organizations were of great value to respond to "the particular evils caused by present circumstances."

All the participants in those debates perceived prostitution as an evil, not work. They understood work as something positive, which could keep men and women at a safe distance from an immoral life. Since the nineteenth century, voluntary associations had established non-profit employment bureaus and rescue homes where training and workrooms for women were organized. Yearly reports informed the League's anti-traffic committee of their continuous efforts to secure jobs and to "inculcate in young girls a love of work."[49] As stated in one chapter authored by the ILO in the committee's 1939 study on the prevention of prostitution, the idea was to provide "protection by means of work."[50]

---

48   This and the following quotes are taken from: Committee, Minutes of the Thirteen Session, Second Meeting, Geneva, 4 April 1934, 16–27, 26–27, LNA CTFE/13th Session/PV (Revised).

49   Committee, Minutes of the Fourteenth Session, Third Meeting, Geneva, 3 May 1935, 7, LNA CTFE/14th Session/PV.3.

50   This and the following quotes are taken from: "The moral protection of young women drawn up by the International Labour Office," in *Prevention of Prostitution: A Study of Preventive Measures, Especially Those which Affect Minors* (Geneva, League of Nations Advisory Committee on Social Questions, 15 May 1939), 60–61, LNA, CQS/A/19(a). The report was published in 1943 and also contains a chapter by the renowned Danish eugenicist

THE ILO AND THE OLDEST NON-PROFESSION 103

The ILO had come to the conclusion that although certain forms of employment (such as domestic service or jobs in bars, dance halls, and other public places) "may cause moral danger," a lack of occupation was no less risky. It also demanded attention for working conditions. Wages and the status of some occupations needed improvement to protect women against the "temptation to find a way out by taking up a shameful but profitable trade." Within the ILO, Thibert was making great efforts to improve domestic work, but admitted that progress was slow. In her view, "it was of the utmost importance that girls taking up domestic service should feel that they had a real vocation and should not be ashamed of their work."[51]

Work was thus to be made attractive to women, but it needed to be monitored. The League's anti-traffic committee applauded the efforts of voluntary organizations, which sought cooperation with ministries of labor and private employment agencies to obtain not only working permits for foreign girls but also "moral guarantees" for jobs abroad.[52] The ILO, too, promoted itself as a crucial partner for the task of supervising female labor. In its contribution to the League's study on the prevention of prostitution, the ILO's analysis focused on three measures: Regulation of placing operations, protection in the workplace, and protection of female workers during their spare time.

A measure for the regulation of job placement was adopted in 1933, when the International Labour Conference adopted an international convention to abolish all fee-charging employment agencies and to supervise non-profit bureaus working under the mask of philanthropy. Among the important provisions for the protection of women in the workplace were conventions on the minimum age for industrial and non-industrial employment. Supervision of employment in the entertainment industry, restaurants, and domestic service in particular called for greater attention. Only a few countries (e.g. France) had established inspectorates to intervene in cases where "a girl's morals may be endangered by the employment provided for her."[53]

With regard to the protection of young women outside of working hours and during holidays, the ILO had to admit that legislation on the subject was restricted. Since spare time did not belong to the employer-employee

---

Dr. Tage Kemp, on the "physical and psychological causes of prostitution and the means of combatting them."

51 Committee, Minutes of the Fifteenth Session, Fifth Meeting, 22 April 1936, 4, LNA CTFE/15th Session/PV.5.

52 Committee, Minutes of the Third Session, Geneva, 7–11 April 1924, 83, LNA C.217.M.71.1924.IV.

53 The following quotes and information are taken from: "The moral protection of young women drawn up by the International Labour Office," 60–61, 70–73.

relationship, the recreation activities organized by charitable associations were of crucial importance. The ILO found four types of private initiatives that at the time of writing (1939) were apparently worth mentioning: Youth hostels, Christian workers' organizations, social service or adult education associations, and institutions organized by political parties, such as the socialist women's groups in Belgium and the Hitler Youth in Germany. Among the activities organized by public authorities, the ILO took the German, Italian, and Soviet tourist services as examples.[54] Obviously, the ILO explained, the objective of all these initiatives was not merely recreational. The educational aim was to teach "young persons of both sexes to live in normal, healthy friendship."

Health concerns remained a priority for the ILO, which explains the repeated call for increased cooperation between the League's anti-traffic committee and the LNHO. In addition, the UIPV's leader, J.A. Cavaillon, was in favor of coordinated action between the Geneva specialized organizations, and agreed to contribute with a chapter on the reduction of demand for the League's study into the prevention of prostitution—a Swedish model *avant la lettre*.[55] In the immediate post-war period, the ILO agreed to join hands with the LNHO's successor, the World Health Organization (WHO). As the role played by private associations diminished, the ILO/WHO campaigns against STDs became more technical and based on purely medical foundations.[56]

3.2   *After 1976*

As the previous section demonstrates, the ILO's early views on prostitution were neither static nor monolithic, and the post-war period shows no difference. Further archival research is required in order to find out whether the ILO considered prostitution directly (that is, not indirectly, such as within the Joint ILO/WHO Committees on the Hygiene of Seafarers, and on Occupational Health) in the 1950s and 1960s. To my knowledge, the theme returned to the ILO agenda in the mid-1970s, when an Office for Women Workers' Questions was set up by the director-general. During the World Employment Conference of 1976, special attention was paid to the working and living conditions of rural

---

54   In Europe, leisure time became increasingly formalized, regularized, and institutionalized from the eighteenth century onward. During the interwar period, the organization of leisure was a powerful control mechanism of authoritarian regimes. For analyses of the organization of leisure time in Italy and Germany, see Victoria de Grazia, *The Culture of Consent: Mass Organisation of Leisure in Fascist Italy* (Cambridge, 2002); Shelley Baranowski, *Strength Through Joy: Consumerism and Mass Tourism in the Third Reich* (Cambridge, 2007).

55   J.A. Cavaillon, "Reduction of demand," in *Prevention of prostitution*, LNA CQS/A/19(c).

56   Weindling, "The Politics of International Co-ordination," 102.

women in developing countries.[57] The establishment of U.S. military bases in Thailand in the mid-1960s led to a mushrooming of "go-go" bars and to the growth of the phenomenon of "hired wives"—many of them recruited from rural areas—for American servicemen.[58] In the aftermath of the American departure, the development of erotic tourism attracted the attention of international organizations. In the late 1970s, the ILO's "Programme on Rural Women" focused first on the involvement of young women as masseuses in the sex trade of Bangkok.

This was perhaps the first time the ILO—or at least one of its branches—described prostitution as a form of work. Interestingly, the idea of prostitution as work entered the ILO via its Asian connections. In his preface to the study, Dharam Ghai (head of research at the ILO World Employment Programme) praised the investigation on Thai masseuses as "an important contribution to understanding a highly publicised but under-researched dimension of women's work."[59] Its author, Pasuk Phongpaichit (a Thai Ph.D. in economy from Cambridge University) delivered an analysis based on fundamental details obtained from in-depth interviews with fifty masseuses. She focused on the causes of migration, the women's experiences, and the impact on their families once they left the countryside. Contrary to previous studies on prostitution produced in Geneva, Phongpaichit's research stressed the economic motives of the women involved and the negative impact of the Thai market economy on rural households. The wide income gap between urban and rural landscapes provided the setting for migration. She concluded:

> It is within an economic system structured in this particular way that the actions of the migrant girls must be understood. They were not fleeing from a family background or rural society which oppressed women in conventional ways. Rather they were engaging in an entrepreneurial move designed to sustain the family units of a rural economy which was coming under increasing pressure ... The returns available in this particular business, rather than in other business accessible to an unskilled

---

57   "Activities of the ILO, 1976. Report of the Director-General (Part 2)," International Labour Office, Geneva, 1977, 68–69, accessed January 5, 2017, http://www.ilo.org/public/portugue/region/eurpro/lisbon/pdf/09383_1977_63_part2.pdf.

58   Leslie Ann Jeffrey, *Sex and Borders: Gender, National Identity and Prostitution Policy in Thailand* (British Columbia, 2007).

59   Pasuk Phongpaichit, "Rural Women of Thailand: From Peasant Girls to Bangkok Masseuses," International Labour Organisation, World Employment Programme Research—Working Paper, November 1980, iii, accessed January 5, 2017, http://www.ilo.org/public/libdoc/ilo/1980/80B09_876_engl.pdf?gathStatIcon=true.

and uneducated person, had a powerful effect on their choices. Our survey clearly showed that the girls felt they were making a perfectly rational decision within the context of their particular social and economic situation.[60]

In subsequent decades, the blooming of sex tourism and the fear of the spread of HIV infection strengthened the ILO's interest in the issue. Lin Lim, ILO Senior Specialist on Women Workers' Questions for Asia and the Pacific, took up the subject in the 1990s and coordinated the work for an edited volume that further antagonized the rivalling camps within the prostitution debate. It is not clear whether or to what extent Lin Lim was influenced by the sex workers' movement. However, the book she helped to produce shows many commonalities not only with the research conducted by Pasuk Phongpaichit, but also with the conclusions drawn by activists and scholars who called for the redefinition of prostitution as work. The study examines the social and economic factors that influenced the growth of the sex industry in four Southeast Asian countries (Indonesia, Malaysia, the Philippines, and Thailand). It emphasizes the economic bases of prostitution and stresses the material and non-material advantages it provided to young (uneducated) women: Higher wages, flexibility, and increased mobility.[61]

The ILO authors argued that since commercial sex had developed into a full-blown industry providing employment to millions of people worldwide, it should be recognized as an economic sector. In their view, the official recognition of the sex industry would imply the maintenance of records and statistics, which would in turn be beneficial for the preparation of development plans and government budgets, as well as for securing accurate assessments of the health impact and general working conditions in the sector. The study made a clear distinction between adult and child prostitution, the latter being described as a human rights violation and an intolerable form of labor to be eradicated. In her introduction to the report, Lin Lim acknowledged the "wide range of circumstances of those in prostitution,"[62] but grouped adults engaged in the sex trade into three categories:

---

60   Phongpaichit, "Rural Women of Thailand," 141–142. For a comparative analysis that mentions "filial duty" as strong motivation for engagement in prostitution, see: Heerma van Voss, "'The Worst Class of Workers': Migration, Labor Relations and Living Strategies of Prostitutes Around 1900."

61   Lin Leam Lim, ed., The Sex Sector: The Economic and Social Bases of Prostitution in Southeast Asia (Geneva, 1998).

62   This and the following quotes are taken from: Lin Leam Lim, "The economic and social bases of prostitution in Southeast Asia," in Lin Leam Lim, The Sex Sector, 2–3.

THE ILO AND THE OLDEST NON-PROFESSION 107

> Some adults make a relatively 'free' personal choice or choose to work as prostitutes as their right to sexual liberation; others 'choose' sex work because of economic pressures or because there are no better-paying alternatives; and yet others are overtly pressured by third parties in the form of deception, violence and/or debt bondage.

Hence she concluded that "in the case of adults it may be possible to make a distinction between 'voluntary' prostitution and prostitution through coercion." A harsh criticism of the abolitionist approach was implicit in her analysis. "Many current studies," she wrote, "highlight the pathetic stories of individual prostitutes, especially of women and children deceived or coerced into the sector. Such an approach tends to sensationalize the issues and to evoke moralistic, rather than practical, responses."

Lin Lim's stance gained her the praise of (feminist) advocates of the sex work perspective,[63] but it also drew a rebuke from the abolitionist camp. In an essay published by the Coalition Against Trafficking in Women, shortly after the publication of Lin Lim's book, the radical feminist Janice Raymond deplored that the ILO had "become the latest and most questionable group urging acceptance of the sex industry," because legalization of the sex sector necessarily implied a "recognition of prostitution and related forms of sexual entertainment as sex work."[64] However, in the book's preface, Lin Lim explicitly stated that it was "outside the purview of the ILO to take a position on whether prostitution should be legalized."[65] When she received the 1998 International Nike Award at the Frankfurt Book Fair in Germany, Lin Lim reiterated that "recognition of prostitution as an economic sector does not mean that the ILO is calling for the legalization of prostitution."[66] Raymond took some abstracts from the book to criticize Lin Lim's alleged call for the recognition of prostitution as "a

---

63 See for example, Laura María Agustín and Jo Weldon, "The Sex Sector: A Victory for Diversity," *Global Reproductive Rights Newsletter* 66/67 (2003): 31–34, accessed January 5, 2017, http://www.nswp.org/sites/nswp.org/files/The%20Sex%20Sector%20-%20%20A%20 Victory%20for%20Diversity.pdf.

64 Janice G. Raymond, "Legitimating Prostitution as Sex Work: UN Labour Organization (ILO) Calls for Recognition of the Sex Industry," Coalition Against Trafficking in Women, July 1999, accessed January 6, 2017, http://www.catwinternational.org/Home/Article/61 -legitimating-prostitution-as-sex-work-un-labour-organization-ilo-calls-for-recognition -of-the-sex-industry. See also: Janice G. Raymond, *Not A Choice, Not A Job: Exposing the Myths about Prostitution and the Global Sex Trade* (Washington, DC, 2013).

65 Lin Leam Lim, "Preface", in Lim, *The Sex Sector*, v.

66 "ILO Report on the Sex Sector Receives Prestigious Prize at Frankfurt Book Fair," International Labour Organization, 10 October 1998, accessed January 6, 2017, http://www.ilo.org/ global/about-the-ilo/newsroom/news/WCMS_007999/lang--en/index.htm#N_1_.

legal occupation,"[67] but Lin Lim's quote in its entirety shows a more nuanced stance:

> In the case of adults, prostitution could be viewed as a matter of personal choice and a form of work, in which case the policy issues are mainly concerned with whether prostitution should be recognized as a legal occupation with protection under labour law and social security and health regulations.[68]

In the last chapter of the book, Lin Lim provided "some policy considerations" and explained the different possible legal approaches and the pros and cons of criminalization/prohibition, legalization, and decriminalization of prostitutes.[69] In its public communication, the ILO insisted that, "it is for countries themselves to decide on the legal stance to adopt."[70]

3.3 Recent Decades[71]

National responsibility continues to be the ILO's official position on prostitution. In the new millennium, the entry point into the debate on commercial sex became HIV/AIDS prevention. The ILO's involvement with the issue had already started in the late 1980s, when it held a joint consultation with the WHO on AIDS and the workplace, but the ILO Programme on HIV/AIDS (ILO/AIDS) was formally established in November 2000.[72] In 2010, the ILO Recommendation (No. 200) concerning HIV and AIDS and the World of Work was adopted at the 99th International Labour Conference (ILC) with the aim of strengthening national policies and programs to combat the pandemic.[73]

---

67 Raymond, "Legitimating Prostitution as Sex Work," point 7 of section "Arguments and Answers."

68 Lim, "The economic and social bases of prostitution in Southeast Asia," 2.

69 Lin Leam Lim, "Whither the Sex Sector? Some Policy Considerations," in Lim, The Sex Sector, 206–222.

70 "ILO Report on the Sex Sector Receives Prestigious Prize."

71 I am grateful to Dorothea Hoehtker from the ILO Century Project, and Richard Howard, Director of the ILO Country Office for Nepal, for the information on the ILO initiatives to combat HIV/AIDS and forced labor, and the exchange of views on the recent ILO position on prostitution. My attempts to talk to Beatee Andrees, former head of the ILO Special Action to Combat Forced Labour, on the issue of voluntary vs. forced prostitution led to no result.

72 For an analysis of the relationship between labor and the spread of HIV infection, as well as the response to the pandemic by the powerful International Transport Federation, see: Michel Pigenet, "Le VIH-Sida, nouveau terrain d'intervention syndicale dans les transports internationaux," Le Mouvement Social 241, no. 4 (2012): 185–203.

73 "ILOAIDS' History," International Labour Organization, accessed January 6, 2017, http://www.ilo.org/aids/Aboutus/WCMS_DOC_AIDS_ABO_BCK_EN/lang--en/index.htm.

During the debates within the ILC's Committee on HIV/AIDS, a government member from the Netherlands proposed an amendment to the recommendation's draft to insert an extra clause—"(d) sex workers"—in paragraph 2, which described the instrument's scope. Paragraphs 2(a) and 2(c) listed the categories of workers and services covered by the recommendation: "Persons in any employment or occupation; those in training, including interns and apprentices; volunteers; job seekers and job applicants; laid-off and suspended workers; armed forces and uniformed services."[74] The Dutch representative argued that it was difficult to develop effective programs for an important target group such as sex workers if they remained unrecognized. The worker's representative, J. Sithole (Swaziland), supported the amendment, but governmental representatives were divided on the issue. The French representative stated that his government "could not support the amendment, since sex workers were not a legal category of workers."[75] All the members of the committee agreed that an explicit reference to sex workers was unnecessary, since they could be considered to be covered by Paragraph 2(b): "all sectors of economic activity, including the private and public sectors and the formal and informal economies." The Dutch delegate withdrew the amendment on the understanding that sex workers were also included in the general description of Paragraph 2(a): "all workers working under all forms or arrangements, and at all workplaces."

The ILO/AIDS program focuses on the factors that enhance the risks of HIV infection, and that pose barriers to access to treatment facilities. It emphasizes the vulnerabilities of sex workers and aims at "reducing stigma and discrimination, promoting economic empowerment of women and men and addressing gender dimensions."[76] It does not advocate launching an international convention on sex work, but follows a bottom-up approach to promote "decent work" in the sex industry.[77] Richard Howard, former ILO senior specialist on HIV and AIDS in the Asia-Pacific region, described Recommendation 200 as "an intermediary strategy for addressing the working conditions and improved

---

74   "Recommendation concerning HIV and AIDS and the World of Work, 2010 (No. 200)," (Geneva, 2010), 3, accessed January 6, 2017, http://www.ilo.org/wcmsp5/groups/public/---ed_protect/---protrav/---ilo_aids/documents/normativeinstrument/wcms_142706.pdf.

75   "Fifth item on the agenda: HIV/AIDS and the world of work," Report of the Committee on HIV/AIDS, International Labour Conference, 99th Session, Geneva, June 2010, 27–28, accessed January 10, 2017, http://www.nswp.org/sites/nswp.org/files/ILO%20Report%20of%20the%20Committee%20on%20HIV%20AIDS.pdf.

76   "HIV and work. Getting to Zero through the world of work."

77   "Viet Nam's Sex Industry—A Labour Rights Perspective," ILO Country Office for Viet Nam, 16 September 2016, accessed January 11, 2017, http://www.ilo.org/wcmsp5/groups/public/---asia/---ro-bangkok/---ilo-hanoi/documents/publication/wcms_524918.pdf.

HIV prevention, treatment and services for sex workers."[78] In his view, the role of the ILO is to facilitate partnerships with trade unions. During the XIX International Aids Conference of 2012, he mentioned Cambodia as a model.

During the same event, Marijke Wijnroks, the Netherlands Special Ambassador for HIV/AIDS and Sexual Reproductive Health, described the Dutch approach to prostitution. She explained that sex work is legal in her country and stressed the government's support of international programs aimed at the protection of sex workers' rights. However, she added a critical note on a recent evolution that is also being felt in the Netherlands:

> Over the last couple of years we've seen an increasing tendency to more strictly regulate sex work in an attempt to control human trafficking ... This is doomed to fail because sex work and human trafficking are two very different issues, and should not be confused. Still, this is happening.

Indeed, the issue of trafficking returned to the agendas of national governments and international organizations at the end of the twentieth century. Within the ILO, the starting point for discussing forced prostitution was the observation made by the Osaka Fu Special English Teachers' Union (OFSET) in 1995, on the Japanese violation of the Forced Labour Convention during the years prior to and during the Second World War. The allegations referred to the so-called "comfort women," and OFSET asked for appropriate compensations to be made. The ILO's Committee of Experts ruled that Japan's system of military sexual slavery violated the Forced Labour Convention (No. 29) of 1930, but that it did not have the power to order the relief sought.[79] By the turn of the century, the ILO had created its Special Action Programme to Combat Forced Labour, and has subsequently contributed to the conceptual confusion in

---

78   This and the following quotes are taken from: "IAC Washington/Kolkata joint session: The Oldest Profession: is Sex Work, Work?" XIX International Aids Conference, 22–27 July 2012, accessed January 10, 2017, http://www.nswp.org/news/iac-washington kolkata-joint-session-the-oldest-profession-sex-work-work.

79   Observation (CEACR)—adopted 1996, published 85th ILC Session (1997): Forced Labour Convention, 1930 (No. 29)—Japan (Ratification: 1932), accessed January 10, 2017, http://www.ilo.org/dyn/normlex/en/f?p=1000:13100:0::NO:13100:P13100_COMMENT_ID:2152098. See also: Sayoko Yoneda, "Sexual and Racial Discrimination: An Historical Inquiry into the Japanese Military's 'Comfort' Women System of Enforced Prostitution," in *Nation, Empire, Colony: Historicizing Gender and Race*, eds. Ruth Roach Pierson and Napur Chaudhuri (Bloomington, 1998), 237–250; Heisoo Shin, "Seeking Justice, Honour and Dignity: Movement for the Victims of Japanese Military Sexual Slavery," in *Global Society 2011: Globality and the Absence of Justice*, eds. Helmut Anheir et al. (New York, 2011), 14–28.

international law and to the conflation of human trafficking and prostitution.[80] In a recent study on sexual exploitation and prostitution requested by the European Parliament's Committee on Women's Rights and Gender Equality, the authors stated that international law provisions such as those provided by the ILO point to the thin dividing line between prostitution and trafficking.[81]

Article 2(1) of the 1930 convention defines forced or compulsory labor as "all work or service which is exacted from any person under the menace of any penalty and for which the said person has not offered himself voluntarily,"[82] yet on its website, the ILO introduces confusion. "The forced labour definition encompasses," the website states:

> Traditional practices of forced labour, such as vestiges of slavery or slavery-like practices, and various forms of debt bondage, as well as new forms of forced labour that have emerged in recent decades, such as 'human trafficking,' also called 'modern slavery,' to shed light on working and living conditions contrary to human dignity.[83]

Hence, the ILO has expanded its definition of the term "forced labour" to include "modern slavery" and "human trafficking," even though the former has no legal standing and the latter is, in legal terms, not a form of (labor) exploitation but a process.[84]

---

80   Magaly Rodríguez García, "On the Legal Boundaries of Coerced Labor," in *On Coerced Labor: Work and Compulsion after Chattel Slavery*, eds. Marcel van der Linden and Magaly Rodríguez García (Leiden, 2016), 11–29.

81   Erika Schulze et al., "Sexual Exploitation and Prostitution and its Impact on Gender Equality" (Brussels, 2014), 16, accessed January 10, 2017, http://www.europarl.europa.eu/RegData/etudes/etudes/join/2014/493040/IPOL-FEMM_ET(2014)493040_EN.pdf. This report lay at the basis of the EU Resolution approved in February 2014, which calls EU states to criminalize clients of prostitution.

82   "Forced Labour Convention, 1930 (No. 29)," International Labour Organization, accessed January 10, 2017, http://www.ilo.org/dyn/normlex/en/f?p=NORMLEXPUB:12100:0::NO::P12100_ILO_CODE:C029.

83   "What is forced labour, modern slavery and human trafficking," International Labour Organization, accessed January 10, 2017, http://www.ilo.org/global/topics/forced-labour/definition/lang--en/index.htm.

84   Human trafficking only came to be defined in the 2000 UN Protocol to "Prevent, Suppress and Punish Trafficking in Persons, Specially Women and Children," accessed January 10, 2017, http://www.ohchr.org/EN/ProfessionalInterest/Pages/ProtocolTraffickingInPersons.aspx. Following the definition described in Art. 3(a), human trafficking is understood as a process which consists of three elements: A method (recruitment, transportation, transfer, harbouring, or receipt of persons), a means (threats, use of force, coercion, abduction,

This broad interpretation of forced labor reifies the mental binaries of victim/perpetrator without taking into account the fluidity and complexity of labor relationships in the sex industry.[85] It negates the agency of sex workers, who often "respond to push factors ... rather than the pull factor of trafficker enticement."[86] It also simplifies labor arrangements that often result in both progress and subjugation, improving workers' economic opportunities and at the same time submitting them to exploitative working conditions. Akin to analyses and international tools to combat trafficking during the early twentieth century, the ILO instruments on forced labor stress the danger presented to women and girls, and establish a dichotomy between forced sexual exploitation and forced labor exploitation.[87]

Siddharth Kara is an important advisor to the ILO's program against forced labor. He is a well-known anti-trafficking activist, who promotes the criminalization of clients, the destruction of the economic basis of the industry that produces "sex slaves," and the establishment of "community vigilance committees" to rescue trafficked women and girls.[88] The ILO's 2014 publication on the economics of forced labor relies heavily on Kara's methodology.[89] In spite of the harsh criticism of his statistical methods, qualitative analysis and proposed solutions,[90] his affiliation to the Harvard Kennedy School as Fellow of

---

fraud, deception, abuse of power or of a position of vulnerability, or of the giving or receiving of payments or benefits to achieve consent), and a purpose (exploitation).

85   Kimberly Kay Hoang and Rhacel Salazar Parreñas, "Introduction," in *Human Trafficking Reconsidered. Rethinking the Problem, Envisioning New Solutions*, eds. Kimberly Kay Hoang and Rhacel Salazar Parreñas (New York, 2014), 1–18, 7–9.

86   Ronald Weitzer, "New Directions in Research on Human Trafficking," *The ANNALS of the American Academy of Political and Social Science* 653, no. 6 (2014): 6–24, 16.

87   Eileen Boris and Heather Berg, "Protecting Virtue, Erasing Labor: Historical Responses to Trafficking," in Hoang and Salazar Parreñas, *Human Trafficking Reconsidered*, 19–29. In 2014, the International Labour Conference approved the Protocol to the Forced Labour Convention, 1930, and the Forced Labour (Supplementary Measures) Recommendation (No. 203).

88   Siddharth Kara, *Sex Trafficking. Inside the Business of Modern Slavery* (New York, 2009).

89   "Profits and Poverty: The Economics of Forced Labour," International Labor Organization (Geneva, 2014), accessed January 10, 2017, http://www.ilo.org/wcmsp5/groups/public/---ed_norm/---declaration/documents/publication/wcms_243391.pdf.

90   Ann Jordan, "Sex Trafficking: The Abolitionist Fallacy," *Foreign Policy in Focus*, 18 March 2009, accessed January 10, 2017, http://fpif.org/sex_trafficking_the_abolitionist_fallacy/; Laura Agustín, "Review of Kara, Siddharth, *Sex Trafficking: Inside the Business of Modern Slavery*," H-LatAm, H-Net Reviews, February 2012, accessed January 10, 2017, http://www.h-net.org/reviews/showpdf.php?id=35320. In his review on Kara's campaigning book on sex trafficking and modern slavery, Jonathan Birchall ("Sex Trafficking," *Financial Times*, 24 January 2009) asked himself: "So would Kara's 'community vigilance committees' working with 'the moral rigour of tens of thousands of committed citizens' be seen by the sex

THE ILO AND THE OLDEST NON-PROFESSION   113

the Carr Center for Human Rights Policy has accorded Kara's work *and* abolitionist campaigns a standing of scientific authority.

The popular language of trafficking is used by abolitionist activists who understand prostitution as gender-based violence, as well as by public authorities that present themselves as defenders of human rights to justify stringent
migration policies and to arbitrarily remove people or businesses deemed un-
desirable. It is therefore doubtful whether the ILO campaigns against forced
labor will boost the efforts of ILO/AIDS to improve the working and living conditions of sex workers.

4   Concluding Remarks

"The issue of prostitution has always been controversial," wrote Lin Lim in the
first lines of the preface to the ILO's publication on the sex sector in Southeast
Asia. Almost one hundred years after its foundation, the ILO still has difficulties
in positioning itself in the prostitution debate.[91] Instead of taking a clear and
unified stance on the issue, it has opted for decentralization and for the development of programs aimed at tackling problems linked to prostitution: STDs
and trafficking. Further research—particularly of unpublished material—is
needed in order to analyze whether the members of the various ILO's sections
competed or cooperated with each other, and to gauge the extent to which advocates of the sex-work perspective and the abolitionist approach influenced
the ILO's health and forced labor programs. Judging from its published sources,
the ILO seems to have become a battleground for competing views on commercial sex.

The ILO's health branch has been more inclined to take a pragmatic approach. During the interwar period, it supported the hegemonic view on prostitution, but from the 1950s onward, and particularly after the increased AIDS
incidence through the 1980s, the ILO programs became focused on treatment
and prevention, rather than on the morality of sex work. Learning—perhaps
inadvertently—from the controversy caused by the publication of the sex-
sector book, the ILO/AIDS program's staff have adopted a more gradual strategy. Instead of proposing measures that could be interpreted as a call for the
legalization of prostitution, they have concentrated on the development of
national HIV/AIDS workplace legislation and policies, the expansion of social

---

       trade as allies and defenders, seeking to eradicate violence and compulsion, or as moralist
       enemies of the sex trade itself?"

91   Skype conversation with Richard Howard, Brussels-Lalitpur (Nepal), 12 January 2017.

protection for people affected by HIV and AIDS, and the reduction of workers' vulnerability to HIV through economic empowerment. While their activities around sex workers do not feature prominently on the website, it seems that they are primarily concerned with the promotion of grass-roots initiatives to improve knowledge of legal rights and to forge partnerships with authorities and trade unions. Whether this strategy will lead to the integration of sex workers in national trade unions in more countries than is now the case, and whether such recognition will translate into the decriminalization or legalization of sex work, will depend on two factors: The strength of the abolitionist movement, and more importantly, the resilience of sex workers' organizations.

In spite of the growth of the sex workers' movement during recent decades, a unified voice has not yet been achieved. While the best-organized groups lobby for legalization, others advocate only for decriminalization.[92] Some social organizations active in the Global North stress the risks of legalization for migrant sex workers who have no residency permits. This is one of the main criticisms of the Dutch system, which created a legal framework that only applies to EU subjects. Some sex workers also point at the disadvantages of both schemes. While some dislike the idea of having to do paperwork and pay taxes, others complain about the increased competition from more *laissez-faire* commercial sex markets. In Zimbabwe, for example, after the sex trade became decriminalized in 2015 a flood of women joined it, driving the prices down.[93] During conversations with sex workers, I have noticed in some of them a slight temptation to adopt the human trafficking discourse in an attempt to reduce the flow of migrants who may push locals out of business or lead to a worsening of working conditions. Furthermore, the persistent stigma results in sex workers' continued hesitance to become involved in public manifestations or to provide first-hand testimonies that would support comprehensive analyses of prostitution.

These are all thorny issues that make the development of strong and unified sex workers' movement difficult. As long as this does not occur, the universal recognition of prostitution as work will remain utopia.

---

92 See e.g. Juno Mac, "The laws that sex workers really want," TED-talk 13 June 2016, accessed September 19, 2017, https://www.ted.com/talks/juno_mac_the_laws_that_sex_workers_really_want.

93 "Less stigma, more competition," *The Economist*, 7–13 January 2017, 26.

CHAPTER 6

The Great Fear of 1852: Riots against Enslavement in the Brazilian Empire

Sidney Chalhoub

1 Introduction

Recent studies on the history of slavery have often started off from the concept of Second Slavery, that is, the transformation of Atlantic slavery as part of the expansion of capitalism during the first decades of the nineteenth century, which resulted in "the opening of new zones of slave commodity production—most prominently the U.S. cotton zone, the Cuban sugar zone, and the Brazilian coffee zone—and the decline of older zones of slave production" (French and British Caribbean).[1] There are several merits to the concept of Second Slavery, but I mention just two of them that are of special significance for this text.

First, it draws attention to the fact that the first half of the nineteenth century did not involve the weakening of slavery in the Americas at all. Actually, there was a partial relocation of it; a persistence of slaveholding economies and societies that brings into sharp relief the indeterminacy of the historical process of slave emancipation. The concept of Second Slavery made it impossible to conceive the nineteenth century as the time of a linear transition from slavery to freedom, or from unfree to free forms of labor regimes. Second, it has made historians more aware of the interconnectedness and interdependence of the worlds of free and unfree labor. These two characteristics of the concept of Second Slavery seem to encapsulate an approach to labor history in capitalist societies that has been articulated by Marcel van der Linden in several of his works. According to him, the boundaries between free and unfree labor in capitalist societies tend to be "rather finely graded or vague";

---

* A first draft of this text was written in the winter of 2013, while I was a fellow at IGK Work and Human Lifecycle in Global History, Humboldt Universität, Berlin. Research in Brazil was funded by the Conselho Nacional de Pesquisa (CNPq) and the Fundação de Amparo à Pesquisa do Estado de São Paulo (FAPESP).

1 Dale W. Tomich, "Introduction," in *The Politics of Second Slavery*, ed. Dale W. Tomich (Albany, 2016).

© SIDNEY CHALHOUB, 2018 | DOI:10.1163/9789004386617_007

This is an open access chapter distributed under the terms of the prevailing CC-BY-NC License.

in reality, "there are extensive and complicated 'grey areas' replete with transitional locations between the 'free' wage laborers and the slaves, the self-employed and the lumpenproletarians." Van der Linden proceeds to say that these "variegated" groups of "subaltern workers," who often gravitate between free and unfree worlds of labor, are the "multitude" that "labor historians should try to understand."[2]

In the case of Brazilian and U.S. slave societies, the experience of freed and free people of African descent seemed to be shaped, to a great extent, by the mere fact of the continuation of slavery. In both countries in the 1850s, free and freed people of African descent experienced an acute sense of precariousness, through being made aware of the vulnerability of their freedom. In the U.S., demand for labor in cotton production caused a huge increase in the number of slaves sold from the Upper South (Virginia, Maryland) to the Deep South (Mississippi, Louisiana). This intensification of the internal slave trade brought "unfathomable suffering" to the enslaved population (50 percent of slave sales in the antebellum period caused the separation of families),[3] concentrated slave property in the hands of fewer whites, increased the number of slaves in some areas, and heightened a feeling of insecurity among the white population. One of the consequences was a hardening of whites' attitudes toward free and freed blacks. In addition to measures to make manumission virtually impossible, southern whites made plans for the deportation of free blacks, for their re-enslavement, and for resuming the slave trade.[4]

In Brazil, the 1850s saw the end of the African slave trade, which had continued as contraband for almost twenty years after a law that had formally prohibited it in November 1831. As a result, there was a huge increase in the internal slave trade from the northern to the southern provinces of the Brazilian Empire in order to meet the demand for labor in coffee production. During the years of the contraband African trade, illegal enslavement had become routine; actively condoned by politicians and public authorities. With the ending of the African trade and the surge in the internal trade, free and freed people of African descent felt threatened, and seemed to have reason to suspect that the government might be plotting their re-enslavement. Accordingly, free and

---

2   Marcel van der Linden, *Workers of the World: Essays toward a Global Labor History* (Leiden and Boston, 2008), 32; see also Tom Brass and Marcel van der Linden, eds., *Free and Unfree Labour: The Debate Continues* (Bern, 1997) and Carolyn Brown and Marcel van der Linden, "Shifting Boundaries between Free and Unfree Labor: Introduction," *International Labor and Working-Class History*, 78 (2010): pp. 4–11.

3   Walter Johnson, *River of Dark Dreams: Slavery and Empire in the Cotton Kingdom* (Cambridge, 2013), 14.

4   Ira Berlin, *Slaves Without Masters: The Free Negro in the Antebellum South* (Oxford, 1974), Ch. 11.

freed blacks offered their perceptions of the period of Second Slavery, and told a history of it from the bottom up: As we will see, they articulated a political view of their situation, which showed an understanding of the connection between the national and the international contexts. They believed that their freedom was at risk, and decided to struggle to uphold it.

2 The Riots

On 1 January 1852, a bill enacted by the Brazilian government on 18 June the previous year was to come into effect, establishing the mandatory civil registration of births and deaths. Another bill enacted on the same day scheduled a general population census to take place in June and July 1852. With the two decrees, the government intended to solve the problem of the lack of information about the country's population, deemed to be a major obstacle to devising public policies.[5]

Justices of the peace were to become responsible for the registries of births and deaths. Entries for newborns who were free needed to include the date, time, and place of birth, the name and sex of the child, and the names of both parents in the case of legitimate children, or just the mother's otherwise. With regard to slave children, almost all the requirements were the same, except for the need to write down the name of the master and the color of the newborn. If freedom was granted upon birth, a proper annotation needed to be made to that effect. The law required that priests demand a birth certificate in order to perform the baptism of any child. In respect of death certificates, they needed to contain a wealth of information: Name of the deceased, date and place of death, age, marital status, place of birth, profession, address, names of parents and spouse, cause of death (citing disease if applicable), as well as whether a last will and testament existed. However controversial the requirement that priests asked for a birth certificate in order to perform baptisms, it seems that people were also worried about and angry at the necessity of presenting a death certificate to bury their dead in cemeteries or churchyards.

Instead of the law coming into effect, what happened in January 1852 was a "calamity," according to public authorities that reported on the events in the following months: Police chiefs, justices of the peace, judges, military officers,

---

5 Decree no. 797, 18 June 1851, "Manda executar o Regulamento para a organização do Censo geral do Império"; decree no. 798, 18 June 1851, "Manda executar o Regulamento do registro dos nascimentos e óbitos," in *Collecção das Leis do Imperio do Brasil*, tome 14, Part 2, Section 3, 161–173.

118   SIDNEY CHALHOUB

priests, provincial presidents, and government ministers.[6] The "people" rose up in riots that spread through several of the northern provinces of the Empire. There followed a state of unrest and apprehension throughout the country,

---

6   My account is based on the following printed sources: *Relatório apresentado à Assembléa Geral Legislativa na quarta sessão da oitava legislatura pelo ministro e secretário D'Estado dos Negócios da Justiça Eusébio de Queiróz Coitinho Mattoso Camara* (Rio de Janeiro: Typographia Nacional, 1852); *Relatório apresentado à Assembléa Geral Legislativa na quarta sessão da oitava legislatura pelo ministro e secretário d'Estado dos Negócios do Império Visconde de Mont'alegre* (Rio de Janeiro: Typographia Nacional, 1852); *Relatório apresentado à Assembléa Geral Legislativa na primeira sessão da nona legislatura pelo ministro e secretário d'Estado dos Negócios do Império Francisco Gonçalves Martins* (Rio de Janeiro: Typographia Nacional, 1853); *Relatorio que à Assembléa Legislativa Provincial de Pernambuco apresentou na sessão ordinaria do 1. de março de 1852 o excellentissimo presidente da mesma provincia, o dr. Victor de Oliveira* (Pernambuco: Typ. de M.F. de Faria, 1852); *Relatorio apresentado à Assembléa Legislativa Provincial da Parahyba do Norte pelo excellentissimo presidente da provincia, o dr. Antonio Coelho de Sá e Albuquerque em 3 de maio de 1852* (Parahyba: Typ. de José Rodrigues da Costa, 1852); *Falla dirigida à Assembléa Legislativa da provincia das Alagoas, na abertura da primeira sessão ordinaria da nona legislatura, pelo exm. presidente da mesma provincia, o conselheiro José Bento da Cunha e Figueiredo em 26 de abril de 1852* (Maceió: Typ. Constitucional, 1852); *Relatorio apresentado à Assembléa Legislativa Provincial de Sergipe na abertura de sua sessão ordinaria no dia 8 de março de 1852 pelo exm. snr. presidente da provincia, dr. José Antonio de Oliveira Silva* (Sergipe: Typ. Provincial, 1852); *Relatorio do excellentissimo senhor doutor Joaquim Marcos d'Almeida Rego, presidente da provincia do Ceará, à respectiva Assembléa Legislativa na abertura da 1.a sessão ordinaria de sua 9.a legislatura, em o 1.o de setembro de 1852* (Ceará: Typ. Cearense, n.d.); *Relatorio que à Assembléa Provincial da provincia de Minas Geraes apresentou na sessão ordinaria de 1852, o doutor Luiz Antonio Barboza, presidente da mesma provincia* (Ouro Preto: Typ. do Bom Senso, 1852). In addition, in the following manuscript sources, consulted in the National Archive, Rio de Janeiro (thereafter ANRJ), which consist basically of correspondence between the Ministry of Justice and the presidency of several provinces of the Empire: IJ1-360, Alagoas, ofícios dos presidentes, 1851–2; IJ1-698, Alagoas, ofícios dos presidentes ao ministério da Justiça, 1852–5; IJ1-265, Ceará, ofícios dos presidentes, 1852–3; IJ1-721, Ceará, ofícios dos presidentes ao ministro da Justiça, 1850–5; IJ1-618, Minas Gerais, ofícios dos presidentes, 1851–2; IJ1-771, Minas Gerais, ofícios dos presidentes ao ministério da Justiça, 1850–3; IJ1-303, Paraíba, ofícios dos presidentes, 1851–2; IJ1-304, Paraíba, ofícios dos presidentes, 1853–4; IJ1-798, Paraíba, ofícios dos presidentes ao ministro da Justiça, 1850–6; IJ1-325, Pernambuco, ofícios dos presidentes, 1851–2; IJ1-326, Pernambuco, ofícios dos presidentes, 1853–4; IJ1-824, Pernambuco, ofícios dos presidentes ao ministro da Justiça, 1850–3. I refer to the aforementioned sources in abbreviated form in the notes that follow. See also: Guillermo Palacios y Olivares, "Revoltas camponesas no Brasil escravista: a 'Guerra dos Maribondos' (Pernambuco, 1851–1852)," *Almanack Braziliense* 3 (2006): 9–39; Mara Loveman, "Blinded Like a State: The Revolt Against Civil Registration in Nineteenth-Century Brazil," *Comparative Studies in Society and History* 49 (2007): 5–39; Maria Luiza Ferreira de Oliveira, "Resistência popular contra o decreto 798 ou a 'lei do cativeiro': Pernambuco, Paraíba, Alagoas, Sergipe, Ceará, 1851–1852," in *Revoltas, Motins, Revoluções: Homens Livres Pobres e Libertos no Brasil do Século XIX*, ed. Monica Duarte Dantas (São Paulo, 2011). I have related these events before in *A Força da Escravidão: Ilegalidade e Costume no Brasil Oitocentista* (São Paulo, 2012), Ch. 1.

leading the Imperial government to move quickly and, on 29 January, suspend the application of both the decree on mandatory civil registration and the one concerning the national census.

The "people" acted deliberately to prevent the law from coming into effect. According to the customs of the time, priests announced new laws to their parishioners at Sunday mass. Thus, rioters watched nearby roads to keep official correspondence from reaching clerics and the local authorities in villages and towns. Furthermore, armed men and women invaded churches during mass to threaten priests and stop them from reading the decree. The mobs persecuted and attacked justices of the peace and notarial officers because they were in charge of preparing birth and death certificates. Several stories appeared about protesters who deprived police officers of their weapons and locked them up in jail. Rioters hiding in the woods would suddenly gather by the hundreds to run through the main streets of villages and towns, sometimes on their way to attack the rural properties belonging to local grandees.

These raids went on for a couple of weeks in January, an itinerant and intermittent pattern of skirmishes; from one village to another, from one province to the next. A rebellion on the move, decentralized, and composed of protesters with no formal leadership, but incredibly determined to resist the mandatory registration of births and deaths. Provincial governments deployed heavily-armed military and police units, called on the National Guard for emergency service, and resorted to missionaries. The latter went to meet the "turbulent crowds," preached to them, prayed, talked a lot, and often managed to appease rioters, therefore preventing the military from slaughtering scores of demonstrators. After a month, it seemed difficult to account for the numbers of dead and wounded, although the figures reported by authorities appear suspiciously low. A dozen people had been killed in the province of Pernambuco, and fewer in Paraíba and Alagoas, with some authorities and military among them. However, the authorities alleged that it had become difficult to distinguish between victims directly linked to the riots, from others deemed to be associated with private conflicts and crimes that increased as a consequence of the breakdown of public order. Certainly, official reports carry plenty of stories of police and justices on the run, threatened by protesters.

Once the decrees had been suspended and the people had calmed down, the authorities sought to understand what had happened. The minister of justice attempted to relate the events to the rivalries between the two political parties, the Conservatives and the Liberals. Nonetheless, it proved difficult to attribute any major influence over the "seditious" crowds to the liberal opposition, because the riots sprang up here and there, without leaders who could be identified beyond the space and duration of particular episodes. Furthermore, according to the minister himself, these were "rustic" folk, most of them poor peasants, "plus a carpenter, a cooper."[7] Although the minister admitted that there were practical difficulties in the application of the law on civil registration, he did so in a cursory manner, asserting that the complaints remained restricted to "the inhabitants of distant villages." However, several skirmishes had taken place in the rural belt around Recife, the capital of Pernambuco, including some of its parishes. For the minister of justice and his ilk to consider the popular uprising as comprising people coming from the backwoods was a way of disdaining its importance. According to his reasoning, these people were "ignorant," thus prone to manipulation by "agents of propaganda and anarchy," by which he meant the Liberal opposition. The minister referred to the riotous lot in colorful language: They were "less enlightened people," "deceived folk," possessed by "fatal and absurd hallucinations," "foolish crowds," and "swarms of men and women in arms" who did not know what they wanted to achieve.[8] Nevertheless, in an apparent contradiction, he concluded his narration of events in the several provinces by remarking that the rebels had "similar goals" everywhere, and presented "the same motives" for their actions. With regard to their "goals," these seemed clearly aimed at thwarting the application of the law that required the registration of births and deaths. In addition, the protesters did not want to submit to the enrollment of family and household members in a national population census. However, the other questions remain: What were their shared motives? What experiences did these people have in common—beyond the "ignorance" attributed to them—that justified their widespread animosity towards government initiatives regarding the registration and gathering of information about the population?

The minister of the interior, perhaps because his office was charged with the obligation of attending to the practical matters associated with the application of the law, described in more detail the difficulties pertaining to mandatory civil registration.[9] He said that the initiative suffered from its own novelty, from the isolation caused by the lack of roads and proper means of communication, in addition to the "eccentric" modes of living prevailing among the population of the interior. During the second semester of 1851, the Imperial government had been receiving information from provincial authorities that anticipated problems regarding the application of the civil registry law. The Conservative

---

7   *Relatório apresentado ... pelo ministro e secretário D'Estado dos Negócios da Justiça Eusébio de Queiróz Coitinho Mattoso Camara*, 1852, 3.

8   *Relatório apresentado ... pelo ministro e secretário D'Estado dos Negócios da Justiça Eusébio de Queiróz Coitinho Mattoso Camara*, 1852, 4–5.

9   *Relatório apresentado ... pelo ministro e secretário d'Estado dos Negócios do Império Visconde de Mont'alegre*, 1852, 16–18.

cabinet considered such warnings exaggerated at first, although it did take the precaution of analyzing the complaints to study possible changes in the law. A visit paid to the ministry by the bishops of the provinces of Mato Grosso and Pernambuco, both alarmed by the strong opposition to the law among their flock, convinced the government that changes had to be made.

While the Council of State studied the issue of proposing amendments to the law, news arrived of the "extraordinary events taking place in the province of Pernambuco and four others, three of them its neighbors," forcing the government to take immediate action. Resistance to civil registration meant "threats" to the authorities, "criminal acts," and gatherings of people brandishing arms, therefore making it necessary for the rioters to be repressed and dispersed. On reading the correspondence sent to the ministry in January 1852, the minister of interior learned that the cause of the disturbances had been "the rumor, artfully spread, and crazily believed by the ignorant people, that civil registration was a means to enslave the colored folk." The minister did not give much credence to the hypothesis that members of the Liberal Party might have infiltrated the ranks of the rebels to instill such allegedly crazy ideas in their minds. Instead, he elaborated on the point that protesters indeed believed the purpose of the law was to reduce the free people of African descent to slavery: They even called it "the law of slavery."

Therefore, there seems to have been a shared understanding that motivated the actions of thousands of individuals, spread over a vast area of the Brazilian Empire, who went on rioting against the law on civil registration: Free people of color were afraid of being forced into slavery and freed persons were scared of returning to it. Regardless of the fact that ministerial reports displayed the usual class hatred that made state officials oblivious to the reasoning of ordinary, poor folk, they revealed clearly the goal of the crowds (to prevent the application of the law on civil registration), their strategy (to prevent priests publicizing the law from the pulpit and justices of the peace from applying its dispositions), and their motive (to resist illegal enslavement).

With regard to the fear of enslavement, the protesters believed that a connection existed between civil registration and the end of the African slave trade, which had been achieved shortly beforehand as a consequence of the application of the law of 4 September 1850. Perhaps the rioters thought the cessation of the African trade was merely the result of British pressure, which would have made them more insecure in respect of the intentions of the Imperial government to obtain labor for coffee cultivation. On 6 January 1852, a judge from the province of Pernambuco wrote to the provincial president to say that "the reason why the people are so restless and threatening is that it is said generally that the dispositions of the Decree are designed to enslave their children, since the British no longer permit the coming of Africans."[10] In fact, it seems that the rebels saw a relationship between the end of the African slave trade and the two decrees regarding civil registration and the census: Birth certificates had been envisaged as reducing future generations to slavery, and the enrollment associated with the national census would make it possible to organize the enslavement of free and freed adult persons of color.[11]

The president of the province of Paraíba, after an introduction in the customary style of these official reports, made his point objectively: "The idea that the enslavement of men of color was the purpose of civil registration became widespread, and to some weak minds it gave rise to a sort of fanaticism."[12] This was in print. In his confidential exchanges with the minister of justice, to which he appended a wealth of correspondence received from other provincial authorities—such as the police chief and the judge of the first district— the president of Paraíba offered chilling accounts of what the rebels had been saying and doing. On 7 February 1852, the president wrote to the minister to relate that in the villages of Campina Grande and Ingá, according to the judge who had visited those places, the people, carrying weapons, insisted "that authorities gave them the Book, which they called the Book of slavery, as well as the boxes with ropes and ferules, and made other wild demands."[13]

Despite the repeated acknowledgement by authorities from the top to the bottom of the Brazilian governmental hierarchy that poor people of African descent resorted to riots in 1852 because they thought that they would be enslaved or re-enslaved, official documents reveal a deafening silence regarding what made so many people share the experience of such fear. In order to understand the great fear of 1852, the confluence of two historical processes must be approached: That is, the practices within Brazilian slavery that rendered insecure the freedom of free and freed people of color, and the political and social aspects that created a kind of interdiction concerning the representation of that very situation.

---

10   Cited in Guillermo Palacios y Olivares, "Revoltas camponesas no Brasil escravista," 22.

11   The president of the province of Minas Gerais clarified this point: "the wickedness of some men, which made them abuse the ignorance of the inhabitants of some villages in the interior of Pernambuco, persuaded the population that the enrollment of citizens and the registration of births had the purpose of enslaving the parents and the children [respectively]"; *Relatorio ... da provincia de Minas Geraes*, 1852, 4.

12   *Relatorio ... da Parahyba do Norte*, 1852, 3.

13   Maço IJ1-798, ANRJ. The citations that follow refer to this.

RIOTS AGAINST ENSLAVEMENT IN THE BRAZILIAN EMPIRE

3 The Practice of Illegal Enslavement

In 1826, in exchange for British diplomatic support for the recognition of Brazilian independence (obtained in 1822), the Brazilian government agreed to sign a treaty promising to end the African slave trade within three years of the treaty's ratification.[14] As a consequence, the slave trade became illegal beginning in March 1830. Moreover, on 7 November 1831, the Brazilian parliament passed a law prohibiting it. In spite of the legal ban, and after a temporary decrease in the first half of the 1830s, the slave trade—now contraband—resumed. It peaked in the following years, furthered by labor demand in the coffee plantations, counting on the corruption of public officials and the support of ample sectors of the population to elude British efforts to curb it. By the early 1850s, when changed political and social conditions brought about the enactment of a new law and the effective cessation of the slave trade, more than 750,000 Africans had been smuggled into the country, thus comprising the great majority of the labor force in Brazilian plantations in the provinces of Rio de Janeiro, São Paulo, and Minas Gerais.[15] It follows that the wealth and power of coffee planters, the major symbol of the alleged economic prosperity and political stability of the Brazilian Empire, originated in the acquisition of slave labor illegally, by means of the contraband African trade.

Given the obvious fact, recognized by government authorities and planters, that slave property originating from the importation of Africans was illegal after the law of 1831, it remains to be seen how it became possible to shape institutions, conduct everyday business transactions pertaining to a slave society, and maintain slave discipline under these circumstances.

It appears that the seigneurial class considered access to slave labor a customary right, to be guaranteed by the government especially at an economic juncture in which coffee expanded throughout the southeastern provinces and conquered international markets.[16] Furthermore, the contraband trade may have benefited from the fact that the institution of slavery enjoyed wide social backing during the first half of the nineteenth century; that is, access to slave property was not restricted to the wealthy, as people of relatively

---

14 The traditional accounts of the story summarized in this paragraph are: Leslie Bethell, *The Abolition of the Brazilian Slave Trade: Britain, Brazil and the Slave Trade Question, 1807–1869* (Cambridge, 1970); Robert Edgar Conrad, *World of Sorrow: The African Slave Trade to Brazil* (Baton Rouge/London, 1986).

15 For this estimate, see www.slavevoyages.org (24 May 2017).

16 Beatriz Galotti Mamigonian, "O direito de ser africano livre: os escravos e as interpretações da lei de 1831," in *Direitos e Justiças no Brasil. Ensaios de História Social*, eds. Silvia H. Lara and Joseli M.N. Mendonça (Campinas, 2006), 129–160.

modest means—freed people among them—often had one or two slaves of their own. In order to carry on with their activities, slave traders depended on a vast network of partners and services, ranging from inhabitants of distant coastal areas willing to support the clandestine landing of Africans— therefore feeding, healing, and hiding them until they could proceed to their final destination—to conniving local authorities and planters determined to acquire African labor irrespective of the law. However, there were risks involved in every step of such undertakings. The British government demanded compliance with international treaties and sought to repress the contraband trade. Furthermore, it maintained that the right to freedom pertained not only to Africans actually apprehended on board captured slave ships, but to all those already successfully smuggled into the country, whose situation should be investigated and addressed by the Imperial government.

The high rate of illegal enslavement that occurred after 1831 affected the daily experience of freedom for people of African descent in general, as it caused insecurity and rendered freedom precarious. The connection between illegal enslavement and the precariousness of freedom is crucial, both to understand the logic permeating public policies and to observe the strategies used by blacks and *pardos* (mixed-race people)—slaves, free, and freed—in dealing with it.[17] Slave owners' interests in not abiding by the law of 1831 necessarily meant increasing slackness in property requirements thereafter. For example, in the early 1830s, when attempts to curb the illegal trade were still in place, police authorities in the city of Rio realized that they needed to prevent the transportation of Africans to where they were in demand: To the interior of the provinces of Rio de Janeiro, São Paulo, and Minas Gerais. However, the alleged owners of the slaves to be transported were not required by law to present documents of the transaction that brought them into possession of the enslaved people in the first place.[18] The absence of this requirement is significant, since it alone made it relatively easy to claim ownership of recently-arrived Africans, who after 1831 could no longer be introduced through the *alfândega* (customs), with the ensuing certificates and receipts associated with the collection of due taxes. With government revenue from slave property on the wane, laxity regarding primary documentation of ownership became commonplace, with

---

17 Sidney Chalhoub, "Illegal Enslavement and the Precariousness of Freedom in Nineteenth-Century Brazil," in *Assumed Identities: The Meanings of Race in the Atlantic World*, eds. John D. Garrigus and Christopher Morris (College Station, 2010), 88–115.

18 Secretaria de Polícia da Corte, Ofícios com Anexos (1831–1832), maço IJ6-165, ANRJ. In the rest of this paragraph and in the subsequent one, I summarize arguments previously made in Sidney Chalhoub, "The Precariousness of Freedom in a Slave Society (Brazil in the Nineteenth Century)," *International Review of Social History* 56 (2011): 425–426.

authorities in Rio and elsewhere eager to have proprietors pay taxes on their slaves.[19] Hence, a law enacted on 11 April 1842, establishing rules for slave registration and for the payment of annual and sale taxes on slave property, reassured owners, stating that "On the occasion of the first registration, nobody can be required to present the title through which [he or she] came to the possession of a slave."[20]

Rules and procedures making it possible not to "see" illegally enslaved Africans and giving the appearance of legality to property originating in contraband had two consequences. First, it encouraged slave stealing, an activity that seems to have acquired epidemic proportions in the 1830s and 1840s, judging from the amount of time and effort the police dedicated to preventing it during this period. Slave stealing necessarily involved establishing networks with the participation of a variety of individuals, beginning with the captives themselves. They often agreed—and sometimes asked—to be taken away, therefore turning the slackness regarding proof of slave ownership to their own advantage, by negotiating better conditions for themselves within slavery. The second consequence of the looseness concerning proof of slave property was that illegal enslavement became a greater threat to free and freed people of color in general; both African and Brazilian born. Although it is not possible to know the frequency of such events, they are mentioned in police correspondence, prison books, and trial records frequently enough to suggest that potential victims had to deal with this, calculating their moves and remaining vigilant.

As noted, the rioters of 1852—identified as free blacks and *pardos*—related the cessation of the illegal importation and enslavement of Africans to their supposition that the Brazilian government intended to enslave them as a substitute labor force thereafter, presumably for southeastern coffee plantations. A question follows from this—an intriguing one at least from the point of view of a social historian—which is, what did the Africans who arrived after 1831 and their descendants, also held in illegal bondage, know about their situation

---

19   Wilma Peres Costa, "Estratégias ladinas: o imposto sobre o comércio de escravos e a 'legalização' do tráfico (1831–1850)," *Novos Estudos CEBRAP* 67 (2003): 57–75.

20   *Collecção das leis do Imperio do Brasil*, decree no. 151, 11 April 1842, article 6: "No acto da primeira matricula a ninguem se exigirá o titulo porque possue o escravo." As late as June 1869, deputies resisted the approval of a bill that proposed the creation of national slave registration, despite the fact that the deputy who presented it argued that proprietors would not be required "to exhibit the titles under which they possess their slaves." He added that fiscal authorities would not have the right to raise questions concerning the list of slaves presented by each owner: That is, they should take their word for it; *Annaes do Parlamento Brazileiro. Camara dos Srs. Deputados*, 1869, tome 2, 192.

vis-à-vis the laws of the country? Further, what did they do, if anything, with whatever knowledge they had gained?

There is a glimpse of what government authorities believed slaves knew about their legal situation in a formal response offered by the council of state, to a complaint sent to the Imperial government by the São Paulo Provincial Assembly in October 1854.[21] Assuming overtly the role of representatives of the coffee planters in the province, the deputies argued that slave crimes against masters, their families, and overseers had been growing lately because captives had acquired a sense of impunity for such deeds. According to the deputies from São Paulo, the problem was the non-application of the death penalty against slaves condemned according to the law of 10 June 1835. This law, enacted after two major slave insurrections in the provinces of Minas Gerais and Bahia, provided special dispositions intended to send slaves who had attacked masters, their families, and overseers to a certain and speedy death by hanging, in public ceremonies designed to dissuade others from engaging in similar acts of violence. However, by the late 1840s the Imperial government seemed to have reached the conclusion that the law of 1835 had become ineffective in deterring slave violence against masters. Furthermore, it had caused repeated judicial errors because it did not give defendants the right to appeal a sentence, as the law was inspired by the notion of swift, exemplary punishment. Hence, beginning in the late 1840s, the emperor used the powers granted to him by the Brazilian Constitution of 1824 to impede the application of capital punishment against the majority of slaves condemned according to the law of 1835, sending them instead into forced labor in shackles for life. The deputies from São Paulo thought that it did not make sense to condemn slaves to forced labor. They contended that slaves preferred to serve a sentence of that kind to toiling in coffee cultivation; thus they committed horrendous crimes and deliberately turned themselves in to public authorities, unafraid of the punishment to come.

The Council of State replied to the deputies from São Paulo with a mixture of condescending irony and lessons regarding how to maintain slave discipline. They found the argument specious that there were captives who preferred to serve sentences of forced labor for life in state prisons than to remain slaves on coffee plantations. If this were indeed the case, it meant that planters had

---

21   José Prospero Jehovah da Silva Caroatá, *Imperiais resoluções tomadas sobre consultas da seção de Justiça do Conselho de Estado. Desde o anno de 1842, em que começou a funccionar o mesmo Conselho, até hoje*, ed. B.L. Garnier Livreiro (Rio de Janeiro, 1884), Part I, 507–509. For a detailed analysis of this document, see Sidney Chalhoub, *A Força da Escravidão*, 144–152.

not been giving slaves appropriate treatment and had neglected their religious instruction. Moreover, slaves were not endowed with "a ferocious perversity," as the deputies alleged, but became that way as a result of excessive physical punishment. Considering the bad treatment suggested by the deputies themselves, and aware of "notions of freedom" that they heard about from those among them who were able to read newspapers, had the slaves been really "ferocious," they would have already attempted in Brazil something similar to what had taken place in Haiti. Further elaborating on this point about what the slaves knew, the councilors argued that the rigorous application of capital punishment against the slaves would have led them to desperation. The problem of the politics of domination under Brazilian slavery had to be approached within the context of "the thousands of blacks that were annually imported to the country irrespective of the law that forbade such abominable trade. It is not possible that the slaves did not come to perceive the illegality of their bondage."[22] After all, many of them had inevitably witnessed the clandestine arrival of slave ships, had seen occasional apprehensions of recently-arrived Africans subsequently declared free, and had heard the revelations of their "false protectors" and fellow captives who knew better. In sum, "everything has been concurring for them to come to learn of their situation"; therefore, it did not make sense to worsen matters by using excessive force against enslaved people.

The councilors may have reacted against the *paulistas* (people from the province of São Paulo), perhaps irritated by the complaint from the main beneficiaries of a monarchical regime that had condoned the contraband slave trade for two decades and continued to guarantee the slave property thus acquired. Possibly therefore, it was an exaggeration to suggest that slaves in general were aware of the widespread illegality pertaining to the institution of slavery at that time. In fact, if they knew of their right to freedom, why did they not demand such right in the courts? Or did they?

Certainly, in addition to the occasions of slave ships caught in the process of disembarking scores of Africans ashore in some more or less hidden locations, there were relatively frequent cases of recently-arrived Africans captured on land. This was sometimes as a consequence of their running away from slavers, thus getting lost on the streets of Rio, for example, until taken to a police station or to some public authority, such as a police official or a neighborhood inspector. Police authorities might find several reasons to believe that an individual African was a recent arrival: For instance, they knew that a clandestine

---

22   José Prospero Jehovah da Silva Caroatá, *Imperiais resoluções tomadas sobre consultas da seção de Justiça do Conselho de Estado*, Part I, p. 508.

disembarkation had just happened, the African did not speak or understand any Portuguese, had skin diseases and other illnesses associated with crossing the Atlantic in dire conditions, and so on. The police would then send the African to a municipal judge, who would interrogate him or her with the help of an interpreter of the same ethnic origin, if possible, to reach a decision about his or her legal status. If the conclusion was that the person had been introduced by contraband, he or she would be declared an *africano livre* (liberated African), which meant that—now under the authority of the Brazilian government—they would be sent to public works or rented out to private citizens.[23] Liberated Africans had to serve fourteen years before becoming able to apply for full emancipation. Their number at the time is estimated at approximately 11,000 individuals, a sharp contrast with the 750,000 reduced to slavery during the years of the contraband trade. Their lot was often compared with and taken to be similar to that of people in bondage;[24] as a consequence, it may have made more sense, to many Africans, to reckon with bondage and seek manumission, instead of staging an uphill legal battle to become a liberated African.

The usual story, in any case, was that hundreds of thousands of Africans introduced through the illegal trade remained slaves, and became invisible, so to speak. As a British diplomat once observed, "These illegal slaves are at every moment and everywhere in presence of the Brazilian authorities, but are not seen."[25] Africans—and certainly also *crioulos* (Brazilian-born blacks)—who came to the attention of authorities were presumed slaves unless otherwise proven. Africans who spoke and understood a little Portuguese and who did not show clear signs of having recently experienced crossing the Atlantic on a slave ship, were considered *ladinos*, that is, taken to have been introduced a long time ago, or at least at a time in the past impossible to determine, therefore taken to be earlier than the law of 7 November 1831. Police authorities and the judicial system tended to dismiss outright allegations of a right to freedom originated in a supposedly illegal importation that occurred after the law of 1831.

---

23   This summary of what happened in the case of individual Africans seized on the streets of Rio and suspected of having been recently introduced to the country by contraband is based on the systematic reading of police correspondence and jail papers pertaining to the 1830s and 1840s, especially the following series: IJ6, Secretaria de Polícia da Corte. Ofícios com anexos; IIIJ7, Registro de ofícios relativos ao Calabouço; IJ7, Casa de Correção da Corte. Ofícios com anexos; all in the collection of the ANRJ.

24   Charles Pradez, *Nouvelles études sur le Brésil* (Paris, 1872), 133–136. For an official estimate of the number of *africanos livres* (10,719): *Relatorio do Ministerio da Justiça apresentado à Assembéa Geral Legislativa na segunda sessão da decima terceira legislatura, 1868*, Minister Martim Francisco Ribeiro de Andrada, 16.

25   W.D. Christie, *Notes on Brazilian Questions* (London/Cambridge, 1865), 82.

RIOTS AGAINST ENSLAVEMENT IN THE BRAZILIAN EMPIRE 129

Moreover, there needed to appear a clear link between a given African claiming freedom and a determined clandestine disembarkation. This constituted a legal trap since, as a rule, a clandestine disembarkation was one that did not receive the proper recognition and formal procedures pertaining to police, fiscal, and judicial authorities.

In 1854, in the interior of the province of São Paulo, a runaway slave called Bento was caught and taken to a local judge. Someone appeared soon afterwards, claiming to be his owner. The judge, however, for unknown reasons, thought that the captured African might have been smuggled into the country, and therefore investigated the situation, interrogated witnesses, and concluded that Bento had a formal right to freedom and should be declared a liberated African. Alarmed, the police chief and the provincial president wrote to the minister of justice to seek guidance regarding what to do in this situation. In a confidential, carefully-worded reply, Minister Nabuco de Araújo, a prominent politician, lawyer, and a towering statesman of the Brazilian Empire, praised the concern of provincial authorities and explained to them that, on the one hand, it did not seem appropriate for the judge to reach a conclusion against the law. On the other hand, in practice and for the security of the best interests of Brazilian society, the Imperial government had established a proscription of the application of the law of 1831. The minister proceeded to say that "the empire of circumstances requires that something be done, directly or at least indirectly, to defend the collective interests of society." In other words, the minister ordered the provincial authorities to do something to silence the overzealous local judge.[26]

4 From the African Slave Trade to the Internal Slave Trade

In September 1850, the Brazilian parliament approved a new law to abolish the African slave trade, in a changed context that suggested the government's determination to apply its dispositions. In 1848, a slave conspiracy in the coffee-producing Paraíba Valley scared planters and authorities, who were at the time acutely aware of the growing demographic imbalance brought about by the huge number of enslaved Africans arriving in the country in the late 1840s (it was common that more than 80 percent of slaves in coffee plantations at the

---

26   Joaquim Nabuco, *Um Estadista do Império. Nabuco de Araújo, sua Vida, suas Opiniões, sua Época*, ed. H. Garnier Livreiro, 2 vols. (Rio de Janeiro/Paris, 1897), vol I, 242–243.

time were Africans).[27] In the summer of 1849–1850, a severe yellow fever outbreak in several coastal cities of the country, including Rio de Janeiro and Salvador, was thought to have originated in ships linked to the African slave trade. Since the epidemic was particularly devastating to European immigrants and whites in general, affecting blacks only marginally, it increased white people's feelings of insecurity with regard to the large African presence in the country.[28] Last but not least, in the first months of 1850 the British campaign against the African slave trade turned to seizing and destroying Brazilian ships, deemed to be linked with the contraband trade, found in national territorial waters and even anchored in ports. In July 1850, it was clear that the situation had become untenable and that the Brazilian government would finally move firmly towards ending the contraband slave trade.[29]

Ministerial and provincial reports and correspondence pertaining to 1851—thus in the months immediately preceding the riots of January 1852—leave no doubt about the intensity of government efforts to curb the illegal trade. What had been allegedly impossible in the 1830s and 1840s seems to have been achieved in a matter of months, perhaps in little more than a year, with intense vigilance and repression going on during 1851.[30] In the late 1840s, the last years of the contraband trade, the number of Africans introduced into the country annually was appalling: 52,395 were illegally reduced to bondage in 1846; 61,731 in 1847; 61,757 in 1848; and 57,504 in 1849. In 1850, with British warships patrolling the Brazilian coast more aggressively than ever before, slavers still managed to smuggle 31,161 Africans into the country, which meant a reduction to the level of contraband observed in the early 1840s. In 1851, the year in which the Brazilian government's repression of the trade took shape, some 5,595 Africans were introduced illegally, followed by just 984 in 1852, and none in the

---

27   Robert W. Slenes, "'Malungu, Ngoma's Coming': Africa Hidden and Discovered in Brazil," in *Mostra do Redescobrimento: Negro de Corpo e Alma—Black in Body and Soul*, ed. Nelson Aguilar (São Paulo, 2000), 221–229; Robert W. Slenes, "L'arbre Nsanda Replanté. Cultes d'Affliction Kongo et Identité des Esclaves de Plantation dans le Brésil du Sud-Est (1810–1888)," *Cahiers du Brésil Contemporain* 67/68 (2007): Partie II, 217–313.

28   Sidney Chalhoub, "The Politics of Disease Control: Yellow Fever and Race in Nineteenth Century Rio de Janeiro," *Journal of Latin American Studies* 25, Part 3 (1993): 441–463; Dale T. Graden, "An Act 'Even of Public Security': Slave Resistance, Social Tensions, and the End of the International Slave Trade to Brazil, 1835–1856," *Hispanic American Historical Review* 76, no.2 (1996): 249–282.

29   Leslie Bethell, *The Abolition of the Brazilian Slave Trade, 1807–1869* (Cambridge, 1970).

30   See, for example, *Relatório apresentado ... pelo ministro e secretário D'Estado dos Negócios da Justiça Eusébio de Queiróz Coitinho Mattoso Camara*, 1852, 9–10; also, maços IJ1-379, IJ1-824, IJ1-840, IJ1-865, IJ1-910.

RIOTS AGAINST ENSLAVEMENT IN THE BRAZILIAN EMPIRE 131

following years until 1856, in which a last episode resulted in the introduction of 320 Africans.[31]

How were the would-be rioters of January 1852 affected by the aggressive campaign against the slave trade in 1851? The ostensible measures to prevent the contraband trade must have had a strong impact countrywide, considering the dimensions such business had acquired, the network of services and communications it required, and the enormous amount of capital invested. The raids against perpetrators conducted during 1851 sought to abort specific instances of contraband and to dissuade traders from making further attempts. For instance, in November 1851, the president of Pernambuco wrote to the minister of justice to report that in the village of Garanhuns, where there would be riots in the following January, there had been an apprehension of 39 Africans who had been recently disembarked in the nearby province of Alagoas and taken there to be sold. The provincial president alleged that the success of the operation was due to the fact that he had fired supposedly conniving police officials and taken other measures to make proprietors shy away from buying smuggled Africans, forcing the slave dealer to keep them longer than he had planned and facilitating his arrest.[32] According to the minister of justice, in his official report to the parliament pertaining to 1852, the central government feared that the large apparatus of repression deployed in the southern part of the Empire would divert slave traders to northern provinces, where Africans would be disembarked and later sent to southern provinces by means of the coastal maritime trade.[33] As a consequence, the correspondence sent to the minister of justice by the presidents of the northern provinces in the early 1850s shows that they were under pressure to remain vigilant regarding possible clandestine disembarkations, and were asked to supervise carefully the issuing of passports to slaves being transported from one province to the other.[34] Furthermore, slave prices soared in the southern provinces during 1851, causing an immediate growth in the internal slave trade. According to the minister of justice, just 940 slaves had arrived in Rio from other provinces

---

31   www.slavevoyages.org (24 May 2017).

32   Maço IJ1-325, ANRJ.

33   *Relatório apresentado ... pelo ministro e secretário D'Estado dos Negócios da Justiça Eusébio de Queiróz Coitinho Mattoso Camara*, 1852, 9–10.

34   See note 6 above. For a description of measures to prevent the transportation to southern provinces of Africans recently arrived by contraband, see the letter of the president of the province of Alagoas to the minister of justice, 28 April 1852, maço IJ1-910, ANRJ.

in 1849; in 1850, there were 1,074, but the number jumped to 3,088 in 1851, and 1,473 had already entered from January to mid-April 1852.[35]

The significant growth of the internal slave trade in the context of the intense repression and actual cessation of the African trade must have caused alarm among the free and freed population of African descent in the northern provinces. The kidnapping and selling away into slavery of children of African descent were not unheard of events in those provinces. In fact, in February when the riots were still unfolding in some places, the police of the province of Rio Grande do Norte investigated "the kidnapping of a child named João, six years old, free, son of the *crioula* [a Brazilian-born black woman] Galdina," who they suspected had already been sent to another province.[36] Two years later, in September 1854, during a discussion in the chamber of deputies concerning the continued growth of the internal slave trade and about whether the central government should do something to bring it under control, a deputy from Bahia alleged that, in addition to the threat to the economic prosperity of the northern provinces, there should be a law to regulate such trade because it had caused "the appearance of a new kind of speculation in the northern provinces—namely, to reduce free people to bondage." He proceeded to say that "helpless children, *pardos* and blacks, are sold by people to whom they are entrusted"; other criminals "resort to violence to kidnap children and sell them!"[37]

Moreover, the rioters' apprehension concerning birth certificates must be seen in the context of repeated episodes of children of freed and free women of African descent being baptized as slaves by abusive landlords willing to take advantage of the vulnerability and dependence of poor people of color. On 24 December 1851, the Director General of Indians wrote to the president of the province of Pernambuco regarding concerns for his personal safety, as he was about to return to Recife, the provincial capital.[38] According to him, "anarchists"—that is, members of the Liberal Party—had spread rumors that the decree on civil registration was intended "to reduce people of color to slavery," and that he had gone to Rio de Janeiro in person to propose the decree to the Imperial government. More interestingly, however, he also attributed the animosity against him to the supposedly false contention that free children of African descent to whom he had become a godparent recently appeared

---

35   *Relatório apresentado ... pelo ministro e secretário D'Estado dos Negócios da Justiça Eusébio de Queiróz Coitinho Mattoso Camara*, 1852, 9.

36   Maço IJ1-287, ANRJ.

37   *Annaes do Parlamento Brasileiro, Camara dos Srs. Deputados*, 1 September 1854.

38   Maço IJ1-824, ANRJ.

RIOTS AGAINST ENSLAVEMENT IN THE BRAZILIAN EMPIRE   133

"in the book of the parish priest as his slaves."[39] Hence the rioters' suspicion regarding birth certificates may suggest that they thought their children would become even more vulnerable to illegal enslavement than they already were in baptisms performed in local parishes.

5   Telling Histories of Illegal Enslavement

Although the rule in public discourse was to maintain silence about the pervasiveness and scale of illegal enslavement—or the frequent threat of it—as a structural conditioning of the lives of free and freed people of African descent, there are plenty of narratives of illegal enslavement produced by blacks themselves in nineteenth-century Brazil, most (but not all) of them accounts submitted to police and judicial authorities in criminal and civil court cases. Luiz Gama, a well-known black abolitionist and republican, wrote an autobiographical letter in 1880, in which illegal enslavement appeared as the major turning point in his life history. Gama became a self-taught lawyer and a journalist who professed to hate all masters and kings. He built his fame beginning in the late 1860s, when he filed successive appeals for freedom in the province of São Paulo, arguing that the captives he represented had been smuggled into the country after the enactment of the law of 1831. In addition, he wrote newspaper articles denouncing judges who refused to acknowledge and investigate these claims. It appears that the daring of Luiz Gama remained an isolated case in the 1860s; however, it may have played a part in the coming of the gradual emancipation law of 1871, which created a national slave registry intended to stabilize the existing slave property.[40]

Luiz Gama wrote his autobiographical letter at the request of a friend, a journalist like himself, who wanted to publish a piece about Gama's life.[41] He related that he had been born free in Salvador in 1830, the son of an *africana livre*—a liberated African woman—and a white man belonging to a wealthy and traditional Bahian family of Portuguese origin. According to him, his mother, often suspected of being involved in slave insurrections, had to leave

---

39   For further examples, see Sidney Chalhoub, *A Força da Escravidão*, 263–268.
40   Elciene Azevedo, *O Direito dos Escravos. Lutas Jurídicas e Abolicionismo na Província de São Paulo* (Campinas, 2010); Elciene Azevedo, *Orfeu de Carapinha: a Trajetória de Luiz Gama na Imperial Cidade de São Paulo* (Campinas, 1999).
41   The first book to have reproduced the letter and studied its content was Sud Menucci, *O Precursor do Abolicionismo no Brasil (Luiz Gama)* (São Paulo, 1938); see also Lígia Fonseca Ferreira, "Luiz Gama por Luiz Gama: carta a Lúcio de Mendonça," *Tereza. Revista de Literatura Brasileira da USP* 8/9 (2008): 300–321.

the Bahian capital in 1837. Luiz Gama remained with his father until 1840, when economic troubles hit the family hard and he was sold as a slave by his own father, thus sent along with others to Rio and then to bondage in coffee plantations in the province of São Paulo. He proceeded to tell of his experiences in São Paulo, of how his Bahian origin made it difficult for him to be sold, given the reputation for rebelliousness of slaves from there, resulting in his staying in the capital of the province where he learned to read and write and managed to obtain his freedom. Luiz Gama's autobiographical letter is fraught with silences of his own, such as the name of his father and the precise circumstances of his regaining his freedom. These omissions seem to have prevented historians from checking the veracity of key details of Gama's story, although several passages of it are supported by other contemporary documents. Although I would not suggest that checking the accuracy of such details is unimportant—at the very least it can help us to explore further the intentions of the author—it is clear that the letter aimed at a deeper truth: That is, portraying a more collective dimension of the experience of people of African descent in nineteenth-century Brazil, and how it remained marked by the vulnerability of freedom associated with the widespread practice of illegal enslavement.

The life history of Luiz Gama, combined with so many others found especially in civil and criminal court cases, may help us to revise what has become perhaps the master narrative of the history of Brazilian slavery in the recent past. Studies on the subject have consistently emphasized the fact that slaves in Brazil had a better chance of achieving freedom than their counterparts in other slave societies, leading historians to seek sources in notarial archives to offer dense descriptions and interpretations of both the masters' ideology regarding freedom and the slaves' strategies for securing their liberty.[42] Nonetheless, the narrative of Luiz Gama, politically informed and self-conscious as it is, suggests that the precariousness and even the loss of freedom constituted, paradoxically, an equally relevant dimension of the experience of people of African descent living in the slave society in which manumission rates were perhaps the most significant in modern slavery.

This way of looking at the available evidence allows a fresh perspective on the life history told by José, supposedly a slave of João Goulart, thirty-seven years old, single, and a shoemaker. José was arrested in the city of Rio on

---

42   For example, Sidney Chalhoub, *Visões da Liberdade: Uma História das Últimas Décadas da Escravidão na Corte* (São Paulo, 1990). For recent reviews of the vast body of literature on Brazilian slavery, see Robert Slenes, "Brazil," in *The Oxford Handbook of Slavery in the Americas*, eds. Robert Paquette and Mark Smith (Oxford/ New York, 2010), 111–133; Herbert Klein and João José Reis, "Slavery in Brazil," in *The Oxford Handbook of Latin American History*, ed. José Moya (Oxford/New York, 2011), 181–211.

27 April 1865, accused of murdering his alleged master's son-in-law.[43] He confessed to having stabbed the victim out of despair caused by harsh physical punishment imposed by his master. Answering questions from a police officer, José declared that he had been born free and that his mother was still alive in the county of Pau d'Alho, in Pernambuco. José probably belonged to a family whose members had recently obtained freedom; perhaps the first generation of a family of freed people. His mother carried the names of "Maria" and "Conceição," alluding to the Blessed Virgin Mary, and very common among freed women.[44] In addition, she had managed to have her son baptized by a person of a higher social status, a "Lieutenant Colonel of the National Guard," a strategy to bring recognition to her child's status as free or freed. However, poverty and destitution, and perhaps the hope of achieving better economic means, made José take his chances in the nation's capital, therefore falling prey to criminal gangs willing to enslave free people and sell them to coffee planters.

José's narrative brings us full circle in this text. Pau d'Alho, the county he came from in Pernambuco and where his mother still lived, was considered the main propagation center of the riots against enslavement in January 1852. If José had been 37 years old when arrested in 1865, then he would have been 24 in 1852; old enough to have participated in the riots, or at least to have had strong memories of the event. Finding details of his life history in the archive is a stroke of luck that leads us to think of how much of his narrative of having been illegally enslaved exposed a social logic he could not escape from, and the articulation of a political culture that helped to interpret and deal with the situation in daily life; by himself and others who shared similar experiences and anxieties.

---

43 Arquivo Edgard Leuenroth, UNICAMP, processo criminal (1865–6), Tribunal da Relação do Rio de Janeiro, reel 84.0.ACR.163 (microfilm copy of original belonging to the Arquivo Nacional). I have analyzed this document before in Sidney Chalhoub, "The Precariousness of Freedom," 427–429.

44 Jean Hébrard, "Esclavage et dénomination: imposition et appropriation d'un nom chez les esclaves de la Bahia au XIXe siècle," *Cahiers du Brésil Contemporain* 53/54 (2003), 31–92.

CHAPTER 7

Driving out the Undeserving Poor

Jan Breman

At the beginning of the 21st century, historical research about the toil, troubles and achievements of workers and labor movements is undergoing an exciting transition to a truly *Global* Labor History.[1]

1   Dealing With Vulnerability in the Pre-capitalist Past

Peasant life based on a simple mode of production dominated the pre-capitalist history of a large part of humankind for millennia. Stone-age economics revolving around hunting and gathering, although continuously practiced in many zones of our planet, were steadily surpassed by more sedentary forms of work and living. Lack of control over natural resources did not allow for much more than precarious survival, but the condition of poverty that prevailed was a shared experience. Arrangements for production and livelihood took place in small-scale communities, and the majority of the world's population lived in households that remained embedded in these primary anchor points of ancient civilizations. With a surplus siphoned off at the behest of supra-local lords engaged in early state formation, the peasantry produced for its own frugal subsistence. A communitarian ethos saw to it that they helped each other out in times of hardship; this redistribution was facilitated by the still cashless character of the localized economy. With an increase in output—the result of technological advancements that led to better control over the forces of nature—differentiation in the ownership of means of production set in and gave rise to a more varied life style, also at the local level. This was the beginning of a social divide, which according to Alexis de Tocqueville arose in a new stage of settled—that is, domesticated—agriculture following slash-and-burn cultivation. In his first *Memoir on Pauperism* (1834), he argued that:

> from the moment that landed property was recognized and men had converted the vast forests in fertile land and rich pastures, from this

---

1   Marcel van der Linden, *Workers of the World; Essays Toward a Global Labor History* (Leiden/Boston, 2008), 1.

© JAN BREMAN, 2018 | DOI:10.1163/9789004386617_008

This is an open access chapter distributed under the terms of the prevailing CC-BY-NC License.

DRIVING OUT THE UNDESERVING POOR

moment, individuals arose which accumulated more land than they requited to feed themselves and so perpetuated property in the hands of their progeny.[2]

Although the peasantry became more stratified, a common fund remained in place to deal with periods of collective adversity caused by the failure of harvests. While coping with calamities such as famine, war, or plague was all but impossible on a communal basis, the usual practice was to assume joint responsibility for individualized instances of indigence, and to take care of vulnerable households that were temporarily or indefinitely unable to provide for their livelihood. In these agrarian and still cashless economies, deserving cases for entitlement to rations handed out in kind ran the gamut from illness to old age and other forms of disability. Underlying such support was a binding code of reciprocity, which enabled people in dire straits to fulfil their subsistence needs. Redistributive mechanisms used to be endorsed by religious tenets advocating charity as a pious duty expressed in the collection of *zakat* under Islamic law or the tithe in the world of Christianity. Institutionalized in the Poor Laws throughout Europe from the Late Middle Ages onward, the prime recipients of relief were members of the local community. It is important to add that for the provision of communal care it was not only the non-working poor who qualified, but also people out of work and income at the low tide of the agrarian cycle. To keep them alive was also in the best interests of the nonpoor, who at the peak of agricultural activity might need those idle hands laid off in reserve. It was a situation in which labor power used to be scarcer than land, a large amount of which still remained uncultivated and classified for that reason as an open resource. Landowners needed to protect themselves in such circumstances against the shortage of workers by keeping them attached in bondage.[3]

To prevent or at least slow down an unwelcome trend toward progressive dispossession, many peasant societies were familiar with the custom of the commons, which implied open access to resources jointly held nearby, such as waste land or water, to people acknowledged as shareholding members of the same rural locality. A periodic redistribution of the cultivated land, as for instance in the traditional Russian *mir* or among native tribes in South America, was a more rigorous way to pre-empt progressive differentiation in property,

---

2 Alexis de Tocqueville, *Alexis de Tocqueville's Memoir on Pauperism*, trans. Seymour Drescher (London, 1997), 19, http://www.civitas.org.uk/pdf/Tocqueville_rr2.pdf.

3 Herman Jeremias Nieboer, *Slavery as an Industrial System: Ethnological Researches* (The Hague, 1910).

power, and status. Were such customary forces that pressed for some modicum of compulsory redistribution a feature of all peasant societies? It seems more likely, as Tocqueville surmised, that a large part of humankind used to or came to live and work in societies marked by more or less inequality in all walks of life. In different parts of the world, varieties of feudalism had eroded the free disposal of gains from peasant holdings while silencing the voice of the victimized dispossessed. With large tracts of waste land still lying unproductive, labor was much in demand and had to be appropriated by extra-economic force. Agrestic serfs were at the beck and call of landlords, who attached landless households to their domain in a relationship of patronage and exploitation. Even then, while a set of notables engaged in surplus extraction and imposed their elevated ranking as a gentry in the maximization of power and status, the moral imperative of togetherness in a frame of proximity and familiarity prescribed that the patrons felt bound to allot a minor part of their proceeds, which allowed them a carefree existence and to take care of their clients who lacked the bare essentials required for survival.[4]

For the sake of keeping social cohesion intact, as well as justified from all sides, some form of entitlement had to be apportioned to the hapless needful bereft of the ability to stock up and stay alive independently. Thus, deprivation and accumulation did not become separated dynamics of adversity and prosperity, but instead remained intertwined in a corporate circuit of calibrated give and take. It was essentially an attempt to safeguard the inclusion of all stakeholders who could rightfully claim to belong to the community. Their interdependence rested on a face-to-face relationship, and was facilitated by an exchange of goods and services in kind rather than in cash. Consolidation of the trend toward unequal distribution was made conditional on granting the right to the inclusion of households lagging behind in the generation of surplus due to mishaps beyond their will or control. Of major significance was a clause in the customary social contract that acknowledged the claim for relief when out of work. Facing bouts of unemployability in the erratic agrarian cycle—leading to a livelihood deficit that could not be bridged by savings set aside—was met by support from the common fund.

2   The Undeserving Poor

However small scale in nature the communal membership may have been, outsiders were identified who remained excluded from whatever transfers

---

4   Jan Breman, *Patronage and Exploitation: Changing Agrarian Relations in South Gujarat, India* (Berkeley, 1974).

DRIVING OUT THE UNDESERVING POOR

took place at the local level. These were able-bodied people who either did not prefer to or did not manage to find admittance as fully-fledged members of a community in a relationship meant to be reciprocal. Many of those effectively excluded were victims of adversities that drove them to cut loose from wherever their origin had been. However, there were also people who, in order to escape being tied down in bondage, opted to remain footloose and did not want to settle down indefinitely. Habituated to wander around sourcing whatever occasional reprieve that happened to come their way, they turned up at weekly markets, annual fairs, and religious festivals to beg for alms, to offer their services as bards, conjurers, quacks, tinkers, fortune tellers, or tricksters, but also as ordinary workers willing to do a fair day's labor in or outside of agriculture. Their movement followed the rhythm of the seasons and they traveled around in search of any makeshift employment. This was a contingent of wage hunters and gatherers remaining on the margins of the localized economy, who peddled whatever they could lay their hands on or just chose to stay put waiting for a windfall to come their way and otherwise resorted to petty pilfering, They made off when their presence was no longer required, or were chased away when inhabitants of the locality turned against them. Blamed for shirking and loitering, these drifters found no access to mainstream society because of their wayward, abrasive, and shady character. In this stigmatized view, they were not torn loose from their social origin due to some misfortune, but had opted for a life of vagrancy. It is a portrait that takes sedentarism for granted and is apt to treat a taste for wandering—such as practiced by nomads, transporters, and other kinds of itinerant labor—with dismay and suspicion. The norm was settlement, and the acceptance of bondage in one form or the other. Those who remained footloose and opted for that unsettled way of life stood accused of escaping from social dependency and control.

> Society was ordered in hierarchies that were unified by paternalism. Every man had his place, his function and his master in this scheme of things. There was no room for the vagrant: he was "masterless," and thus had broken away from the established order. He was idle, too, and thus not performing a useful function in the Common Weal.[5]

Such people were held in disrepute for having absconded from a regular existence; the label attached to them was that of the "undeserving poor." As long as they remained small in number, this "parasitic" residuum did not really pose

---

5 A.L. Beier, "Vagrants and the Social Order in Elizabethan England," *Past & Present* 64 (August 1974): 3–29, here: 27.

a danger to the established order. Nevertheless, their floating around constituted a nuisance difficult to tolerate, since this good-for-nothing lot adroitly refused to bow down in docile subservience. Such was expected to be the habitus befitting the people without means who were rewarded for being willing to demonstrate their subaltern state: Because the incidental support the "deserving poor" were entitled to when confronted with adversity had to be accepted with gratitude, deference, and a show of allegiance. Another understanding of gestures of beneficence was that these prevented the recipients from stoking unrest and resorting to illegally appropriating what they were denied. Suspected of attempting to resist their commodification as a dispossessed underclass, itinerant people may have preferred a life of vagrancy rather than settling down in dependency or even servitude. All said and done, the divide between insiders eligible for communal relief and outsiders cut off from the local dole was not a hard and fast one but ranged over a continuum of restrictiveness to leniency, which used to be practiced in an arbitrary fashion, either mercilessly withheld or on the spur of the moment generously granted.

In the course of time, the linkage between the small-scale community and the outside world did increase. A decisive feature in the enlargement of scale was the loss of autonomy to settle matters and issues at the local level. This mandate tended to become usurped from seats of power higher up, and was made manifest in the downward imposition of administrative and political authority. Although the peasant community never had the self-sufficiency ascribed to it in an image which portrayed the village as autarkic—a closed system of production for consumption—there is no lack of evidence that with growing control over the resource base, goods and services came to be exchanged in widening networks of circulation. Domination and interference from outside over the local order, and infrastructural development with improved means of transport, allowed for trade routes to be established over longer distances than before. Agriculture still dictated life and work, and peasant society remained intact, although restructured into greater complexity. In addition to a growing division of labor and a lengthening of the chain of dependency, the outcome was a more differentiated economic-cum-social fabric marked by starker contrasts separating a local elite equipped with a disproportionate share of the means of production, from a sizable segment at the bottom made more dispossessed. The trend toward marketization meant not only that an increasing part of the output realized left the locality, but also that commodities and services previously unknown became available to those who could afford them. The inevitable result was a divergence class-wise in lifestyle, and a growing conflict of interests between winners and losers. The surge in

DRIVING OUT THE UNDESERVING POOR

commerce was accompanied by monetization, ultimately leading to a drastic change in the relations of production. It was a shift that found expression both in more pronounced swings in the demand for labor due to increased seasonality, and the replacement of payment in kind for labor rendered in cash. The proximity and familiarity that were the hallmarks of the peasant locality broke down to make way for a contractual distancing between the segments that had been tied to each other from generation to generation in a setting of complementarity and reciprocity.

One of the consequences of the loss of cohesion that kept the households in the small-scale community connected to each other, was a rapid increase in the number of people cut loose from wherever they belonged in terms of work and livelihood. From the sixteenth to the nineteenth century, this denigrated contingent, for a variety of reasons unsettled from their roots and habitat, increased in many parts of the world to a much larger footloose army than had existed previously. Again, a substantial contingent among them may have taken to the road in order to shy away from becoming entrapped as a sedentarized commodity, tied down in debt bondage. They joined the ranks of the multi-class riffraff that Karl Marx identified as the *Lumpenproletariat*, which in his all too scornful imagery was prone to criminality.

> Alongside decayed roués with dubious means of subsistence and of dubious origin, alongside ruined and adventurous off shoots of the bourgeoisie, were vagabonds, discharged soldiers, discharged jailbirds, escaped galley slaves, swindlers, mountebanks, lazzaroni [homeless idlers], pickpockets, tricksters, gamblers, maquereaux [pimps], brothel keepers, porters, literati, organ grinders, rag-pickers, knife grinders, tinkers, beggars—in short the whole indefinite, disintegrated mass, thrown hither and thither, which the French call la bohème.[6]

Commitments of mutuality that used to bond households together no longer matched—or were even antagonistic to—concerns resulting from differential involvement in networks of exchange that reached beyond local leverage. Systems of poor relief, as they had operated in the past, came under pressure; the consequence of a spiraling clash of interests between dominant stakeholders engaged in a strategy of accumulation while the dominated ones were forced to make do with the wherewithal left to them. The increased vulnerability of subordinated households was compounded by the loss of bargaining power

---

6 Karl Marx, "The Eighteenth Brumaire of Louis Bonaparte (1851–52)," *Karl Marx/Frederick Engels Collected Works (MECW)* 11 (1976): 99–197, here: 149.

142 JAN BREMAN

they had earlier enjoyed in a localized frame. Intruding market forces from higher up were fortified by a more encompassing and effective span of control, which required the exercise of jurisdiction within a much wider setting.

3 Capitalism in the Countryside

The dissolution of communal coalescence in the agrarian-rural order preceding the capitalist one, has first and foremost to be understood as heralding changes in the relations of production caused by the advancement of the new mode of accumulation facilitated by new storage and transport techniques. What had gone on before, patterned and institutionalized in vast diversity, was not immediately and contemporaneously obliterated, but lingered on, also in economic zones that were the first to yield to the spreading march of capitalism. The shift that found its impetus in a trend toward the commodification of land and labor was first described and analyzed for different parts of Europe. Karl Polányi aptly phrased the gist of the new deal that came about:

> No relief any longer for the able-bodied unemployed, no minimum wages either, not a safeguarding of the right to live. Labor should be dealt with as that which it was, a commodity which must find its price in the market.[7]

His succinct statement indicates how the balance between capital and labor became more tilted, prioritizing the interests of the former and victimizing those of the latter. Much of the literature on the subject consists of accounts specifying what was going on in different parts of Great Britain. The transformation that materialized gave rise to a major increase in labor mobility, and may already have taken shape in the agrarian-rural landscape before catching on in other sectors mainly concentrated in the, until then, relatively small urban economy.

In a rationalization drive from the second half of the eighteenth century onward, British rural magnates introduced new farming technology and crop rotation. They added to their property land that had been part of the village commons, forcing enclosure either in private deals or legislated by a parliament in which landlords called the shots. What used to be open fields, subdivided into holdings that the agrarian poor had cultivated for their mainstay, were now fenced off and managed by the owners of large estates. As a

---

7   Karl Polányi, *The Great Transformation. The Political and Economic Origins of Our Times* (Boston, 1944), 117.

DRIVING OUT THE UNDESERVING POOR

consequence of the enclosure movement, the yield of land was made more productive and commercially more profitable. The spirit of accumulation was well served by the concentration of ownership into fewer hands; those of the rural gentry and a peasant segment consisting of well-to-do freeholders mixed with more powerful tenant farmers. At the polar opposite end of the hierarchy, a very sizable class of petty cultivators lost their holdings to join the ranks of the landless proletariat and make a mean living as waged workers in a tight and seasonally fluctuating labor market. The congestion that built up at the bottom of the rural-agrarian economy was a major cause of rising destitution.

The "Speenhamland Ordinance," passed at the end of the eighteenth century, was a regional regulation resorted to in South England in an attempt to redress rural distress caused by soaring grain prices. Laboring households unable to afford their regular food ration received a supplement to make up their budget deficit; a subsidy that was charged to the landowners of the parish. This add-on, dependent on the price of bread and the size of the household, was granted to allay fears of growing discontent among the rural proletariat, and was made when the French Revolution was in full swing. It enabled landowners to keep the reservoir of cheap labor intact, which could be tapped whenever required. Although the subsidy did not last long—the cash supplement was withdrawn again when the Napoleonic wars were over and the threat of social revolt subsided—it must have whetted the appetite of the underclass for a guaranteed minimum income with which to satisfy their basic needs throughout the annual cycle. Once the threat of revolution started to fade away in the early nineteenth century, the rural poor in England also were back to being exposed to the vagaries of an overcrowded labor market.

Could communal support as provided under the Poor Laws at least keep the immiseration of a huge and expanding underclass within bounds? This was this question that, quite unforeseen, came to preoccupy Alexis de Tocqueville. In an essay that for a long time remained fairly unnoticed, the French aristocrat gave vent to his views on pauperism and how to deal with it. Like many of his contemporaries around the mid-nineteenth century, the political philosopher expressed his belief that public welfare demoralized the laboring poor, rather than alleviating their unfortunate plight. In his considered opinion, it debased them to a condition of permanent inferiority. On his return from the famed trip made to the New World, he paid a short and private visit to England in 1833. The estate owner with whom he stayed in south England was a peer, like him a landlord who also acted as a justice of the peace. At his invitation, Tocqueville attended court sessions in which suits were brought by the poor against the parish or the other way round. He astutely observed that the ire felt by the payers of the poor rate was not only directed against the indolent underclass, but also extended to the local overseers empowered to tax the non-poor of the parish for the levy they were obliged to contribute, and who made decisions on granting or rejecting claims for benefit made by impoverished inhabitants. Tocqueville contrarily argued that:

> Any measure which establishes legal charity on a permanent basis and gives it an administrative form thereby creates an idle and lazy class, living at the expense of the industrial and working class.[8]

The voices clamoring for amendments to the Poor Laws had already prevailed when Tocqueville was still busy writing up the findings of his first tour. The revision parliament debated and in 1834 enacted reduced the cost of looking after the poor by taking away the right to public relief when no local employment could be found. The benefit was forthwith withheld from the poor of working age and exclusively provided to the deserving non-laboring poor: All those of old age, widows, the handicapped, and the chronically ill; at least, when they were fortunate enough to pass the "means test," confirming that they were not receiving support from relatives or other donors. The decision to make poor relief conditional on proper behavior, attach conditions such as workfare under surveillance in poor houses, and add penal sanctions to prevent or at best restrain false claims, was much inspired by the need to show the better-off public that support would only be extended to deserving cases and even then under duress. Access to social assistance was given a coercive twist. As Peter Townsend summarized, the rationale of the Poor Laws amendment was to place the burden of destitution upon the individual and to treat that individual's poverty as simply a question of his or her moral fault.[9] Those with a right to relief before, able to work but previously acknowledged as being part and parcel of the deserving poor, were reclassified as non-deserving for their incidental failure to find gainful employment. That stigma would last under the by now rapidly expanding regime of capitalism.

> The emphasis given to selective assistance—together with the continued refusal to compare conditions of the poor with those of the rich and match their rights—reflected the distrust and lack of acquaintance of

---

8 De Tocqueville, *Memoir on Pauperism*, 30.

9 Peter Townsend, "The Right to Social Security and National Development; Lessons from OECD experience for low-income countries," Issues in Social Protection. Discussion Paper No.18, Social Security Department, ILO. (Geneva, 2007).

DRIVING OUT THE UNDESERVING POOR

leading classes and administrators with the poor that had marked English class attitudes for generations.[10]

The author's observation is no less valid for the manner in which poverty came to be dealt with elsewhere in Europe's past.

The growing reluctance of the non-poor to contribute to a common fund spent on labor labeled as unwilling to search for waged work and thus take care of their own sustenance, seemed to be the immediate ground for the reform of the Poor Laws that was carried through. More hidden sentiments behind expressing annoyance at what was portrayed as a "free riders'" mentality were inspired by a steadfast refusal in the drawn-out capitalist transformation to accept maintenance of the idle poor as a burden on the localized commonwealth in which all must share. It was certainly no coincidence that the revisions to the Poor Laws were passed by parliament two years after the Reform Act of 1832 was approved, which gave suffrage to the middle class. A covertly held consideration of the revision was the widely felt need to drive the land-poor and landless out of their habitat in times of distress. Waiting until their labor power would be in demand again, they had been accustomed to make do with what local relief provided. Thomas Hardy wrote that in the aftermath of the ordinance, agricultural laborers wandered around like birds of passage and trekked to towns and cities in desperate search of a job.[11] Uprooted from where and how they used to work and live, this reserve army now stood accused of escaping into vagrancy, and of a stubborn unwillingness to resettle in sedentary dependency. In a case study on pauperism in the late-Victorian decades, Elizabeth Hurren discusses how the makeshift economy that arose— with work available off and on or not at all—heightened reliance on public relief. However, under the new amendment, the agrarian poor were cut off from such support to alleviate their immiseration. In the county Hurren focused on, the landless laborers tenaciously and in collective action resisted becoming excluded from what they had fought for as their customary right since the late-medieval centuries.[12]

In Germany, Max Weber's treatise on the agrarian question toward the end of the nineteenth century is of equal relevance for understanding how the social question was handled in rural Europe on the verge of the transition to

---

10   Townsend, *The Right to Social Security*, 28.
11   Thomas Hardy, "The Dorsetshire Labourer," *Longman's Magazine* (1883). Republished as *The Dorset Farm Labourer: Past and Present* (Dorchester, 1884).
12   Elizabeth T. Hurren, *Protesting About Pauperism. Poverty, Politics and Poor Relief in Late-Victorian England, 1870–1900* (Woodbridge, 2015).

capitalism. Elaborating on the concept of patrimonial rule practiced in the eastern provinces, he characterized the relationship between the landlord (*Junker*)—who tended to maximize power and status instead of production—and his farm servant, as one of bondage that took the form of a beck-and-call relationship. These servants had previously been attached to their master's household on an annual contract according to which they received discretionary benevolence for the ongoing though erratic use made of their labor power. It was a form of servitude that modified ruthless exploitation with features of patronage.

> The master 'owes' the subject something as well, not juridically, but morally. Above all—if only in his own interest—he must protect him against the outside world, and help him in need. He must also treat him 'humanely,' and especially he must restrict the exploitation of his performance to what is 'customary.' On the ground of a domination whose aim is not material enrichment but the fulfillment of the master's own needs, he can do so without prejudicing his own interest because, as his needs cannot expand qualitatively and, on principle, unlimitedly, his demands differ only quantitatively from those of his subjects. And such restriction is positively useful to the master, as not only the security of his domination, but also its results greatly depend on the disposition and mood of the subordinates. The subordinate morally owes the master assistance by all the means available to him.[13]

The *Verein für Sozialpolitik* (Social Policy Association) took the initiative to launch an inquiry into agrarian labor relations in different parts of the country. In the voluminous questionnaire sent out in 1890, only landowners were addressed—over 3,000 of them—but no data was collected from the farmworkers themselves. Their omission from the investigations was criticized by Weber, who accepted the request to analyze the findings reported for the eastern provinces.[14] In this first and only empirical research project he handled, he focused his attention on the inroads capitalism had made in the rural economy east of the Elbe river during the previous few decades. A drastic change in the crop pattern caused by a higher volume of international grain trade had led to a pronounced seasonality in the cultivation cycle. In reaction

---

13   Max Weber, *Wirtschaft und Gesellschaft, Grundriss der Sozialökonomik, III Abteilung* (Tübingen, 1922), 682.

14   Paul F. Lazarsfeld and Anthony R. Oberschall, "Max Weber and Empirical Social Research," *American Sociological Review* 30, no. 2 (1965): 185–199.

DRIVING OUT THE UNDESERVING POOR

to the accelerated pace of commercialization, the estate owners in Prussia had started to replace their servile workforce by free, though casual, labor hired only when their presence was required in the peak periods. Gangs from Poland and Russia—"barbarian hordes" in Weber's vocabulary—with less physical strength, but willing to work on very low wages, flooded the countryside of eastern Germany in the busy months, to disappear again when employment fell. In the migrant worker, the landlord found what he wanted: A commodity. In Weber's view, the seasonal arrival of this floating segment made manifest the class struggle waged in the countryside of eastern Germany.

> The migrant worker, torn from his family and usual environment, is regarded as simple labour power both by the landlords and by himself. The barracks of the migrant workers are the money-equivalents of the slave trade barracks of antiquity. The estate owner saves on workers' housing, since accommodation for the migrants costs little or nothing. He also has no need to allocate plots of land, but above all he is not regulated by laws governing conditions of work and pay. Thus while the seasonal wage rates are higher, taken over the year the employer lays out no more, usually less, than he used for a resident worker throughout the year.[15]

Landlords were no longer willing to guarantee the livelihood of their farm servants in the relentless drive for proletarianization. While circulating migrants from far away were hired whenever required, the local landless could not survive on intermittent casual work. They had become superfluous to demand, and took off to the city to find work in industry, construction, transport, or any other sector of the now rapidly expanding and booming urban economy. However, farmhands did not opt out of agrarian employment only to avoid a decline in their living standards. Weber argued that an additional reason for the land flight of the attached farmhands was motivated by a lust for freedom; their craving to get out of personal subservience to a master and his whimsical commands.

4 How to Deal with Pauperism?

Dissatisfied with what he had come to know during his first short visit to England, Tocqueville decided to probe more deeply into the causes and impact

---

15 Max Weber, "Development Tendencies in the Situation of East Elbian Rural Labourers," trans. Keith Tribe, *Economy and Society* 8, no. 2 (1979): 177–205, here: 193.

of the ongoing pauperization. He returned in 1835 on a second tour, which brought him to Manchester where the land flight of many people hailing from the countryside in Middle England and Ireland ended. He showed himself to be horrified by what he saw and heard in this brutal heartland of capitalist industrialism, and described in vivid detail the immense squalor of industrial work and life as well as the stark contrast between wealth and misery:

> you will see the huge palaces of industry. You will hear the noise of furnaces, the whistle of steam. These vast structures keep air and light out of the human habitation which they dominate; they envelop them in perpetual fog; here is the slave, there is the master; there the wealth of some, here the poverty of most; there the organized efforts of thousands produce, to the profit of one man, what society has not learnt to give. Here the weakness of the individual seems more feeble and helpless even than in the middle of a wilderness; here the effects, there the causes ... From this foul drain the greatest stream of human industry flows out to fertilise the whole world. From this filthy sewer pure gold flows. Here humanity attains its most complete development and its most brutish; here civilization works its miracles, and civilized man is turned back almost into a savage.[16]

His portrait was strikingly similar to the one Friedrich Engels would publish ten years later.[17] Pauperism was the inevitable outcome of this hellish kind of industrialism, and the by now well-known author tersely commented that the condition of the poor was nowhere as abysmal as in England. His judgement was that the laboring poor had become entrapped in a new form of servitude. From his sojourn in industrial England, Tocqueville journeyed on to agrarian Ireland where in July and August 1835 he took stock of the disastrous impact the enclosure movement had on the dispossessed victims. From his coach— the seasoned traveler carefully abstained from coming too close to the scene of pauperism—Tocqueville glimpsed the hand-to-mouth existence he came across. The subhuman standard to which the Irish peasantry had sunk preceded the Great Famine that broke out barely ten years later, leading to the death of about one million Irish, while another million left home to emigrate. In the ensuing havoc, the country lost a fifth to a quarter of its population.

16　Alexis de Tocqueville, *Journeys to England and Ireland*, ed. J.P. Mayer (Forge Village, MA, 1958), 107–108.

17　Friedrich Engels, *The Condition of the Working Class in England in 1844*, trans. F.K. Wischnewetzky (New York, 1887).

DRIVING OUT THE UNDESERVING POOR 149

In his first *Memoir on Pauperism*, the aristocrat had spoken out in favor of private charity to alleviate poverty, arguing that personalized transfers strengthened the moral bond between donors and recipients. While voluntary gifts contributed to social harmony, he posited that public relief was disgruntledly given as well as received. Its effect was to raise resentment on both sides, and would instigate a class struggle erupting in revolution.[18] Tocqueville had second thoughts, however, when confronted on his second tour with the abominable plight of the workforce in the "satanic mills" in Manchester, and in Ireland, with the callous behavior of the estate owner who could not care less about the destitution of the tenants chased off by him.

> He will take walks in immense grounds surrounded by high walls. Within his park everything breathes splendor; outside misery groans, but he does not notice it. His doormen take care to keep the poor from his sight and if by accident he meets one, he answers his entreaties by saying, 'I make it a duty not to encourage begging.' He has big, fat dogs, and his fellows die at his door. Not only do they not help the poor in any way, but they profit from their needs by charging enormous rents which they spend in France or Italy. If for a short time one returns among us, it is only to evict a farmer who is behind with the rent and chase him from his home.[19]

When asking one of his high-class informants about agrarian relationships in the country's past, Tocqueville was given to understand that the peasants also hated their landlords then. However, they used to submit to their ordeal with a patience they had since lost. The problem arose, he was told, from the destruction of the moral tie between rich and poor, who had come to live far apart from each other. He ended his second tour to England and Ireland convinced of the devastating impact the new and spreading mode of production was having in urban as well as rural settings.

What about private charity to solve what the social question is all about? On his initial confrontation with widespread destitution, Tocqueville had no doubt that this was a better alternative to public relief. Today's neoconservative apostles of market fundamentalism could not agree more with the stance taken by him, which is why his first *Memoir on Pauperism* surfaced again in 1997. Long ignored in Tocqueville's body of work, the conservative think tank Civitas released it on their website for dissemination free of charge. The reprint from the original edition was augmented with an introduction by

---

18   De Tocqueville, *Memoir on Pauperism*, 17.
19   De Tocqueville, *Journeys to England and Ireland*, 165.

Gertrude Himmelfarb, a stalwart of the American caucus spreading the reactionary dogma of market fundamentalism. In her comments, she stresses not only the vices of the paupers, then as well as now, but also "the undue degree of state control and centralization" to which mandatory public welfarism gives rise.[20] This historian's main attention is clearly focused on the social question in today's global order and, of course, all forms of public action or agency—from the New Deal in the United States to the welfare state in Britain and Europe—are anathema to her. In the neoconservative scenario, the poor and paupers are bid welcome to join the better-off in the race to accumulation and are then lambasted for their failure to do so. Tocqueville's unequivocal condemnation of public welfare explains why the Institute for the Study of Civic Society decided to republish *Memoir on Pauperism* as a *Rediscovered Riches* publication. Its renowned author was praised not only for his objection to the way in which the undeserving poor were pampered out of the common fund, but also for his critique of the government machinery set up to cater to the needs of this underclass clientele. He minced no words in taking these public officials to task, and it comes as no surprise that his scornful exposure of the costly, bossy, but useless bunch of officials in charge of public relief is much appreciated by today's anti-state cabal. Its proponents are clamoring for the empowerment of civic society, by which they mean something quite different from the usual brand of non-government organizations that advocate all forms of welfare interventions. While such agencies advocate on behalf of people whose voice is not heard and whose interests are not served, the former are neoconservative apostles of a civic society preaching the gospel of individual freedom. Their main objective behind the virtuous façade is not to upset the excessively skewed distribution of wealth and privilege.

Tocqueville decided on a more in-depth study of the problem of pauperism, which was very much *en vogue* and debated in Great Britain, and had already returned two years after his first visit for a second tour. Taking stock of what was going on, which included consulting policymakers and front-rank figures, led him to a fundamentally different opinion. As in England, Tocqueville did not trouble himself to meet with the outcasts when touring around Ireland, but put on record what he found out about their plight by keeping the company of the upper-class authorized to know. In his interview with the bishop of Carlow, he learned that the land in this county was basically the property of two families. The new system of cultivation that had been introduced meant the end of smallholdings parceled out in a tenancy relationship. One of the landowners had evicted 150 families. The bishop's colleague in Kilkenny told

---

20   Gertrude Himmelfarb, "Introduction," in *De Tocqueville's Memoir on Pauperism,* 1–16.

DRIVING OUT THE UNDESERVING POOR

his guest a similar story. All the arable land had been turned into grassland, so that 10 shepherds were now enough where there had previously been 150 laborers. The dispossession, which had already been going on for decades, ended in wide-scale impoverishment and the absence of public relief in Ireland, and to the starvation of the people. Was the gist of his much more nuanced reappraisal dealt with fairly and fully in the introductory commentary of the 1997 edition of his *Memoir*? Not really, and I fully agree with other critics who have taken Himmelfarb to task for having misreported the author's thoughts on how to tackle the social question (see for example Keslassy and Cruikshank).[21] In summarizing Tocqueville's stance, the current brand of neoconservative historians have grossly understated both his incisive—though low-key—admonitions of capitalism, and his firm stance that the privileged rich to a large extent bear responsibility for the adversity of the poor. Tocqueville's sociological imagination induced him to highlight pauperism as the outcome of a civilizational trend toward increasing inequality in the transition from an agrarian-rural to an urban-industrial way of life. In his opinion, dispossession was a major reason for the growing social divide. That verdict, already reached in the early stage of capitalist development, has with its spread over the global economy become more topical and relevant than ever before.

The transition from an agrarian to an industrial mode of production played an important role in Tocqueville's understanding of why, when, and how pauperism came about. The gap between the rich and the poor grew wider, because the class at the top developed new tastes, which in order to be satisfied, required the production of manufactured commodities. The gratification of what became an insatiable penchant for consumerism triggered a more diversified system of production. These dynamics led to a restructuring of the workforce, which meant that "men left the plow for the shuttle and the hammer; they moved from the thatched cottage to the factory."[22] The industrial economy that emerged made the working classes more vulnerable, since it increased their dependency on market forces over which they had no control. This was due to fluctuating demand ending in job loss or displacement when artisanal skills became outdated and replaced by new crafts and wares. The industrial class, which gives so much impetus to the well-being of others, is thus much more exposed to sudden and irremediable evils, Tocqueville surmised, with

---

21   Barbara Cruikshank, "Tocqueville's Authority: Feminism and Reform 'Between Government and Civil Society,'" in *Feminist Interpretations of Alexis de Tocqueville*, eds. J. Locke and E.H. Bunting (State College, PE, 2009), 305–335; Eric Keslassy, *Le Libéralisme de Tocqueville à l'épreuve du Paupérisme* (Paris, 2000).

22   De Tocqueville, *Memoir on Pauperism*, 22.

the paradoxical consequence that "the richer a nation is, the more the number of those who appeal to public charity must multiply."[23] So what should be done to enable the victims of destitution to live up to their human condition? With keen insight, Tocqueville observed that the needs of the impoverished are elastic and cannot be fixed and kept constant at a minimum level that is indispensable for sheer survival. The class in destitution is prone to emulate the lifestyle of the non-poor, and what used to be the desires of yesteryear for elite comfort is bound to change over time into habits which shortly also become daily necessities for those at the bottom of the pile. Tocqueville formulated what in sociological jargon is known as the phenomenon of relative deprivation, which suggests that who you are and what you do not have, but want, should be seen in the wider frame of inter-class relationships. The basic message his memoir conveys is that prosperity and pauperism are interdependent and have to be contextualized in the total social fabric. Having initially rejected public relief as an ineffective or even counterproductive palliative, Tocqueville was more positive about private charity, which encourages individual transfers from the well-to-do to the impoverished. On the other hand, at the end of his first tour he had already conceded that this discretionary remedy cannot be relied upon, does not deliver timely or adequately when and where required, and is "not aroused by every cry of pain." Having weighed both options, the author's starting point in his consideration of welfare provisioning is that the poor have an absolute and pre-emptive right to help from society in coping with their misfortune.

5 Redistribution

If pauperism cannot be redressed by either public or private welfare, what other course of action then remains to solve the social question? This was the query that brought Tocqueville back for his second visit to Great Britain. The findings resulting from his travel to industrial England and agrarian Ireland did not appear in print straightaway, and this is why the latter-day proponents of neoconservative policies are apt to conclude that Tocqueville's treatise on pauperism remained a project that he failed to finish. This is a misconceived assessment, underrating the importance of the manuscript that the author did produce but never published. As Himmelfarb states, "because the problem of industrial pauperism seemed to him intractable." She follows up this erroneous judgement with the lament that the second essay lacks the sweep

---

23   De Tocqueville, *Memoir on Pauperism*, 22–25.

DRIVING OUT THE UNDESERVING POOR 153

and passion of the first one. Once again, this interlocutor's final conclusion is out of tune with Tocqueville's recommendations. Her complaint is his failure to apprehend the potentialities of industrialism to improve the condition of the poor without recourse to charity; private or public. The author, so highly praised for what he condemned—the moral hazards of public welfarism— now stands accused for his stubborn refusal to profess unconditional faith in the virtues and blessings of capitalism. The same disappointment is expressed more forcefully in the foreword by Max Hartwell to the 1997 edition of the first memoir:

> Tocqueville, however, did not foresee that economic growth, largely the consequence of private enterprise, would raise all living standards, and that continuing private charity would help to alleviate hardship. He clearly recognized the moral hazard of public welfare, but too easily accepted that its consequence was universal degradation. He did anticipate, however, the problems of the welfare state that are still with us.[24]

The criticism expressed was directed at Tocqueville's opinion that the growing disparity in the world at large—further enrichment at the top and steady impoverishment below—could only be halted and reversed by a fundamental reallocation of what produces welfare and well-being for all. To start with, redistribution of land was the forceful recipe he prescribed for redressing immiseration in the English and Irish countryside. In the same vein was his proposal to encourage industrial laborers to have a stake in the enterprises in which they work, to create space for voluntary associations along both vertical and horizontal lines of collaboration, to establish workshops on their own, and to set up savings banks funded with contributions out of the wealth generated by industrial production. While Tocqueville was skeptical about the short-term viability of initiatives taken on the basis of collective action from below, he predicted that in due course, with increased exposure to education and growing tolerance for workers' cooperatives, impediments to self-management could be overcome. This remedy of worker's emancipation—essentially a plea in favor of small-scale manufacture and commodity production in partnership—is glossed over rather than discussed by today's critics of public agency and by institutions who keep hammering on the immorality of pauperism. No doubt, this is not the sweep and passion which Himmelfarb wants to find back in Tocqueville's writings, but that is because in her ideological lexicon, enrichment and impoverishment should not be seen as progressing in tandem, but as

---

24   Max Hartwell, "Foreword," in *De Tocqueville's Memoir on Pauperism*, vi.

contrasts that testify to a behavioral divide deserving respectively praise versus blame. In a scathing review, Michael Katz has shown how in the late-twentieth century, reactionary voices came to dominate the debate on poverty in America and why, in the prevailing policies and politics, a regime of welfare grounded in equality as the organizing principle of the social fabric was jettisoned.[25]

Did Tocqueville's reservations and warnings of the dangers of a looming class conflict, discussed at length in his notebooks as well as in the manuscript of his second memoir, show him to be adverse to capitalism? Not at all, because the question he raised was how to imbibe the paupers with the accumulative instinct on which the spirit of capitalism is founded. Redistribution of property was his plain and straightforward solution; a remedy that he specified by pointing out the imperative need for land reforms to mitigate the impact of agrarian dispossession, and thus prevent the exodus from the countryside of a proletarianized class in desperate search of regular work and income. My reading of his work, the first and second memoirs, leads me to conclude that Tocqueville rested his case and gave up writing about the social question. Not because he had failed to find a solution to the problem, but because the policy of redistribution, which he proposed for redressing pauperism, was rejected out of hand by the powers that be. He reported on wage levels going down rather than up, and on the substitution of women and children for men in the Manchester mills because they were cheaper to employ as well as easier to exploit. In his second memoir, Tocqueville placed in the foreground that accumulation and sharing should be seen as complementary and not contradictory. The inequality that he found in his travels around Britain frightened him, and the reforms he advocated aimed to defuse the widening gap between poverty and prosperity as well as to reduce the increase in distance between the classes at the top and bottom of society. At the end of his first visit to England he had already expressed his amazement about land concentration in the hands of a small aristocratic elite leading to a ceaseless growth of the proletarian class:

"The English are still imbued with that doctrine, which is at least debatable, that great properties are necessary for the improvement of agriculture, and they still seem convinced that extreme inequality of wealth is the natural order of things."[26]

Of course, redistribution of property—rural and urban as well as agrarian and industrial—as the way out of the dilemma fell on deaf ears, and this was why he quit. Was his soft-spoken warning heeded later on? What Tocqueville

---

25   Michael B. Katz, *The Undeserving Poor: America's Enduring Confrontation With Poverty* (New York, 2013), second and revised edition, 156–202.

26   De Tocqueville, *Journeys to England and Ireland*, 72.

DRIVING OUT THE UNDESERVING POOR

diagnosed as a broken moral bond, an alliance of trust between elite and underdogs that he projected back to a rustic past, has failed to be repaired. The nascent capitalism that Tocqueville found in Great Britain in 1835 would become the dominant mode of production in the world at large. The crux of his analysis is that accumulation and sharing must expand hand in hand, while in reality the former has tended to increase at the cost of the latter. Tocqueville realized that he had reached a dead end; the steadfast refusal of the owners of capital to compromise on their accumulative drive when that also implied the denial of stakes held in the lower echelons of the economy. It happens to be an unwillingness regimenting the capitalist mode of existence in the past and the present.

CHAPTER 8

Area Studies and the Development of Global Labor History

Andreas Eckert

1 Risen from the Dead

During the 1980s and 1990s, area studies and labor history both experienced a period of "*baisse*" and were given numerous obituaries. Harry Harootunian, a historian of Japan, labeled area studies a "dinosaur" and regarded, for instance, Asian studies as an illusion because, as he argued, there is no such thing as "Asia."[1] David Ludden, a specialist of South Asia, lamented that "there is no theory of area studies or of area-specific knowledge, only a set of institutional, personal, and fragmented disciplinary, market and professional interests that converge chaotically in questions of funding."[2] Mahmood Mamdani, a political scientist from Uganda teaching in New York, stated that the area studies enterprise is underpinned by two problematic core methodological claims. "The first sees state boundaries as boundaries of knowledge, thereby turning political into epistemological boundaries." This led to the rule that every area studies specialist "must cultivate his or her own 'local' patch." The second methodological claim he criticized is "that knowledge is about the production of facts. This view translates into a stubborn resistance to theory in the name of valorizing the fact." However, "the single most important failing of area studies is that it has failed to frame the study of the 'third world' in broad intellectual terms."[3] After 9/11, Middle Eastern Studies in particular were suspected of cooperating

---

1 See Harry Harootunian, *History's Disquiet: Modernity, Cultural Practice, and the Question of Everyday Life* (New York, 2000), 41ff. See also Miyoshi Masao and Harry Harootunian, eds., *Learning Places: The Afterlives of Area Studies* (Durham, NC, 2002). For a more ambivalent view of the example of Africa, see Paul Tiyambe Zeleza, ed., *The Study of Africa, Vol. I: Disciplinary and Interdisciplinary Encounters* (Dakar/Oxford, 2006); *Vol. II: Global and Transnational Encounters* (Dakar/Oxford, 2007).

2 David Ludden, *Area Studies in the Age of Globalization* (January 1998), http://www.sas.upenn.edu/~dludden/GlobalizationAndAreaStudies.htm.

3 Mahmood Mamdani, *When Victims Become Killers. Colonialism, Nativism, and the Genocide in Rwanda* (Oxford, 2001), XXII–XIV. This type of critique follows the path set by Edward Said's *Orientalism* (New York, 1978). A good introduction to the effects of Said's study is provided by Ulrike Freitag, "The Critique of Orientalism," in *Companion to Historiography*, ed. Michael

---

© ANDREAS ECKERT, 2018 | DOI:10.1163/9789004386617_009

This is an open access chapter distributed under the terms of the prevailing CC-BY-NC License.

AREA STUDIES AND THE DEVELOPMENT OF GLOBAL LABOR HISTORY   157

with "the enemy."[4] The "crisis" of labor history began somewhat earlier. One could even say that rarely has a sub-discipline been buried so often and with such vigor as has labor history.[5] A widespread disillusionment about the possibilities of labor history has emerged since the 1980s. As Marcel van der Linden argues:

> Many labour historians have viewed the state of their discipline as a protracted crisis. First, the emerging paradigms of women's and ethnic history showed that there had been giant blank spots on labour history's maps, and that filling in these blanks would necessitate a complete rewriting of the old narratives. Second, the unilinear conception of class consciousness that had long been dominant came into question.[6]

Due to growing uncertainty about its organizing categories, labor history began to lose its character as a discipline. The distinction between labor history and historiographical branches, such as women's history, ethnic studies, anthropology, and sociology, began to dissolve. Conceptual difficulties and political disappointments further fueled the impression of a state of crisis. According to William Sewell Jr., this "crisis" was due to the fact that labor history was too embedded in the metanarrative of proletarianization. The thesis of proletarianization brings together, as Sewell points out, a number of processes, and while acknowledging variation, treats the overall trend as universal: Cultivators and artisans are deprived of access to means of production, they move to cities or are forced into insecure wage labor jobs on farms, their skills are devalued, and even tighter forms of managerial control are devised. Meanwhile, workers acquire a sense of their collective identity as the sellers of labor power, and their traditions of artisanal autonomy or republican assertiveness are rechanneled into class identity; they build organizations, go on strike, and collectively challenge capital. According to Sewell, this proletarianization thesis pays "insufficient attention to the profoundly uneven and contradictory

---

Bentley (London/New York, 1997), 620–638; as a short introduction, Conor McCarthy, *The Cambridge Introduction to Edward Said* (Cambridge, 2010).

4 This was especially true in the United States. See Joel Beinien, "The New McCarthyism: Policing Thought about the Middle East," in *Academic Freedom after September 11*, ed. Beshara Doumani (New York, 2006), 237–266. For the long term effects of 9/11 on Middle Eastern Studies, see Seteney Shami and Cynthias Miller-Idriss, eds., *Middle East Studies for the new Millennium. Infrastructures of Knowledge* (New York, 2016).

5 Kim Christian Priemel, "Heaps of Work. The ways of labour history," in *H-Soz-Kult*, 23 January 2014, http://www.hsozkult.de/literaturereview/id/forschungsberichte-1223.

6 Marcel van der Linden, *Transnational Labour History. Explorations* (Aldershot, 2003), 2.

character of changes in productive relations, not to mention the role of discourse and politics in labor history."[7]

More recently, there has been a recurrent interest in area studies as well as in themes related to labor and work. This trend is closely linked with the rise of global history.[8] For a while, conceptual debates very much dominated this field. The discussions about various approaches oscillated between two kinds of ideal types: Relatively rigorous distinctions between world history, global history, and transnational history contrasted with more fluid conceptualizations of the field.[9] Jürgen Osterhammel represents the former approach by insisting on a clear distinction between transnational, world-historical, and global approaches. Transnational history, he suggests, is primarily concerned with inter-European relationships and their transatlantic connections. Moreover, transnational histories generally examine shorter time periods and are less concerned with universal patterns of connectivity. Notwithstanding its careful attention to historical multiplicity, by contrast, world history aims specifically to explain such general tendencies. Hence, as Osterhammel argues, it examines developments over the *longue durée* and across much larger regions, as it privileges transcultural relations. He conceived global history in much narrower terms: As an approach that historicizes global entanglements. Thus it examines developments that originated in the middle of the nineteenth century, and that still characterize the interconnectedness of the word today. Osterhammel carefully distinguishes global history, then, from the history of globalization. While the former in his view explores the contacts and

---

7   See William Sewell, Jr., "Toward a Post-materialist Rhetoric for Labor History," in *Rethinking Labor History: Essays in Discourse and Class Analysis*, ed. Lenard A. Berlanstein (Urbana, 1993), 15–38 (quote: 18). On the "crisis" of labor history see also, among many others, David Brody, "Labor History, Industrial Relations, and the Crisis of American Labor," *ILR Review* 43, no. 1 (1989): 7–18; Marcel van der Linden, ed., *The End of Labour History?* (Cambridge, 1994).

8   The literature on global history is vast by now. Among many others, see Sebastian Conrad, *What is Global History?* (Princeton, 2016); Dominic Sachsenmeier, *Global Perspectives on Global History. Theories and Approaches in a Connected World* (Cambridge, 2010), 112; James Belich et al., eds., *The Prospect of Global History*, (Oxford, 2016); Maxine Berg, ed., *Writing the History of the Global. Challenges for the 21st Century* (Oxford, 2013); Sven Beckert and Dominic Sachsenmaier, eds., *Global History Globally* (London/New York, 2018).

9   See Katja Naumann, "(Re)Writing World History in Europe," in *A Companion to World History*, ed. Douglas Northrup (Oxford, 2012), 478–496, here: 483f. In addition, one finds numerous debates and suggestions for neologisms. One was coined by area studies researches at the Center for Modern Oriental Studies in Berlin: "'Translocal history' expresses the desire to treat neither 'cultures' nor 'regions' nor 'nations' as fixed entities, but to view all definitions of locality as constructs and—at least partly—as the results of global entanglements." See Ulrike Freitag and Achim von Oppen, eds., *Translocality. The Study of Globalizing Processes from a Southern Perspective* (Leiden, 2010); Sachsenmaier, *Global Perspectives*, 159.

interactions between various global networks, the history of globalization suggests a master narrative chronicling the continuous intensification of exchange and interdependencies.[10]

Other authors have opted for a more integrative approach, stressing the common elements between world, global, and transnational histories. They argue that all these approaches share some perspectives: Whether they are inspired by world-system theory, analyze different civilizations, insist on multiple modernities, write the history of globalization, or build on postcolonial studies, they all reject modernization theory and seek to reconstruct "modernity" as a fully relational category. Moreover, these authors insist that world and global history no longer postulate a universal past, no longer mean a teleological view of historical development, and no longer attempt to represent the world in its spatial and temporal reality.[11] Building on these thoughts, Sebastian Conrad later defined the core concerns of this field:

> ... with mobility and exchange, with processes that transcend borders and boundaries. It takes the interconnected world as its point of departure, and the circulation and exchange of things, people, ideas, and institutions are among its key subjects. A preliminary and rather broad definition of global history might describe it as a form of historical analysis in which phenomena, events, and processes are placed in global contexts.[12]

Dominic Sachsenmaier even refers to the "necessary impossibility of defining global history" and argues that despite the growing prominence of global history during the past two decades, the various field designations have not crystallized into a set of rivalling schools but, on the contrary, have become increasingly enmeshed with each other. Therefore, he continues, it is not possible to categorically distinguish global history from fields such as transnational history or world history. "Rather, global history—like many other terms—can

---

10 Jürgen Osterhammel, *Geschichtswissenschaft jenseits des Nationalstaates. Studien zur Beziehungsgeschichte und Zivilisationsvergleich* (Göttingen, 2001); Jürgen Osterhammel, "Weltgeschichte. Ein Propädeutikum," *Geschichte in Wissenschaft und Unterricht* 56 (2005): 452–479; Jürgen Osterhammel, "World History," in *The Oxford History of Historical Writing, Vol.5*, eds. Axel Schneider and Daniel Woolf (Oxford, 2011), 93–112. See also Margarete Grandner et al., eds., *Globalisierung und Globalgeschichte* (Vienna, 2005).

11 Sebastian Conrad and Andreas Eckert, "Globalgeschichte, Globalisierung, multiple Modernen: Zur Geschichtsschreibung der modernen Welt," in *Globalgeschichte. Theorien, Ansätze, Themen*, eds. Sebastian Conrad, Andreas Eckert, and Ulrike Freitag (Frankfurt, 2007), 7–49.

12 Conrad, *What is Global History?* 5.

be taken as shorthand for a larger academic trend which we may also choose to call the 'global trend' in historiography."[13]

This chapter argues that both area studies and labor history profited from the emergence of global history, while at the same time these two fields fueled and shaped global approaches in historiography. The chapter will first analyze more broadly the entanglements between area studies and global history before looking more closely at the crucial role of area based history writing for global labor history. A set of questions structure this essay: Did labor history employ a particular sensitivity to the knowledge and insights of area studies and thus avoid some of the pitfalls of the global turn? And which complications did the combination of global perspectives and the incorporation of area based knowledge create in the field of labor history? What are the effects of the huge differences between world regions in the availability of relevant data and source material on the writing of global labor history? Did the global turn only include working *on* areas beyond the North Atlantic realm, or also working *with* scholars from these areas?

2 Scenes from a Marriage: Area Studies and Global History

Area Studies have been an important factor in the rise of global history in many parts of the world. It is even safe to say that a crucial impulse behind the (re-)emergence of global history in the European academy was a reaction against Eurocentrism of agency (the assumption that it has been mostly Europeans, or at least Westerners, who have changed the world) and Eurocentrism of concept (the dominance in history and social sciences of models derived from the analysis of European/Western experience, even when the object of investigation is experience elsewhere).[14] While the former exaggerates European exceptionalism, the latter entails the opposite: The long-standing tendency to "naturalize" European history by treating it as the norm, and the histories of other world regions as exceptions that need explanation. Hence the arguably most fundamental intellectual requirement for the development of global history as a field or as an approach was the massive growth of historical research on the non-Western world that has occurred since 1945, and especially since

---

13   Sachsenmaier, *Global Perspectives*, 70, 78.

14   As Eric Vanhaute puts it: "Much of the drive for a 'new' global history started with the aim to surpass or delegitimize the 'old' Eurocentric stories of the rise of a unified world." Eric Vanhaute, "Who is afraid of global history? Ambitions, pitfalls and limits of learning global history," *Österreichische Zeitschrift für Geschichtswissenschaft* 20, no. 2 (2009): 22–39, here: 22.

1960. In the UK, for example, specialists on parts of Asia and Africa such as Christopher Bayly, William Gervase Clarence-Smith, and Gareth Austin became early protagonists in the writing and institutionalizing of global history.[15]

According to David L. Szanton, the task of area studies is to know, analyze, and interpret another culture, a multidisciplinary effort in translating and "to make the assumptions, meanings, structures, and dynamics of another society and culture comprehensible to an outsider."[16] Conventional wisdom has it that area studies were "invented" in post-World War II North America, but this field has earlier roots, not only in the United States, but also in Europe.[17] Nevertheless, the U.S. was crucial as a pacemaker for developing institutional frameworks for area studies.[18] Cold War concerns, and the conviction of North American elites that the country would need to play a considerably larger international role after World War II than it had done before, provided the major impetus in founding and funding area studies in the U.S. However, many scholars involved in this field soon criticized the link between their research and teaching and the "national interest" of the United States. The different views most dramatically clashed during the Vietnam War, but were also apparent, for instance, in the context of Latin America.[19]

The events of 9/11 and their aftermath triggered a considerable growth of political demand for area expertise, especially for the regions from North Africa to Southeast Asia shaped by Islam. In this context, the "culturalization" of global conflicts, most effectively promoted by Samuel Huntington's

---

15 Gareth Austin, "Global History in (Northwestern) Europe: Explorations and Debates," in Beckert and Sachsenmaier, *Global History Globally*, 21–44: here: 24. For a broader picture, see Andreas Eckert, "Area Studies and the Writing of Non-European History in Europe," in *Transnational Challenges to National History Writing*, eds. Matthias Middell and Lluís Roura (Houndsmill and Basingstoke, 2013), 140–163.

16 David L. Szanton, "Introduction. The Origins, Nature and Challenges of Area Studies in the United States," in *The Politics of Knowledge. Area Studies and the Disciplines*, ed. David L. Szanton (Berkeley, 2004), 1.

17 Eckert, *Area Studies*; Anne Kwaschik, *Der Griff nach dem Weltwissen. Normative Ordnungen, kognitive und institutionelle Praktiken der Area Studies im 19. und 20. Jahrhundert*, unpublished Postdoctoral [Habilitation] thesis, Free University, Berlin 2016.

18 Thus, area studies in the United States are the best-researched example. See for instance Immanuel Wallerstein, "The Unintended Consequences of the Cold War Area Studies," in *The Cold War and the University: Toward an Intellectual History of the Postwar Years*, ed. Noam Chomsky (New York, 1997), 195–232; Vincente L. Rafael, "Regionalism, area studies, and the accidents of agency," *American Historical Review* 104, no. 4 (1999): 1208–1220; David Engerman, *Know Your Enemy. The Rise and Fall of America's Soviet Experts* (New York, 2009); Szanton, *The Politics of Knowledge*.

19 See Mark Berger, *Under Northern Eyes. Latin American Studies and US Hegemony in the Americas, 1895–1980* (Bloomington, IN, 1995).

concept of a "clash of civilizations," proved to be particularly challenging.[20] At the same time, the end of the Cold War produced considerable effects. As mentioned above, the emergence of area studies after World War II was partly due to strategic interests of Western and Eastern governments in the era of competition of ideological systems. Political interests changed after 1989. Local and supranational concerns at least partly replaced the demand for information exclusively related to nation states. Moreover, the old holistic understanding of a territorially bounded culture, which was constitutive for area studies, gave way to a concept of culture as process and practice; of culture as a "work in progress."[21] The detachment of culture from its spatial references led to a new focus on processes such as cultural globalization and diaspora.[22] These phenomena led to the dissolution of the traditional idea of culture and space as being congruent. On the other hand, it is impossible to conceptualize "diaspora" without any symbolic spatial structure. What does this mean for area studies? There is a growing insight that "culture" cannot be defined as a spatial container, but that the various "areas" must be understood as the result of processes of cultural marking. "What is African about Africa" should be the question, not a given assumption. The analysis of social networks, diasporas, cultural entanglements, and affinities should follow concrete movements in space instead of distinguishing between already defined "localities" or "regions" and a vague idea of "the global."[23] While numerous new studies follow this path and demonstrate a fruitful cooperation between area studies and global history,[24] another eternal problem is still much disputed: The relationship between area studies and the so-called systematic disciplines such as history, sociology, economics, or political sciences. Area studies specialists tended to make efforts to follow the standards of the disciplines regarded as "systematic" and they produced "evidences of achievement" meant to prove their contributions to the "mother disciplines."[25] However, few scholars

---

20 Samuel P. Huntington, *The Clash of Civilization and the Remaking of World Order* (New York, 1996). One of the many critics was Amartya Sen, *Identity and Violence. The Illusion of Destiny* (New York, 2006).

21 Ulf Hannerz, "The World in Creolization," *Africa* 57 (1987): 546–559, here: 550.

22 One by now classic example is Paul Gilroy, *The Black Atlantic. Modernity and Double Consciousness* (Cambridge, MA, 1993).

23 See Frederick Cooper, "Africa's Past and Africa's Historians," *Canadian Journal of African Studies* 34, no. 2 (2000): 298–336, here: 299.

24 See the articles in Birgit Schäbler, ed., *Area Studies und die Welt. Weltregionen und neue Globalgeschichte* (Wien, 2007).

25 A good example of this is the volume Robert Bates et al., eds., *Africa and the Disciplines. The Contributions of research in Africa to the Social Sciences and Humanities* (Chicago, 1993). See also Cooper, *Africa's Past.*

AREA STUDIES AND THE DEVELOPMENT OF GLOBAL LABOR HISTORY   163

systematically discussed to what extent knowledge about a specific area could question the theories, epistemologies, and boundaries of a discipline.[26] In addition, it could be asked whether the massive attacks on area studies,[27] which were launched in the 1980s and 1990s especially in the United States, resulted from the considerable self-confidence of certain disciplines, or whether the contrary is true: That representatives of certain disciplines were worried that external input could be threatening. In turn, area studies scholars as well as historians of non-European regions complained about the growing devaluation of language training, field research, and lack of cooperation with researchers in the localities. Even those who agree that area studies could never provide a serious alternative to disciplinary practices insist on the fact that area studies have always been a valuable enlargement, because in the context of area studies intellectual communities were formed, which stressed that scholars should "know something about someplace."[28]

The case of Germany is an interesting example of the complex relationship between area studies and global history. In Germany too, "an area specialization within Non-western history ... has been by far the most important avenue towards global history."[29] However, the specific institutional parameters of German academia resulted in a kind of outplacing of expertise on non-European world regions. While in the overall majority of history departments the proportion of scholars exploring history outside Europe is very low (in many cases there is not even a single tenured position devoted to these parts of the world), the task of studying Africa, Asia, the Americas, and the Middle East is largely relegated to small specialized fields such as Islamic Studies or Sinology, still characterized by strong philological traditions and mostly organized in "area studies" departments. To date, these small disciplines have tended to nurture their own forms of academic training. Furthermore, they

---

26   Steve Feiermann, "African History and the Dissolution of World History," in *Africa*, eds. Bates et al., 167–212 does this very effectively in the case of history.

27   These attacks were mainly orchestrated by economists and social scientists, but historians also took the opportunity to put into question the usefulness of dealing with the past of non-European areas. In the early 1990s, the seventeenth-century specialist John Kenyon noted with satisfaction that in "history departments hastily cobbled-up courses on Indochina or West Africa faded away as soon as these areas ceased to be of immediate current concern." Quoted in Richard J. Evans, *In Defence of History* (London, 1997), 178.

28   For recent debates about the relations between area studies and other approaches such as transregional studies, but also about a definition of area studies that goes beyond the "Global South," see Katja Mielke and Anna Katharina Hornidge, eds., *Area Studies at the Crossroads. Knowledge Production after the Mobility Turn* (New York, 2017).

29   Jürgen Osterhammel, "Global history in a national context: the case of Germany," *Österreichische Zeitschrift für Geschichtswissenschaft* 20, no. 2 (2009): 40–58, here: 44–45.

entertain their own disciplinary public spheres through separate journals, conferences, and associations. As a consequence, the bulk of area expertise in Germany remains somewhat fragmented, which prevents researchers focusing on other parts of the world from building an intellectual counterweight to predominantly Eurocentrically structured fields such as historiography.[30]

Despite these structural limitations, the number of collaborative projects between representatives from area studies and history departments has been growing slowly but steadily. This process has met with support from influential academic and political circles, which came to promote interregional and interdisciplinary research. In this regard, one major step was the recommendation of the German Science Council in 2005 to establish interdisciplinary area studies centers at some universities. During the past few years, and due to comparatively substantial funding for the humanities and particularly area studies, a richer institutional landscape has started to emerge, with the possibility and purpose of strengthening interdisciplinary cooperation by fostering global and transnational historical research. There are reasons to assume that the growing interest in transnational and transcultural themes will provide new connecting points between the field of history, area studies, and subfields such as Atlantic or Indian Ocean history. In this way, the historiography of China, India, Africa, and other parts of the world may ultimately start to lose its character as a garden of marginal "orchid fields" and gain significance within the professional community of German historians.[31] On the other hand, historians of India or Africa who stress the importance of source-based empirical research, note with concern the fact that global historians often rely on generalizations of secondary literature. Margrit Pernau, for instance, warns against the widespread ignorance of sources written in non-European languages. According to her, the exclusive use of source material in European languages implies the danger of reproducing colonial views or becoming caught up in absurdities; then global history runs the risk of degenerating into "historiography light."[32]

While global history currently seems to be everywhere and is celebrated "to be one of the most significant developments in the discipline of history since the social history revolution of the 1970s,"[33] some protagonists of global history are increasingly turning to a modus of self-criticism. Most notably, Princeton historian Jeremy Adelman, an eminent historian of Latin America and one of

---

30   Sachsenmeier, *Global Perspectives*, 122–125; Matthias Middell, "Area Studies under the Global Condition. Debates on Where to Go with regional or Area Studies in Germany," in *Self-reflexive area studies*, ed. Matthias Middell (Leipzig, 2013), 7–57.

31   Sachsenmeier, *Global perspectives*, 161.

32   Margrit Pernau, "Global History—Wegbereiter für einen neuen Kolonialismus," *geschichte transnational*, 17 December 2004, http://geschichte-transnational.clio-online.net/forum.

33   Becker and Sachsenmaier, "Introduction," in *Global History Globally*, 1.

the promoters of global history in the United States, recently published an essay in which he laments that suddenly global historians seem out of step with their time. "A powerful political movement arose against 'globalism.' White-supremacists and Vladimir Putin fans from the Traditionalist Worker Party in the US proclaim as their slogan that 'Globalism is the poison, nationalism is the antidote.'" Adelman takes this political movement as a starting point for substantial self-critique. Despite the mantras of integration and the inclusion on the planetary scale, he argues, global history came with its own segregation, starting with language. Historians working across borders merged their mode of communication in ways that created new walls; in the search for academic cohesion, English became "Globish." Global History would not be possible without the globalization of the English languages. On the other hand, Adelman writes, it is hard not to conclude that global history is another Anglospheric invention to integrate the Other into a cosmopolitan narrative "on our terms, in our tongues." According to Adelman, global history faces two seemingly opposite challenges for an interdependent, overheating planet:

> If we are going to muster meaningful narratives about the togetherness of strangers near and far, we are going to have to be more global and get more serious about engaging other languages and other ways of telling history. Historians and their reader-citizens are also going to have to re-signify the place of local attachments and meanings. Going deeper into the stories of Others afar and Strangers at home means dispensing with the idea that global integration was like an electric circuit, bringing light to the connected. Becoming inter-dependent is not just messier than drawing a wiring diagram. It means reckoning with dimensions of networks and circuits that global historians—and possibly all narratives of cosmopolitan convergence—leave out of the story: lighting up corners of the earth leaving others in the dark.[34]

Adelman articulates a number of points of criticism concerning global history regularly expressed by area historians, such as the obsession for mobility and entanglement while ignoring immobility as a crucial feature of the global condition; or the dominance of English that usually comes along with the neglect of sources and literature in other languages. These are also challenges for the field of global labor history.

---

34 Jeremy Adelman, "What is global history now?" https://aeon.co/essays/is-global-history-still-possible-or-has-it-had-its-moment. For a forceful rejoinder: David Motadel and Richard Drayton, "Discussion: The Future of Global History," Journal of Global History 13, no.1 (2018): 1–21.

3   Global Labor History and the World Regions

More generally, many of the "scenes" presented in the previous paragraphs are also relevant in order to understand the relationships between current efforts to employ global perspectives in writing histories of work and area-based historical research. One of the virtues of labor history in recent decades has been its micro-historical focus on workers and work in relation to the range of social processes in a particular milieu, for example race, gender, and ethnicity. If we increasingly look beyond both locality and region toward wider spatial relationships, what do we learn apart from the insight that we are confronted with fuzzy categories and fuzzy constellations? Labor historians face the difficulty of focusing on the necessarily specific historical trajectories in certain localities in Europa, Asia, or Africa and across specific patterns of regional migration, without losing sight of the wider context. A growing number of labor historians have attempted to write a history of labor and work infused with both specificity and comparison; that sees shared entanglements as bi- or multi-directional rather than unidirectional, and that does not impose a model from one period, nation, or region onto another. These efforts have been subsumed under the rubric of Global Labor History.[35]

As far as its methodological status is concerned, it is more an "area of interest" than a theory or school to which everyone must subscribe. It is not "a vertical organization, but a network continuously assembling and breaking up in relation to specific research projects; it does not aim for a new 'grand narrative,' but rather to partial syntheses based on multiple empirical research and various intellectual interpretations."[36] One of its main concerns so far has been to integrate more systematically the "Global South" into labor historiography, at both the intellectual and the institutional level. Widening the focus— moving beyond workers in the West to look at those in Asia, Latin America, and Africa—formed one of the starting points of global labor history and implied

---

35   The key text in this field is still Marcel van der Linden, *Workers of the World. Essays Toward a Global Labor History* (Leiden, 2008). He also produced numerous essays to map the field, most notably "The Promise and Challenges of Global Labor History," *International Labor and Working Class History* 82 (2012): 57–76. For other efforts in mapping see Leo Lucassen, "Working Together: New Directions in Global Labour History," *Journal of Global History* 11, no. 1 (2016): 66–87; Andreas Eckert, "Why all the fuss about Global Labour History?" in *Global Histories of Work,* ed. Andreas Eckert (Berlin/Boston, 2016), 3–22; Andreas Eckert and Marcel van der Linden, "New Perspectives on Workers and the History of Work: Global Labor History," in *Global History Globally*, 145–161.

36   Christian G. De Vito, "New Perspectives on Global Labour History. Introduction," *Workers of the World* 1, no. 3 (2013): 7–31, here: 12.

the incorporation of scholarship on and from these areas. It soon became evident that North-Atlantic-focused labor history, with its emphasis on wage workers, industries, and cities, has provided a highly incomplete picture of labor and has ignored the vast amount of labor in the countryside, outside of wage relations, and in agriculture. In a global labor perspective, the slave and the sharecropper are put next to the wage worker, and the focus is on the complex entanglements between them. This understanding of the global scope of labor history undermines a core narrative that emphasizes the development of labor toward contract, freedom, and formalization. In addition, via the "detour" of the "Global South," historians of the West re-discovered the importance of agrarian or different forms of non-wage labor and began to locate, for Europe and North America, the extensive and complicated "grey areas" replete with transitional locations between the "free" wage laborers and other forms of labor, to take into consideration that households often combine several modes of labor, and to have an eye for the possibility that individual laborers can combine different modes of labor, both synchronically and diachronically.[37]

These more recent efforts, however, should not let us ignore the fact that, for instance, Latin American historians, like their colleagues in North America and Europe, have been studying the particularities of labor in their regions for decades.[38] African and Indian historians have done this more recently, but with a focus either on area or on specific types of labor, for example plantation labor.[39] For a long time, European and Western labor historians tended to "universalize" their views, often based on rather specific examples. They ignored for instance the work of Caribbean specialists, for whom the relationship between plantation labor and global capitalism has been central since the work of C.L.R. James and Eric Williams in the 1930s and 1940s.[40] Perspectives in the context of (post-)colonialism have been central in many attempts to globalize historical studies.[41] This appears also to be true with regard to labor history. In this field, the mutual relationship between social change with the colonizing

---

37 Van der Linden, *Workers of the World*, 32.

38 See James P. Brennan, "Latin American Labor History," in *The Oxford Handbook of Latin American History*, ed. José C. Moya (Oxford, 2011), 342–366.

39 Rana Behal, *One Hundred Years of Servitude: Political Economy of Tea Plantations in Colonial Assam* (New Delhi, 2014); Abdul Sheriff, *Slaves, Spices and Ivory in Zanzibar* (London, 1987). Much of the literature on plantation labor in Africa has been produced by North American scholars. See e.g. Frederick Cooper, *From Slaves to Squatters. Plantation Labor and Agriculture in Zanzibar and Colonial Kenya, 1890–1925* (New Haven, 1980).

40 Eric Williams, *Capitalism and Slavery* (Chapel Hill, 1944); C.L.R. James, *The Black Jacobins. Toussaint L'Ouverture and the San Domingo Revolution* (New York, 1938).

41 Conrad, *Global History*, 53–57.

countries and the colonized territories continues to be of interest. The crucial question that remains open is how colonization shapes labor history. One important reference here is the slave plantation as a formative experience in developing large-scale, closely supervised enterprises.[42] How did this experience shape the ideas, organization, and practice of labor in the world? Another is the point Karl Marx made: According to him, the availability of land and the possibility of migration are obstacles to original accumulation. Why did this problem remain even after relatively long-term and intense colonization efforts? In fact, there is some reason to argue that this concept from Marx might gain new importance in the African context, given for example the rush for land in Africa and the political and economic conflicts this entails.[43]

One of the major insights of global approaches to the history of labor has been the emphasis on numerous hybrid constellations and on the ambiguity of established concepts, definitions, and distinctions. Area-based studies have played a major role here. For example, historians of Brazil show that slaves were ordered by their owners to leave the mansion or the plantation and work for wages, but to bring back part of their earnings.[44] Other combinations of slave and wage labor, or serfdom and capitalism (such as in Russia around 1900), would seem to relativize Karl Marx's and other classical writers' theses of the outstanding importance of contractually free wage labor as a defining element of capitalism.[45] Comparing Russia and England between 1780 and 1850, Alessandro Stanziani highlights: "Servants, wage earners, the poor, criminals, slaves, and serfs all had to respond to common general principles of utility and efficiency."[46] In societies where slavery was central—as in the Americas, Africa, and elsewhere—the distinction between "free" and "unfree" became essential, especially once slavery as an "institution" became a public abomination, at least from the late eighteenth century onward. In these contexts, the clear

---

42 Sidney Mintz, *Sweetness and Power. The Place of Sugar in Modern History* (Harmondsworth, 1985).

43 Catherine Boone, *Property and Political Order. Land Rights and the Structure of Conflict in Africa* (New York, 2014).

44 João José Reis, "The Revolution of the Ganhadores: Urban Labor, Ethnicity and the African Strike of 1857 in Bahia, Brazil," *Journal of Latin American Studies* 29 (1997): 355–393.

45 Alessandro Stanziani, "The Legate Statute of Labour from the Seventeenth to the Nineteenth Century. Russia in a Comparative European Perspective," *International Review of Social History* 54 (2009): 359–389; Alessandro Stanziani, *Bondage. Labor and Rights in Eurasia from the Sixteenth to the Early Twentieth Century* (New York/Oxford, 2014); Alessandro Stanziani, ed., *Le Travail Contraint en Europe et en Asie, XVI–XXe siècles* (Paris, 2010).

46 Alessandro Stanziani, "The travelling panopticon: labor institutions and labor practices in Russia and Britain in the eighteenth and nineteenth century," *Comparative Studies in Society and History* 51, no. 4 (2009): 715–741, here: 732.

AREA STUDIES AND THE DEVELOPMENT OF GLOBAL LABOR HISTORY 169

divide between "slavery" and "freedom" turned into the source of all sorts of social and political anxieties and fostered various logics of continuity and discontinuity. On this topic, again, not the least Brazilian historians have stressed that during the nineteenth century no distinct division existed between slaves and "freed" workers with regard to the utilization of extra-economic coercion. On the other hand, as their studies show, the ambivalence of the concept of "freedom" indicated sharp social conflict on the ground, related to specific work arrangements. Among former slaves, "freedom" was usually experienced as precarious, limited, or even spurious, but it nevertheless constituted a relevant category and a crucial aspiration.[47] One insight from this research is that even if there seems to be a long-term trend towards "free wage labor," so-called free labor "cannot be seen as the only form of exploitation suitable for modern capitalism, but rather as one alternative among several."[48]

The study of regions outside the North Atlantic realm very much shaped debates about the global rise of precarious and informal work, currently an intensely discussed theme both in scholarly and political fields. Although some Africanists insist that "African economies are the most informalized in the world," non-waged economic activities, unregulated by law and unprotected by social regulations or services, became increasingly visible in many parts of the world, including the core regions of the North Atlantic world.[49] "Precarity"

---

47 See Henrique Espada Lima, "Freedom, Precariousness, and the Law: Freed Persons contracting out their Labor in Nineteenth-Century Brazil," *International Review of Social History* 54, no. 3 (2009): 391–416; Marcelo Badaró Mattos, "Experiences in Common: Slavery and 'Freedom' in the Process of Rio de Janeiro's Working Class Formation (1850–1910)," *International Review of Social History* 55, no. 2 (2010): 193–213; Sidney Chaloub, "The Precariousness of Freedom in a Slave Society (Brazil in the Nineteenth Century)," *International Review of Social History* 56, no. 3 (2011), 405–439; Sidney Chaloub, "The Politics of Ambiguity. Conditional Manumission, Labor Contracts and Slave Emancipation in Brazil (1850s to 1888)," *International Review of Social History* 60, no. 2 (2015): 161–191. For a thoughtful reflection on the unfree-free divide referring to the crucial contribution of Brazilian historians, see Ravi Ahuja, "A Freedom Still Enmeshed in Servitude. The Unruly 'Lascers' of the *SS City of Manilaor*, a Micro-History of the 'Free Labour' Problem," in *Working Lives and Worker Militancy. The Politics of Labour in Colonial India*, ed. Ravi Ahuja (New Delhi, 2013), 97–133, especially 97.

48 Marcel van der Linden, "Labour History Beyond Borders," in *Histories of Labour. National and International Perspectives*, eds. Joan Allen et al. (Pontypool 2010), 353–383, here: 368.

49 Kate Meagher, "The Scramble for Africans: Demography, Globalization and Africa's Informal Labor Markets," *Journal of Development Studies* 52 (2016): 483–497, here: 485. For an insightful analysis of the categories "informal" and "precarious" in the African context, see Frederick Cooper, "From Enslavement to Precarity? The Labour Question in African History," in *The Political Economy of Everyday Life in Africa. Beyond the Margins*, ed. Wale Adebawi (Oxford, 2017), 135–156. For a powerful argument about the global importance of informal labor relations, see Jan Breman and Marcel van der Linden, "Informalizing the

has also become a fashionable new concept in labor studies. It seems to imply the view that while in the past, capital was striving to systematically extract surplus value from a large and growing work force that at the same time had to be tamed, today more and more workers have apparently become unnecessary. However, some scholars have drawn attention to the fact that precarity does not represent a particular phase of capitalism, but that it is an inherent characteristic of capitalist labor.[50] The discovery of the "informal" and "precarity" went hand in hand with the observation that full-time wage labor with relatively good social benefits over the course of an entire career was not a global norm, but instead the exception in many parts of the world; the contingent product of a particular conjuncture in twentieth-century world history. This in turn led to the insight that the male proletarian does not represent the quintessential worker, but is instead one among a number of categories of workers whose histories are connected.[51] Rather than being exceptions confirming the rule, parts of Africa and Asia represent contexts in which capitalist production regimes and their related forms of employment have confronted social practices and cultural forms that questioned the normative pretenses of the wage relation and challenged the universalism inherent in ideologies of "free" commodity-producing work.

Lastly, area studies were also crucial in creating a new impetus for rethinking central concepts of labor history. All the core concepts of "traditional" labor history are primarily based on experiences in the North Atlantic region and are thus in need of critical re-evaluation.[52] There is no simple solution to this problem, but a growing consciousness that we should not implicitly assume how "labor" and "work" are to be understood, but define and trace much more precisely their changing and varying meanings.[53] In a recent article, Anne Kelk Mager shows a competition for semantic ground between two main concepts pertaining to the domain of "work" among isiXhosa speakers in South Africa. This competition took place against the backdrop of their being increasingly affected by European notions of "work" and "labor." As Mager demonstrates, the renegotiation of ideas of "work" in isiXhosa was a much more complex

---

economy: the return of the social question at a global level," *Development and Change* 45, no. 5 (2014): 920–940.

50 Marcel van der Linden, "San Precario: A New Inspiration for Labor Historians," *Labor* 11 (2014): 9–21.

51 This is one of the major points made by van der Linden, *Workers of the World.*

52 Van der Linden, *Labor History beyond Borders*, 365.

53 See Jörn Leonhard and Willibald Steinmetz, "Von der Begriffsgeschichte zur historischen Semantik von 'Arbeit,'" in *Semantiken von Arbeit. Diachrone und vergleichende Perspektiven*, eds. Jörn Leonhard and Willibald Steinmetz (Cologne, 2016), 9–59.

process than colonial notions unilaterally affecting pre-existing concepts. Indeed, labor and employment in this region were not just abstract ideas, but concrete arenas of negotiation of economic conditions. Mager's analysis shows how linguistic understandings of concepts of "work" were shaped by the events of the nineteenth century, including the expansion of colonial rule, but also how these concepts themselves influenced isiXhosa speakers' decisions and actions during this period.[54]

A fundamental challenge for global perspectives on the history of labor is the globally very uneven existence of source material and the availability of data. A large project by the International Institute of Social History in Amsterdam entitled "Global Collaborative on the History of Labour Relations" shows both the possibilities and limits of large-scale, data-based global labor history enterprises. The core of this project is a universal taxonomy of labor relations that aims to map different types of labor relations in various world regions between 1500 and 2000.[55] The taxonomy basically distinguishes between four forms of labor: Non-work, reciprocal labor, tributary labor, and commodified labor; either connected with the household, the community, or the market. These types are further elaborated in nineteen different types of labor relations at the individual level, for instance in the category of the household: Leading producers, kin producers, kin non-producers, servants, and redistributive laborers. The project chose five cross-sections in time: 1500, 1650, 1800, 1900, and 2000, as well as 1950 for Africa. On the basis of the data collected by the participating specialists on specific regions and cross-sections, the collaboratory attempts to analyze major shifts in labor relations by asking, for instance, when a specific type of labor relation gave way to another, or how these transitions could be explained and connected in a global context. Without any doubt, this project offers a solid base from which to analyze shifts in labor relations over time within societies, and which allows for interregional and worldwide comparisons. One drawback seems to be the strong role of demographical data as a starting point for examining each geographical unit and cross-section, given

---

54 Anne Kelk Mager, "Tracking the Concept of 'Work' on the North Eastern Cape Frontier, South Africa," in: *Doing Conceptual History in Africa*, eds. Axel Fleisch and Rhianoon Stephens (New York/Oxford, 2016), 73–90.

55 My presentation of the project follows Lucassen, *New Directions*, 68–70. For detailed information see https://collab.iisg.nl/labourrelations/about. Among the publications that emerged from this project are: Karin Hofmeester and Christine Moll-Murata, eds., *The Joy and Pain of Work. Global Attitudes and Valuation 1500–1650* (Cambridge, 2012); Marcelo Badaró Mattos et al., eds., *Relações Laborais em Portugal et no Mundo Lusófono. História e Demografia* (Lisbon, 2014); Karin Hofmeester and Pim de Zwart, eds., *Colonialism, Institutional Change, and Shifts in Global Labor Relations* (Amsterdam, 2017).

the fact that for a continent such as Africa, this data is very sketchy and unreliable until right into the twentieth century. Moreover, the taxonomy does not really allow the capturing of overlaps and "grey zones" in individual labor relations. The Africa-related publications emerging from this project so far provide interesting new insights, but also refer to the limits of the database-driven approach for the history of African labor and its global connections, especially for the periods before 1900.[56]

The project sets an example for collaboration between scholars from many parts of the world, including historians from what is now called the "Global South." Despite various and successful efforts, however, one cannot ignore the structural inequalities that shape the field of Global Labor History in many ways: For scholars in Asia or Africa, access to sources and literature is limited, and funding for research and conferences is rarely available. The important thing for the practice of Global Labor History is, according to Van der Linden, "to follow the traces of interest to us wherever they may lead: across political and geographical frontiers, time frames, territories and disciplinary boundaries."[57] This journey presents a considerable demand not only on the intellectual and linguistic skills of the researcher, but also on their finances. Skepticism about global history approaches is not only due to frustrations about the lack of resources though. In many parts of the "Global South," the persistent preoccupation with national history also represents an obstacle to global perspectives. In essence, given the long history of Eurocentric knowledge production and academic hierarchies, there is a widespread sense of Global (Labor) History as just another hegemonic Western project.

4   A Luta Continua

Although some protagonists of Global (Labor) History come along as missionaries, most representatives of this field would agree that this is not the only game in town, but one perspective among others. To consider Africa, Asia, or Latin America in relation to global history suggests valuable lines of connection to other fields of history and new perspectives on a number of topics, but also jumping on bandwagons. There is no need for historians of the "Global South" to prove that they are also capable of employing a global perspective, and thus entitled to historiographical citizenship, although some seem to

---

56   See Karin Hofmeester et al., "No Global Labor History without Africa: Reciprocal Comparison and Beyond," *History in Africa* 41 (2014): 249–276.

57   Van der Linden, *Promise*, 62.

feel a kind of pressure and even react defensively. In fact, as we have seen, there is a long tradition of placing these world regions in the long sweep of global history, not the least in the realm of labor. Global histories of labor require the cooperative spirit of teamwork and conversations transcending all kinds of boundaries—language boundaries and others—although the Global Collaborative on the History of Labor Relations indicates that collaborative projects focusing on numerous world regions imply a set of methodological problems that are not easy to solve. It is still worth taking the trouble to write histories of labor that put the subsistence laborer, the slave and the sharecropper next to the wageworker, and that keep the entire world in mind, even when focusing on a specific area. Finally, it is important to emphasize that global labor history not only gained momentum from good intentions, intellectual declarations, and the energy of a number of historians. During the past years, a growing institutional and financial fundament has been built that supported a further expansion of historical research at a global and transnational level. It is currently unclear how stable this fundament is, but without any doubt, global historical perspectives gained an important place in the historiography of labor within a relatively short period of time. The esteem of area studies as well as the increasing (though still limited) incorporation of historians from the South into new global communities of scholars are crucial elements in this context. The global turn might lose some of its dynamics, but the insights and perspectives that came with it will continue to shape historical research on labor and other topics.

CHAPTER 9

Beyond Labor History's Comfort Zone? Labor Regimes in Northeast India, from the Nineteenth to the Twenty-First Century

Willem van Schendel

1 Introduction

What is global labor history about? The turn toward a world-historical understanding of labor relations has upset the traditional toolbox of labor historians. Conventional concepts turn out to be insufficient to grasp the dizzying array and transmutations of labor relations beyond the North Atlantic region and the industrial world. Attempts to force these historical complexities into a conceptual straitjacket based on methodological nationalism and Eurocentric schemas typically fail.[1]

A truly "global" labor history needs to feel its way toward new perspectives and concepts. In his *Workers of the World* (2008), Marcel van der Linden provides us with an excellent account of the theoretical and methodological challenges ahead. He makes it very clear that labor historians need to leave their comfort zone. The task at hand is not to retreat into a further tightening of the theoretical rigging: "we should resist the temptation of an 'empirically empty Grand Theory' (to borrow C. Wright Mills's expression); instead, we need to derive more accurate typologies from careful empirical study of labor relations."[2] This requires us to place "all historical processes in a larger context, no matter how geographically 'small' these processes are."[3]

This chapter seeks to contribute to a more globalized labor history by considering such "small" labor processes in a mountainous region of Asia. My aim is to show how these processes challenge us to explore beyond the comfort zone of "labor history," and perhaps even beyond that of "global labor history"

---

* International Institute of Social History and University of Amsterdam. I wish to thank Joy L.K. Pachuau for her advice. This chapter uses visual material collected jointly for our book *The Camera as Witness: A Social History of Mizoram, Northeast India* (Delhi, etc, 2015).

1 Marcel van der Linden, *Workers of the World: Essays toward a Global Labor History* (Leiden/ Boston, 2008), 3–10.

2 Van der Linden, *Workers of the World*, 36.

3 Van der Linden, *Workers of the World*, 6.

© WILLEM VAN SCHENDEL, 2018 | DOI:10.1163/9789004386617_010

This is an open access chapter distributed under the terms of the prevailing CC-BY-NC License.

BEYOND LABOR HISTORY'S COMFORT ZONE 175

as outlined by Van der Linden.[4] We are reminded of the urgency of studying such regions—and the long road ahead for "global history"—when we see "the mismatch between our historical curiosity and the population of the world's major regions." Clossey and Guyatt suggest that over three quarters of historical research in North America and the UK deals with the North Atlantic region, home to 17 percent of humankind, and only 4 percent of historical research deals with South and Southeast Asia, home to a third of humankind.[5]

The region in question is Mizoram, one of the 29 states (or provinces) of India. It is in the far northeast of that country, and on three sides lie territories governed by Myanmar (Burma) and Bangladesh. Mizoram is a good place to reassess methodological nationalism, as culturally it is starkly different from the "India" that labor historians have so far studied and theorized. Historically, labor relations in this region have much in common with those in an expanse sometimes referred to as the Extended Eastern Himalayas, a culture area stretching from northeast India and Bangladesh to Myanmar and southwest China.[6] By looking at the evolution of labor relations in Mizoram over the last 150 years, we can provide a modest corrective to the ills of both Eurocentrism and Indiacentrism in labor history. Van der Linden identifies "neglect," "prejudice," and "implicit assumptions" as the major ills of Eurocentrism;[7] these can be applied equally to what inhabitants of Northeast India might call Mainland-India-centrism.

The case of Mizoram alerts us to similarities in labor relations across borders and within culture areas, reminds us of the historical contingency of contemporary nation states, and points to a lack of consideration given to labor in many local historiographies. Labor relations in Mizoram also draw our

---

4   See also Marcel van der Linden, "The 'Globalization' of Labour and Working-Class History and its Consequences," *International Labor and Working-Class History* 65 (2004): 136–156; Willem Van Schendel, "Stretching Labour Historiography: Pointers from South Asia," *International Review of Social History* 51 (2006): 229–261; Van der Linden, *Workers of the World*, 360.

5   Luke Clossey and Nicholas Guyatt, "It's a Small World After All: The Wider World in Historians' Peripheral Vision," American Historical Association, accessed July 11, 2018, https://www.historians.org/publications-and-directories/perspectives-on-history/may-2013/its-a-small-world-after-all and http://smallworldhistory.org/.

6   Stuart Blackburn, "Oral Stories and Culture Areas: From Northeast India to Southwest China," *South Asia: Journal of South Asian Studies* 30, no. 3 (2007): 419–437.

7   *Neglect*: "There is only attention for part of the world; the author assumes that the history of 'his piece of the world' can be portrayed without giving any attention to the rest." *Prejudice*: "The authors do consider global connections, but nevertheless believe Greater Europe (including in this North America and Australasia) 'shows the way.'" *Implicit assumptions*: "General beliefs about historical experience which, allegedly, have been confirmed time and again by previous scientific research, and therefore can be taken for granted": Van der Linden, *Workers of the World*, 8–9.

attention to both the difficulties in generalizing familiar categories (for example, "slavery"[8]), and the dangers of applying evolutionary typologies. Lastly, the case of Mizoram throws light on an enduring type of labor relation, voluntary communal labor, which historians of labor rarely scrutinize.

I present brief sketches of Mizoram's labor regime as it evolved during three successive periods. The purpose is to show that global labor history cannot advance unless we shed assumptions of unilinear transformation, and until we recognize the importance of dealing with the cultural meanings of labor— and not just its economic forms—in any attempt at comparing labor relations across time and space. This requires labor historians to improve their cross-cultural sensibilities, re-examine their methodologies, and broaden their use of sources.[9]

2 Pre-colonial Labor Relations

In the 1890s, the British invaded the territory of what is now Mizoram (up to the 1950s: Lushai Hills[10]). Before this time, the region had never been under state control. Its village-sized polities were self-governing and the regional labor regime combined household self-employment (mainly subsistence agriculture), servile labor, and communal labor. All households had access to land, so they acted as largely self-providing production teams. This was a region of abundant land and perennial labor shortages and—in the absence of a labor market—such shortages were met by servitude and communal labor.

---

8 For a recent critique of definitions of slavery, see Marcel van der Linden, "Dissecting Coerced Labor," in *On Coerced Labor: Work and Compulsion after Chattel Slavery*, eds. Marcel van der Linden and Magaly Rodriguez García (Leiden/Boston, 2016), 293–322.

9 Van der Linden makes this point when discussing changing labor relations in Papua New Guinea: "ethnographers have much to offer labor historians, including over 21,000 brief and extended studies on Papua New Guinea alone. Global Labor History can access much more relevant information than one might think." Van der Linden, *Workers of the World*, 358.

10 The British named the region after the largest language community, the Lushai. They defined speakers of this language as a "tribe," even though the term was highly problematic and many fluid group identities were subsumed under it. Over time, tribal self-identification flourished and solidified, partly because Lushai became the language of education: Lushai speakers developed a sense of belonging and attempted (quite successfully) to bring other groups into the fold. They insisted on the appellation of "Mizo" for this larger grouping. Today not all groups in Mizoram [Mizo Land] identify as Mizo, however, and self-identification remains remarkably malleable.

BEYOND LABOR HISTORY'S COMFORT ZONE

3   Servitude

Various forms of servitude were practiced in pre-colonial Mizoram, and they bore a family resemblance to practices across the Extended Eastern Himalayas. The exact evolution of these regional practices is hard to establish, because most societies were preliterate. Historical evidence is scarce: whatever we know comes from oral traditions and external, often post-invasion, written sources. It is clear, however, that servitude took different shapes across the region.[11] In Mizoram it comprised two types, servitude-by-capture (*sal*) and servitude-by-refuge (*bawi*, pronounced "boi").[12]

Servitude-by-capture (*sal*). The small polities of the region engaged in what has been called "slave-gathering warfare."[13] They raided the villages of other groups to safeguard their own autonomy and in search of labor power. Such conflicts became more frequent in the nineteenth century. Some involved hunting in areas in the foothills[14] where European tea planters had intruded, and which British authorities claimed as colonial territory.[15] Construed as

---

11   Gordon P. Means, "Human Sacrifice and Slavery in the 'Unadministered' Areas of Upper Burma During the Colonial Era," *Sojourn: Journal of Social Issues in Southeast Asia* 15, no. 2 (2000): 184–221; Mandy Sadan, *Being and Becoming Kachin: Histories Beyond the State in the Borderworlds of Burma* (Oxford, 2013), 59–63, 80–82, 223–224.

12   These are the terms in the Duhlian dialect of the Lushai language. The Mizoram region was (and is) multilingual, so it is important to acknowledge that there were many local terms for forms of servitude. Today the Duhlian dialect (now known as the Mizo language) is the official language of Mizoram. When missionaries first attempted to write down this language in Roman script, they chose to transcribe the "o" as "aw," mirroring the practice in their native Welsh. See Indrani Chatterjee, "Slavery, Semantics and the Sound of Silence," in *Slavery and South Asian History*, eds. Indrani Chatterjee and Richard M. Eaton (Bloomington, 2007), 287–316. Probably the first written reference to the terms ("*sul*" and "*boi*") can be found in T.H. Lewin, *Progressive Colloquial Exercises in the Lushai Dialect of the "Dzo" Or Kúki Language, with Vocabularies and Popular Tales* (notated) (Calcutta, 1874), 80–81 and *passim*.

13   Bryce Beemer, "Southeast Asian Slavery and Slave-Gathering Warfare as a Vector for Cultural Transmission: The Case of Burma and Thailand," *Historian* 71, no. 3 (2009): 481–506; Andrew Turton, "Violent Capture of People for Exchange on Karen-Tai Borders in the 1830s," *Slavery & Abolition* 24, no. 2 (2003): 69–82.

14   Guite argues that large forested areas, which the British considered uninhabited, were in fact hunting grounds that the hill people deliberately left uncultivated, a strategy well understood by lowlanders. British incursions into these buffer zones challenged the hill people's spatial and sacred notions of sovereignty—and thereby triggered negotiations and, more rarely, warfare: Jangkhomang Guite, "Colonialism and Its Unruly? The Colonial State and Kuki Raids in Nineteenth Century Northeast India," *Modern Asian Studies* 48, no. 5 (2014).

15   N.E. Parry, *The Lakher* (London:, 1932), 7–12, 202–221; David Vumlallian Zou, "Raiding the Dreaded Past: Representations of Headhunting and Human Sacrifice in North-East India,"

178   WILLEM VAN SCHENDEL

attacks on "British subjects," these conflicts triggered brutal British invasions of the highlands.[16] Between the 1890s and 1930s, these invasions succeeded in subjugating the many polities in Mizoram.[17]

Before colonization, captives taken in war—predominantly children and women because enemy men were often killed in combat[18]—became the personal property of their captors (Figure 9.1).[19] Their labor power was an important economic and social resource. A challenge to the master's ownership would meet with strong village opposition, as British officials found out.

> On one occasion [in the early 1860s] my predecessor, Captain Graham, was visiting a Kookie [Lushai or Mizo] village, and he discovered that they held some British subjects in captivity. On demanding their release,

---

Contributions to Indian Sociology 39, no. 1 (2007); Soong Chul Ro, *Naming a People: British Frontier Management in Eastern Bengal and the Ethnic Categories of the Kuki-Chin, 1760–1860* (Ph.D. thesis: University of Hull, 2007), Chapter 6; Jangkhmang Guite, "Civilisation and its Malcontents: The Politics of Kuki Raid in Nineteenth Century Northeast India," *The Indian Economic and Social History Review* 48, no. 3 (2011): 339–376; Guite, "Colonialism and Its Unruly." Among the Mara (Lakher), war captives were known as *sei*. For the eighteenth century, see Willem van Schendel, ed., *Francis Buchanan in Southeast Bengal (1798): His Journey to Chittagong, the Chittagong Hill Tracts, Noakhali and Comilla* (Dhaka, 1992), 16, 93, 112–113. For examples of "raids into British-held territory," see *Annual Report on the Administration of the Bengal Presidency for 1863–64* (O.T. Cutter, Military Orphan Press, 1865), 164–168; "Copy of Correspondence between the India Office and the Government of India, on the Subject of the Irruption of Hill Tribes into Cachar," *Accounts and Papers of the House of Commons (Session 9 February-21 August 1871)*, vol. 14 (London: House of Commons, 1871); "Copy of Further Correspondence on the Subject of the Looshai Raids and the Consequent Hostilities," in *Continuation of Parliamentary Paper, No. 398, of Session 1871* (London: House of Commons, 1872); Alexander Mackenzie, *History of the Relations of the Government with the Hill Tribes of the North-East Frontier of India* (Calcutta, 1884), 287–365; Guite "Colonialism and Its Unruly."

16   R.G. Woodthorpe, *The Lushai Expedition, 1871–1872* (London, 1873); Mackenzie, *History of the Relations.*

17   The southernmost villages remained "independent and unadministered until the last few years" and they were "loosely administered" in the 1930s (Parry, *The Lakher*, vii, 12; cf. ix). The persistence of *sal* servitude here is attested to by the British declaration that its signing of the Slavery Convention of the League of Nations (1926) was not binding for "a small tract in the South of the Lushai Hills District [Mizoram]": League of Nations, *Slavery Convention* (Geneva, 1926), 6.

18   J. Shakespear, *The Lushei Kuki Clans* (London, 1912), 50. Lorrain indicated that the Mara (Lakher) in southern Mizoram preferred to capture children because these were less likely to escape: Reginald A. Lorrain, *Five Years in Unknown Jungles for God and Empire* (London, 1912), 166.

19   Parry, *The Lakher*, 222–223; Lian H. Sakhong, *In Search of Chin Identity: A Study in Religion, Politics and Ethnic Identity in Burma* (Copenhagen, 2003), 41–42; Lalhrilmoi Hrangchal "Sal: Slavery in the Lushai Hills," *International Journal of Research* 1, no. 10 (2014): 1903–1931.

FIGURE 9.1 A war captive (*sal*), 1866.
PHOTOGRAPH BY T.H. LEWIN, REPRODUCED BY PERMISSION OF THE LEWIN FAMILY PAPERS, UNIVERSITY OF LONDON LIBRARY, UK
Note: This woman, whose name is unknown, was a Lushai who was taken in war by a neighboring group, the Shendu (Mara). See also Joy L.K. Pachuau and Willem van Schendel, *The Camera as Witness: A Social History of Mizoram, Northeast India* (New Delhi, etc., 2015), 27.

however, the Chief refused to let them go; and Captain Graham equally refusing to go without them, things began to look mischievous. At length the Chief in a rage betook himself off to his house, and the big gong began to toll. Captain Graham describes the effect as miraculous: every woman and child disappeared from sight as if by magic, and the Lhoosai, with their weapons in their hands, came crowding to the Chief. Matters, however, were eventually arranged on a peaceable footing, and the captives were released.[20]

Captives did not own possessions and their servitude was heritable. They could be traded, but it is unclear whether or not this was a rare occurrence.[21] Pre-colonial Mizoram had a barter economy, so the price of captives was not expressed in money, but in terms of *gayals* (semi-wild bison, also known as *mithuns*) or guns. "A slave among them [the Shendu or Mara] is valued at eight muskets or two guyals. They appear to be ignorant of money or its value."[22] "I am told that when guns first made their appearance in the hills the western tribes used to exchange their sāl with the eastern tribes for guns, one strong sāl being worth two guns."[23] There is considerable evidence that captives were well treated.[24] According to Lewin,

> A remarkable circumstance transpired with reference to the people held in captivity by the Lushais, viz., that all unite in describing the treatment they received as kind in the extreme. In no case has it been ascertained that any violence had been offered to a female captive, while, as the list shows, many of them have actually married, and becoming incorporated with the tribe, decline positively to be released. The captives given up by

---

20   T.H. Lewin, *The Hill Tracts of Chittagong and the Dwellers Therein; with Comparative Vocabularies of the Hill Dialects* (Calcutta, 1868), 104, cf. 35–36. The text of this book is largely the same as Lewin 1870.

21   Lewin, *Progressive Colloquial Exercises*, 80.

22   Lewin, *The Hill Tracts*, 114.

23   Shakespear, *The Lushei*, 50. See also Parry, *The Lakher*, 205, 585. For more on the connection between the spread of guns and the trade in *sal*, see Hrangchal, "Sal: Slavery."

24   The term *sal* was also employed in a figurative way: "Should several children have died young, the parents will carry the next baby and deposit it in a friend's house, and then come and ask, 'Have you a slave to sell,' and purchase it for a small sum. This is supposed to deceive the Huais [demons causing sickness]. Such children's names always begin with Suak, and, judging from the frequency with which such names are met, the custom must be a very common one": Shakespear, *The Lushei*, 126. The practice was known as *salah zuar* or *suakah zuar*: Reginald A. Lorrain, *Dictionary of the Lushai Language* (Calcutta, 1940), 410, 420.

BEYOND LABOR HISTORY'S COMFORT ZONE

the Southern Howlongs had to be brought forcibly into the camp, and clung to their Lushai friends, weeping piteously and entreating that they might not be made over to us.[25]

Those captives who attempted to flee, however, were severely dealt with. Masters would punish those whom they recaptured by hobbling them, by means of wooden fetters, or even putting them to death.[26]

Servitude-by-refuge (*bawi*). The second, much larger servile category was known as *bawi*. People in this category were in a better position than war captives, not least because they could not be sold and because they were from within the community.[27] This type of servitude came in three different forms: distress servants, sanctuary servants, and deserter servants. Only village chiefs were entitled to keep servants of these categories.[28]

Distress servants, or dependents "living in the village chief's house," formed the majority of *bawi*.[29] They were villagers who could not support themselves—orphans, widows without relatives, or people who had incurred debts—and therefore took refuge in the chief's house.[30] This form of servitude

---

25 Report from Captain T.H. Lewin, Civil Officer, Right Column Lushai Expedition, to the Secretary to the Government of Bengal, No. 22, dated Chittagong, the 26th March, 1872: Reproduced in Mackenzie, *History of the Relations*, 469. See also Lewin, *Progressive Colloquial Exercises*, 80–81; Woodthorpe, *The Lushai Expedition*, 237–238, 317; A.G.E. Newland and J.D. MacNabb, *The Image of War, or Service on the Chin Hills* (Calcutta, 1894), 54; Bertram S. Carey and H.N. Tuck, *The Chin Hills: A History of the People, Our Dealings with Them, Their Customs and Manners, and a Gazetteer of Their Country* (Rangoon, 1896), 230.

26 Lorrain, *Five Years*, 8, 82, 165–166. See also Woodthorpe, *The Lushai Expedition*, 181; Parry, *The Lakher*, 11, 222–223.

27 Shakespear, *The Lushei*, 46–49. Earlier indications of the *bawi* system can be gleaned from the observations of Buchanan in the 1790s and Lewin in the 1860s: Van Schendel (ed.), *Francis Buchanan*, 89–90, 93; Lewin, *The Hill Tracts*, 33–35.

28 Chiefs could afford to keep large numbers of dependents, because even if their labor did not entirely provide for their upkeep, the chief had various sources of income in addition to returns from the land: a rice tax on each cultivator, a share in each animal shot or trapped in the village, a due on salt, and fines that rule-breaking villagers had to pay. This extra income was also expended on prestige-enhancing feasts. Parry, *The Lakher*, 5–6, 12–13.

29 These were known by various names, such as *chhungte, inawm*, and *inpuichhung* (living in the big house), *lalchhung* (living in the chief's house), or *chhiahhlawh* (servant).

30 There are no indications that such debts were in money, because little or no money seems to have been circulating in this region, unlike in the adjacent Chittagong and Arakan hills, which were in direct contact with the thoroughly monetized coastal plains. For more information on barter and the absence of money in pre-colonial Mizoram: Lewin, *The Hill Tracts*, 114; Woodthorpe, *The Lushai Expedition*, 319; R.C. Temple, "Beginnings of Currency," *The Journal of the Anthropological Institute of Great Britain and Ireland* 29, no. 1/2

constituted the pre-colonial social security system: *Bawi* servants were guaranteed shelter and food for the rest of their life.[31] They were treated reasonably well, because they were free to move from one chief's house to another. Other chiefs welcomed *bawi*, because a large number of servants increased the importance of their village and their household's labor power.[32] *Bawi* were allowed to own property and they could set up their own households after having worked for the chief for a number of years.[33] Such "separate dependents" still owed their master certain services and gifts, and one or more of their children would be *bawi*. There were two ways of ending this form of servitude: by buying freedom—the price often being a *gayal* or its equivalent in other goods—or by being adopted by the chief.[34]

Sanctuary servants were those who had committed a serious crime, for example, murder or theft, and had sought refuge in the chief's house to escape revenge.[35] This form of servitude was part of the pre-colonial system of justice.[36] Sanctuary servants were not absorbed into the chief's household, but were settled nearby, under his or her protection. Their children were always considered *bawi*.

Deserter servants were men who, during a war, had deserted the losing side to join the victors by promising that they and their descendants would be servants.[37] They did not live in the chief's house, but unlike the "separate dependents" and sanctuary servants, their daughters were usually not servants.

4   Communal Labor

The system of distress servitude meant that pre-colonial Mizoram lacked footloose workers, but this was not an egalitarian society. The village chiefs, who belonged to a few lineages, considered their fellow villagers—self-providing

---

(1899): 101–102; Lorrain, *Five Years*, 89–90; Zalawra, "Titi Phungleng," *Mizo leh Vai* (December 1922): 135.

31   Shakespear, *The Lushei*, 47; Lorrain, *Five Years*, 166. According to Verghese and Thanzawna, "to the Lushai [Mizo], the word '*Bawi*' meant 'Pauper'": C.G. Verghese and R.L. Thanzawna, *A History of the Mizos*, 2 vols. (New Delhi, 1997), I, 39; A.G. McCall, *Lushai Chrysalis* (London, 1949), 130.

32   For an example, see Lewin, *Progressive Colloquial Exercises*, 80.

33   They were known as *inhrang bawi* or "separate servant."

34   Lewin, *Progressive Colloquial Exercises*, 80; Shakespear, *The Lushei*, 47–48.

35   Known as *chem-sen bawi*, referring to a large axe or machete used as a weapon.

36   Servitude of this kind can be understood as an addition to the ten variants already identified in Van der Linden, "Dissecting Coerced Labor": 298–306.

37   They were known as *tuklut bawi*, or "enter by promising" servants.

BEYOND LABOR HISTORY'S COMFORT ZONE

agriculturalists—as their subjects, and they thought of their servants being significantly below that status. This was a pattern of social distinction throughout the region, but among the Lushai (the majority population of Mizoram) it appears to have been comparatively muted. Commoners were relatively self-assured, and chiefs less powerful than in some neighboring communities: "A chief who disregards custom and oppresses the villagers will speedily lose the bulk of his subjects. The Lushai are accustomed to migrate freely from village to village and this custom affords a very salutary check on too arbitrary a use of power."[38]

Even so, the chief could commandeer the labor power of fellow villagers to have his house built and his fields cultivated, but also for community work, such as repairing the bachelors' communal living quarters (*zawlbuk*),[39] cutting a path through the jungle, making a tiger trap, or constructing a weir in the river. In addition, all able-bodied men were at his disposal for warfare or hunting expeditions.[40] None of this work was paid for, but in return the chief would occasionally give a village feast.[41]

Community service (*hnatlang*[42]) was public work in which everyone was expected to take part. Much of it took place without the chief's involvement. Neighbors helped each other in constructing a hut or weeding a plot of land, the reward being a meal or helpings of rice beer and the promise of returning the favor when needed.[43] Voluntary communal labor was the everyday social expression of the local ethical code (*tlawmngaihna*), which stressed the obligation to be self-sacrificing, stoical, brave, industrious, generous, and sharing. One characterization of *tlawmngaihna* is "an ideal of life in which a man could not be outdone in doing well to others. When a man is Tlawmngai, one cannot

---

38   N.E. Parry, *A Monograph on Lushai Customs and Ceremonies* [1928] (Calcutta, 1976), 1–2, 14–17. See also Lewin, *The Hill Tracts*, 100. According to Shakespear, "The Lakhers, in common with the Chins, are less democratic than the Lushais and their cognates. The power of the chiefs is greater, and the chiefs' relatives and other wealthy people form a kind of peerage and lord it over the lesser fry, being seldom interfered with unless their doings endanger the interests of the chief": Shakespear, *The Lushei*, 216.

39   Often the largest hut in a village; unmarried young men socialized, learned, and slept there.

40   This was especially true of the residents of the bachelors' living quarters: "As all the young men are concentrated there, they are always available for any unexpected emergency or for any urgent work": Parry, *A Monograph*, 9.

41   Parry, *A Monograph*, 6, 12.

42   Zaichhawna Hlawndo, "A Study of the Cultural Factors in the Foreign Missions Thinking of the Mizoram Presbyterian Church" (Ph.D. Thesis, University of Birmingham, 2011), 41.

43   C. Nunthara, *Impact of the Introduction of Grouping of Villages in Mizoram* (Guwahati, 1989), 53–54.

184   WILLEM VAN SCHENDEL

defeat him in doing well to others, and that self-sacrifice sometimes demands life itself."[44] Such community-sustaining behavior was essential in these tough mountains: Its inescapability was reflected in the popular saying *"sem sem, dam dam, ei bil, thi thi"*[45] (share equally, otherwise you die).

5   The Pre-colonial Labor Regime

Before the 1890s, the labor regime of Mizoram consisted of *household self-employment, servile labor,* and *communal labor* (see Table 9.1); wage labor was absent and so was proletarianization.[46] There was no "free labor." The local economy had long been influenced by the expansion of world capitalism—mainly through trade—but this had effected neither a transformation of labor relations nor a monetization of the local economy.

TABLE 9.1   Mizoram. Pre-colonial labor regime. Pre-colonial labor relations ended in the 1890s, except for some areas in the south, where they continued up to c. 1930.

Household labor			
Servitude	Servitude-by-capture		*sal*
	Servitude-by-refuge (*bawi*)	Distress servants	*inpuichhung bawi, lalchhung bawi*
		Sanctuary servants	*chem-sen bawi*
		Deserter servants	*tuklut bawi*
Communal labor			*hnatlang*

---

44   R.L. Thanmawia, "The Mizo Value (As Reflected in Oral Traditions)," in *History and Identity Formation in North-East India,* ed. J.V. Hluna (New Delhi, 2013), 273–279 (quoting K.C. Lalvunga). For various other definitions of this mindset, see Hlawndo, "A Study of the Cultural Factors," 44–46; Parry, *A Monograph,* 19–21.

45   Hlawndo, "A Study of the Cultural Factors," 43.

46   In each village there were a few individuals who did some work that was remunerated, but it would be a misnomer to refer to their services as wage labor. The blacksmith, the priest, and (sometimes) the herald would get a basket of paddy from each household annually in exchange for their services to the community. Parry, *A Monograph,* 6–7.

BEYOND LABOR HISTORY'S COMFORT ZONE   185

6   Colonial Labor Relations

The 1890s were a period of rapid and violent transformation. The British managed to establish their rule in most of Mizoram, disrupting and reordering the labor regime.

6.1   *Servitude*

Servitude-by-capture (*sal*) came to an end, because the colonial rulers prohibited it and because the internecine warfare that had provided a fresh supply of captives had become a thing of the past.[47] Some *sal* stayed with their former masters and became integrated into their villages, others returned to their own villages.[48]

Servitude-by-refuge (*bawi*) underwent considerable change. One of the three subgroups, *deserter servants*, was formally discontinued "but their duties weigh so lightly on them that they seldom claim their release, and in their case, as in that of the 'sāl,' the class, receiving no fresh recruits, will soon cease to exist."[49] The second subgroup, *sanctuary servants*, was also disallowed and "whenever one has claimed protection he has been released."[50] A new colonial justice system was gradually taking over, and those who committed serious crimes could no longer take refuge in a chief's house and live nearby under his or her protection.

It was the third and largest subgroup, *distress servants*, that was allowed to persist. This was remarkable, because the British understood this form of servitude-by-refuge quite well and had abolished it when they took over neighboring areas: the Chittagong Hill Tracts, the Chin Hills, and Arakan.[51]

---

47   According to Turton, this was a more general pattern: "the violent 'razzia' form of slave raiding and trading was the first to disappear with the expansion of European influence in the region [Southeast Asia]": Turton, "Violent Capture," 70.

48   On the fluidity of pre-colonial group identities and the ease with which individuals could take on a new identity by means of the practice of *saphun*, which involved adopting the guardian spirit (*sakhua*) of another group, see Joy L.K. Pachuau, *Being Mizo: Identity and Belonging in Northeast India* (New Delhi, 2014). On former *sal* returning to their old villages, see Shakespear, *The Lushei*, 41. See also Parry, *The Lakher*, 228; McCall, *Lushai Chrysalis*, 64–65.

49   Shakespear, *The Lushei*, 49.

50   Shakespear, *The Lushei*, 49.

51   It was not a case of failed recognition, as Jacobsen argues for Cambodia: Trude Jacobsen, "Debt Bondage in Cambodia's Past—and Implications for its Present," *Studies in Gender and Sexuality* 15 (2014): 33. On the Chittagong Hill Tracts (now in Bangladesh), see Lewin, *The Hill Tracts*, 34–35; Parry, *The Lakher*, 18. On the Chin Hills (now the Chin State of Myanmar), see Bertram S. Carey and H.N. Tuck, *The Chin Hills*, 203–204; C. Crosthwaite,

One reason for preserving it in Mizoram was the specific "light" form of colonial administration there, in which a small cohort of British soldiers-administrators relied heavily on the power of local chiefs who, in turn, relied on the labor of their servants and on the prestige these bestowed on their masters (Figure 9.2).[52] Fear of revolt by chiefs and the cost of releasing servants (and consequently having to deal with Mizoram's poor) made the colonial authorities take a lenient view of this form of servitude: "the custom seems well suited to the people and provides for the maintenance of the poor, old, and destitute, and it would be extremely unwise to attempt to alter it."[53]

Not all observers shared this indulgent view. In what became known as the "Bawi Controversy," a missionary, faced with chiefs who forbade their *bawi* servants to become Christians, publicly challenged the colonial authorities by asserting that *bawi* servants were, in fact, slaves.[54] He proceeded to liberate several of them.[55] He also urged Christian chiefs to free their *bawi*—and some did (Figure 9.3).

The colonial establishment was not amused. The highest local official flatly denied that *bawi* servitude could be equated with slavery, and eventually forced the missionary to leave Mizoram.[56] This controversy was not, however, merely a definitional squabble between a zealous missionary activist and local officials. It had far-reaching consequences, because it touched on well-established legal provisions prohibiting slavery in both Britain and India. The controversy led to a campaign in Britain and debates in Parliament during

---

The Pacification of Burma (London, c. 1912), 324. On Arakan (now the Rakhine State of Myanmar), see Gwynne W. Hughes, *The Hill Tracts of Arakan* (Rangoon, 1881), 20–21.

52   Most distress servants (*inpuichhung bawi*) appear to have been women and children. Chatterjee, *Slavery and South Asian History*, 330.

53   Shakespear, *The Lushei*, 49. See also McCall, *Lushai Chrysalis*, 121–131, who describes *bawi* servitude as "in most cases, almost paternal care."

54   Chatterjee, "Slavery, Semantics"; Sajal Nag, "Rescuing Imagined Slaves: Colonial State, Missionary and Slavery Debate in North East India (1908–1920)," *Indian Historical Review* 39, no. 1 (2012): 57–71; Sajal Nag, *The Uprising: Colonial State, Christian Missionaries, and Anti-Slavery Movement in North-East India (1908–1954)* (New Delhi, 2016); Kyle Jackson, "Colonial Conquest and Religious Entanglement: A Mizo History from Northeast India (c. 1890–1920)" (Ph.D. thesis, University of Warwick, 2016), 276n.

55   The colonial authorities had modified the rule that offering a *gayal* to the master terminated a family's servitude; now a sum of money (40 rupees) could be paid instead. Parry, *The Lakher*, 13.

56   McCall, *Lushai Chrysalis*, 121–131; Chatterjee argues that mission authorities told him to leave: Indrani Chatterjee, *Forgotten Friends: Monks, Marriages, and Memories of Northeast India* (New Delhi, 2013), 320–324, 330.

FIGURE 9.2 Mara woman and her servant pounding rice in Saikao (Serkawr), southern Mizoram.
PHOTOGRAPHER UNKNOWN. REPRODUCED BY PERMISSION OF THE LAKHER PIONEER MISSION COLLECTION, SAIKAO (SERKAWR), MIZORAM, INDIA

1913 and 1914.[57] After World War I, the League of Nations began to scrutinize *bawi* servitude under its remit to abolish slavery worldwide, and Britain was

---

57 Nag "Rescuing Imagined Slaves"; Nag, *The Uprising*; Suhas Chatterjee, *Mizo Chiefs and the Chiefdom* (Delhi, 1995), 42–44; House of Commons Debates, 12 June 1913 (vol. 53, 1789–90); 7 August 1913 (vol. 56, 1887–8, 1899–1900); 7 July 1914 (vol. 64, 867); 23 July 1914 (vol. 65, 657–9); 3 August 1914 (vol. 65, 1800–2).

FIGURE 9.3 Anti-slavery activist with his wife and helper, together with a Christian chief who freed his *bawi* servants in 1909.
LEFT TO RIGHT: MARY FRASER, DR. PETER FRASER, WATKIN R. ROBERTS, AND KHAWVELTHANGA. PHOTOGRAPHER UNKNOWN. REPRODUCED BY PERMISSION OF SYNOD ARCHIVES COLLECTION, AIZAWL, MIZORAM, INDIA

obliged to reiterate its disavowal of *bawi* servitude being a form of slavery.[58] Meanwhile, back in Mizoram, the authorities discontinued using the word *bawi* "due to its association with the wider sense of slavery."[59]

6.2   Communal Labor

The British maintained communal labor for the chief, but codified and circumscribed chiefs' rights to demand it for their own benefit.[60] Instead, communal tasks directed by the chief were to focus on repairing the bachelors' living

---

58   Gordon P. Means, "Human Sacrifice," 184–221. By contrast, when signing the Convention on Slavery in 1926, the British government implicitly acknowledged that they regarded *sal* servitude (which persisted in the southernmost region of Mizoram until they gained control there around 1930) as genuine slavery. See League of Nations, *Slavery Convention*, 6.
59   McCall, *Lushai Chrysalis*, 129.
60   Superintendent, Lushai Hills [A.G. McCall], *Lushai Hills District Cover* (Aizawl Theological College Archives, Aizawl, Mizoram, India, 1938), 23, 24.

BEYOND LABOR HISTORY'S COMFORT ZONE

quarters (*zawlbuk*), the village forge (*pum*), the village school and teacher's house, clearing jungle, and fencing off the water supply.[61]

Throughout the colonial period, communal labor without the chief's involvement continued to be an essential social institution. "It is the custom in Lushai villages for all people to help each other ... it is very shameful if people refuse to help."[62] Reciprocal cooperation was especially important in agriculture, because without mutual assistance the work could not be done in time.[63]

6.3   *Forced Labor*

Under colonial rule, the two older labor relations—servitude and communal labor—were combined with two new forms: state-imposed forced labor and wage labor. Forced labor (corvée, impressed labor) was the most controversial.[64] The new rulers saw it as a form of taxation that was fully justified and they made light of it:

> You forced us to occupy your hills, we had no wish to come up here but you would raid our villages, so we had to come, and so now you have got [to] bear as much of the occupation as possible, you cannot expect us [to] spend the money of the people of the plains on importing coolies to do the work that you are too lazy to do except under compulsion.[65]
>
> Labour by impressment is a part of the people's reasonable contributions to the Government in return for the services provided and on account of the almost insurmountable difficulty that would attend any attempt to create communications through the Hills capable of sustaining mechanical Transport ... The scale of impressed labour is a maximum of 10 days per year per house. A Lushai house generally contains 4 to 6 members of whom two may be males. There are at the time of writing some 22500 houses. From these figures it will easily be seen that even the maximum liability is very small and when it is realized further that the maximum has never yet had to be exacted the incidence of hardship can be said to be infinitesimal.[66]

---

61   Superintendent, *Lushai Hills*, 24.
62   Superintendent, *Lushai Hills*, 24–25.
63   C. Nunthara, *Impact*, 53–54.
64   There was also some privately imposed forced labor, mainly of children in missionary schools. Pachuau and Van Schendel, *The Camera as Witness*, 178–179. See also Catherine Koonar, "Using Child Labor to Save Souls: the Basel Mission in Colonial Ghana, 1855–1900," *Atlantic Studies* 11, no. 4 (2014): 536–554.
65   J. Shakespear, *Annual Report of the Lushai Hills for 1898–1899* (Shillong, 1899), 4, quoted in Sangkima, *Mizos: Society and Social Change* (1890–1947) (Guwahati, 1992), 78.
66   Superintendent, *Lushai Hills*, 97, 106.

If we go by these figures, the *annual* forced-labor demand in colonial Mizoram came to some 600 man years, and the system involved the labor of tens of thousands of male villagers.[67] People deeply resented and opposed coerced labor, not only because it was backbreaking work, but also because it came with the destruction of social hierarchies, humiliation, physical abuse, billeting, demands for women's sexual services, theft of livestock and rice, and disruption of agricultural work.[68]

A major task of coerced laborers was to act as porters for officials who regularly toured the area (Figure 9.4).[69] Because of the very steep terrain—and the lack of level roads and wheeled traffic—travelers had to move arduously along trails, beds of rivulets, and bridle paths.[70] Porters were supposed not to be forced to carry loads exceeding 50 lb., or to march for more than 15 miles a day, "except in very special circumstances."[71] In the 1930s, porters were remunerated at the rate of half a rupee a day.[72]

Forced labor took other forms as well, such as house building, clearing the jungle around military settlements, and carrying heavy building materials and agricultural produce.[73] Officially, women were not to be recruited as forced

---

67   Kyle Jackson, "Globalising an Indian Borderland Environment: Aijal, Mizoram, 1890–1919," *Studies in History* 32, no. 1 (2016): 39–71; Jackson, "Colonial Conquest," 75, 109.

68   McCall, *Lushai Chrysalis*, 288; Parry, *A Monograph*, 6; Lalngurliana Sailo, "Economic Changes and Social Evolution: Mizoram (1870–1960)" (Ph.D. Thesis, Shillong, 2004), 116–118, 217; Chatterjee, *Forgotten Friends*, 295–296, 299; Pachuau and Van Schendel, *The Camera as Witness*, 121–122, 154–156, 159–160, 178, 180; Jackson, "Colonial Conquest," 68–78, 109–113. Guite suggests that when, in World War II, the Japanese appeared on the borders of Mizoram, local people were attracted to them partly because they promised to relieve them of forced labor: Jangkhomang Guite, "Representing Local Participation in INA-Japanese Imphal Campaign: The Case of the Kukis in Manipur, 1943–45," *Indian Historical Review* 37, no. 2 (2010): 307–308.

69   Britain ratified the League of Nations' *Forced Labour Convention* in 1931 (ILO 1930; www .ilo.org). Its Article 18 states: "Forced or compulsory labour for the transport of persons or goods, such as the labour of porters or boatmen, shall be abolished within the shortest possible period," but proceeds to list exemptions. Colonial officials continued to use forced labor for porterage until the end of British rule in 1947. For strategies to withstand international pressures to abolish forced labor in another British colony, see Kwabena Opare Akurang-Parry, "Colonial Forced Labor Policies for Road-Building in Southern Ghana and International Anti-Forced Labor Pressures, 1900–1940," *African Economic History* 28 (2000): 1–25.

70   Pachuau and Van Schendel, *The Camera as Witness*, 145–167.

71   Superintendent, *Lushai Hills*, 112.

72   "[E]xcept in the case of the stages below Kolasib when 12 annas [three-quarters of a rupee] a day will be paid." Superintendent, *Lushai Hills*, 112. Initially payments were much lower, and laborers sometimes refused to accept them as being "beneath their dignity to retain." R.B. McCabe (1892), quoted in Jackson, "Colonial Conquest," 80.

73   Jackson, "Colonial Conquest," 75, 122.

BEYOND LABOR HISTORY'S COMFORT ZONE 191

FIGURE 9.4   "Empire on their backs": More than 30 coerced porters carrying the belongings of an official on tour, 1896.
PHOTOGRAPH PROBABLY BY F.W. SAVIDGE. REPRODUCED BY PERMISSION OF THE BAPTIST CHURCH MISSION COLLECTION, SERKAWN, MIZORAM, INDIA
Note: Expression taken from the title of Lipokmar Dzüvichü, "Empire on their Backs: Coolies in the Eastern Borderlands of the British Raj," *International Review of Social History* (2014): 89–112.

laborers in Mizoram, although they were in other parts of the mountainous frontier regions.[74] However, in reality, women and children in Mizoram were at times compelled to work as porters.[75] The following categories were excused

---

74   Superintendent, *Lushai Hills*, 108; Lipokmar Dzüvichü, "Empire on their Backs," 106.
75   Jackson, "Colonial Conquest," 75–76.

from forced labor: men who went to France in World War I, government servants, those with a physical deformity, schoolmasters, chiefs and their assistants (*upa*), the chief's official (assistant) priest, and certain members of the Salvation Army ("on account of their industrial work and not in connection with any religious aspect of their calling").[76] In an attempt to boost cash cropping, in the early years those who started rubber plantations or potato farms were also exempted.[77]

Even more onerous was the notorious *melveng* system, introduced in 1903.[78] Villages were made responsible for constructing and maintaining almost all paths, roads, and roadside camps in Mizoram. To this end, fixed labor gangs of villagers (*melveng*, or *awmpui*) were formed. These were to settle near the road for which they were responsible. They, or their village chief, were "paid twice annually at some fixed mileage rate." The authorities were very pleased with this system of forced relocation and labor exploitation, because it was cheap and efficient, and because it stimulated the market economy by "distributing money among the villagers."[79]

The pressure of forced labor could be so intense that people migrated to areas where they could escape it.[80] Some villages in Mizoram joined the rebellion against forced labor that broke out in neighboring areas in 1917.[81] Initially, the chiefs resisted the imposition of forced labor, but in the long run the system eroded their legitimacy.[82] The British made them responsible for the supply of laborers,[83] and because the chiefs could not protect the villagers, popular resentment converged on them.

---

76 Superintendent, *Lushai Hills*, 115–116; Parry, *A Monograph*, 1.

77 Pachuau and Van Schendel, *The Camera as Witness*, 175; Thialret, "Thialret thu," *Mizo leh Vai* (October 1908): 183; Jackson, "Globalising," 64; Jackson, "Colonial Conquest," 122, 187, 245. See also Parry, *A Monograph*, 5, 6.

78 "Hodgkins was the first District Engineer, a very competent man who did much good work. It was under him that the Melveng system of road maintenance was brought to perfection": J. Shakespear, "The Making of Aijal" http://aizawl.nic.in/makingofaijal.htm (July 11, 2018). Reprinted in Hluna (ed.). (2013), 410–416.

79 Superintendent, *Lushai Hills*, 199–201. See also Parry, *A Monograph*, 18; Jackson, "Colonial Conquest," 113.

80 Darthuami, "Mihring thih tam saithuk-a," *Mizo leh Vai* (March 1907): 55–56; Jackson, "Colonial Conquest," 96–97, 99–100.

81 Known as Zou Gal or the Kuki Uprising. See Manju Bezbaruah, *The Pursuit of Colonial Interests in India's Northeast* (Guwahati, 2010), 140, 142; Guite, "Representing Local," 304.

82 Jackson, "Colonial Conquest," 92, 95–96, 99–100.

83 "Chiefs are responsible for seeing that the incidence of impressment falls evenly on all the villagers and on none more than others." Superintendent, *Lushai Hills*, 25, see also 33. "Every chief and Headman shall be bound to supply labour on requisition of the Superintendent or his Assistants at such rates of payment as may be fixed by the Superintendent

BEYOND LABOR HISTORY'S COMFORT ZONE

6.4   *Wage Labor*

Colonial rule also ushered in wage labor. All those who were involved in the British occupation—soldiers, officials and imported laborers[84]—were wage earners. It was in the fortified British settlements of Aizawl and Lunglei that a cash economy first developed.[85] Wage labor soon spread among the subject population as well, because the authorities encouraged it by various means. Denial of essential items was one way of compelling people to seek wage employment, as in this case (described by an early missionary) in which payment was in kind:

> To bring a refractory Chief to his senses the government stopped the sale of salt in the bazaars. For the first 5 weeks did not care a straw. But when salt had all gone in their houses they began to feel the pinch. We gave out that we would pay workmen in salt (when building our house). We thus got all things up from Sairang by giving salt (we had wondered how we were going to get our good[s] up) also plenty [of] materials for building our house—simply besieged by men, women & children bringing wood, pumpkins, sweet potatoes, beans, sugarcane, fowls, eggs, etc. in exchange for salt until our storeroom was full up & our backyard one great pile of wood. Workmen would sleep on verandah in order to be sure of work next morning.[86]

In 1909, the authorities promised that those who undertook wage labor for ten days would be excused from forced labor for the year.[87] Taxation was another way in which the authorities encouraged working for wages. They levied a

---

with the sanctions of the Governor." Superintendent, *Lushai Hills*, 105. See also Sailo "Economic Changes," 103. Such policies were common in colonized societies with labor shortages across the Global South. For African examples, see Akurang-Parry, "Colonial Forced Labor Policies," 5–7, 10–12; Jeremy Ball, "Colonial Labor in Twentieth-Century Angola," *History Compass* 3, no. 1 (2005): 3–4.

84   Soldiers came from all over South Asia; notable categories were Sikhs from the Punjab and Gorkhas from Nepal. Officials were generally from the British Isles. Imported laborers were mostly Khasis from what is now Meghalaya, Santals from Central India, Cacharis from the lowlands to the north, and Bengali boatmen.

85   Pachuau and Van Schendel, *The Camera as Witness*, 168–188. The commercialization of labor soon extended to hunting as well, when district authorities began offering large bounties for killing tigers, bears, leopards, and other large forest animals. Jackson, "Colonial Conquest," 135–143.

86   Pu Buanga (Lorrain) 14 March 1894.

87   H.W.G. Cole, "Hlawh-fa kuli hna thawh," *Mizo leh Vai* (August 1909): 133.

household tax (and a grazing tax on some households[88]) and demanded it in cash.[89] As cash would remain scarce here for decades,[90] this drove numerous people to the labor market.[91] Sometimes the household tax was increased to accelerate this process.[92] Wage labor was greatly advanced after famine struck in 1911, because many were forced to take government loans that took years to pay off.[93]

British employers could be rough with wage laborers. One irate missionary admitted to beating up the boatmen who brought him to Mizoram.

> You can have no idea how terribly trying Bengali boatmen are. They are the laziest set of men under the sun ... The Bengalis do not appreciate kindness. Nothing but cross words & blows will make (many of) them do an honest day's work ... The spectacle of a missionary of Peace thrashing a poor heathen is perhaps enough to make many pious people at home shudder but I would invite such to come to spend a few years in Bengal & see if they would not speedily resort to the same as *the only way* to deal with the natives, especially when they are employed as workers.[94]

To such employers, the practices of local laborers came as a surprise. When the first missionaries arrived in Aizawl, they found that the locals included them in their institution of *hnatlang* (communal labor):

> Voluntary Lushai workmen come to us to help build [the] house. Everyone who sees the work says that the men have worked harder & accomplished more in the time than they would have done for any of the officials ... They love to hear us praise what they have done & are proud of the work they have done. They often say, 'A tha maw?' (Is it good?) and are

---

88 Superintendent, *Lushai Hills*, 104–105; Sailo, "Economic Changes," 115–116.

89 After 1904, house tax had to be paid in cash. Sailo, "Economic Changes," 205.

90 Parry, *A Monograph*, 2.

91 Commuting the compensation for the emancipation of *bawi* servants to a fee of Rs. 40 is likely to have had a similar effect.

92 "In the case of one village, Chaltlang near Aijal, the house tax was raised from Rs. 2/- to Rs. 4/- in view of the fact that in normal and prosperous times the villagers had shown themselves incapable of repaying loans taken from Government in times of distress. It is hoped that this poverty stri[c]ken people will migrate to easier conditions or if they remain will become more industrious and therefore be able to pay this enhanced rate of tax, which will reduce any future irrecoverable losses sustained by Government." Superintendent, *Lushai Hills*, 98.

93 Jackson, "Colonial Conquest," 278–283.

94 Pu Buanga (Lorrain) 5 January 1895. Emphasis in the original.

hurt if we do not praise them. It is a treat to find people take an interest in what they do.[95]

When the missionaries did not reciprocate and the authorities proceeded to introduce forced labor, however, the locals quickly stopped offering their labor voluntarily. Henceforth, they excluded the Europeans from their system of mutual cooperation. They worked only for cash payments or evaded employment altogether.[96]

7 The Colonial Labor Regime

After colonial annexation, the labor regime in Mizoram retained some elements of its pre-colonial precursor (see Table 9.2), but these were turned to new ends. *Household self-employment* remained the most prevalent, but following policies to make agriculture more market oriented (or "developed"), it became increasingly connected to a cash economy.[97] New cash crops (such as rice, potatoes, oranges, and rubber) linked cultivators to local and external markets, forcing adaptations in labor deployment within household production units. *Servile labor* had changed considerably and only one category, distress servitude, continued to thrive. *Communal labor* flourished, but with changes. First, the authorities restricted communal labor for the chief by curtailing the private benefits to village chiefs. Second, communal labor became the cultural idiom by which many in Mizoram understood and subsequently appropriated Christianity, allowing rapid indigenous church growth.[98] This, in turn, led to some communal labor in Mizoram being channeled through British and mission-inspired associations such as the Boy Scouts, first aid groups, Sunday schools, and the Young Lushai Association. Communal labor emerged as a core element of a new identity: being a Christian Mizo.

New forms of labor dominated the colonial labor regime. The British imposed *forced labor*, mainly in the form of compulsory porterage and work on roads. In addition, *wage labor* spread rapidly, but by the end of colonial rule few people completely depended on it, and a proletarian underclass had not developed.

---

95   Pu Buanga (Lorrain) 29 January and 14 February 1894.
96   Jackson, "Colonial Conquest," 84–85, 185–186.
97   Pachuau and Van Schendel, *The Camera as Witness*, 171–176.
98   Hlawndo, "A Study of the Cultural Factors."

TABLE 9.2   Mizoram. Colonial labor regime.

Household labor			
Servitude	Servitude-by-refuge (*bawi*)	Distress servants	*inpuichhung bawi, lalchhung bawi*
Communal labor			*hnatlang*
Forced labor			
Wage labor			

8   Post-colonial Labor Relations

In 1947, India gained independence and Mizoram became incorporated into it (rather than into Burma or Pakistan, which absorbed neighboring districts). Independence had no immediate effect on labor relations, however, because the entire colonial setup continued for some time, including a British top official and rule by chiefs in the villages. Even forced labor continued: post-colonial dignitaries made use of it during their tours.[99]

It was not until 1955 that—after much political pressure and an election—rule by chiefs was abolished in Mizoram.[100] With its disappearance, distress servitude and communal labor for the chief also became labor arrangements of the past.

Household self-employment remained important, and wage labor expanded vastly. This was a result of an increase in market-oriented production, but also of war. In 1966 an armed revolt broke out in Mizoram, and the rebels declared the area an independent republic. The Indian armed forces retaliated

---

99   Nari Rustomji, *Enchanted Frontiers: Sikkim, Bhutan and India's Northeastern Borderlands* (Calcutta, 1973), 97–98. The District Council abolished it in 1953. *Zoram Hriattirna* (District Information), 15 November 1952, 3, cited in Sailo, "Economic Changes," 145. India did not ratify the *Forced Labour Convention* of the International Labour Organisation until 1954 (ILO 1930; see also www.ilo.org).

100   J. Zorema, *Indirect Rule in Mizoram 1890–1954 (The Bureaucracy and the Chiefs)* (New Delhi, 2007), 169–170; Pachuau and Van Schendel, *The Camera as Witness*, 257. For resistance to communal labor for the chief during this period, see Sailo, "Economic Changes," 136–138.

BEYOND LABOR HISTORY'S COMFORT ZONE   197

with draconian measures. One that affected the majority of inhabitants was involuntary resettlement. The population of over 500 villages was driven into 110 "grouping centers" under military control. Most of the original villages were destroyed. This counterinsurgency policy affected 87 percent of Mizoram's rural population (and 82 percent of its total population). Resettlement cut people off from their fields and livelihoods, and hunger compelled them to look for wage labor or depend on government handouts.[101] Many drifted into towns in search of work. Between 1961 and the end of the war in 1986, the urban population increased from 5 to 25 percent, and today more than half of the inhabitants live in cities and towns, making Mizoram one of the most urbanized states in India. By the early twenty-first century, wage work had become the dominant element of Mizoram's labor regime.

8.1   *The Return of Forced Labor*

The war also led to the reintroduction of forced labor, which had been discontinued in the 1950s.[102] The Indian military compelled local men and women to carry loads,[103] and this time there were no rules with respect to the weight of burdens, length of marches, or the treatment of porters; let alone remuneration.[104] There were added dangers, too: Indian soldiers used porters as human shields against rebel attacks by having them walk between them and, if an attack happened anyway, as hostages killed in revenge.[105] The "grouping centers" have been described as forced labor camps: all able-bodied internees were put to work under military supervisors and could be whipped if they disobeyed. They dug bunkers and built fences; constructed roads and cleared jungles; and carried water, food, firewood, and ammunition.[106] Forced labor came to an end

---

101   Nunthara, *Impact*, 7–8, 17–18, 55–56; J.V. Hluna and Rini Tochhawng, *The Mizo Uprising: Assam Assembly Debates on the Mizo Movement, 1966–1971* (Newcastle, 2012), 166, 222.

102   In 1966, Mizoram was declared a "disturbed area" under both the Assam Disturbed Areas Act of 1955 and the Armed Forces (Special Powers) Act of 1958. Neither of these acts allowed the authorities to impose forced labor. This was different in nearby Nagaland, where they actually legalized compulsory porterage in 1965.

103   On women being forced to act as porters during the Mizoram War of Independence, see Denise Adele Ségor, "Tracing the Persistent Impulse of a Bedrock Nation to Survive within the State of India: Mizo women's response to War and Forced Migration" (Ph.D. thesis, Santa Barbara, CA, 2006), 265, 268–269, 278, 289, 327, 341, 343, 363, 384, 484.

104   Earlier generations of Indian soldiers had also mistreated porters: "The Lushais [Mizos] greatly resented having to carry what they called the sepoys' [soldiers'] 'Fat wives' and their children, while the sepoys behind them kick and beat them along the roads": McCall, *Lushai Chrysalis*, 288.

105   Sailo, "Economic Changes," 92–93; Hluna and Tochhawng, *The Mizo Uprising*, 159, 200.

106   Hluna and Tochhawng, *The Mizo Uprising*, 200, 158–159, 164.

20 years later, with the signing of a peace treaty between the rebels and the Indian government in 1986.

8.2   *Communal Labor*

The post-colonial labor regime did not consist merely of self-employment, wage labor, and (in the early post-independence days as well as between 1966 and 1986) forced labor. It featured a special characteristic: the continued importance of unpaid voluntary communal labor. This practice had adapted to new circumstances and urban surroundings. Today, in some wealthy neighborhoods, certain recurrent forms have been replaced by wage labor, which exposes these neighborhoods to criticism about losing Mizo authenticity and the community spirit. In most neighborhoods and villages, however, voluntary communal labor continues to flourish. Local groups mobilize the labor of women, men, and children to perform tasks for the public good. These groups include churches, charitable institutions, schools, and neighborhood chapters of the Young Mizo Association (YMA).[107] The technology of mobilizing voluntary labor has changed over time; from word of mouth and church gongs, to public address systems and digital social media.

Communal labor takes many forms. People gather to organize a funeral[108] or a Christmas feast; construct a clinic, church, clubhouse, or private house for a family whose house has burnt down; repair a road; clean and polish; or form a rescue party in the aftermath of an earthquake or landslide (Figures 9.5 to 9.10). Communal labor may also include law and order tasks, when a group checks the neighborhood for unlawful behavior (for example, drinking).[109] Lastly, groups may offer their free labor to clear an agricultural plot or wash people's blankets in return for a donation to a charitable fund. In Mizoram, voluntary labor provides a variety of services that salaried state or commercial agents take charge of elsewhere.

9   The Post-colonial Labor Regime

Compared with Mizoram's pre-colonial and colonial labor regimes (and the 20-year war regime), the post-1986 labor regime was relatively simple (see Table 9.3). Old labor relations, such as servitude and forced labor, had withered away and wage labor had burgeoned. What remained constant throughout these three

---

107   The Young Lushai Association (YLA) changed its name to YMA in 1947.
108   Pachuau, *Being Mizo*, Ch. 5.
109   The Mizoram Liquor (Total Prohibition) Act was in force until 2014, after which a new act allowed permit holders the consumption of alcohol under stringent conditions.

FIGURE 9.5 Communal labor. Planing planks for a new clinic in Pukzing village, 1956.
PHOTOGRAPHER UNKNOWN (POSSIBLY GWEN REES ROBERTS). REPRODUCED BY PERMISSION OF AIZAWL THEOLOGICAL COLLEGE COLLECTION, AIZAWL, MIZORAM, INDIA

FIGURE 9.6 Communal labor. Boys repairing a road in Sihfa village, c. 1956.
PHOTOGRAPHER UNKNOWN (POSSIBLY GWEN REES ROBERTS). REPRODUCED BY PERMISSION OF AIZAWL THEOLOGICAL COLLEGE COLLECTION, AIZAWL, MIZORAM, INDIA

FIGURE 9.7 Communal labor. Constructing a new church in Aizawl town, 1964.
PHOTOGRAPHER UNKNOWN. REPRODUCED BY PERMISSION OF LALHRUAI-
TLUANGA RALTE COLLECTION, AIZAWL, MIZORAM, INDIA

FIGURE 9.8 Communal labor. Improving the Presbyterian Hospital in Durtlang village, 1980.
PHOTOGRAPHER UNKNOWN. REPRODUCED BY PERMISSION OF PRESBYTE-
RIAN HOSPITAL COLLECTION, AIZAWL, MIZORAM, INDIA

BEYOND LABOR HISTORY'S COMFORT ZONE 201

FIGURE 9.9 Communal labor. Cleaning a sacred statue in Aizawl in 2012.
PHOTOGRAPH BY WILLEM VAN SCHENDEL

FIGURE 9.10 Communal labor. Smartening a college campus in Durtlang in 2016.
PHOTOGRAPH BY WILLEM VAN SCHENDEL

202   WILLEM VAN SCHENDEL

TABLE 9.3   Mizoram. Post-1955 labor regime. The period between India's independence
(1947) and the abolition of chiefdom in Mizoram (1955) was a transitional
one in which vestiges of servitude and forced labor persisted.

Household labor	
Wage labor	
Communal labor	*hnatlang*
Forced labor (1966–1986)	

periods, however, was household self-employment and, quite remarkably, communal labor. It was this form of voluntary unpaid labor that gave the labor regime in Mizoram its singular character. The ethic of *tlawmngaihna* (being self-sacrificing, stoical, brave, industrious, generous, and sharing), now grounded in Christian convictions, endured as a core value. Its principal praxis was community service.

10   Labor Regimes in Mizoram

Over the last 150 years, labor relations in Mizoram have undergone astonishing change. By the early twenty-first century, some forms had faded away, together with the forms of power that had supported them (servitude and communal labor for chiefs), others had been introduced (wage labor and forced labor), and yet others had endured (household labor and communal labor).

Significantly, at no time did Mizoram's labor regimes resemble those in other parts of India. In other words, any general pronouncements about labor relations in colonial or post-colonial "India" need to take on board the Mizoram case (and many others that still suffer from labor historians' "neglect, prejudice and implicit assumptions"[110]).

The serial imposition of forced labor—by an "authoritarian" colonial state (1890s to 1950s) and by a "democratic" post-colonial state (1960s to 1980s)—is of particular interest, because it reminds us of the iterative nature of this labor relation, which signals a state's withholding of citizens' rights to certain categories of inhabitants. For this reason, the re-emergence of forced labor

---

110   Van der Linden, *Workers of the World*, 8–9.

under post-colonial states in the wider Extended Eastern Himalayas region is of particular comparative interest.[111]

More than anything, however, it is the vigorous persistence of unpaid voluntary communal labor that is of distinct analytical importance. Rooted in pre-capitalist methods of production, it survived the transition from rural to urban, from barter to cash, and from high levels of autarky to a market economy. Today it coexists with wage labor and household subsistence labor.

As we have seen, voluntary communal labor (*hnatlang*) is an economic activity that expresses the ethical code of *tlawmngaihna*; to be self-sacrificing, stoical, brave, industrious, generous, and sharing. Figure 9.11 invokes this code as the essence of being Mizo. We have also seen that communal labor became

FIGURE 9.11 *"Tlawmngaihna is what makes being Mizo so wonderful!"* Roadside poster in Durtlang (Mizoram), 2016.
PHOTOGRAPH BY WILLEM VAN SCHENDEL

---

111 The best-studied example is Burma (Myanmar). See Patrick Bollé, "Supervising Labour Standards and Human Rights: The Case of Forced Labour in Myanmar (Burma)," *International Labour Review*, 137 no. 3 (1998): 391–418; : Karen Women Organization, *Walking Amongst Sharp Knives: The Unsung Courage of Karen Women Village Chiefs in Conflict Areas of Eastern Burma* (Mae Sariang, 2010); Richard Horsey, *Ending Forced Labour in Myanmar: Engaging a Pariah Regime* (Abingdon, Oxon, 2011); Ken Maclean, "Lawfare and Impunity in Burma since the 2000 Ban on Forced Labour," *Asian Studies Review* 36, no. 2 (2012): 189–206.

the cultural idiom by which many in Mizoram understood and appropriated Christianity.[112] Today the code of *tlawmngaihna* forms the core of the self-ascribed identity of Mizo Christians (or Christian Mizos).[113]

In recent decades, the salience of Mizo self-ascription has increased because of mainland Indian insistence on Mizo "tribal" differences, and because of the 20-year armed struggle for independence. Today, communal labor is a manifestation of proud self-sufficiency and religious merit. To see people routinely offering their labor power for the public good is especially striking in an era in which neo-liberal policies—in India as elsewhere—seek to spread a free-market form of capitalism that encourages a calculus of individual gain.

11   Communal Labor and the Reach of "Global Labor History"

Is voluntary communal labor to be studied as part of "global labor history"? Marcel van der Linden defines the field as researching "not the history of all forms of human labor through the centuries, but *the history of labor insofar that labor is part of the global process of commodification*."[114] However, theorizing voluntary communal labor as being "part of the global process of commodification" is a bit of a stretch. It is not commodified. As a rule, it does not produce commodities. Nor does it generate commodity production or incubate wage labor. It has held out amidst the rise of wage labor and commodity production, but it is of a different order. It presents global labor historians with some conceptual issues. Does contemporary Mizoram fit the assumptions about a "capitalist society," and if so, since when; and how should we deal analytically with non-commodified labor at its very core? Further, how should we calibrate economic and cultural aspects in explaining the persistence of communal labor?

Social scientists have sought to explain unpaid voluntary work in various ways: As an individual "conscience good," as an expression of "warm-glow" non-market transfers, or as embedded in global development interventions.[115]

---

112   Hlawndo, "A Study of the Cultural Factors."

113   Pachuau, *Being Mizo*.

114   Van der Linden, *Workers of the World*, 366–367 (emphasis in the original).

115   For introductions, see Lorenzo Cappellari and Gilberto Turati, "Volunteer Labour Supply: The Role of Workers' Motivations," *Annals of Public and Cooperative Economics* 75, no. 4 (2004): 619–643; Deborah A. Schmedemann, "Pro Bono Publico as a Conscience Good," *William Mitchell Law Review* 35, no. 3 (2008–2009): 977–1010; Ruth J. Prince, "Seeking Incorporation? Voluntary Labor and the Ambiguities of Work, Identity, and Social Value in Contemporary Kenya," *African Studies Review* 58, no. 2 (2015): 85–109; Sergio Destefanis

BEYOND LABOR HISTORY'S COMFORT ZONE 205

Labor historians have focused mainly on the entanglement of wage labor and unpaid household labor for subsistence and the reproduction of labor power.[116] This is what makes the case of Mizo—and others like it across the world[117]—so interesting. Those who regularly offer their labor power for *hnatlang* see this as a free contribution to the community, as a labor of love, and as a confirmation of cultural identity. Their labor is not for personal use nor for close kin, but for a wider community with which they identify: village, urban neighborhood, association, church, and ultimately, Mizo nation (*hnam*). Communal labor does not sustain people's own households, nor is it a survival strategy. Further, it is voluntary: redistributive pressure is low and sanctions for non-involvement are minimal.[118] Moreover, participants in *hnatlang* cannot be subsumed under the rubrics of the "working poor" or "subaltern workers." They have all kinds of class positions and degrees of autonomy (wage laborers, housewives, unemployed, employers, and self-employed).

Voluntary labor poses questions about basic concepts in global labor history: the transformative force of capitalism, extra-economic coercion, peripheral areas,[119] the degree of commodification that makes a society capitalist, and

---

     and Marco Musella, eds., *Paid and Unpaid Labour in the Social Economy: An International Perspective* (Heidelberg, 2009). These deal with non-profit ("third-sector") organizations and "social enterprises," rather than with the type of unpaid voluntary labor addressed in this chapter.

116   For example, the Bielefeld or Entanglement School, which evolved out of the modes-of-production debate. Van der Linden, *Workers of the World*, 320–337. In the "Taxonomy of Labour Relations," an ongoing venture aiming to categorize labor relations worldwide over the past 500 years, there is as yet no place for communal labor relations of the type encountered in Mizoram; instead the taxonomy links "reciprocal labor" to households: Global Collaboratory on the History of Labour Relations, 1500–2000, 2015, *Taxonomy of Labour Relations*, http://www.historyoflabourrelations.org. (July 11, 2018).

117   For example, *tequio* in Mexico and *vuimi/kikwa* in Tanzania: Danièle Dehouve, "Le travail gratuit au Mexique: Les communautés tlapanèques et l'équipement," *Études rurales* 113/114 (1989): 119–130; Michael J. Sheridan, "An Irrigation Intake Is Like a Uterus: Culture and Agriculture in Precolonial North Pare, Tanzania," *American Anthropologist* 104, no. 1 (2002).

118   For a definition of voluntary labor for statistical purposes ("the measurement of volunteer work"), see ILO, *Report of the Conference, 18th International Conference of Labour Statisticians Geneva, 24 November–5 December 2008* (Geneva: International Labour Organisation), 18–19.

119   According to Wallerstein, free labor is "a defining feature of capitalism, but not free labor throughout the productive enterprises. Free labor is the form of labor control used for skilled work in core countries whereas coerced labor is used for less skilled work in peripheral areas." Immanuel Wallerstein, *The Modern World System I: Capitalist Agriculture and the Origins of the European World-Economy in the Sixteenth Century* (Berkeley etc., 1974), 127.

collective action. For example, could we interpret voluntary labor as collective action; as a form of resistance against expansive capitalism? Such questions promise new dialogues and insights, especially regarding the balancing of economic and cultural factors in explaining labor relations in the world today. As Hagan and Wells point out in a review of conceptual debates about free and unfree labor: "Workers are as steeped in the cultural meanings derived from language, religion, ethnicity, and gender as in those created by their location in the relations of production."[120]

If we find it hard to see communal labor as part of "the global process of commodification," it can only be part of what Van der Linden calls "the history of all forms of human labor through the centuries." He emphasizes that these two research domains are compatible, but not of equal urgency. It is a question of priority. "If Global Labor History would in time extend its horizons beyond capitalist civilization, it would deepen our understanding of the specificity (or non-specificity) of capitalist developments."[121] His motivation for endorsing this time lag is twofold:

> both Old and New labor historians have always centrally focused on labor in capitalist societies; it is obvious that Global Labor History dovetails with that interest ... [The] approach directly contributes to understanding the world in which we live now—to [offer] better insight into the tendencies which have brought us to where we are today.[122]

Both points exemplify the theoretical and methodological challenges that Van der Linden elucidates so skillfully. Furthermore, both merit a discussion that goes well beyond the scope of this chapter. The first contains a tactical warning: if we broaden the field of global labor history to include the history of all forms of human labor through the centuries, we run the risk of forfeiting labor historians' attention. However, why should global labor history wait for "Old and New labor scholars" to be ready? Should their current interests really constrain the pursuit of global labor history, at least for some time to come? It might be better to face up to the tension between the ambition to "write the history of labor on a world scale"[123] and its provisional delimitation to "the global process of commodification."

---

120 Jim Hagan and Andrew Wells, "Brassed-Off: The Question of Labour Unfreedom Revisited," *International Review of Social History* 45 (2000): 484.

121 Van der Linden, *Workers of the World*, 361.

122 Van der Linden, *Workers of the World*, 360.

123 Van der Linden, *Workers of the World*, 360.

The second point begs the question of who the "we" are in the phrase "the tendencies which have brought us to where we are today." Presumably, this is a worldwide "we" that includes present-day Mizoram society and its thriving practice of unpaid voluntary communal labor. In other words, if labor historians doubt whether unpaid voluntary communal labor appertains to the global process of commodification, they can only study it by stepping out of their comfort zone. It seems impracticable counsel to neglect non-commodified labor relations until the field of global labor history is ready "in time ... to extend its horizons."

Marcel van der Linden's clarion call for "more accurate typologies from careful empirical study of labor relations" is well taken, as is his assertion that we need to abandon teleological perspectives in order to study the histories of labor as an "open dialectic" without fully predetermined outcomes.[124] But does this not necessarily broaden the field to the history of labor on a world scale, without preconditions or restrictions? How else can we overcome the field's "implicit assumptions"?[125] Surely, global labor history is too important to have us wait for historians to reach agreement on what type, or degree, of commodification makes a society capitalist; or on how to delineate "the global process of commodification." Let us broaden the comfort zone of global labor history to comprise analyses of all histories of labor.

---

124   Van der Linden, *Workers of the World*, 36, 369.
125   Van der Linden, *Workers of the World*, 8–9, 28–32.

Bibliography

Absi, Pascal. "The Future of an Institution from the Past: Accommodating Regulationism in Potosí (Bolivia) from the Nineteenth to Twenty-First Centuries." In *Selling Sex in the City: A Global History of Prostitution, 1600s–2000s*, edited by Magaly Rodríguez García, Lex Heerma van Voss, and Elise van Nederveen Meerkerk, 466–489. Leiden, 2017.

Adelman, Jeremy. "What is global history now?" https://aeon.co/essays/is-global-history -still-possible-or-has-it-had-its-moment.

Agustín, Laura María. "Review of *Sex Trafficking: Inside the Business of Modern Slavery*, by Siddarth Kara." *H-LatAm, H-Net Reviews*, February 2012. Accessed January 10, 2017. http://www.h-net.org/reviews/showpdf.php?id=35320.

Agustín, Laura María, and Jo Weldon. "The Sex Sector: A Victory for Diversity." *Global Reproductive Rights Newsletter* 66/67 (2003): 31–34. Accessed January 5, 2017. http://www.nswp.org/sites/nswp.org/files/The%20Sex%20Sector%20-%20%20A%20Victory%20for%20Diversity.pdf.

Ahuja, Ravi. "A Freedom Still Enmeshed in Servitude. The Unruly 'Lascers' of the *SS City of Manilaor*, a Micro-History of the 'Free Labour' Problem." In *Working Lives & Worker Militancy. The Politics of Labour in Colonial India*, edited by Ravi Ahuja, 97–133. New Delhi, 2013.

Akurang-Parry, Kwabena Opare. "Colonial Forced Labor Policies for Road-Building in Southern Ghana and International Anti-Forced Labor Pressures, 1900–1940." *African Economic History* 28 (2000): 1–25.

Allen, Martin, and D'Maris Coffman, eds. *Money, Prices and Wages. Essays in Honour of Professor Nicholas Mayhew*. Houndmills, Basingstoke, 2015.

Amable, B. *The Diversity of Modern Capitalism*. Oxford, 2003.

American Historical Association. Luke Clossey, and Nicholas Guyatt. "It's a Small World After All: The Wider World in Historians' Peripheral Vision." Accessed August 3, 2016. https://www.historians.org/publications-and-directories/perspectives-on-history/may-2013/its-a-small-world-after-all.

Amin, Shahid, and Marcel van der Linden. "Introduction." In *"Peripheral" Labour? Studies in the History of Partial Proletarianization*, edited by Amin and Van der Linden, 4–5. Cambridge, 1997.

Anderson, Keven B. *Marx at the Margins. On Nationalism, Ethnicity, and Non-Western Societies*. Chicago/London, 2010.

Appleby, J. *The Relentless Revolution: A History of Capitalism*. New York, 2010.

Aston, T.H., and C.H.E. Philpin, eds. *The Brenner Debate. Agrarian Class Structure and Economic Development in Pre-Industrial Europe*. Cambridge, 1985.

Atkinson, A.B. *Inequality. What Can be Done?* Cambridge, MA, 2015.

Austin, Gareth. "Global History in Europe." In *Global History Globally*, edited by Sven Beckert, and Dominic Sachsenmaier, 140–163. London/New York, 2017.

Austin, Gareth. "The Return of Capitalism as a Concept." In *Capitalism. The Reemergence of a Historical Concept*, edited by Jürgen Kocka and Marcel van der Linden, 207–234. London, 2016.

Avineri, Shlomo. *The Social and Political Thought of Karl Marx*. Cambridge, 1968.

Azevedo, Elciene. *O Direito dos Escravos. Lutas Jurídicas e Abolicionismo na Província de São Paulo*. Campinas, 2010.

Azevedo, Elciene. *Orfeu de Carapinha: a Trajetória de Luiz Gama na Imperial Cidade de São Paulo*. Campinas, 1999.

Backhaus, Wilhelm. *Marx, Engels und die Sklaverei*. Düsseldorf, 1974.

Ball, Jeremy. "Colonial Labor in Twentieth-Century Angola." *History Compass* 3, no. 1 (2005): 1–9.

Banaji, Jairus. *Theory as History. Essays on Modes of Production and Exploitation*. Leiden/Boston, 2010.

Baptist, E.E. *The Half Has Never Been Told: Slavery and the Making of American Capitalism*. New York, 2014.

Baranowski, Shelley. *Strength Through Joy: Consumerism and Mass Tourism in the Third Reich*. Cambridge, 2007.

Barbieri-Low, Anthony J. *Artisans in Early Imperial China*. Seattle/London, 2007.

Barker, Robert, Kathleen Wininger, and Frederick Elliston. *The Philosophy of Sex*. New York, 1984.

Barona, Josep L. "The emergence of venereal diseases in the international agenda (ca. 1900)," paper presented at the European Social Science History Conference. Valencia, 2016.

Barry, Kathleen. *Female Sexual Slavery*. Englewood Cliffs, 1979.

Bates, Robert, et al., eds. *Africa and the Disciplines. The Contributions of Research in Africa to the Social Sciences and Humanities*. Chicago, 1993.

Bavel, B.J.P. van, "The transition in the Low Countries: Wage labour as an indicator of capitalism in the countryside, 1300–1700." *Past and Present* 195 (2007): 286–303.

Bavel, B.J.P. van. "Rural wage labour in the sixteenth-century low Countries: An assessment of the importance and nature of wage labour in the countryside of Holland, Guelders and Flanders." *Continuity and Change* 21 (2006): 37–72.

Bavel, B.J.P. van. *The Invisible Hand? How Market Economies have Emerged and Declined since AD 500*. Oxford, 2016.

Becker, G.S., and G.N. Becker. *The Economics of Life: From Baseball to Affirmative Action to Immigration. How Real-World Issues Affect Our Everyday Life*. New York, 1997.

Beckert, Jens. *Imagined Futures. Fictional Expectations and Capitalist Dynamics*. Cambridge, MA, 2016.

Beckert, Sven, and Dominic Sachsenmaier, eds. *Global History Globally*. London/New York, 2017.

BIBLIOGRAPHY

Beckert, Sven. "The New History of Capitalism." In *Capitalism. The Reemergence of a Historical Concept*, edited by Jürgen Kocka, and Marcel van der Linden, 235–249. London/New York, 2016.

Beckert, Sven. *Empire of Cotton: A Global History*. New York, 2014.

Beemer, Bryce. "Southeast Asian Slavery and Slave-Gathering Warfare as a Vector for Cultural Transmission: The Case of Burma and Thailand." *Historian* 71, no. 3 (2009): 481–506.

Behal, Rana. *One Hundred Years of Servitude: Political Economy of Tea Plantations in Colonial Assam*. New Delhi, 2014.

Behal, Rana P., and Marcel van der Linden. "Preface." *International Review of Social History* 51 (Supplement) (2006): 1–5.

Beier, A.L. "Vagrants and the Social Order in Elizabethan England." *Past & Present* 64 (August 1974): 3–29.

Beinien, Joel. "The New McCarthyism: Policing Thought about the Middle East." In *Academic Freedom after September 11*, edited by Beshara Doumani, 237–266. New York, 2006.

Belich, James, et al., eds. *The Prospect of Global History*. Oxford, 2016.

Berend, Ivan T. *An Economic History of Nineteenth-Century Europe*. Cambridge, 2013.

Berg, Maxine, ed. *Writing the History of the Global. Challenges for the 21st Century*. Oxford, 2013.

Berger, Mark. *Under Northern Eyes. Latin American Studies and US Hegemony in the Americas, 1895–1980*. Bloomington, IN, 1995.

Berlin, Ira. *Slaves Without Masters: The Free Negro in the Antebellum South*. Oxford, 1974.

Bethell, Leslie. *The Abolition of the Brazilian Slave Trade: Britain, Brazil and the Slave Trade Question, 1807–1869*. Cambridge, 1970.

Bezbaruah, Manju. *The Pursuit of Colonial Interests in India's Northeast*. Guwahati, 2010.

Bidet, Jacques. *Exploring Marx's Capital. Philosophical, Economic and Political Dimensions*. Leiden/Boston, 2007.

Birchall, Jonathan. "Sex Trafficking." *Financial Times*, January 24, 2009.

Blackburn, Robin. *An Unfinished Revolution. Karl Marx and Abraham Lincoln*. London/New York, 2011.

Blackburn, Robin. *The Making of New World Slavery. From the Baroque to the Modern, 1492–1800*. London/New York, 1997.

Blackburn, Stuart. "Oral Stories and Culture Areas: From Northeast India to Southwest China." *South Asia: Journal of South Asian Studies* 30, no. 3 (2007): 419–437.

Blaut, J.M. *Eight Eurocentric Historians*. New York/London, 2000.

Blaut, J.M. "Fourteen ninety-two." *Political Geography* 11, no. 4 (1992): 355–412.

Bollé, Patrick. "Supervising Labour Standards and Human Rights: The Case of Forced Labour in Myanmar (Burma)." *International Labour Review* 137, no. 3 (1998): 391–418.

Bolton, J.L. *Money in the Medieval English Economy, 973–1489*. Manchester, 2012.

Boone, Catherine. *Property and Political Order. Land Rights and the Structure of Conflict in Africa*. New York, 2014.

Booth, Charles. *Life and labour of the people in London*. 14 vols. London, 1902–1904.

Boris, Eileen, and Heather Berg. "Protecting Virtue, Erasing Labor: Historical Responses to Trafficking." In *Human Trafficking Reconsidered. Rethinking the Problem, Envisioning New Solutions*, edited by Kimberly Kay Hoang and Rhacel Salazar Parreñas, 19–29. New York, 2014.

Boris, Eileen, and Jennifer N. Fish. "Decent Work for Domestics: Feminist Organizing, Worker Empowerment, and the ILO." In *Towards a Global History of Domestic and Caregiving Workers*, edited by Dirk Hoerder, Elise van Nederveen Meerkerk, and Silke Neunsinger, 530–552. Leiden, 2015.

Brantlinger, Patrick. *Fictions of State: Culture and Credit in Britain, 1694–1994*. Ithaca, NY, 1996.

Brass, Tom, and Marcel van der Linden, eds. *Free and Unfree Labour. The Debate Continues*. Bern etc., 1997.

Breman, Jan. *Outcast Labour in Asia: Circulation and Informalization of the Workers at the Bottom of the Economy*. Oxford, 2012.

Breman, Jan. *Patronage and Exploitation: Changing Agrarian Relations in South Gujarat, India*. Berkeley, 1974.

Breman, Jan, and Marcel van der Linden. "Informalizing the economy: the return of the social question at a global level." *Development and Change* 45, no. 5 (2014): 920–940.

Brennan, James P. "Latin American Labor History." In *The Oxford Handbook of Latin American History*, edited by José C. Moya, 342–366. Oxford, 2011.

Brenner, Robert. "The Agrarian Roots of European Capitalism." *Past & Present* 97 (1982): 16–113.

Brenner, Robert. *Merchants and Revolution. Commercial Change, Political Conflict, and London's Overseas Traders, 1550–1653*. Princeton, 1993.

Brick, H. *Transcending Capitalism: Visions of a New Society in Modern American Thought*. Ithaca, NY, 2006.

Britnell, Richard. "Labour Turnover and Wage Rates on the Demesnes of Durham Priory, 1370–1410." In: *Money, Prices and Wages. Essays in Honour of Professor Nicholas Mayhew*, edited by Martin Allen, and D'Maris Coffman, 158–179. Houndmills, Basingstoke, 2015.

Brody, David. "Labor History, Industrial Relations, and the Crisis of American Labor." *ILR Review* 43, no. 1 (1989): 7–18.

Brown, Carolyn, and Marcel van der Linden. "Shifting Boundaries between Free and Unfree Labor: Introduction." *International Labor and Working-Class History* 78 (2010): 4–11.

Brown, Heather A. *Marx on Gender and the Family. A Critical Study*. Leiden/Boston, 2012.

BIBLIOGRAPHY

Bureau international du travail. *La protection de la santé des marins contre les maladies vénériennes.* Etudes et documents, Series P. (Marins), no. 2. Geneva, 1926.

Bureau International du Travail. "Amélioration des conditions de séjour des marins dans les ports." Genève, 1931.

Buxton, Th.F. "The African Slave Trade." In *Marx Engels Gesamtausgabe* Abt. 4, Bd. 9, edited by the International Marx-Engels Foundation, 494–501. Berlin 1991.

Callinicos, Alex. *Deciphering Capital. Marx's Capital and its Destiny.* London, 2014.

Cappellari, Lorenzo, and Gilberto Turati. "Volunteer Labour Supply: 'The Role of Workers' Motivations." *Annals of Public and Cooperative Economics* 75, no. 4 (2004): 619–643.

Carey, H.C. "The Past, the Present and the Future." In *Marx Engels Gesamtausgabe* Abt. 4, Bd. 8, edited by Institute for Marxism-Leninism, 740–752. Berlin, 1986.

Carey, Bertram S., and H.N. Tuck. *The Chin Hills: A History of the People, Our Dealings with Them, Their Customs and Manners, and a Gazetteer of Their Country.* Rangoon, 1896.

Caroatá, José Prospero Jehovah da Silva. *Imperiais resoluções tomadas sobre consultas da seção de Justiça do Conselho de Estado. Desde o anno de 1842, em que começou a funccionar o mesmo Conselho, até hoje, part I*, edited by B.L. Garnier Liveiro. Rio de Janeiro, 1884.

Chalhoub, Sidney. "Illegal Enslavement and the Precariousness of Freedom in Nineteenth-Century Brazil." In *Assumed Identities: The Meanings of Race in the Atlantic World*, edited by John D. Garrigus and Christopher Morris, 88–115. College Station, 2010.

Chalhoub, Sidney. "The Politics of Disease Control: Yellow Fever and Race in Nineteenth Century Rio de Janeiro." *Journal of Latin American Studies* 25, Part 3 (1993): 441–463.

Chalhoub, Sidney. "The Precariousness of Freedom in a Slave Society (Brazil in the Nineteenth Century)." *International Review of Social History* 56, no. 3 (2011): 405–439.

Chalhoub, Sidney. *A Força da Escravidão: Ilegalidade e Costume no Brasil Oitocentista.* São Paulo, 2012.

Chalhoub, Sidney. *Visões da Liberdade: Uma História das Últimas Décadas da Escravidão na Corte.* São Paulo, 1990.

Chaloub, Sidney. "The Politics of Ambiguity. Conditional Manumission, Labor Contracts and Slave Emancipation in Brazil (1850s to 1888)." *International Review of Social History* 60, no. 2 (2015): 161–191.

Chatterjee, Indrani. "Slavery, Semantics and the Sound of Silence." In *Slavery and South Asian History*, edited by Indrani Chatterjee and Richard M. Eaton, 287–316. Bloomington, 2007.

Chatterjee, Indrani. *Forgotten Friends: Monks, Marriages, and Memories of Northeast India.* New Delhi, 2013.

Chatterjee, Suhas. *Mizo Chiefs and the Chiefdom*. Delhi, (1995).

Chayanov, A.V. *The Theory of Peasant Economy*, edited by Daniel Thorner, Basile Kerblay and R.E.F. Smith. Homewood, IL, 1966.

Christie, W.D. *Notes on Brazilian Questions*. London/Cambridge, 1865.

Cole, H.W.G. "Hlawh-fa kuli hna thawh." *Mizo leh Vai* (1909).

Conrad, Robert Edgar. *World of Sorrow: The African Slave Trade to Brazil*. Baton Rouge/London, 1986.

Conrad, Sebastian. *What is Global History?* Princeton, 2016.

Conrad, Sebastian, and Andreas Eckert. "Globalgeschichte, Globalisierung, multiple Modernen: Zur Geschichtsschreibung der modernen Welt." In *Globalgeschichte. Theorien, Ansätze, Themen*, edited by Sebastian Conrad, Andreas Eckert, and Ulrike Freitag, 7–49. Frankfurt, 2007.

Cooper, Frederick. "Africa's Past and Africa's Historians." *Canadian Journal of African Studies* 34, no. 2 (2000): 298–336.

Cooper, Frederick. "From Enslavement to Precarity? The Labour Question in African History." In *The Political Economy of Everyday Life in Africa. Beyond the Margins*, edited by Wale Adebawi, 135–156. Oxford, 2017.

Cooper, Frederick. *From Slaves to Squatters. Plantation Labor and Agriculture in Zanzibar and Colonial Kenya, 1890–1925*. New Haven, 1980.

Crosthwaite, C. *The Pacification of Burma*. London, c. 1912.

Crouch, Colin. *Industrial Relations and European State Tradition*. Oxford, 1993.

Crowhurst, Isabel. "Troubling Unknowns and Certainties in Prostitution Policy Claims-Making." In *Prostitution Research in Context: Methodology, Representation and Power*, edited by May-Len Skilbrei and Marlene Spanger, 47–63. Oxford, 2017.

Cruikshank, Barbara. "Tocqueville's Authority: Feminism and Reform 'Between Government and Civil Society.'" In *Feminist Interpretations of Alexis de Tocqueville*, edited by J. Locke and E.H. Bunting, 305–335. State College, PA, 2009.

Cutter, O.T. *Annual Report on the Administration of the Bengal Presidency for 1863–64*. Military Orphan Press, 1865.

Darthuami. "Mihring thih tam saithuk-a." *Mizo leh Vai* (1907).

Davids, Karel, and Jan Lucassen, eds. *A Miracle Mirrored. The Dutch Republic in European Perspective*. Cambridge, 1995.

Deaton, Angus. *The Great Escape: Health, Wealth, and the Origins of Inequality*. Princeton, 2013.

Dehouve, Danièle. "Le travail gratuit au Mexique: Les communautés tlapanèques et l'équipement." *Études rurales* 113/114 (1989): 119–130.

Desan, Christine. *Making Money. Coin, Currency, and the Coming of Capitalism*. Oxford, 2014.

Destefanis, Sergio, and Marco Musella, eds. *Paid and Unpaid Labour in the Social Economy: An International Perspective*. Heidelberg, 2009.

BIBLIOGRAPHY

Dobb, Maurice. *Studies in the Development of Capitalism*. 1946.

Dore, R. *Stock Market Capitalism, Welfare Capitalism: Japan and Germany versus the Anglo-Saxons*. Oxford, 2000.

Draper, Hal. *Karl Marx's Theory of Revolution, vol. II: The Politics of Social Classes*. New York, 1978.

Dubois, Page. *Slavery. Antiquity and its Legacy*. London/New York, 2010.

Dureau de la Malle, M. *Économie Politique des Romains*. Paris, 1811.

Dussel, Enrique. *La Producción Teórica de Marx. Un Comentario a los Grundrisse*. Madrid etc., 1985.

Dussel, Enrique. *Towards an Unknown Marx. A Commentary on the Manuscripts of 1861–63*. London/New York, 2001.

Dyer, Christopher. "A Golden Age Rediscovered: Labourers' Wages in the Fifteenth Century." In *Money, Prices and Wages. Essays in Honour of Professor Nicholas Mayhew*, edited by Martin Allen, and D'Maris Coffman, 180–195. Houndmills, Basingstoke, 2015.

Dzüvichü, Lipokmar. "Empire on their Backs: Coolies in the Eastern Borderlands of the British Raj." *International Review of Social History* (2014): 89–112.

Eckert, Andreas. "Area Studies and the Writing of Non-European History in Europe." In *Transnational Challenges to National History Writing*, edited by Matthias Middell and Lluís Roura, 140–163. Houndsmill and Basingstoke, 2013.

Eckert, Andreas. "Capitalism and Labor in Sub-Saharan Africa." In *Capitalism. The Reemergence of a Historical Concept*, edited by Jürgen Kocka and Marcel van der Linden, 165–185. London/New York, 2016.

Eckert, Andreas. "Why all the fuss about Global Labour History?" In *Global Histories of Work*, edited by Andreas Eckert, 3–22. Berlin/Boston, 2016.

Eckert, Andreas, and Marcel van der Linden. "New Perspectives on Workers and the History of Work: Global Labor History." In *Global History Globally*, edited by Sven Beckert, and Dominic Sachsenmaier, 145–161. London/New York, 2017.

Editorial Committee. "Editorial." *International Review of Social History* 32, no. 2 (1987): 107–108.

Edlund, Lena, and Evelyn Korn. "A Theory of Prostitution." *Journal of Political Economy* 110 (2002): 181–214.

Eisenberg, Christiane. *The Rise of Market Society in England, 1066–1800*. New York, 2014.

Engels, Friedrich. *The Condition of the Working Class in England in 1844*. Translated by F.K. Wischnewetzky. New York, 1887.

Engerman, David. *Know Your Enemy. The Rise and Fall of America's Soviet Experts*. New York, 2009.

Epstein, S.R. "Rodney Hilton, Marxism and the Transition from Feudalism and Capitalism." *Past and Present* 195 (Supplement 2, 2007): 248–269.

Evans, Richard J. *In Defence of History*. London, 1997.

Fanfani, Amintori. *Catholicism, Protestantism, and Capitalism*. Norfolk, VA, 2002.

Feiermann, Steve. "African History and the Dissolution of World History." In *Africa and the Disciplines. The Contributions of Research in Africa to the Social Sciences and Humanities*, edited by Robert Bates et al., 167–212. Chicago, 1993.

Ferreira de Oliveira, Maria Luiza. "Resistência popular contra o decreto 798 ou a 'lei do cativeiro': Pernambuco, Paraíba, Alagoas, Sergipe, Ceará, 1851–1852." In *Revoltas, Motins, Revoluções: Homens Livres Pobres e Libertos no Brasil do Século XIX*, edited by Monica Duarte Dantas, 391–427. São Paulo, 2011.

Fischer, Eric. "The International Institute of Social History—Reorganization after fifty years." *International Review of Social History* 33, no. 3 (1988): 246–257.

Fonseca Ferreira, Lígia. "Luiz Gama por Luiz Gama: carta a Lúcio de Mendonça." *Tereza. Revista de Literatura Brasileira da USP* 8/9 (2008): 300–321.

Foucault, Michel. *Histoire de la sexualité: La volonté de savoir*. Paris, 1976.

Frances, Raelene. "Prostitution: The Age of Empires." In *A Cultural History of Sexuality in the Age of Empire*, edited by Chiara Beccalossi and Ivan Crozier, 145–170. Oxford, 2011.

Freitag, Ulrike. "The Critique of Orientalism." In *Companion to Historiography*, edited by Michael Bentley, 620–638. London/New York, 1997.

Freitag, Ulrike, and Achim von Oppen, eds. *Translocality. The Study of Globalizing Processes from a Southern Perspective*. Leiden, 2010.

Frentrop, P.A. *History of Corporate Governance, 1602–2002*. Amsterdam, 2002.

Galotti Mamigonian, Beatriz. "O direito de ser africano livre: os escravos e as interpretações da lei de 1831." In *Direitos e Justiças no Brasil. Ensaios de História Social*, edited by Silvia H. Lara, and Joseli M.N. Mendonça, 129–160. Campinas, 2006.

Genovese, Eugene D. "Marxian Interpretations of the Slave South." In *In Red and Black. Marxian Explorations in Southern and Afro-American History*, edited by Eugene D. Genovese, 315–353. New York, 1968.

Gielkens, Jan, ed. *"Was ik maar weer in Bommel." Karl Marx en zijn Nederlandse Verwanten*. Amsterdam, 1997.

Gilroy, Paul. *The Black Atlantic. Modernity and Double Consciousness*. Cambridge, MA, 1993.

Glahn, Richard von. *Fountain of Fortune. Money and Monetary Policy in China, 1000–1700*. Berkeley etc., 1996.

Glazebrook, Allison. "Prostitution." In *A Cultural History of Sexuality in the Classic World*, edited by Mark Golden and Peter Toohey, 145–168. Oxford/New York, 2011.

Glazebrook, Allison. "The Bad Girls of Athens: The Image and Function of *Hetairai* in Judicial Oratory." In *Prostitutes & Courtesans in the Ancient World*, edited by Christopher A. Faraone and Laura K. McClure, 125–138. Madison, 2006.

BIBLIOGRAPHY

Global Collaboratory on the History of Labour Relations, 1500–2000. "Taxonomy of Labour Relations." Accessed November 27, 2016. http://www.historyoflabourrelations.org.

Global Network of Sex Work Projects. "A Labour Rights Approach to HIV and Sex Work." Accessed December 27, 2016. http://www.nswp.org/news/labour-rights-approach-hiv-and-sex-work.

Goff, Jacques Le. *La Bourse et la Vie: Economie et Religion au Moyen Age.* Paris, 1986.

Goff, Jacques Le. *Le Moyen Age et l'Argent.* Paris, 2010.

Goff, Jacques Le. *Marchands et Banquiers au Moyen Age.* Paris, 1956.

Graden, Dale T. "An Act 'Even of Public Security': Slave Resistance, Social Tensions, and the End of the International Slave Trade to Brazil, 1835–1856." *Hispanic American Historical Review* 76, no.2 (1996): 249–282.

Gramlich-Oka, Bettina, and Gregory Smits, eds. *Economic Thought in Early Modern Japan* Leiden/Boston, 2010.

Grandner, Margarete, et al., eds. *Globalisierung und Globalgeschichte.* Vienna, 2005.

Grassby, Richard. *The Idea of Capitalism before the Industrial Revolution.* Lanham, 1999.

Grazia, Victoria de. *The Culture of Consent: Mass Organisation of Leisure in Fascist Italy.* Cambridge, 2002.

Gronewold, Sue. "Prostitution in Shanghai." In *Selling Sex in the City: A Global History of Prostitution, 1600s–2000s,* edited by Magaly Rodríguez García, Lex Heerma van Voss, and Elise van Nederveen Meerkerk, 567–593. Leiden, 2017.

Guite, Jangkhomang. "Civilisation and its Malcontents: The Politics of Kuki Raid in Nineteenth Century Northeast India." *The Indian Economic and Social History Review* 48, no. 3 (2011): 339–376.

Guite, Jangkhomang. "Colonialism and Its Unruly? The Colonial State and Kuki Raids in Nineteenth Century Northeast India." *Modern Asian Studies* 48, no. 5 (2014): 1188–1232.

Guite, Jangkhomang. "Representing Local Participation in INA-Japanese Imphal Campaign: The Case of the Kukis in Manipur, 1943–45." *Indian Historical Review* 37, no. 2 (2010): 1291–1309.

Guy, Donna J. *Sex and Danger in Buenos Aires. Prostitution, Family and Nation in Argentina.* Lincoln, 1991.

Hagan, Jim, and Andrew Wells. "Brassed-Off: The Question of Labour Unfreedom Revisited." *International Review of Social History* 45 (2000): 475–485.

Haider, Najaf. "Fractional pieces and non-metallic monies in medieval India (1200–1750)." In *Money in Asia (1200–1900). Small Currencies in Social and Political Contexts,* edited by Kate Leonard, and Ulrich Theobald, 86–107. Leiden/Boston, 2015.

Hall, P.A., and D. Soskice, eds. *Varieties of Capitalism: The Institutional Foundations of Comparative Advantage.* Oxford, 2001.

Hammad, Hahan, and Francesca Biancani. "Prostitution in Cairo." In *Selling Sex in the City: A Global History of Prostitution, 1600s–2000s*, edited by Magaly Rodríguez García, Lex Heerma van Voss, and Elise van Nederveen Meerkerk, 233–260. Leiden, 2017.

Hannerz, Ulf. "The World in Creolization." *Africa* 57 (1987): 546–559.

Hardy, Thomas. "The Dorsetshire Labourer." *Longman's Magazine* (1883). Republished as *The Dorset Farm Labourer in Past and Present*. Dorset Agricultural Workers' Union, Dorchester, 1884.

Harman, Chris, and Robert Brenner. "The Origins of Capitalism." *International Socialism. A quarterly review of socialist theory* 111 (2006). Accessed November, 17, 2017. http://isj.org.uk/the-origins-of-capitalism/.

Harootunian, Harry. *History's Disquiet: Modernity, Cultural Practice, and the Question of Everyday Life*. New York, 2000.

Hartwell, Max. "Foreword." In *Alexis de Tocqueville's Memoir on Pauperism*. Translated by Seymour Drescher, iv–vi. London, 1997. http://www.civitas.org.uk/pdf/Tocqueville_rr2.pdf.

Hébrard, Jean. "Esclavage et dénomination: imposition et appropriation d'un nom chez les esclaves de la Bahia au XIXe siècle." *Cahiers du Brésil Contemporain* 53/54 (2003): 31–92.

Heerma van Voss, Lex. "'The Worst Class of Workers': Migration, Labor Relations and Living Strategies of Prostitutes Around 1900." In *Working on Labor: Essays in Honor of Jan Lucassen*, edited by Marcel van der Linden and Leo Lucassen, 153–170. Leiden, 2012.

Heinrich, Michael. *An Introduction to the Three Volumes of Karl Marx's Capital*. New York, 2004.

Hertroijs, Frasie. *Hoe kennis van China naar Europa kwam. De rol van Jezuïeten en VOC-dienaren, circa 1680–1795*. PhD diss., Vrije Universiteit Amsterdam, 2014.

Hilferding, Rudolf. *Das Finanzkapital*. Vienna, 1910.

Hilton, Rodney, ed. *The Transition from Feudalism to Capitalism*. London, 1976.

Hilton, Rodney. *The English peasantry in the later Middle Ages: The Ford lectures for 1973, and related studies*. Oxford, 1975.

Himmelfarb, Gertrude. "Introduction." In *Alexis de Tocqueville's Memoir on Pauperism*. Translated by Seymour Drescher, 1–16. London, 1997. http://www.civitas.org.uk/pdf/Tocqueville_rr2.pdf .

Hirschman, Albert O. *Rival Views of Market Society and Other Recent Essays*. Cambridge, MA, 1992.

Hlawndo, Zaichhawna. "A Study of the Cultural Factors in the Foreign Missions Thinking of the Mizoram Presbyterian Church." PhD Diss., University of Birmingham, 2011.

Hluna, J.V., and Rini Tochhawng. *The Mizo Uprising: Assam Assembly Debates on the Mizo Movement, 1966–1971*. Newcastle, 2012.

BIBLIOGRAPHY

Hoang, Kimberly Kay, and Rhacel Salazar Parreñas. "Introduction." In *Human Trafficking Reconsidered. Rethinking the Problem, Envisioning New Solutions*, edited by Kimberly Kay Hoang and Rhacel Salazar Parreñas, 1–18. New York, 2014.

Hofmeester, Karin, and Christine Moll-Murata, eds. *The Joy and Pain of Work. Global Attitudes and Valuation 1500–1650*. Cambridge, 2012.

Hofmeester, Karin, and Pim de Zwart, eds. *Colonialism, Institutional Change, and Shifts in Global Labor Relations*. Amsterdam, 2017.

Hofmeester, Karin, et al., "No Global Labor History without Africa: Reciprocal Comparison and Beyond." *History in Africa* 41 (2014): 249–276.

Holthoon, Frits van, and Marcel van der Linden, eds. *Internationalism in the Labour Movement 1830–1940*. Leiden, 1988.

Holton, R.J. *The Transition from Feudalism to Capitalism*. Houndmills, Basingstoke, 1985.

Honegger, C., et al., eds. *Strukturierte Verantwortungslosigkeit: Berichte aus der Bankenwelt*. Frankfurt, 2010.

Horace. *Satires*. Book I, Satire 1.

Horsey, Richard. *Ending Forced Labour in Myanmar: Engaging a Pariah Regime*. Abingdon, Oxon, 2011.

House of Commons. "Assam (Lushai Tribes)." *House of Commons Debates (London, 12 June 1913)* vol. 53 (1913): 1789–90.

House of Commons. "East India Revenue Accounts (Indian Budget)." *House of Commons Debates (London, 7 August 1913)* vol. 56 (1913): 1887–1900.

House of Commons. "Semi-Slavery (Lushai Hills)." *House of Commons Debates (London, 7 July 1914)* vol. 64 (1914): 867.

House of Commons. "Slavery and Ransom—Written Answers." *House of Commons Debates (London, 23 July 1914)* vol. 65 (1914): 657–9W.

House of Commons. "Tribal Customs—Written Answers." *House of Commons Debates (London, 3 August 1914)* vol. 65 (1914): 1800–2W.

Howell, M.C. *Commerce Before Capitalism in Europe, 1300–1600*. Cambridge, 2010.

Hrangchal, Lalhrilmoi. "Sal: Slavery in the Lushai Hills." *International Journal of Research* 1, no. 10 (2014): 1903–1931.

Hughes, Gwynne W. *The Hill Tracts of Arakan*. Rangoon, 1881.

Huntington, Samuel. *The Clash of Civilization and the Remaking of World Order*. New York, 1996.

Hurren, Elizabeth T. *Protesting About Pauperism. Poverty, Politics and Poor Relief in Late-Victorian England, 1870–1900*. Woodbridge, 2015.

ILO Country Office for Viet Nam. "Viet Nam's Sex Industry—A Labour Rights Perspective." 2016. Accessed January 11, 2017. http://www.ilo.org/wcmsp5/groups/public/---asia/---ro-bangkok/---ilo-hanoi/documents/publication/wcms_524918.pdf.

International Committee on the Rights of Sex Workers in Europe. "Under the red umbrella." Accessed December 28, 2016. http://www.sexworkeurope.org/campaigns/red-umbrella-campaigns.

International Labour Conference, 99th Session. "Fifth item on the agenda: HIV/AIDS and the world of work," Report of the Committee on HIV/AIDS. Geneva, 2010. Accessed January 10, 2017. http://www.nswp.org/sites/nswp.org/files/ILO%20Report%20of%20the%20Committee%20on%20HIV%20AIDS.pdf.

International Labour Office. "Activities of the ILO, 1976. Report of the Director-General (Part 2)." Geneva, 1977. Accessed January 5, 2017. http://www.ilo.org/public/portugue/region/eurpro/lisbon/pdf/09383_1977_63_part2.pdf.

International Labour Office. *Profits and Poverty: The Economics of Forced Labour.* Geneva, 2014. Accessed January 10, 2017. http://www.ilo.org/wcmsp5/groups/public/---ed_norm/---declaration/documents/publication/wcms_243391.pdf.

International Labour Organization. "HIV and work. Getting to Zero through the world of work." Accessed January 10, 2017. http://www.ilo.org/wcmsp5/groups/public/@ed_protect/@protrav/@ilo_aids/documents/genericdocument/wcms_185717.pdf.

International Labour Organization. "ILO Report on the Sex Sector Receives Prestigious Prize at Frankfurt Book Fair." Accessed January 6, 2017. http://www.ilo.org/global/about-the-ilo/newsroom/news/WCMS_007999/lang--en/index.htm#N_1_.

International Labour Organization. "ILOAIDS' History." Accessed January 6, 2017. http://www.ilo.org/aids/Aboutus/WCMS_DOC_AIDS_ABO_BCK_EN/lang--en/index.htm.

International Labour Organization. "Recommendation concerning HIV and AIDS and the World of Work (No. 200)." Geneva, 2010. Accessed January 6, 2017. http://www.ilo.org/wcmsp5/groups/public/---ed_protect/---protrav/---ilo_aids/documents/normativeinstrument/wcms_142706.pdf.

International Labour Organization. "What is forced labour, modern slavery and human trafficking." Accessed January 10, 2017. http://www.ilo.org/global/topics/forced-labour/definition/lang--en/index.htm.

International Labour Organization. *Forced Labour Convention* no. 29 (1930). Accessed January 10, 2017. http://www.ilo.org/dyn/normlex/en/f?p=NORMLEXPUB:12100:0::NO::P12100_ILO_CODE:C029.

International Labour Organization. *Report of the Conference, 18th International Conference of Labour Statisticians Geneva, 24 November–5 December 2008.* Geneva.

Jackson, Kyle. "Colonial Conquest and Religious Entanglement: A Mizo History from Northeast India (c. 1890–1920)." PhD diss., University of Warwick, 2016.

Jackson, Kyle. "Globalising an Indian Borderland Environment: Aijal, Mizoram, 1890–1919." *Studies in History* 32, no. 1 (2016): 39–71.

Jacobsen, Trude. "Debt Bondage in Cambodia's Past—and Implications for its Present." *Studies in Gender and Sexuality* 15 (2014): 32–43.

BIBLIOGRAPHY

James, C.L.R. *The Black Jacobins. Toussaint L'Ouverture and the San Domingo Revolution.* New York, 1938.

Jeffrey, Leslie Ann. *Sex and Borders: Gender, National Identity and Prostitution Policy in Thailand.* British Columbia, 2007.

Jeffreys, Sheila. *The Idea of Prostitution.* North Melbourne, 1997.

Johnson, Walter. *River of Dark Dreams: Slavery and Empire in the Cotton Kingdom.* Cambridge, 2013.

Jordan, Ann. "Sex Trafficking: The Abolitionist Fallacy." *Foreign Policy in Focus,* March 18, 2009. Accessed January 10, 2017. http://fpif.org/sex_trafficking_the_abolitionist_fallacy/.

Jursa, Michael. "Babylonia in the first millennium BCE—economic growth in times of empire." In *The Cambidge History of Capitalism,* edited by Larry Neale, and Jeffrey G. Williamson, 24–42. 2 vols. Cambridge, 2014.

Kara, Siddharth. *Sex Trafficking. Inside the Business of Modern Slavery.* New York, 2009.

Karen Women Organization, *Walking Amongst Sharp Knives: The Unsung Courage of Karen Women Village Chiefs in Conflict Areas of Eastern Burma.* Mae Sariang, 2010.

Katz, Michael B. *The Undeserving Poor: America's Enduring Confrontation With Poverty.* New York, 2013. Second and revised edition.

Keslassy, Eric. *Le Libéralisme de Tocqueville à l'épreuve du Paupérisme.* Paris, 2000.

Kindleberger, C.P. and R. Aliber. *Manias, Panics and Crashes: A History of Financial Crises.* Hoboken, NJ, 2005. Fifth edition.

Klein, Naomi. *This Changes Everything. Capitalism vs. the Climate.* New York, 2014.

Klein, Herbert, and João José Reis. "Slavery in Brazil." In *The Oxford Handbook of Latin American History,* edited by José Moya, 181–211. Oxford/New York, 2011.

Kloosterman, Jaap, and Jan Lucassen. *Rebels with a Cause. Five centuries of social history collected by the IISH.* Amsterdam, 2010.

Kocka, Jürgen, and Marcel van der Linden, eds. *Capitalism. The Reemergence of a Historical Concept.* London/New York, 2016.

Kocka, Jürgen. "Capitalism: The History of the Concept." In *International Encyclopedia of the Social & Behavioral Sciences,* edited by James D. Wright, vol. III, 2nd edition, 105–110. Amsterdam, 2015.

Kocka, Jürgen. "Introduction." In *Capitalism. The Reemergence of a Historical Concept,* edited by Jürgen Kocka and Marcel van der Linden, 1–10. London, 2016.

Kocka, Jürgen. "Kapitalismus und Demokratie. Der historische Befund." *Archiv für Sozialgeschichte* 56 (2016): 39–50.

Kocka, Jürgen. *Arbeiterleben und Arbeiterkultur. Die Entstehung einer sozialen Klasse.* Bonn, 2015.

Kocka, Jürgen. *Arbeitsverhältnisse und Arbeiterexistenzen: Grundlagen der Klassenbildung im 19. Jahrhundert.* Bonn, 1990.

Kocka, Jürgen. *Capitalism is not Democratic and Democracy not Capitalistic. Tensions and Opportunities in Historical Perspective.* Florence, 2015.

Kocka, Jürgen. *Capitalism. A Short History.* Princeton/Oxford, 2016.

Koonar, Catherine. "Using Child Labor to Save Souls: the Basel Mission in Colonial Ghana, 1855–1900." *Atlantic Studies* 11, no. 4 (2014): 536–554.

Krätke, Michael. "Journalisme et Science. L'importance des Travaux Journalistiques de Marx pour la Critique de l'Économie Politique." *Actuel Marx* 42, no. 2 (2007): 128–163.

Krätke, Michael. "Marx and World History." *International Review of Social History* 63, no. 1 (April 2018): 91–125

Kriedte, P. et al. *Industrialization before Industrialization: Rural Industry in the Genesis of Capitalism.* Cambridge, 1981.

Krippner, G.R. *Capitalizing on Crisis: The Political Origins of the Rise of Finance.* Cambridge, 2011.

Kulischer, Josef. *Allgemeine Wirtschaftsgeschichte des Mittelalters und der Neuzeit, vol. I.* Munich, 1965. Third edition.

Kwaschik, Anne. *Der Griff nach dem Weltwissen. Normative Ordnungen, kognitive und institutionelle Praktiken der Area Studies im 19. und 20. Jahrhundert.* Unpublished Postdoctoral [Habilitation] thesis, Free University, Berlin 2016.

Laite, Julia. "Traffickers and Pimps in the Era of White Slavery." *Past & Present* 237, no. 1 (2017): 237–269.

Laite, Julia. *Common Prostitutes and Ordinary Citizens: Commercial Sex in London, 1885–1960.* London, 2011.

Lazarsfeld, Paul F., and Anthony R. Oberschall. "Max Weber and Empirical Social Research." *American Sociological Review* 30, no. 2 (1965): 185–199.

League of Nations Advisory Committee on Traffic in Women and Children. "Report of the Special Body of Experts on Traffic in Women and Children (two parts)." Geneva, 1927.

League of Nations Commission of Enquiry into Traffic of Women and Children in the East. "Report to the Council." Geneva, 1932.

Lebowitz, Michael A. *Beyond Capital. Marx's Political Economy of the Working Class.* London, 1992.

Ledbetter, James. "Introduction." In *Dispatches for the New York Tribune. Selected Journalism of Karl Marx*, edited by James Ledbetter, xvii–xxvii. London, 2007.

Lenger, Friedrich. "Die neue Kapitalismusgeschichte. Ein Forschungsbericht als Einleitung." *Archiv für Sozialgeschichte* 56 (2016): 3–37.

Leonhard, Jörn, and Willibald Steinmetz. "Von der Begriffsgeschichte zur historischen Semantik von 'Arbeit.'" in *Semantiken von Arbeit. Diachrone und vergleichende Perspektiven*, edited by Jörn Leonhard and Willibald Steinmetz, 9–59. Cologne, 2016.

"Less stigma, more competition." *The Economist*, January 26, 2017.

BIBLIOGRAPHY

Lewin, T.H. *Progressive Colloquial Exercises in the Lushai Dialect of the 'Dzo' Or Kúki Language, with Vocabularies and Popular Tales* (notated). Calcutta, 1874.

Lewin, T.H. *The Hill Tracts of Chittagong and the Dwellers Therein; with Comparative Vocabularies of the Hill Dialects.* Calcutta, 1868.

Lim, Lin Leam, ed. *The Sex Sector: The Economic and Social Bases of Prostitution in Southeast Asia.* Geneva, 1998.

Lim, Lin Leam. "Preface." In *The Sex Sector: The Economic and Social Bases of Prostitution in Southeast Asia*, edited by Lin Leam Lim, v. Geneva, 1998.

Lim, Lin Leam. "The economic and social bases of prostitution in Southeast Asia." In *The Sex Sector: The Economic and Social Bases of Prostitution in Southeast Asia*, edited by Lin Leam Lim, 2–3. Geneva, 1998.

Lim, Lin Leam. "Whither the Sex Sector? Some Policy Considerations." In *The Sex Sector: The Economic and Social Bases of Prostitution in Southeast Asia*, edited by Lin Leam Lim, 206–226. Geneva, 1998.

Lima, Henrique Espada. "Freedom, Precariousness, and the Law: Freed Persons contracting out their Labor in Nineteenth-Century Brazil." *International Review of Social History* 54, no. 3 (2009): 391–416.

Limoncelli, Stephanie. *The Politics of Trafficking: The First International Movement to Combat the Sexual Exploitation of Women.* Stanford, 2010.

Linden, Marcel van der, ed. *The End of Labour History?* Cambridge, 1994.

Linden, Marcel van der. "Charles Tilly's Historical Sociology." *International Review of Social History* 54, no. 2 (2009): 237–274.

Linden, Marcel van der. "Connecting Household History and Labour History." *International Review of Social History*, Supplement 1 (1993): 163–173.

Linden, Marcel van der. "Die neue Zusammensetzung der Weltarbeiter Innenklasse und das Problem der Solidarität." In *Die Wiederkehr der Proletarität. Dokumentation der Debatte*, edited by Karl Heinz Roth, 83–94. Köln, 1994.

Linden, Marcel van der. "Dissecting Coerced Labor." In *On Coerced Labor: Work and Compulsion after Chattel Slavery*, edited by Marcel van der Linden and Magaly Rodríguez García, 293–322. Leiden, 2016.

Linden, Marcel van der. "Editorial." *International Review of Social History* 38 (Special Issue; 1993): 1–3.

Linden, Marcel van der. "Final Thoughts." In *Capitalism. The Reemergence of a Historical Concept*, edited by Jürgen Kocka and Marcel van der Linden, 251–266. London/ New York, 2016.

Linden, Marcel van der. "Forced Labour and Non-Capitalist Industrialization: The Case of Stalinism (c. 1929–c. 1956)." In *Free and Unfree Labour. The Debate Continues*, edited by Tom Brass and Van der Linden, 351–362. Bern, 1997.

Linden, Marcel van der. "Histoire Comparée des Sociétés de Secours Mutuels." *Revue de l'économie sociale* 19 (1990): 169–179.

Linden, Marcel van der. "Keeping Distance: Alf Lüdtke's "Decentred" Labour History." *International Review of Social History* 40 (1995): 287–296.

Linden, Marcel van der. "Labour History and Organizational Ecology." *International Review of Social History* 35 (1990): 273–280.

Linden, Marcel van der. "Labour History Beyond Borders." In *Histories of Labour. National and International Perspectives*, edited by Joan Allen et al., 353–383. Pontypool, 2010.

Linden, Marcel van der. "Methodologische Probleme vergleichender Sozialgeschichte: Eine Erwiderung auf Christiane Eisenbergs 'methodenkritische Bemerkungen' zu einem IISG-Projekt." *Archiv für Sozialgeschichte* 35 (1995): 231–239.

Linden, Marcel van der. "San Precario: A New Inspiration for Labor Historians." *Labor* 11 (2014): 9–21.

Linden, Marcel van der. "The 'Globalization' of Labour and Working-Class History and its Consequences." *International Labor and Working-Class History* 65 (2004): 136–156

Linden, Marcel van der. "The Aftermath of '1968': 'Interactions of Workers,' Youth and Women's Movements." In *Transnational Labour History. Explorations*, edited by Van der Linden, 117–141. Aldershot, 2003.

Linden, Marcel van der. "The Crisis of World Labor." *Against the Current* 176 (2015): 29–34.

Linden, Marcel van der. "The Many Faces of Dutch Revolutionary Trade Unionism." In *Revolutionary Syndicalism: An International Perspective*, edited by Van der Linden and Wayne Thorpe, 45–57. Aldershot, 1990.

Linden, Marcel van der. "The Origins, Spread and Normalization of Free Wage Labour." In *Free and Unfree Labour. The Debate Continues*, edited by Tom Brass and Van der Linden, 501–523. Bern, 1997.

Linden, Marcel van der. "The Promise and Challenges of Global Labor History." *International Labor and Working Class History* 82 (2012): 57–76.

Linden, Marcel van der. *Transnational Labour History. Explorations*. Aldershot, 2003.

Linden, Marcel van der. *Workers of the World. Essays Toward a Global Labor History*. Leiden, 2008.

Linden, Marcel van der, and Magaly Rodríguez García, eds. *On Coerced Labor. Work and Compulsion After Chattel Slavery*. Leiden/Boston, 2016.

Linden, Marcel van der, and Magaly Rodríguez García. "Introduction." In *On Coerced Labor. Work and Compulsion after Chattel Slavery*, edited by Van der Linden and Magaly Rodríguez García, 1–10. Leiden/Boston, 2016.

Linden, Marcel van der, and Jan Lucassen. *Prolegomena for a Global Labour History*. Amsterdam, 1999.

Linden, Marcel van der, and Jürgen Rojahn, eds. *The Formation of Labour Movements 1870–1914. An International Perspective*. 2 vols. Leiden, 1990.

BIBLIOGRAPHY

Linden, Marcel van der, and Karl Heinz Roth. "Introduction." In *Beyond Marx. Theorising the Global Labour Relations of the Twenty-first Century*, edited by Marcel van der Linden and Karl Heinz Roth, 1–20. Leiden/Boston, 2014.

Linden, Marcel van der Linden, and Wayne Thorpe. "The Rise and Fall of Revolutionary Syndicalism." In *Revolutionary Syndicalism: An International Perspective*, edited by Van der Linden and Thorpe, 1–24. Aldershot, 1990.

Linden, Marcel van der, and Lex Heerma van Voss "Introduction." In *Class and Other Identities. Gender, Religion and Ethnicity in the Writing of European Labour History*, edited by Van der Linden and Heerma van Voss, 1–39. New York/Oxford, 2002.

Linden, Marcel van der, Angelika Ebbinghaus, and Max Henninger, eds. *1968—A View of the Protest Movements 40 Years After, from a Global Perspective*. Leipzig, 2009.

Lis, Catharina, and Hugo Soly. *Worthy Efforts: Attitudes to Work and Workers in Pre-Industrial Europe*. Leiden/Boston, 2012.

Lis, Catharina, Jan Lucassen, and Hugo Soly, eds. "Before the Unions. Wage earners and collective action in Europe, 1300–1850." *International Review of Social History* 39 Supplement 2 (1994).

Liu, William Guanglin. *The Chinese Market Economy, 1000–1500*. Albany, 2015.

Lordon, Frédéric. *Willing Slaves of Capital. Spinoza and Marx on Desire*. London/New York, 2014.

Lorrain, Reginald A. *Dictionary of the Lushai Language*. Calcutta, 1940.

Lorrain, Reginald A. *Five Years in Unknown Jungles for God and Empire*. London, 1912.

Lourens, Piet, and Jan Lucassen. "Marx als Historiker der niederländischen Republik." In *Die Rezeption der Marxschen Theorie in den Niederlanden*, edited by Marcel van der Linden, 430–454. Trier, 1992.

Loveman, Mara. "Blinded Like a State: The Revolt Against Civil Registration in Nineteenth-Century Brazil." *Comparative Studies in Society and History* 49 (2007): 5–39.

Löwy, Michael. *The Theory of Revolution in the Young Marx*. Leiden/Boston, 2003.

Lucassen, Jan, ed., *Wages and Currency. Global Comparisons from Antiquity to the Twentieth Century*. Bern, 2007.

Lucassen, Jan. "Deep Monetization: The Case of the Netherlands 1200–1940," TSEG 11, no. 3 (2014): 73–121.

Lucassen, Jan. "Deep Monetization, Commercialization and Proletarianization. Possible Links, India 1200–1900." In *Towards a new History of Work*, edited by Sabyasachi Bhattacharya, 17–55. New Delhi, 2014.

Lucassen, Jan. "Deep Monetization in Eurasia in the long run." In *Money, Currency and Crisis. In Search of Trust 2000 BC to AD 2000*, edited by Bert van der Speck and Bas van Leeuwen. London, 2018, forthcoming.

Lucassen, Jan. "Free and Unfree Labour Before the Twentieth Century: A Brief Overview." In *Free and Unfree Labour. The Debate Continues,* edited by Tom Brass and Marcel van der Linden, 45–56. Bern, 1997.

Lucassen, Jan. "Working at the Ichapur Gunpowder Factory in the 1790s." *Indian Historical Review* 39 (2012): 19–56 and 251–271.

Lucassen, Jan. "Writing Global Labour History c. 1800–1940: A Historiography of Concepts, periods, and Geographical Scope." In *Global Labour History. A State of the Art,* edited by Jan Lucassen, 39–89. Bern, 2006.

Lucassen, Jan. *Jan, Jan Salie en diens kinderen. Vergelijkend onderzoek naar continuïteit en discontinuïteit in de ontwikkeling van arbeidsverhoudingen.* Amsterdam, 1991.

Lucassen, Jan. *Migrant Labour in Europe 1600–1900. The Drift to the Norh Sea.* London, 1987.

Lucassen, Jan. *Outlines of a History of Labour. IISH Research Paper* 51. Amsterdam, 2013.

Lucassen, Jan. *Tracing the Past. Collections and research in social and economic history: The International Institute of Social History, the Netherlands Economic History Archive and related institutions.* Amsterdam, 1989.

Lucassen, Leo. "Working Together: New Directions in Global Labour History." *Journal of Global History* 11, no. 1 (2016): 66–87.

Lucassen, Jan, and Leo Lucassen, eds. *Globalising Migration History. The Eurasian Experience (16th–21st centuries).* Leiden/Boston, 2014.

Lucassen, Jan, and Rinus Penninx. *Newcomers. Immigrants and their Descendants in the Netherlands 1550–1995.* Amsterdam, 1997.

Ludden, David. "Area Studies in the Age of Globalization." (January 1998). http://www.sas.upenn.edu/~dludden/GlobalizationAndAreaStudies.htm.

Mac, Juno. "The laws that sex workers really want." TED-talk 13 June 2016, accessed September 19, 2017. https://www.ted.com/talks/juno_mac_the_laws_that_sex_workers_really_want.

Machiels, Christine. *Les féminismes et la prostitution (1860–1960).* Rennes, 2016.

Mackenzie, Alexander. *History of the Relations of the Government with the Hill Tribes of the North-East Frontier of India.* Calcutta, 1884.

Mackey, J. *Conscious Capitalism: Liberating the Heroic Spirit of Business.* Cambridge, MA, 2013.

Maclean, Ken. "Lawfare and Impunity in Burma since the 2000 Ban on Forced Labour." *Asian Studies Review* 36, no. 2 (2012): 189–206.

Mager, Anne Kelk. "Tracking the Concept of 'Work' on the North Eastern Cape Frontier, South Africa." In *Doing Conceptual History in Africa,* edited by Axel Fleisch and Rhianoon Stephens, 73–90. New York/Oxford, 2016.

Mamdani, Mahmood. *When Victims Become Killers. Colonialism, Nativism, and the Genocide in Rwanda.* Oxford, 2001.

Mandel, Ernest. *The Formation of the Economic Thought of Karl Marx.* London, 1971.

BIBLIOGRAPHY

Mann, Michael. "The End May Be Nigh, But for Whom?" In *Does Capitalism Have a Future?* Edited by Immanuel Wallerstein et al., 71–97. Oxford, 2013.

Marx Engels Collected Works (MECW) (London 1974–2001).

Marx, Karl. "Das Kapital. Kritik der politischen Ökonomie." In *Marx Engels Gesamtausgabe* Abt. 2, Bd. 5, edited by Institute for Marxism-Leninism, 1–649. Berlin, 1983.

Marx, Karl. "The British Cotton Trade." In *Dispatches for the New York Tribune. Selected Journalism of Karl Marx*, edited by James Ledbetter, 276–280. London, 2007.

Marx, Karl. "The British Government and the Slave-trade." In *Dispatches for the New York Tribune. Selected Journalism of Karl Marx*, edited by James Ledbetter, 261–266. London, 2007.

Marx, Karl. "The Duchess of Sutherland and Slavery." In *Dispatches for the New York Tribune. Selected Journalism of Karl Marx*, edited by James Ledbetter, 113–119. London, 2007.

Marx, Karl. "The Eighteenth Brumaire of Louis Bonaparte (1851–52)." *Karl Marx/ Frederick Engels Collected Works (MECW)* 11 (1976): 99–197.

Marx, Karl. *Das Kapital. Kritik der politischen Ökonomie.* Marx/Engels Werke, vol. 33. Berlin, 1962.

Masao, Miyoshi, and Harry Harootunian, eds. *Learning Places: The Afterlives of Area Studies.* Durham, NC, 2002.

Mason, Paul. *Post Capitalism: A Guide to the Future.* London, 2016.

Mattos, Marcelo Badaró. "Experiences in Common: Slavery and 'Freedom' in the Process of Rio de Janeiro's Working Class Formation (1850–1910)." *International Review of Social History* 55, no. 2 (2010): 193–213.

Mattos, Marcelo Badaró, et al., eds. *Relações Laborais em Portugal et no Mundo Lusófono. História e Demografia.* Lisbon, 2014.

Mayhew, Nicholas. "Wages and Currency: The Case in Britain up to 1600." In *Wages and Currency. Global Comparisons from Antiquity to the Twentieth Century*, edited by Jan Lucassen, 211–220. Bern, 2007.

Mazo Karras, Ruth. *Common Women: Prostitution and Sexuality in Medieval England.* New York, 1996.

McCall, A.G. *Lushai Chrysalis.* London, 1949.

McCall, A.G., Superintendent, Lushai Hills. *Lushai Hills District Cover.* Aizawl, Mizoram, India, 1938.

McCarthy, Conor. *The Cambridge Introduction to Edward Said.* Cambridge, 2010.

Meagher, Kate. "The Scramble for Africans: Demography, Globalization and Africa's Informal Labor Markets." *Journal of Development Studies* 52 (2016): 483–497.

Means, Gordon P. "Human Sacrifice and Slavery in the 'Unadministered' Areas of Upper Burma During the Colonial Era." *Sojourn: Journal of Social Issues in Southeast Asia* 15, no. 2 (2000): 184–221.

Meiksins Wood, Ellen, *The Origin of Capitalism.* New York, 1999.

Meiksins Wood, Ellen. "Capitalism, Merchants and Bourgeois Revolution: Reflections on the Brenner Debate and its Sequel." *International Review of Social History* 41 (1996): 209–232.

Meiksins Wood, Ellen. *The Origin of Capitalism. A Longer View.* London/New York, 2002.

Menucci, Sud. *O Precursor do Abolicionismo no Brasil (Luiz Gama).* São Paulo, 1938.

Merivale, Herman. "Lectures on Colonization and Colonies, delivered before the University of Oxford in 1839, 1840 and 1841." In *Marx Engels Gesamtausgabe* Abt. 4, Bd. 9, edited by the International Marx-Engels Foundation, 435–453, 461–481. Berlin 1991.

Middell, Matthias. "Area Studies under the Global Condition. Debates on Where to Go with Regional or Area Studies in Germany." In *Self-reflexive area studies*, edited by Matthias Middell, 7–57. Leipzig, 2013.

Mielants, E.H. *The Origins of Capitalism and the "Rise of the West."* Philadelphia, 2007.

Bin Wong, R and J.-L. Rosenthal. *Before and Beyond Divergence: The Politics of Economic Change in China and Europe.* Cambridge, MA, 2011.

Mielke, Katja, and Anna Katharina Hornidge, eds. *Area Studies at the Crossroads. Knowledge Production after the Mobility Turn.* New York, 2017.

Milanovic, Branco. *Global Inequality. A New Approach for the Age of Globalization.* Cambridge, MA, 2016.

Miles, Robert. *Capitalism and Unfree Labour. Anomaly or Necessity?* London/New York, 1987.

Mill, John Stuart. "The Negro Question" (1850). In *The Collected Works of John Stuart Mill, vol. XXI*, edited by John M. Robson, 85–95. London, 1984.

Mintz, Sidney. *Sweetness and Power. The Place of Sugar in Modern History.* Harmondsworth, 1985.

Mirowski, P., and D. Plehwe, eds. *The Road from Mont Pèlerin: The Making of the Neoliberal Thought Collective.* Cambridge, MA, 2009.

Motadel, David, and Richard Drayton, "Discussion: The Future of Global History," *Journal of Global History* 13, no. 1 (2018): 1–21.

Muller, Jerry Z. *The Mind and the Market: Capitalism in Western Thought.* New York, 2002.

Nabuco, Joaquim. *Um Estadista do Império. Nabuco de Araújo, sua Vida, suas Opiniões, sua Época, vol. I*, edited by H. Garnier Livreiro. Rio de Janeiro/Paris, 1897.

Nag, Sajal. "Rescuing Imagined Slaves: Colonial State, Missionary and Slavery Debate in North East India (1908–1920)." *Indian Historical Review* 39, no. 1 (2012): 57–71.

Nag, Sajal. *The Uprising: Colonial State, Christian Missionaries, and Anti-Slavery Movement in North-East India (1908–1954).* New Delhi, 2016.

Naumann, Katja. "(Re)Writing World History in Europe." In *A Companion to World History*, edited by Douglas Northrup, 478–496. Oxford, 2012.

Neale, Larry, and Jeffrey G. Williamson, eds. *The Cambidge History of Capitalism.* 2 vols. Cambridge, 2014.

BIBLIOGRAPHY

Nederveen Meerkerk, Elise van. "Couples cooperating? Dutch textile workers, family labour and the 'industrious revolution,' c. 1600–1800." *Continuity and Change* 23 (2008): 237–266.

Nederveen Meerkerk, Elise van, and Lex Heerma van Voss. "Selling Sex in World Cities, 1600s–2000s: An Introduction." In *Selling Sex in the City: A Global History of Prostitution, 1600s–2000s*, edited by Magaly Rodríguez García, Lex Heerma van Voss, and Elise van Nederveen Meerkerk, 1–21. Leiden, 2017.

Newland, A.G.E., and J.D. MacNabb. *The Image of War, or Service on the Chin Hills*. Calcutta, 1894.

Nieboer, Herman Jeremia. *Slavery as an Industrial System: Ethnological Researches*. The Hague, 1910.

Nimtz Jr., August H. *Marx and Engels. Their Contribution to the Democratic Breakthrough*. New York, 2000.

Nimtz Jr., August H. *Marx, Tocqueville, and Race in America. The "Absolute Democracy" or "Defiled Republic."* Lanham etc., 2003.

Nolte, Paul. "Modernization and Modernity in History." In *International Encyclopedia of the Social and Behavioral Sciences, vol. 15*, edited by Neil J. Smelser and Paul B. Baltes, 9954–9961. Oxford, 2001.

Noordegraaf, Leo. "In gesprek met Marcel van der Linden." In *Waarover spraken zij? Economische geschiedbeoefening in Nederland omstreeks het jaar 2000*, edited by Leo Noordegraaf, 193–203. Amsterdam. 2006.

Nunthara, C. *Impact of the Introduction of Grouping of Villages in Mizoram*. Guwahati, 1989.

Offe, Claus. *Disorganized Capitalism: Contemporary Transformation of Work and Politics*. London, 1985.

openDemocracy. Macioti, P.G., and Giulia Garofalo Geymonat. "Sex workers speak. Who listens?" 2016. https://www.opendemocracy.net/beyondslavery/sws/giulia-garofalo-geymonat-pg-macioti/sex-workers-speak-who-listens.

Osterhammel, Jürgen. "Global history in a national context: the case of Germany." *Österreichische Zeitschrift für Geschichtswissenschaft* 20, no. 2 (2009): 40–58.

Osterhammel, Jürgen. "Weltgeschichte. Ein Propädeutikum." *Geschichte in Wissenschaft und Unterricht* 56 (2005): 452–479.

Osterhammel, Jürgen. "World History." In *The Oxford History of Historical Writing, Vol. 5*, edited by Axel Schneider and Daniel Woolf, 93–112. Oxford, 2011.

Osterhammel, Jürgen. *Geschichtswissenschaft jenseits des Nationalstaates. Studien zur Beziehungsgeschichte und Zivilisationsvergleich*. Göttingen, 2001.

Osterhammel, Jürgen, and N.P. Petersson. *Globalization: A Short History*. Princeton, NJ, 2009.

Pachuau, Joy L.K. *Being Mizo: Identity and Belonging in Northeast India*. New Delhi, 2014.

Pachuau, Joy L.K., and Willem van Schendel. *The Camera as Witness: A Social History of Mizoram, Northeast India*. New Delhi, etc., 2015.

Palacios y Olivares, Guillermo. "Revoltas camponesas no Brasil escravista: a 'Guerra dos Maribondos' (Pernambuco, 1851–1852)." *Almanack Braziliense* 3 (2006): 9–39.

Palat, Ravi. *The Making of an Indian Ocean World-Economy, 1250–1650. Princes, Paddy fields and Bazaars*. Houndmills, Basingstoke, 2015.

Pamuk, Sevket. "Institutional change and economic development in the Middle East, 700–1800." In *The Cambidge History of Capitalism*, edited by Larry Neale, and Jeffrey G. Williamson, 193–224. 2 vols. Cambridge, 2014.

Parent-Duchâtelet, Alexandre. *De la prostitution dans la ville de Paris, considérée sous le rapport de l'hygiène publique, de la morale et de l'administration*. London/Brussels, 1838.

Parliamentary Papers. "Copy of Correspondence between the India Office and the Government of India, on the Subject of the Irruption of Hill Tribes into Cachar." *Accounts and Papers of the House of Commons (Session 9 February-21 August 1871), vol. 14*. London, 1871.

Parliamentary Papers. "Copy of Further Correspondence on the Subject of the Looshai Raids and the Consequent Hostilities." *Continuation of Parliamentary Paper, No. 398, of Session 1871*. London, 1872.

Parry, N.E. *A Monograph on Lushai Customs and Ceremonies* [1928] (Calcutta, 1976).

Parry, N.E. *The Lakher*. London, 1932.

Peres Costa, Wilma. "Estratégias ladinas: o imposto sobre o comércio de escravos e a 'legalização' do tráfico (1831–1850)." *Novos Estudos CEBRAP* 67 (2003): 57–75.

Pernau, Margrit. "Global History—Wegbereiter für einen neuen Kolonialismus." *geschichte transnational*, December 17, 2004. http://geschichte-transnational.clio-online.net/forum .

Perry, Mary Elizabeth. *Gender and Disorder in Early Modern Seville*. New Jersey, 1990.

Peršak, Nina, and Gert Vermeulen. "Faces and Spaces of Prostitution." In *Reframing Prostitution. From Discourse to Description, from Moralisation to Normalisation?* Edited by Nina Peršak and Gert Vermeulen, 13–24. Antwerp, 2014.

Persson, K.G. "Markets and Coercion in Medieval Europe." In *The Cambridge History of Capitalism, vol. I*, edited by L. Neal and J.G. Williamson, 225–266. Cambridge, 2014.

Phongpaichit, Pasuk. "Rural Women of Thailand: From Peasant Girls to Bangkok Masseuses." International Labour Organisation, World Employment Programme Research—Working Paper. 1980. Accessed January 5, 2017. http://www.ilo.org/pub lic/libdoc/ilo/1980/80B09_876_engl.pdf?gathStatIcon=true.

Pigenet, Michel. "Le VIH-Sida, nouveau terrain d'intervention syndicale dans les transports internationaux." *Le Mouvement Social* 241, no. 4 (2012): 185–203.

Piketty, Thomas. *Capital in the Twenty-first Century*. Cambridge, MA, 2014.

BIBLIOGRAPHY 231

Pirenne, Henri. "Les périodes de l'histoire sociale du capitalisme." *Bulletins de la classe des lettres et des sciences morales et politiques et de la classe des beaux-arts. Academie royale de Belgique* (1914): 258–299.

Pirenne, Henri. "The Stages in the Social History of Capitalism." *Americal Historical Review* (1914): 494–515. Reprinted in: *Class, Status and Power. A Reader in Social Stratification*, edited by Reinhard Bendix, and Seymour Martin Lipset, 501–517. London, 1954.

Polányi, Karl. *The Great Transformation. The Political and Economic Origins of Our Times.* Boston, 1944.

Polanyi, Karl, and Abraham Rotstein, *Dahomey and the slave trade; an analysis of an archaic economy.* Seattle, 1966.

Post, Charles. *The American Road to Capitalism. Studies in Class-structure, Economic Development and Political Conflict, 1620–1877.* Leiden/Boston, 2011.

Pradella, Lucia. "Marx and the Global South. Connecting History and Value Theory." *Sociology* 51, no.1 (2017): 146–161.

Pradella, Lucia. *Globalization and the Critique of Political Economy. New Insights from Marx's Writings.* London/New York, 2014.

Pradez, Charles. *Nouvelles études sur le Brésil.* Paris, 1872.

Prescott, W.H. "History of the Conquest of Mexico." In *Marx Engels Gesamtausgabe* Abt. 4, Bd. 9., edited by the International Marx-Engels Foundation, 403–434. Berlin 1991.

Priemel, Kim Christian. "Heaps of Work. The ways of labour history." *H-Soz-Kult*, January 23, 2014. http://www.hsozkult.de/literaturereview/id/forschungsberichte-1223.

Prince, Ruth J. "Seeking Incorporation? Voluntary Labor and the Ambiguities of Work, Identity, and Social Value in Contemporary Kenya." *African Studies Review* 58, no. 2 (2015): 85–109.

PROUD. "Sekswerkers Groningen protesteren tegen illegale registratie." Accessed December 28, 2016. http://wijzijnproud.nl/2016/09/05/sekswerkers-groningen -protesteren-tegen-illegale-registratie/.

Rafael, Vincente L. "Regionalism, area studies, and the accidents of agency." *American Historical Review* 104, no. 4 (1999): 1208–1220.

Raghavan, T.C.A. *Attendant Lords. Bairam Khan and Abdur Rahim Courtiers and Poets in Mughal India.* Delhi, 2016.

Raymond, Janice G. "Legitimating Prostitution as Sex Work: UN Labour Organization (ILO) Calls for Recognition of the Sex Industry." Coalition Against Trafficking in Women, 1999. Accessed January 6, 2017. http://www.catwinternational.org/Home/ Article/61-legitimating-prostitution-as-sex-work-un-labour-organization-ilo-calls -for-recognition-of-the-sex-industry.

Raymond, Janice G. *Not A Choice, Not A Job: Exposing the Myths about Prostitution and the Global Sex Trade.* Washington, DC, 2013.

Reinhard, Wolfgang. *Kleine Geschichte des Kolonialismus*. Stuttgart, 2008. Second edition.

Reis, João José. "The Revolution of the Ganhadores: Urban Labor, Ethnicity and the African Strike of 1857 in Bahia, Brazil." *Journal of Latin American Studies* 29 (1997): 355–393.

Renn, Jürgen, and Bernd Scherer, eds. *Das Anthropozän. Zum Stand der Dinge*. Berlin, 2015.

Richardson, Angelique. *Love and Eugenics in the Late Nineteenth Century. Rational Reproduction and the New Woman*. New York, 2003.

Rifkin, Jeremy. *The Zero Marginal Cost Society: The Internet of Things, the Collaborative Commons, and the Eclipse of Capitalism*. New York, 2015.

Ro, Soong Chul. "Naming a People: British Frontier Management in Eastern Bengal and the Ethnic Categories of the Kuki-Chin, 1760–1860." PhD diss., University of Hull, 2007.

Roberts, Nicky. *Whores in History: Prostitution in Western Society*. London, 1992.

Rockman, Seth. "What Makes the History of Capitalism Newsworthy?" *Journal of the Early Republic* 34, no. 3 (2014): 439–466.

Rodríguez García, Magaly. "Defining Commercial Sexualities, Past and Present." In *The Routledge Research Companion to Geographies of Sex and Sexualities*, edited by Gavin Browne and Kath Brown, 321–329. Oxford, 2016.

Rodríguez García, Magaly. "Ideas and Practices of Prostitution around the World." In *The Oxford Handbook of the History of Crime and Criminal Justice*, edited by Paul Knepper and Anja Johansen, 132–154. New York, 2016.

Rodríguez García, Magaly. "La Société des Nations face à la traite des femmes et au travail sexuel à l'échelle mondiale." *Le Mouvement Social* 241 (2012): 105–125.

Rodríguez García, Magaly. "On the Legal Boundaries of Coerced Labor." In *On Coerced Labor: Work and Compulsion after Chattel Slavery*, edited by Marcel van der Linden and Magaly Rodríguez García, 11–29. Leiden, 2016.

Rodríguez García, Magaly, Davide Rodogno, and Liat Kozma. "Introduction." In *The League of Nations' Work on Social Issues: Visions, Endeavours and Experiments*, edited by Magaly Rodríguez García, Davide Rodogno, and Liat Kozma, 13–28. Geneva, 2016.

Roediger, David R. *The Wages of Whiteness. Race and the Making of the American Working Class*. London, 1991.

Rojahn, Jürgen, and Marcel van der Linden. "Introduction." In *The Formation of Labour Movements, 1870–1914. An International Perspective. Vol. 1*, edited by Jürgen Rojahn and Marcel van der Linden, ix–xviii. Leiden, 1990.

Rosdolsky, Roman. *The Making of Marx's Capital*. London, 1977.

Roth, Karl Heinz. "An Encyclopaedist of Critical Thought: Marcel van der Linden, Heterodox Marxism and Global Labour History." In *On the Road to Global Labour*

History. A Festschrift for Marcel van der Linden, edited by Roth, 263–351. Leiden/ Boston, 2017.

Rustomji, Nari. *Enchanted Frontiers: Sikkim, Bhutan and India's Northeastern Borderlands*. Calcutta, 1973.

Sachsenmeier, Dominic. *Global Perspectives on Global History. Theories and Approaches in a Connected World*. Cambridge, 2010.

Sadan, Mandy. *Being and Becoming Kachin: Histories Beyond the State in the Borderworlds of Burma*. Oxford, 2013.

Sailo, Lalngurliana. "Economic Changes and Social Evolution: Mizoram (1870–1960)." PhD diss., North East Hill University, 2004.

Sakhong, Lian H. *In Search of Chin Identity: A Study in Religion, Politics and Ethnic Identity in Burma*. Copenhagen, 2003.

Sandel, M.J. *What Money Can't Buy: The Moral Limits of Markets*. New York, 2012.

Sangkima. *Mizos: Society and Social Change* (1890–1947). Guwahati, 1992.

Sayer, Derek. *The Violence of Abstraction. The Analytic Foundations of Historical Materialism*. Oxford, 1987.

Schäbler, Birgit, ed. *Area Studies und die Welt. Weltregionen und neue Globalgeschichte*. Vienna, 2007.

Schendel, Willem van, ed. *Francis Buchanan in Southeast Bengal (1798): His Journey to Chittagong, the Chittagong Hill Tracts, Noakhali and Comilla*. Dhaka, 1992.

Schendel, Willem van. "Stretching Labour Historiography: Pointers from South Asia," *International Review of Social History* 51 (2006): 229–261.

Schilling, Heinz. *Martin Luther. Rebell in einer Zeit des Umbruchs*. Munich, 2012.

Schmedemann, Deborah A. "Pro Bono Publico as a Conscience Good." *William Mitchell Law Review* 35, no. 3 (2008–2009): 977–1010.

Schulze, Erika, et al. "Sexual Exploitation and Prostitution and its Impact on Gender Equality." Brussels, 2014. Accessed January 10, 2017. http://www.europarl.europa.eu/ RegData/etudes/etudes/join/2014/493040/IPOL-FEMM_ET(2014)493040_EN.pdf.

Schumpeter, Joseph H. *Capitalism, Socialism, and Democracy*. New York, 1947. Second edition.

Ségor, Denise Adele. "Tracing the Persistent Impulse of a Bedrock Nation to Survive within the State of India: Mizo women's response to War and Forced Migration." PhD diss., Fielding Graduate University, 2006.

Sen, Amartya. *Identity and Violence. The Illusion of Destiny*. New York, 2006.

Sewell, Jr., William. "Toward a Post-materialist Rhetoric for Labor History." In *Rethinking Labor History: Essays in Discourse and Class Analysis*, edited by Lenard A. Berlanstein, 15–38. Urbana, 1993.

Shakespear, J. "The Making of Aijal." Accessed June 10, 2016. http://aizawl.nic.in/mak ingofaijal.htm. Reprinted in Hluna (ed.). 2013, 410–416.

Shakespear, J. *Annual Report of the Lushai Hills for 1898–1899*. Shillong, 1899.

Shakespear, J. *The Lushei Kuki Clans*. London, 1912.

Shami, Seteney, and Cynthias Miller-Idriss, eds. *Middle East Studies for the new Millennium. Infrastructures of Knowledge*. New York, 2016.

Shanin, Theodor, ed. *Peasants and Peasant Societies. Selected Readings*. Harmondsworth, 1971.

Sheridan, Michael J. "An Irrigation Intake Is Like a Uterus: Culture and Agriculture in Precolonial North Pare, Tanzania." *American Anthropologist* 104, no. 1 (2002): 79–92.

Sheriff, Abdul. *Slaves, Spices and Ivory in Zanzibar*. London, 1987.

Shin, Heisoo. "Seeking Justice, Honour and Dignity: Movement for the Victims of Japanese Military Sexual Slavery." In *Global Society 2011: Globality and the Absence of Justice*, edited by Helmut Anheir et al., 14–28. New York, 2011.

Slenes, Robert W. "'Malungu, Ngoma's Coming': Africa Hidden and Discovered in Brazil." In *Mostra do Redescobrimento: Negro de Corpo e alma—Black in Body and Soul*, edited by Nelson Aguilar, 221–229. São Paulo, 2000.

Slenes, Robert W. "L'arbre Nsanda Replanté. Cultes d'Affliction Kongo et Identité des Esclaves de Plantation dans le Brésil du Sud-Est (1810–1888)." *Cahiers du Brésil Contemporain* 67/68, partie II (2007): 217–313.

Slenes, Robert. "Brazil." In *The Oxford Handbook of Slavery in the Americas*, edited by Robert Paquette and Mark Smith, 111–133. Oxford/New York, 2010.

Smith, Adam. *The Wealth of Nations. Books I–III*. London, 1999 [1776].

Sokoll, T. *Europäischer Bergbau im Übergang zur Neuzeit*. Idstein, 1994.

Sombart, Werner. *Das Proletariat. Bilder und Studien*. Berlin, 1906.

Sombart, Werner. *Der moderne Kapitalismus*. Munich/Leipzig, 1924–1927. Second edition.

Stanziani, Alessandro, ed. *Le Travail Contraint en Europe et en Asie, XVI–XXe siècles*. Paris, 2010.

Stanziani, Alessandro. "The Legate Statute of Labour from the Seventeenth to the Nineteenth Century. Russia in a Comparative European Perspective." *International Review of Social History* 54 (2009): 359–389.

Stanziani, Alessandro. "The traveling panopticon: labor institutions and labor practices in Russia and Britain in the eighteenth and nineteenth century." *Comparative Studies in Society and History* 51, no. 4 (2009): 715–741.

Stanziani, Alessandro. *Bondage. Labor and Rights in Eurasia from the Sixteenth to the Early Twentieth Century*. New York/Oxford, 2014.

Steinfeld, Robert J. *The Invention of Free Labor. The Employment Relation in English and American Law and Culture, 1350–1870*. London, 1991.

Steinfeld, Robert J., and Stanley L. Engerman. "Labor—Free or Coerced? A Historical Reassessment of Differences and Similarities." In *Free and Unfree Labour. The Debate Continues*, edited by Tom Brass and Van der Linden, 107–126. Bern, 1997.

Steuart, James. *An Inquiry into the Principles of Political Economy, vol. 1*. London, 1767.

BIBLIOGRAPHY

235

Streeck, Wolfgang. "How will Capitalism End?" *New Left Review* 87 (2014): 35–64.

Sugihara, Kaoru. "Labour-intensive industrialization in global history. An interpretation of East Asian experiences." In *Labour-Intensive Industrialization in Global History*, edited by Gareth Austin and Kaoru Sugihara, 20–64. London/New York, 2013.

Svanström, Yvonne. "Criminalising the John: A Swedish Gender Model." In *The Politics of Prostitution: Women's Movements, Democratic States and the Globalisation of Sex Commerce*, edited by Joyce Outshoorn, 225–244. Cambridge, 2004.

Szanton, David L. "Introduction. The Origins, Nature and Challenges of Area Studies in the United States." In *The Politics of Knowledge. Area Studies and the Disciplines*, edited by David L. Szanton, 1–31. Berkeley, 2004.

Szanton, David L., ed. *The Politics of Knowledge. Area Studies and the Disciplines*. Berkeley, 2004.

Temple, R.C. "Beginnings of Currency." *The Journal of the Anthropological Institute of Great Britain and Ireland* 29, no. 1/2 (1899): 99–122.

Thanmawia, R.L. "The Mizo Value (As Reflected in Oral Traditions)." In *History and Identity Formation in North-East India*, edited by J.V. Hluna, 273–279. New Delhi, 2013.

Thébaud, Françoise. "Construire un espace européen ou construire un espace international. L'exemple de Marguerite Thibert (1886–1982)." In *Les rôles transfrontaliers joués par les femmes en Europe*, edited by Guyonne Leduc, 267–282. Paris, 2012.

Thébaud, Françoise. "Les femmes au BIT: l'exemple de Marguerite Thibert." In *Femmes et relations internationales*, edited by Jean-Marc Delaunay and Yves Denéchère, 177–187. Paris, 2006.

Thialret. "Thialret thu." *Mizo leh Vai* (October 1908).

Tilly, Charles. "Demographic Origins of the European Proletariat." In *Proletarianization and Family History*, edited by David Levine, 26–52. London, 1984.

Tilly, Chris, and Charles Tilly. *Work Under Capitalism*. Boulder, CO, 1998.

Tiyambe Zeleza, Paul, ed. *The Study of Africa, Vol. I: Disciplinary and Interdisciplinary Encounters*. Dakar/Oxford, 2006.

Tiyambe Zeleza, Paul, ed. *The Study of Africa, Vol. II: Global and Transnational Encounters*. Dakar/Oxford, 2007.

Tocqueville, Alexis de. *Alexis de Tocqueville's Memoir on Pauperism*. Translated by Seymour Drescher. London, 1997. http://www.civitas.org.uk/pdf/Tocqueville_rr2.pdf .

Tocqueville, Alexis de. *Journeys to England and Ireland*, edited by J.P. Mayer. Forge Village, MA, 1958.

Tocqueville, Alexis de. *Sur le Paupérisme*. 1835. Republished in: Tocqueville, Alexis de. *Oeuvres Complètes*. Paris, 1989.

Todeschini, Giacomo. "Credit and Debt: Patterns of Exchange in Western Christian Society." In *Europas Aufstieg. Eine Spurensuche im späten Mittelalter*, edited by Thomas Ertl, 139–160. Wien, 2013.

Todeschini, Giacomo. "Theological Roots of the Medieval/Modern Merchants' Self-Representation." In *The Self-Perception of Early Modern Capitalists*, edited by Margaret C. Jacobs and Catherine Secretan, 17–46. London, 2008.

Tomba, Massimiliano. *Marx's Temporalities*. Leiden/Boston, 2013.

Tomich, Dale W. "Introduction." In *The Politics of Second Slavery*, edited by Dale W. Tomich, ix–xi. Albany, 2016.

Tomich, Dale W. *Through the Prism of Slavery. Labor, Capital, and the World Economy*. Lanham etc., 2004.

Tornielli, Andrea, and Giacomo Galeazzi. *This Economy Kills: Pope Francis on Capitalism and Social Justice*. Liturgical Press, 2015.

Townsend, Peter. "The Right to Social Security and National Development: Lessons from OECD experience for low-income countries." Issues in Social Protection. Discussion Paper No. 18, Social Security Department, ILO. Geneva, 2007.

Trexler, Richard. "La prostitution florentine au XVe siècle: patronages et clienteles." *Annales: economies, sociétés, civilisations* 36 (1981): 983–1015.

Tripp, C. *Islam and the Moral Economy: The Challenge of Capitalism*. Cambridge, 2006.

Turton, Andrew. "Violent Capture of People for Exchange on Karen-Tai Borders in the 1830s." *Slavery & Abolition* 24, no. 2 (2003): 69–82.

United Nations General Assembly. *UN Protocol to "Prevent, Suppress and Punish Trafficking in Persons, Specially Women and Children."* New York, 2000. Accessed January 10, 2017. http://www.ohchr.org/EN/ProfessionalInterest/Pages/ProtocolTraffick ingInPersons.aspx.

Vanhaute, Eric. "Who is afraid of global history? Ambitions, pitfalls and limits of learning global history." *Österreichische Zeitschrift für Geschichtswissenschaft* 20, no. 2 (2009): 22–39.

Verghese, C.G., and R.L. Thanzawna. *A History of the Mizos, 2 vols*. New Delhi, 1997.

Vito, Christian G. De. "New Perspectives on Global Labour History. Introduction." *Workers of the World* 1, no. 3 (2013): 7–31.

Vries, Jan de. "The industrious revolutions in East and West." In *Labour-Intensive Industrialization in Global History*, edited by Gareth Austin and Kaoru Sugihara, 65–84. London/New York, 2013.

Vries, Peer. "Europe and the rest: Braudel on capitalism." In *Aufbruch in die Weltwirtschaft: Braudel wiedergelesen*, edited by G. Garner and M. Middell, 81–114. Leipzig, 2014.

Vygodski, V.S. *The Story of a Great Discovery. How Karl Marx Wrote "Capital."* Berlin, 1973.

Wagenaar, Hendrik, and Sietske Altink. "Prostitution as Morality Politics or Why it is Exceedingly Difficult To Design and Sustain Effective Prostitution Policy." *Sexuality Research and Social Policy* 9, no. 3 (2012): 279–292.

BIBLIOGRAPHY

Wagner, Peter. *Modernity as Experience and Interpretation: A New Sociology of Modernity*. London, 2008.

Walkowitz, Judith. "Jack the Ripper and the Myth of Male Violence." *Feminist Studies* 8 (1982): 542–574.

Wallerstein, Immanuel. "Capitalism as an Essential Concept to Understand Modernity." In *Capitalism. The Reemergence of a Historical Concept,* edited by Jürgen Kocka and Marcel van der Linden, 187–204. London, 2016.

Wallerstein, Immanuel. "The Unintended Consequences of the Cold War Area Studies." In *The Cold War and the University: Toward an Intellectual History of the Postwar Years,* edited by Noam Chomsky, 195–232. New York, 1997.

Wallerstein, Immanuel. *The Modern World System I: Capitalist Agriculture and the Origins of the European World-Economy in the Sixteenth Century.* Berkeley etc., 1974.

Weber, Max. "Development Tendencies in the Situation of East Elbian Rural Labourers." Translated by Keith Tribe. *Economy and Society* 8, no. 2 (1979): 177–205.

Weber, Max. *Die Ländliche Arbeitsverfassung,* Verhandlungen des Vereins für Sozialpolitik, Band 58. Leipzig, 1893.

Weber, Max. *Economy and Society: An Outline of Interpretive Sociology,* edited by Guenther Roth and Claus Wittich. Berkeley, CA, 1978, reprinted 2013.

Weber, Max. *General Economic History.* Translated by Frank H. Knight. Glencoe, IL, 1927, reprinted 1950.

Weber, Max. *The Protestant Ethic and the Spirit of Capitalism.* Revised, translated and introduced by Stephen Kalberg. New York, 2010.

Weber, Max. *Wirtschaft und Gesellschaft, Grundriss der Sozialökonomik, III Abteilung.* Tübingen, 1922.

Wee, Herman van der and G. Kurgan-van Hentenryk, eds. *A History of European Banking.* Antwerp, 2000. Second edition.

Weindling, Paul. "The Politics of International Co-ordination to Combat Sexually Transmitted Diseases, 1900–1980s." In *AIDS and Contemporary History,* edited by Virginia Berridge and Philip Strong, 93–107. New York, 1993.

Weitzer, Ronald. "New Directions in Research on Human Trafficking." *The ANNALS of the American Academy of Political and Social Science* 653, no. 6 (2014): 6–24.

Williams, Eric. *Capitalism and Slavery.* Chapel Hill, 1944.

Winkler, Heinrich August, ed. *Organisierter Kapitalismus: Voraussetzungen und Anfänge.* Göttingen, 1974.

Woodthorpe, R.G. *The Lushai Expedition, 1871–1872.* London, 1873.

XIX International Aids Conference. "IAC Washington/Kolkata joint session: The Oldest Profession: is Sex Work, Work?." Washington/Kolkata, 2012. Accessed January 10, 2017. http://www.nswp.org/news/iac-washingtonkolkata-joint-session-the-oldest -profession-sex-work-work.

Yoneda, Sayoko. "Sexual and Racial Discrimination: An Historical Inquiry into the Japanese Military's 'Comfort' Women System of Enforced Prostitution." In *Nation, Empire, Colony: Historicizing Gender and Race*, edited by Ruth Roach Pierson and Napur Chaudhuri, 237–250. Bloomington, 1998.

Zalawra, "Titi Phungleng," *Mizo leh Vai* (December 1922).

Zanden, J.L. van, et al. *How Was Life? Global Well-Being Since 1820*. Paris, 2014.

Zorema, J. *Indirect Rule in Mizoram 1890–1954 (The Bureaucracy and the Chiefs)*. New Delhi, 2007.

Zou, David Vumlallian. "Raiding the Dreaded Past: Representations of Headhunting and Human Sacrifice in North-East India." *Contributions to Indian Sociology* 39, no. 1 (2005): 75–105.

Index

abolitionism/abolitionist   50, 53, 54n28, 68,
    101, 102, 107, 112n90, 113, 114, 133
Abu-Lughod, Janet   31
accumulation of capital   10
accumulator, feudal   28–29
Adelman, Jeremy   165
Africa   5, 31, 39, 49, 156n1, 161–164, 166,
    167n39, 168, 170–172
    African descent (people of)   116, 121, 122,
    124, 132–134
agency   50, 61, 70, 103, 112, 150, 153, 160, 161n18
AIDS   90, 91, 108, 109, 110, 113, 114
alienation, in workplace   80, 85
American Civil War   54, 64, 68, 70
American Historical Association   71
American War of Independence   68
Amin, Samir   30, 31, 31n28
Amin, Shahid   14
Amsterdam   1, 2, 3, 72, 77, 78, 171
anarchism/anarchist   23n3, 51, 132
ancient civilizations   136
Annenkow, P.W.   51
anthropology   1, 157
anti-capitalism/anti-capitalist sentiments
    80, 82, 83
anti-cosmopolitanism   85
anti-liberalism   80
anti-Semitism   80
anti-slavery   50–55, 188
Antwerp   72, 77, 78
Arabia   34, 72, 74
Area Studies   1, 21, 156–173
aristocracy/aristocrat   78, 143, 149, 154
Aristotle   74
artisan   5, 25, 38, 40, 40n56, 75, 151, 157
Asia   26, 74, 78n7, 106, 156, 161, 163, 166, 170,
    172, 174
Association of Indian Labor Historians   15
Assyrian Empire   39
Austin, Gareth   30n26, 31, 34, 161
Australasia   17
autarky   203
autonomy   10, 140, 157, 177, 205
    artisanal   157
    Babylonia   31, 33, 39n55

Banaji, Jairus   59, 65
Bangkok   105
Bangladesh   175, 185n51
barbarism   79
Bayly, Christopher   161
bazaar   193
Becker, Gary   84
Beckert, Sven   71
Behal, Rana   16
Belgium   104
Bentham, Jeremy   61, 70
Big Divergence Debate. *See* Great Divergence
    Debate
Bismarck, Otto von   11
Black Death   46
Blanc, Louis   71
Blaut, James Morris   29, 30, 31
Bolivia   92, 92n8
Bonaparte, Napoleon   11, 93
bondage   107, 111, 125, 127, 128, 130, 132, 134,
    137, 139, 141, 146
Booth, Charles   37
bourgeoisie   19, 30, 64, 95, 141
boycott   10
Boy Scouts   195
Brabant   75
Brandon, Pepijn   19, 47–70
Braudel, Fernand   30, 31, 33, 34
Brazil
    Brazilian Empire   115–135
    Brazilian independence (1822)   123
    Brazilian parliament   123, 129
Breman, Jan   14, 16, 17, 18, 21, 136–155
Brenner Debate   27, 28, 29
brothel   92, 93, 95, 100, 141
Brown, Carolyn   16
Brown, John   55
Brussels   3, 99
Brussels Workers' Association   56
Buenos Aires   93
Bund   9

Cairnes, J.E.   48, 62
Cairo   93
Cambodia   110, 185n51

Cape of Good Hope 77
capital 10, 17, 18, 21, 26, 28, 31–35, 47, 48,
48n6, 49, 55–63, 63n60, 63n62, 64–66,
68–71, 73, 75, 77, 80, 81, 120, 126, 127, 131,
132, 134, 135, 142, 155, 157, 170
  accumulation of 10
capitalism
  agrarian 72, 76
  capitalist expansion. *See* expansion,
  capitalist
  capitalist exploitation. *See* exploitation
  Catholic critique of 85
  coordinated 83
  criticism of 83, 85, 88. *See also*
  Kapitalismuskritik
  finance 72, 75–78, 83
  industrial 72, 80–82
  Marxist critique of 85
  merchant 34, 72, 74, 75
  plantation 72
  print 15
  socialist critique of 80
captive/captivity 178–180
Caribbean 55, 76, 115, 167
Carr Center for Human Rights Policy 113
Cavaillon, J.A. 99, 104
Centesimo Annus (1991) 85
Chalhoub, Sidney 16, 20, 21, 115–135
charity 74, 137, 144, 149, 152, 153
Chicago School 84
chief(s) 122, 129, 180, 181n28, 182, 183, 183n38,
188, 192, 192n83, 193, 195, 196, 196n100
  village 181, 182, 192, 195, 203n111
China 30, 31, 33, 34, 38–40, 43–45, 53, 72,
74–76, 164, 175
Christianity/Christians 23n3, 73–76, 79,
93n13, 104, 137, 186, 188, 195, 202, 204
civil society 78, 79
class
  consciousness 157
  hatred 121
  interests 9
  seigneurial 123
Coalition Against Trafficking in Women 107
coercion 107, 111n84, 169, 205
coffee 115, 116, 121, 123, 125, 126, 129, 134, 135
coins 38–45, 55, 72
Cold War 161, 162
collective action 17, 19, 46, 145, 153, 206

collective bargaining 17
collective identity 157
colonialism/colonization 52–54, 70, 76, 77,
167, 168, 178
commerce/commercialization 27, 79, 141,
147, 193n85
commodification 33, 73, 81, 140, 142,
204–207
commodity 17, 34, 40, 57n41, 59, 61, 77, 115,
141, 142, 147, 153, 170, 204
  chain 17
Common Law 74
Common Weal 139
'concept of difference,' 80
Condorcet, Nicolas de 79
connections
  global 172, 175n7
  international 8
  transatlantic 158
Conrad, Sebastian 159
constitutional government 78
consumption
  consumer 57, 58, 78, 82, 140, 198n109
  consumer cooperatives 10
  consumerism 151
  mass 82
contraband 116, 123–125, 127, 128, 128n23, 130,
131, 131n34
contract 17, 23n3, 80, 138, 146, 167
coolie 189, 191
cooperation 23, 24, 31, 79, 99, 103, 104,
162–164, 189, 195
cooperative 10, 153, 173
corruption 74, 123
cosmopolitanism 16
cotton 51, 52, 57, 58, 63, 64, 67, 115, 116
Counter-Reformation 79
credit 42, 51, 73, 74, 78
criminality 141
crioulos 128
crops 45, 142, 146, 192, 195
  cash 192, 195
Cruikshank, Barbara 151
Cuba 20, 50
cultivation cycle 146

Dahomey 36
de Araújo, Nabuco 129
death penalty 126

INDEX
241

Deep South, USA 116
democracy
   democratic politics 50, 86
   liberal 50
   representative 83
demography/demographical 171
destitution 135, 143, 144, 149, 152
'destruction, creative' 81, 82n12
digital revolution 82
discipline 1, 12, 31, 37, 46, 67, 79, 157, 162–164
   slave 123, 126
Dobb, Maurice 28
domestic work 101, 103
double free wage laborers 59–64
Dyer, Chris 43, 44

Early Modern/Early Modernity 12, 23, 72,
   76–79
East Indies, Dutch 63
Eckert, Andreas 21, 156–173
ecology (of labor organizations) 9, 9n17
economy
   barter 180
   cash 193, 195
   economic theory 51
   political 22, 47, 52, 56, 56n38, 57n41,
      61, 69
education 19, 82, 104, 153, 176n10
Egypt, classical 36, 38
emancipation
   slave 68, 70, 115
   workers 153
Emancipation Act (USA) 54
engagement, political 59
Engels, Friedrich 148
Engerman, Stanley 13
England 25–29, 32, 39n55, 43, 46n71, 49,
   68, 72, 77, 78, 79n9, 143, 147–150, 152,
   154, 168
English South Sea Company 77–78
Enlightenment 36, 76–77
enslavement, illegal 116, 121, 123–129,
   133–135
environment, natural 83
ethical code 183, 203
Eurocentrism 11, 15, 19, 29, 29n24, 30, 31, 35,
   160, 175
Europe 4, 5, 8, 10, 12, 17, 23, 25–32, 32n32, 36,
   37, 40, 44n65, 63n62, 67, 72–76, 78, 82,

   83, 85, 87, 88, 93, 94, 98, 104n54, 137, 142,
   145, 150, 161, 163, 167, 175n7
European Parliament 96
European Parliament's Committee on
   Women's Rights and Gender Equality 111
European Union (EU) 96, 111n81, 114
European Women's Lobby 96
expansion, capitalist 7, 16, 27, 72, 76–79, 86
exploitation 14, 20, 56, 57n41, 60n50, 62,
   64–67, 69, 70, 72, 77, 80, 86, 111, 112, 138,
   146, 169, 192
   capitalist 7, 27, 86

factory 43n70, 50, 58, 62, 64, 67, 81, 151
famine 137, 148, 194
fascism 83
feminism/feminist 95, 96, 100, 101, 107
feudalism 26–28, 29, 36, 43, 138
financial sector 86
First International 5, 11
Fischer, Eric 2, 2n3, 22, 23
Flanders 75
Florence 75
Forced Labour Convention 110, 112n87,
   190n69, 196n99
France 29, 50, 77, 93, 103, 149, 192
Frank, Andre Gunder 29n23, 30, 31,
   31n28
Freeman, John 9

Gama, Luiz 133, 134
gender 12, 20, 23n3, 62n58, 96, 109, 111, 166,
   206
General strike 1903, the Netherlands 10
Geneva 90, 98, 104, 105
Gentry 138, 143
Genua 26, 99
German Empire 37
Germany 45, 49, 90, 104, 104n54, 107, 145,
   147, 163, 164
Gervase Clarence-Smith, William 161
Ghai, Dharam 105
Glazebrook, Allison 92, 92n7
global labor history 3, 12, 13, 15–16, 19, 41–44,
   47, 48n5, 56, 66, 69, 156–174, 176, 176n9,
   204–207
Global Labour History Network 3
Global Network of Sex Work Projects 90,
   97n28

Global South 6, 14, 17, 18, 85, 86, 163*n*28, 166, 167, 172, 193*n*83
Goldstone, Jack 33
Goulart, João 134
Great Depression (1870s) 80
Great Depression (1930s) 100, 101
Great Divergence Debate 31
Great Famine 148
Great Fear of 1852 115–135
Great Recession (2008) 87
Grotius/Groot, Hugo de 79
Gulag 13

Hagan, Jim 206
Haiti 127
Hannan, Michael T. 9
Hardy, Thomas 145
Harootunian, Harry 156
Harris, S.W. 101
Hartwell, Max 153
Hayami, Akira 31
Heerma van Voss, Lex 8, 12, 24
Hilferding, Rudolf 71, 83, 83*n*13
Hilton, Rodney 28, 29
Himmelfarb, Gertrude 150–153
Hirschman, Albert 82
history
    Atlantic 164
    cultural 20, 71
    early modern 12, 23
    ethnic 157
    global 21, 158–165, 160*n*14172, 173, 175
    global labor. *See* global labor history
    Indian Ocean 164
    institutional 8, 9
    labor 1, 3–5, 8, 9, 11–16, 19–48, 56, 66, 69, 86*n*19, 115, 116, 136, 156–207
    old labor 8, 14, 16
    social 4–8, 11, 12, 15, 164
    transnational 158, 159, 164
    Transnational Labor 15
    women's 20, 71, 157
    world 12, 33, 158, 159, 159*n*10, 170
Hitler, Adolf 13
Hitler Youth 104
HIV 90, 91, 106, 108*n*71, 108*n*72, 109, 110, 113, 114
Hobbes, Thomas 79
Hobsbawm, Eric 24*n*6, 27, 82

Hobson, John A. 71
Holthoon, Frits van 8
household 12, 14, 15, 18, 19, 28, 36, 36*n*47, 37–39, 45, 105, 120, 136–138, 141, 143, 146, 167, 171, 176, 182, 184, 184*n*46, 194–196, 202, 203, 205
housing 19, 147
Howard, Richard 90, 108*n*71, 109, 113*n*91
humanism 74
humanitarianism 15
humanities 148, 164
human rights 79, 96, 113
    violation 106
human trafficking 20, 96, 110, 111, 111*n*84, 114
Hume, David 79
hunger 197
Huntington, Samuel 161–162
Hurren, Elizabeth 145

immiseration 85, 143, 145, 153
immobility 165
impoverishment 151, 153
independency/independence/
    independent 3, 5*n*11, 30, 39, 42, 45, 50, 53, 63, 68, 123, 196, 202, 204
India
    British rule in 51, 190*n*69
    Indian Independence (1947) 196, 202
Indiacentrism 175
individualization 86
Indonesia 106
industrialized countries 10, 17
Industrial Revolution 27, 31, 44, 50, 67
    Second Industrial Revolution 10
informal sector 17, 18
Institute for the Study of Civic Society 150
institutional inflexibility 18
interconnectedness 115, 158
interdependence 83, 115, 138
interdisciplinary 14, 164
International Committee on the Rights of Sex Workers 94
International Congress of Historical Studies 26
International Council of Women 99
International Institute of Social History
    (IISH) 1, 5, 7, 8, 12, 15, 19, 22–24, 35, 36, 44, 171, 174
    research department of the 22

INDEX

Internationalism   9, 16, 18, 24
international labor law   90
International Labor Organization (ILO)   20, 90–114, 205
International Review of Social History (IRSH)   12, 14, 22, 191
International Union of Catholic Women's Leagues   102
International Workingmen's Association   54
Iraq   32, 33
Ireland   49, 148–152
Islam   85n18, 161
Islamic Studies   163
Italy   26, 27, 32, 72, 75, 104n54, 149

Jack the Ripper   95
Jacobin   7
James, C.L.R.   167
Japan   17, 30–32, 40, 110, 156
Jong Edz, Frits de   2
Junker   146
justice system   185

Kapitalismuskritik,   85, 88. *See also* capitalism
Kara, Siddarth   112
Katz, Michael   154, 154n25
Kelk Mager, Anne   170
Kepler, Johannes   68
Keslassy, Eric   151
Keynesian welfare state   83
Kloosterman, Jaap   23
Kocka, Jürgen   20, 30n26, 33, 34, 71–89
Krätke, Michael   53chil

labor
    activism   8, 9, 12
    child   63–64, 62n58, 69, 189
    commodified   19, 20, 47, 57, 171
    forced   12, 13, 21, 58n44, 91, 108, 111–113, 126, 189–193, 195–198, 202
    Free and Unfree   12–14, 38, 45, 66, 115, 116, 206
    free wage   12, 14, 19, 47, 48, 64, 65n65, 69, 70, 168, 169
    history   1, 3–5, 8, 11–16, 19–47, 115, 156–158, 160, 166–168, 170, 174, 175
    informal   17, 86, 169, 169n49, 170
    law   90

    movements   3, 4, 8, 17, 18, 23, 24, 51, 51n16, 69, 81, 136
    penal   50
    plantation   167, 167n39
    reciprocal   171, 205n116
    regimes   115, 174–207
    relations   1, 5, 10–17, 19, 24, 35–38, 43, 45, 48, 63, 67, 146, 169n49, 171, 172, 174–176, 184–198, 202, 204–207
    shortages   176, 193n83
    slave. *See* slave, labor
    tributary   38, 171
    unionism   15, 18
    voluntary communal   21, 176, 183, 198, 203, 204, 207
    wage   10–15, 17–19, 28, 30, 35, 38–51, 55–59, 61, 62, 64–67, 69, 70, 75, 81, 157, 168, 170, 184, 189, 193–198, 202–205
Lafargue, François   55
Lafargue, Paul   55
Latin America   6, 15, 161, 161n19, 164, 166, 172
League of Nations   96n22, 98, 101n44, 178, 187
League of Nations' Health Organization (LNHO)   98, 99, 104
legal rights   13, 114
leisure   78, 104n54
liberalism   47, 59, 69
Liebknecht, Wilhelm   71
Lim, Lin   106–108, 113
Lincoln, Abraham   54n28, 68
Linden, Marcel van der, passim
livestock   190
living standards   147, 153
Locke, John   79
London   26, 37, 52, 53, 72, 77, 78, 179
Lucassen, Jan   3, 3n4, 5, 5n9, 12, 15, 19, 22–47, 97n29
Ludden, David   156
Lumpenproletariat   141
Lushai   176n10, 177n12, 178–181, 182n31, 183, 189, 194

Malaysia   106
Mamdani, Mahmood   156
Manchester   148, 149, 154
Mandel, Ernest   2, 18
Mandeville, Bernard de   79
Mansion   168
Mao   45

244 INDEX

Marxism
  Marxist   1, 2, 7, 14, 27, 28n18, 48, 64, 66,
    69, 71, 85
  Marxist orthodoxy/Marxism,
    orthodox   14, 49, 69
Marx, Karl, passim
Masataka, Mino   40
masters and servants act   13
Maus, Isidore   101
media   82, 95, 198
Meiksins Wood, Ellen   29
Mesopotamia   36
Middle Ages   20, 26, 28, 44, 137
Middle East   31, 38, 163
Middle Eastern Studies   156, 157n4
Mill, John Stewart   50, 60, 70
minimum wage   142
Mizoram   21, 175–178, 176n10, 177n12, 178n17,
    180–188, 190–192, 194–200, 202–205,
    207
Mobility
  geographical   46
  social   46
modernity/modernization   13, 85, 88, 159
monetization   39–45, 141, 184
monopoly   52, 77, 78
Montesquieu, Charles de   79
mutualism   10, 16
  mutualist societies   10
Myanmar (Burma)   175, 203n111

Napoleonic wars   143
Napoleon III   11
National Council for Combating Venereal
    Disease (UK)   100
nationalism   165
  methodological   19, 21, 174, 175
neoconservative/neoconservatism   149–152
Netherlands, The   10, 14, 23, 42n60, 77, 78, 90,
    94, 109, 110
Neville-Rolfe, Sybil   100
New Deal   142, 150
Newton, Isaac   78
New World   143
New York Tribune   53
nomads   139
non-government organization (NGO)   150
North America   6, 17, 32, 49, 55, 63, 68, 69, 72,
    76, 161, 167, 175, 175n7

Osaka Fu Special English Teachers' Union
    (OFSET)   110
Osterhammel, Jürgen   158
Ownership   57n41, 67, 124, 125, 136, 143, 178

Pacific   36, 68, 106
Pakistan   196
Palat, Ravi   32
Pannekoek, Anton   1
pardos   124, 125, 132
Parent-Duchâtelet, Alexandre   93
Paris   99
paternalism   139
patronage   15, 93, 138, 146
pauperism   143, 145, 147–154
periphery   14, 64
  peripheral areas   205, 205n119
Pernau, Margrit   164
philanthropy/philanthropist   103
Philippines, the   106
Phongpaichit, Pasuk   105, 106
Pirenne, Henri   26–28
Pires, Tomé   42
plantation/planter
  capitalism. See capitalism
  coffee   123, 125, 126, 129, 134, 135
  rubber   192
  tea   177
plant management   12
Poland   147
Polányi, Karl   36, 36n39, 87, 142
political sciences   29, 162
Pomeranz, Ken   31
Poor Laws   137, 143–145
Portuguese/Portugal   42, 128, 133, 171
postcapitalism   87
postcolonialism   167
postmodernism   14
  postmodernist discource   15
poverty   96, 101, 112, 135, 136, 144, 145, 148, 149,
    154, 194, 194n92
pre-capitalism   46, 136–138, 203
precarity   7, 10, 17–19, 169, 169n49, 170
privatization/privatized   19, 58
production   4, 12, 21, 31, 34, 38, 38n54, 43,
    45, 48, 56–67, 71, 75–78, 91, 115, 116, 136,
    140–142, 146, 149, 151, 153, 155–157, 170,
    172, 176, 195, 196, 203, 204, 205n116, 206
productive relations   158

INDEX

profit   17, 57*n*41, 62, 73, 74, 77, 86, 148, 149
progress
   capitalist   51
   proletarianisation   14, 147, 157, 184
proletariat   18, 56, 58, 143
property
   rights   34, 73
   slave   116, 123–125, 127, 133
prostitute   90–93, 95–97, 101, 102, 107, 108
prostitution   20, 90, 91–98, 100–102, 104,
   106–108, 110–111, 113–114
Protestant Ethic   40
proto-industrialization   75
Proudhon, Pierre-Joseph   51
Prussia   147
punishment
   capital   126, 127
   physical   127, 135
Putin, Vladimir   165

Qian, Sima   40

Rahman, Abdur   41
Raymond, Janice   107–108
rebellion   53, 70, 119, 192
redistribution   36, 45, 136–138, 152–155
re-enslavement   21, 116
Reform Act (1832)   145
Reformation   79
registration
   civil   117–122, 132
   slave   125, 133
relief   110, 115, 137, 138, 140–142, 144, 145,
   149–152
   public   144, 145, 149–152
religion   12, 73, 74, 206
relocation, forced   192
remuneration   43, 45, 197
Renaissance   27, 36, 74
Republic, Dutch   24, 26
resettlement   197
revolt
   armed   196
   slave   50, 52, 55, 68
revolution
   Revolution, French   143
   Revolution of 1848–1849   54
   Revolution of 1968   11
Ricardo, David   57

Rice   181*n*28, 183, 187, 190, 195
Rio de Janeiro   123, 124, 130, 132
riots   115–135
Rodriguez, Magaly   20, 58, 90–114
Rojahn, Jürgen   8, 8*n*16, 24*n*4, 81
Roman Empire   26, 33
Roman Law   74
Rome   31, 92
Roth, Karl Heinz   4, 18, 1, 57
Russia   16, 23, 37, 45, 49, 55, 65, 69, 147, 168

Sachsenmaier, Dominic   159
Saich, Tony   22
Sainte-Croix, Avril de   101
Salt   181*n*28, 193
Salvation Army   192
São Paulo   115, 123, 124, 126, 129, 133, 134
Schäffle, Albert   71
Schendel, Willem van   14, 21, 22, 24*n*5
Schumpeter, Joseph A.   81
Second International   9
sedentarism   139
self-employment   17, 198
   household   176, 195, 196, 202
self-management (collective)   9
self-sufficiency   140, 204
Sepoy uprising, India   53
serfdom   16, 26, 36*n*47, 38, 49, 69, 168
servant
   deserter   181, 182, 184, 185
   distress   181, 182, 184–186, 195, 196
   sanctuary   181, 182, 184, 185
servitude
   servitude-by-capture (*sal*)   177, 184, 185
   servitude-by-refuge (*bawl*)   177, 181, 184,
   185
settlement   139, 190, 193
settler colonies   12, 25
Sewell, William Jr.   157, 158
sexuality/sex   20, 90–97, 106–109, 112–114, 117
sexually transmitted diseases (STDs)   91, 98,
   104, 113
sex work   90, 91, 97, 97*n*28, 107, 109, 110, 113,
   114
sharecropping   14
shareholder   77
Silk Road   31
sinology   163
skills   21, 42, 151, 152, 172

slave
  discipline 123, 126
  emancipation 68, 70, 115, 169
  labor 20, 36, 48, 50, 67, 123
  registration 125
  revolt 50, 52, 55, 68
  trade
    African slave 52, 116, 121–123, 129–133
    internal slave 20, 116, 129–133
    transatlantic slave 50
slavery
  Atlantic 115
  Slavery Second 20, 115, 117
smallholder 14
Smith, Adam 20, 57n41, 60, 70, 79, 81, 82
social conflict 77, 169
social hygiene 100
socialism
  socialist 2, 9, 10, 23n3, 50, 71, 80, 85, 99, 100, 104
  socialist state 83, 85
social media 198
social network 19, 162
social revolt 143
social security 15, 18, 108, 182
sociology 2, 157, 162
soldier 39, 141, 193, 193n84, 197, 197n104
solidarity 15, 17, 19, 21, 87
Sombart, Werner 27, 37, 71, 80, 81
South Africa 15, 16, 170
South America 5, 78, 137
Soviet Labor Camps 12
Soviet Union 2, 7, 12, 16, 27
Spartacus 68
spatial relationship 166
speculation 33, 65n65, 75, 78, 132
Spinoza, Baruch 79
Spiritus capitalisticus 27
stable wage labor contract 17
Stalin, Jozef 12, 13, 45
Standard Employment Relationship 17
Stanziani, Alessandro 16, 168
starvation 45, 151
state
  control 150, 176
  formation 11, 75, 136
Steinfeld, Robert 13
Steuart, James 50, 60
Stone Age 136

strangulation laws 10
strike 10, 14, 157
subaltern 56, 140
  workers 116, 205
suffrage 145
sugar 115
Sugihara, Kaoru 30–33, 32n33
suppression in the workplace 80
Sweezy, Paul 28, 29n23
syndicalism 9, 10
  revolutionary 9, 10
Szanton, David L. 161

Taiping rebellion, China 53
tax
  grazing 194
  household 194
technological (changes)/technology 10, 142, 198
Thailand 105, 106
The Poverty of Philosophy (Marx & Engels) 50
Thibert, Marguerite 100, 101n42, 102, 103
Third International 9
'Third World' history 156
Thomas, Albert 99
Thompson, E.P. 8, 27
Tilly, Charles 5, 9, 24n6, 36, 37, 37n53
Tilly, Chris 24, 24n6
Tocqueville, Alexis de 21, 136, 138, 143, 144, 147–155
Townsend, Peter 144, 145n10
trade
  contraband 123, 124, 127, 128, 130, 131
  grain 146
  liberal free 53
  maritime 131
  slave. *See* slave trade
  unionism 17
  wool 75
transaction 75, 123, 124
transcultural relations 158
transgender 94
transnational/transnationalism 9, 11, 16, 18, 77, 78, 83, 158, 159, 164, 173
transport 140, 142, 147, 189, 190n69
tribes 137, 180
trust 10, 74, 154

INDEX

unemployment 100, 102

Union Internationale contre le Péril Vénérien
  (UIPV) 99, 100, 104

United Kingdom 95, 161, 175

United States 5, 33, 50, 52, 62, 68, 150, 157n4,
  161, 161n16, 161n18, 163, 165

University of Amsterdam (UvA) 2, 3, 174

Upper South, USA 116

urbanization/urban/urbanized 10, 18, 67,
  75, 95, 105, 142, 147, 149, 154, 197, 198,
  203, 205

utility 39, 168

vagrancy 139, 140, 145

Varlez, Louis 101

venereal disease 93, 98, 99

Venice 26, 94

Vereenigde Oost-Indische Compagnie
  (VOC) 77

Verein für Sozialpolitik 146

Vietnam War 161

violence 20, 72, 76–79, 95, 96, 107, 112n90,
  113, 126, 132, 180

volunteer/voluntary 21, 60, 96, 98, 102, 103,
  107, 108n71, 109, 149, 153, 176, 183, 194,
  198, 202–204, 205, 205n118, 206, 207

Wals, Henk 23

war/warfare 45, 54, 63, 77, 79, 137, 177n14,
  177n15, 178, 179, 181–183, 185, 196–198

wealth 57n57, 62, 73, 74, 81, 86, 117, 122, 123,
  148, 150, 153, 154

Webb, Beatrice 8

Webb, Sidney 8

Weber, Max 36, 71, 76n5, 79, 80, 80n10, 82,
  145, 146, 147

welfare 84n15, 86, 143, 150, 152–154

welfare state 10, 46, 83, 84, 150, 153

Wells, Andrew 206

West Indies 26

white male industrial wage laborer 11

white-supremacists 165

Wijnroks, Marijke 110

Williams, Eric 167, 167n40

Woerden, Arent van 2, 22

workers
  emancipation 153
  guest 23
  identities 12
  migrant 147
  resistance 16
  seasonal 23
  subaltern 116, 205

Workers of the World (Van der
  Linden) 166n35, 170n51, 174

working class 1, 8, 17, 19, 50, 51, 54–56, 61, 62,
  68–70, 85, 144, 151

working conditions 103, 106, 109, 112, 114

World Employment Conference (1976) 91,
  104

World Health Organization (WHO) 104

world-system 16, 159

World War I 83, 187, 192

World War II 83, 161, 162, 190n68

Wright Mills, C. 174

Young Lushai Association (YLA) 195, 198

Young Mizo Association (YMA) 198

Zakat 137

Zürcher, Eric Jan 22